Life and Death in Captivity

Life and Death in Captivity

The Abuse of Prisoners during War

Geoffrey P. R. Wallace

Cornell University Press

Ithaca and London

First published 2015 by Cornell University Press

Printed in the United States of America

Library of Congress Cataloging-in-Publication Data
Wallace, Geoffrey P. R., 1978– author.
  Life and death in captivity : the abuse of prisoners during war / Geoffrey P.R. Wallace.
    pages cm
  Includes bibliographical references and index.
  ISBN 978-0-8014-5343-4 (cloth : alk. paper)
  1. Prisoners of war—Abuse of.   I. Title.

  UB800.W35 2015
  355.1'296—dc23   2014029093

Cornell University Press strives to use environmentally responsible suppliers and materials to the fullest extent possible in the publishing of its books. Such materials include vegetable-based, low-VOC inks and acid-free papers that are recycled, totally chlorine-free, or partly composed of nonwood fibers. For further information, visit our website at www.cornellpress.cornell.edu.

Cloth printing   10 9 8 7 6 5 4 3 2 1

For Fia

Contents

Figures and Tables

Acknowledgments

Over the course of writing this book, I have benefited immensely from the kindness and generosity of many people. I originally entered graduate school intent on studying a topic far removed from the subject matter of this book, yet the ongoing wars and debates surrounding detainees at the time raised several questions I have sought to address at least partially in the years that followed. Although the project took a long and winding road, with several detours, I am thankful to those who kept me on track and helped in so many respects along the way.

Cornell, where I began researching prisoner abuse, offered an amazing environment for thinking through the many issues that came up during this project in open yet rigorous ways. Peter Katzenstein was always willing to read numerous drafts of every chapter, irrespective of their quality. He constantly challenged my preconceptions on key points and pushed me to consider the broader implications of my argument. Chris Way instilled the need to be my own harshest critic and look at my findings from as many different angles as possible. I may not have always achieved this goal, but his advice on theory and research design gave me something to aspire to. I was also able to draw on Matt Evangelista's insights into international humanitarian law, which played such a large role in informing the central concept of prisoner abuse in this book. When I began venturing somewhat cautiously into the world of Soviet history, I benefited from his extensive knowledge of Russia to make sure any deviations were kept to a minimum. Jonathan Kirshner time and again was able to pinpoint things I took for granted and reveal differences in important concepts or events I had previously thought to be indistinguishable.

Many individuals commented and offered valuable feedback throughout various stages of the project. For their thoughtful suggestions I thank Ben Appel, Laia Balcells, Christian Davenport, Alex Downes, Kristine Eck, Tanisha Fazal, Ryan Grauer, Paul Huth, Stathis Kalyvas, Holger Kern, Michael Koh, Sarah Kreps, Jay Lyall, Walter Mebane, Mark Peffley, Benjamin Valentino, and Justin Wedeking. Jessica Weeks read an entire earlier version of the manuscript and greatly helped in refining the main ideas. Al Tillery did the same and pushed me to think through the contributions that could be made in the book. At Rutgers, I have been fortunate to be surrounded by a wealth of knowledgeable and supportive colleagues: Jan Kubik, Jack Levy, Roy Licklider, Manny Midlarsky, Michael McKoy, and Paul Poast all helped make this a better book than it would have been otherwise. I thank Roger Haydon at Cornell University Press for taking an interest in this project and for guiding me through the formidable process of translating my initial research into a book. Roger more than lived up to his reputation as a devoted and thoughtful editor and offered detailed comments on many parts of the manuscript. I also appreciate the input from two anonymous reviewers whose suggestions were especially useful. Karen Hwa and Deborah Oosterhouse helped enormously in preparing the final version of the manuscript, tightening the prose, and saving me from countless errors. Sarah Kachovec and Laura Shahan provided excellent research assistance and valuable help at key moments of the project. My apologies to anyone I may have overlooked.

Several institutions offered generous financial assistance that greatly facilitated the research and writing of this book. The Social Sciences and Humanities Council of Canada (SSHRC) provided a multiyear fellowship that was immensely helpful in providing the resources necessary to do much of the early research on the historical treatment of prisoners during war. The Judith Reppy Institute for Peace and Conflict Studies at Cornell University awarded me two research fellowships. These fellowships provided important time to think through key points of the project and also a vibrant intellectual community spanning multiple disciplines, which greatly improved my understanding of the dynamics of war and peace. Lastly, a visiting fellowship in the Niehaus Center for Globalization and Governance at Princeton University offered an amazing environment for tying everything together and making the final changes to the book.

Parts of the introduction and chapters 1 through 3 appeared previously in my 2012 article "Welcome Guests, or Inevitable Victims? The Causes of Prisoner Abuse in War," *Journal of Conflict Resolution* 56 (6): 955–81. I thank the journal and the publisher for granting me permission to adapt some of the material from the article into the book.

Acknowledgments

On a more personal note, I thank my parents, Paul and Gisèle Wallace, for their love and support through the years. I am especially appreciative to my Aunt Bern, who showed me the value of always asking questions and finding something interesting in everything. I do not think I would be where I am now if my aunt had not been there every day when I was growing up, reminding me of what could be achieved through a little thought and a lot of effort.

Lastly, I will be forever indebted to my wife, Sophia, who lived through this project just as much as I did, if not more. She offered unending support and encouragement from my first musings on this topic to the final words. She listened patiently as I slowly developed my ideas early on, and read and commented on each and every part of the book several times over. I am thankful that I was fortunate enough to live through this experience with her, a fellow political scientist, and I look forward to sharing many more to come. This book is dedicated to her. Our children, Dahlia and Liam, have grown up over the same period this project moved forward. During the many hard times they provided some much-needed perspective by reminding me there is a world beyond the book, and for this I am most thankful.

[xiii]

Life and Death in Captivity

Introduction

The degree of civilization in a society can be judged by entering its prisons.

—Fyodor Dostoyevsky

Prisons are built to break men, and when a man is broken, society has consummated its revenge.

—Jan Valtin, *Out of the Night*

For soldiers who become prisoners during war, the hellish realities of the battlefield all too often follow them into captivity. As long as there have been wars there have been prisoners, and many of those captured come to suffer in innumerable ways. According to this sinister side of prisoner treatment, enemy combatants are viewed not as mutual human beings deserving of respect, but rather as objects to be dealt with or discarded as captors saw fit. In Roman antiquity prisoners were regarded as a commodity to be sold off as slaves or thrown into the gladiator ring for the entertainment of the masses.[1] Even these captives could be considered fortunate compared to enemy combatants from various German and Asian tribes fighting against the Roman general Germanicus, who followed the strict adage to "Make no prisoners."[2] Unlike Germanicus, in warfare under the Aztec Empire the taking of prisoners in battle was a prized achievement. In fact, one of the few ways a warrior could gain honor and rise through the ranks was by capturing enemy prisoners. Yet the safety and well-being of prisoners was short-lived in a society where ritual killings were the most common eventual outcome. As part of the dedication ceremony of a temple to the god Huitzilopochtli, for example, the king Ahuitzotl commanded that over eighty thousand captives be offered up in sacrifice.[3]

Although enslavement and the ritual killing of wartime captives largely disappeared as common practices over the centuries, captors in modern times have continued to employ violence against prisoners by other means, including torture, hard labor, and a myriad of injustices. The survival chances for Soviet prisoners of Nazi Germany during the Second World War were worse than a cruel flip of a coin, and close to two-thirds would not live to see the end of the war.[4] As the fortunes of the war shifted in the Red Army's favor, captured Wehrmacht soldiers would not fare much better after falling into the hands of their communist foe. The perpetration of extreme levels of abuse is not simply a product of antiquated thinking, as Armenian and Azerbaijani prisoners both found out during the war between their two countries only a few brief years after the end of the Cold War. When facing such dire prospects, it is not surprising that many soldiers have preferred to continue fighting and face almost certain death rather than put themselves at the mercy of their captors, from Soviet soldiers facing the Nazi German onslaught to U.S. troops in the jungles of Vietnam.[5]

Countering these rather vicious maxims of prisoner treatment is an alternative view emphasizing the inherent rights and protections to be enjoyed by prisoners even, and especially, in the midst of armed conflict. Liberal thinkers like Montesquieu underscored that no violations were ever permitted against captives: "The only right that war can give over captives is that they may be imprisoned so that they can no longer do harm."[6] By entering into captivity, prisoners are in effect engaging in a contract where they voluntarily lay down their arms, and their captors in return agree to treat them in a decent manner.[7] As Francis Lieber declared in his instructions for the Union armies later in the American Civil War, which became known as the Lieber Code, "Men who take up arms against one another in public war do not cease on this account to be moral beings, responsible to one another and to God."[8] War may be hell, but according to the liberal tradition combatants who surrender have removed themselves from the heat of battle. Once they do so they are no longer considered instruments of warfare, but rather individual human beings to be granted all of the fundamental rights guaranteeing their health and well-being during their period in captivity. This more humane approach to the treatment of prisoners has been enshrined as a core tenet of modern just war theory and codified in the prevailing laws of war. Beliefs over the proper care of captives are not unique to Western thinking, as similar conventions can be found in ancient Hindu and Islamic texts, among others.[9]

A gentler and kinder vision of the treatment of captured enemy combatants is not merely the purview of philosophers and lawyers but has also been put into practice in numerous conflicts both past and present. Belying the notion that prisoner abuse is inevitable, the code of chivalry

[2]

among Europe's knights witnessed proper care often extended to adversaries seized during battle. During the Middle Ages lofty humanitarian ideals were strongly reinforced by baser pecuniary motives. With a soldier generally considered to belong to his individual captor, the ransoming of prisoners became a commonly accepted practice as higher-ranking captives could command potentially huge sums.[10] Of course, the only way to obtain the reward was to ensure the prisoner was decently treated and would survive his time in custody until payment was negotiated. So lucrative was the ransoming industry that one of the reasons the practice eventually became outlawed was that monarchs found their troops were more concerned with trying to capture prisoners than performing the tasks necessary to win military campaigns.[11]

Even without such direct monetary incentives, prisoners in many conflicts have frequently found themselves well looked after by their captors. The chances of death frequently remain much higher on the battlefield than in captivity across conflicts as varied as the Falklands War of 1982 to the Spanish-American War almost a century earlier. Observing the generous care provided to many captured combatants at the time, James Spaight, a scholar writing in the early twentieth century, went so far as to declare:

> To-day the prisoner of war is a spoilt darling; he is treated with a solicitude for his wants and feelings which borders on sentimentalism. He is better treated than the modern criminal, who is infinitely better off, under the modern prison system, than a soldier on a campaign. Under present-day conditions, captivity . . . is no sad sojourn by the waters of Babylon; it is usually a halcyon time, a pleasant experience to be nursed fondly in the memory, a kind of inexpensive rest-cure after the wearisome turmoil of fighting.[12]

Given the seemingly sumptuous alternative of time spent in captivity rather than taking on the risks of the battlefield, Spaight wondered in amazement why modern troops would even choose to fight! The life of a surrendering soldier apparently betokens more a courteous and refined scene from Austen's *Pride and Prejudice* than the prior wicked side of prisoner treatment more closely resembling Dante's *Inferno*. Far from reflecting the enlightened ideals of a bygone era, one contemporary legal scholar concludes that, "With rare exceptions therefore, no combatant nation can benefit substantially from mistreating prisoners."[13] Although not perpetrated in all wars or at all times, the cruel treatment of captives from many past conflicts, in locations as diverse as the Korean peninsula and the Balkans, suggests that captors in more than the isolated instance seem to find definite advantages from resorting to abuse.

[3]

Over the last century or so of warfare between states, neither the malevolent nor the benevolent perspective on prisoner treatment is entirely convincing. In certain instances captured enemy combatants have been welcomed as honored guests, while in others they are reduced to undeniable victims. What helps to explain the varied ways captors choose to treat prisoners during war? Using an original data set of prisoner abuse during interstate wars from 1898 to 2003 specifically constructed for this book, I find that the historical record reveals some perplexing patterns in who treats their prisoners well or mistreats them across different wars and circumstances. In his astonishment at the good living afforded to most prisoners, one of the cases Spaight points to concerned both sides in the Russo-Japanese War of 1904–5. Considering the war involved Tsarist Russia and Meiji Japan, two autocratic powers from starkly different cultural backgrounds involved in several pitched battles, the prospects for prisoners might be expected to have been dire. Circumstances bore many similarities to (and some of the same autocratic belligerents as in) the Second World War. Yet the treatment of prisoners could not be more different, with Japanese and Russian captors both largely respecting the rights of their captives.

Nondemocracies have traditionally been found to engage in serious violations against their own citizens.[14] Yet the data tell us in fact that more than half of all autocratic captors have limited themselves to little or at most moderate amounts of prisoner abuse. The Russo-Japanese War further highlights some intriguing differences in the treatment of prisoners over time. Decent care for captives by Japan in this conflict and a decade later during the First World War stood in stark contrast to the country's subsequent brutal conduct in the Second World War, culminating in systematic torture, backbreaking labor, and miserable living conditions endured by its captives.[15]

Although some of the most notorious cases of prisoner abuse involve autocratic perpetrators, past conflicts suggest democracy is far from a panacea. States of all varieties have proven more than willing to exact a harsh toll on captives falling under their control during times of war. As revelations continue to surface regarding the full extent of U.S. abuses against detainees at Abu Ghraib, Guantanamo, and elsewhere, democracies appear no more immune from the desire to abuse prisoners. The War on Terror is far from an isolated instance, as French forces likewise resorted to torture and other harsh tactics when confronting rebels during the 1954–62 Algerian War.[16] Data from the last century of interstate warfare reveal that almost one-quarter of democratic belligerents inflicted extreme levels of violence on captives. Looking at past conflicts thus indicates some puzzling trends in the treatment of prisoners, pointing to the need for a more systematic study.

[4]

Existing scholarly work provides little insight for explaining why some prisoners are horribly abused, while others are cared for in a relatively decent manner. The bulk of research into questions of war tends to concentrate on its causes more than any other stage of conflict.[17] In many ways this choice is not without good reason—identifying those factors most likely to lead to the outbreak of hostilities can help avoid later horrors by preventing wars from happening in the first place.[18] A similar motivation is often also behind numerous investigations into how and why wars end.[19] By figuring out what makes the termination of wars more probable, conflicts might be brought to a close in a quicker manner with less violence and bloodshed as a result.

This book instead contributes to the growing literature seeking to explain the conduct of actors in the midst of armed conflict.[20] Warfare of various sorts remains an unfortunate yet enduring reality in the contemporary world.[21] Studying the dynamics of wartime violence has been met with some resistance. As one conflict scholar remarks, "A final obstacle to understanding is the fact that analysing the causes of violence can seem dangerously close to justifying it."[22] Yet inquiring into why belligerents fight in different ways does not necessarily mean unconditionally accepting the brutalities that often accompany hostilities. Comprehending what drives wartime conduct offers the potential to curtail the ferocity of the fighting and improve the outlook for those persons thrust into battle, even if war itself is unlikely to recede for the foreseeable future.

Much of the current body of research on wartime conduct still offers little direct guidance on the dynamics of prisoner treatment. The vast majority of work in this vein centers on the targeting of civilians, whether perpetrated by government forces or nonstate groups.[23] Research on civilian victimization shares many linkages with the more specific study of genocide, where the deaths of noncombatants remain the major focal point for inquiry even though captured combatants are also frequently killed.[24] Even as issues surrounding the treatment of Taliban and al-Qaeda detainees generated widespread public debate, the main legacy of the 9/11 attacks was a renewed interest in the study of terrorism and consequently attacks on civilians.[25]

As the unarmed and innocent, civilians often embody the most visible and sympathetic victims of warfare, deserving the attention devoted in past studies. The killing of noncombatants should certainly be deplored, but a sole focus on civilians can obscure the enormous toll wrought by prisoner abuse. Captured combatants rarely represent a small portion of the humanity swept up in most conflicts. The First World War saw over 2.5 million soldiers from the Austro-Hungarian armed forces surrender,

[5]

equaling one-third of the total number of troops the empire mobilized and over 10 percent of its male population.[26] The Second World War led to the death, dislocation, and forced movement of an enormous number of civilians, yet often overlooked is that hundreds of thousands of German prisoners endured years of hard labor in the Soviet Union, and some of those fortunate enough to survive did not return home until more than a decade after the conflict had ended.[27]

Although emerging norms like the responsibility to protect (R2P) are primarily framed in terms of guaranteeing the safety of civilians, many of the earliest international agreements regulating wartime conduct dealt with caring for the sick and wounded from armies on the battlefield, and later the treatment of prisoners specifically. Even with the four Geneva Conventions of 1949 governing various victims of war, the group enjoying the greatest level of rights and most privileged status were prisoners of war.[28] Despite having taken up arms, combatants are deserving of a corresponding set of rights and protections to those for civilians once they have surrendered and are hors de combat. Looking more closely at the abuse committed against those who have laid down their weapons complements the existing literature on civilians by refocusing attention on another frequently forgotten casualty of war. Furthermore, while some analysts assume the behavior of armed actors is generally the same across various spheres of conduct,[29] I show there exist important differences in the determinants of violence against prisoners.

Research on prisoner affairs in their own right largely comes from the historical and sociological literatures. Many scholars aim less at offering a specific account for why prisoners are treated the way they are, but instead attempt to document and give a fuller sense of the experience of soldiers in captivity, such as through the use of oral histories.[30] Others seek to explain why prisoners have or have not been abused but tend to stress the particularities of individual cases. Some focus on prisoner policies within a specific conflict, with the First World War an especially popular case.[31] A similar captivation with the War on Terror has seen many books dealing with the treatment of captives.[32] Partially as a further attempt to understand current counterterrorism, other analysts investigate the treatment of prisoners by a single country across several wars; the United States remains the favored choice.[33] An alternative tactic instead focuses on specific types of abuse, and recent research centers especially on torture and indefinite detention.[34]

Even if current works differ in precise emphasis, their focus on a handful of cases or certain types of violations limits the ability to produce a broader understanding of the dynamics of prisoner treatment. A more pragmatic reason for the restricted nature of existing studies, especially in comparison to the much larger literature on civilians, is the lack of adequate data.[35] By examining a wider range of cases and practices across more than a century of interstate warfare, I offer a framework that places specific conflicts in their proper theoretical and historical context.

THE QUESTION AND ANSWER IN BRIEF

Even the lauded military theorist General Carl von Clausewitz, not exactly known for a genteel approach to warfare, argued that, "If, then, civilized nations do not put their prisoners to death . . . it is because intelligence plays a larger part in their methods of warfare and has taught them more effective ways of using force than the crude expression of instinct."[36] Unfortunately for Clausewitz, many belligerents have found abusing captives to be a useful strategy, and "civilized" countries like the United States and France have sometimes been at the forefront of prisoner mistreatment. Why are the rights of some prisoners rigorously upheld, while other captives are viewed as expendable? Simply put, why are some prisoners horribly abused, while others are humanely treated? These are the central questions put forward in this book, but the answer is far from straightforward. In particular, the history of prisoner abuse reveals puzzling differences in belligerents' conduct toward combatants taken from various adversaries fighting in the exact same war, as well as changes in their treatment of similar captives over the course of a single conflict. Nazi Germany's approach toward prisoners could never be characterized as humane, but the sometimes austere conditions for prisoner camps on the western front paled in comparison to the Third Reich's exploitation and outright extermination of enemy troops captured in eastern Europe. By contrast, the Western powers' treatment of Axis prisoners was generally more generous, but even here conduct declined methodically as the war neared its end and in the aftermath. We need to account not only for overall trends in the abuse of captured enemy combatants, but also for some of these surprising differences in the treatment of prisoners over time or within the same war.

One of the most common sets of arguments reflects some of Clausewitz's civilizational thinking but emphasizes the importance of cultural differences between adversaries when accounting for patterns of prisoner treatment. Enemies of dissimilar race or religion are more prone to view each other as barbaric and uncivilized, and consequently inflict higher levels of violence upon prisoners.[37] In his account of the fighting in the Pacific during the Second World War, John Dower proposed:

Race hate fed atrocities, and atrocities in turn fanned the fires of race hate. The dehumanization of the Other . . . facilitates killing, not only on the

[7]

battlefield but also in the plans adopted by strategists far removed from the actual scene of combat.[38]

Looking at wartime conduct more broadly, European states may have been more than willing to apply the laws of war to conflicts fought among members of their own community, but those humanitarian precepts apparently disappeared quickly when dealing with non-Western foes.[39]

Another approach also incorporates cultural factors but focuses less on the attributes of society at large than on those specific to a country's armed forces. Organizational culture, commonly described as "the set of basic assumptions, values, norms, beliefs, and formal knowledge that shape collective understandings," can transform the doctrinal choices and conduct of militaries toward war.[40] A military's organizational culture guides the way it will fight—practices that are consistent with the organization's culture will lead belligerents to escalate their use during wars, while for contrary modes of violence the country's armed forces will exercise restraint.[41] Through its embodiment of *Vernichtung* (destruction), the Imperial German Army extended its closely held principle of annihilating the enemy to mean crushing all elements of the adversary rather than just those on the battlefield. The elimination of captured enemy combatants developed into standard practice, as German forces came to see prisoner abuse as part and parcel of their organization's very reason for being.[42] From this perspective, a belligerent's decision over whether to treat prisoners in a brutal or a humane manner ultimately depends on the ideas and beliefs of the coercive apparatus tasked with waging war.

Although these arguments possess many merits, evidence from the last century of warfare shows neither type of cultural argument satisfactorily accounts for the full constellation of prisoner abuse. On civilizational differences, conflicts like Japan's war in the Pacific or Germany's war in the east do indeed expose captors engaging in horrific amounts of abuse against prisoners from dissimilar races. Yet if we look at conduct across a wider range of episodes, cultural differences are not consistently associated with higher levels of prisoner abuse. Relying on organizational culture leads to expectations of a consistency in wartime conduct that belies the enormous differences in prisoner abuse evident in the historical record.[43] Countries as varied as interwar Japan and the post–Cold War United States have shifted dramatically from relatively decent practices in one conflict to violent behavior in another. Organizational culture also has a hard time accounting for changes in the treatment of prisoners within the same conflict, which have also frequently taken place.[44]

Drawing from existing research on the broader study of wartime conduct, along with evidence from the treatment of prisoners across more

[8]

than a century of interstate warfare, I argue instead that two sets of factors are the primary drivers behind violence against captured combatants. First, within the warring parties themselves, a country's regime type generates several internal incentives that influence how a captor chooses to treat captured enemy combatants. Democracies, despite some notable exceptions, are typically more restrained about resorting to greater levels of abuse against their captives. The reasons for this democratic benevolence, however, are rooted less in liberal norms of tolerance and nonviolence than in institutionally driven considerations resulting from democratic leaders' accountability to their publics. Because of a heightened sense of casualty aversion, democracies are more sensitive to the dangers of reprisal and escalation by the enemy that would likely follow prisoner abuse. The proper treatment of enemy combatants thereby acts as a sort of insurance policy, albeit an imperfect one, to limit abuses against their own troops in enemy captivity.

Alongside concerns over retaliation, domestic desires to win quickly and cheaply encourage democracies to take advantage of the strategic benefits that can come from decent conduct. Promises of proper care upon capture, which are likely more credible from democracies since they usually treat their own citizens more humanely than do autocrats, can persuade remaining enemy forces to prefer surrendering over the hazards of continuing to fight. Rather than a liability, humane conduct during war can weaken the ability of the adversary to resist by reducing its effective fighting forces on the battlefield. The military advantages conferred by surrenders may help explain Clausewitz's distaste for prisoner abuse and why he viewed captured enemy combatants as one of the "real trophies of victory."[45]

These more pragmatic rather than principled considerations also help to explain instances where democracies have not adequately cared for their prisoners. Far from always following humanitarian ideals, democracies can be capable of harsh conduct toward captives when institutional incentives are faint or missing. Where fears of retaliation and escalation disappear, or the strategic benefits from good conduct are limited, the conduct of democratic captors may differ little from that of their autocratic counterparts.

The second set of factors turns instead to external incentives resulting from the nature of the conflict itself. The severity of fighting, especially in conflicts that get bogged down into long and costly wars of attrition, shapes how belligerents choose to treat their prisoners. Facing dire circumstances, embattled captors can become increasingly desperate and resort to prisoner abuse as a tool of coercion to make the war more costly and painful for their adversary. Stuck in a full-scale conflict that calls for the mobilization of all available resources, captors are also highly attracted to extracting as much as possible from their prisoner population irrespective of the hardships that will ensue. Caught in the midst of attritional fighting, worries over retaliation or other downsides to abuse thus give way to the frantic necessity of finding any means to intimidate the adversary or obtain more resources for the war effort.

A further characteristic of the nature of the conflict concerns the specific aims states seek to achieve through war and the ways these goals influence decisions over how to treat enemy combatants. Not all aims are created equal, and it is particularly in wars where a belligerent strives to conquer large swathes of territory that prisoners from the adversary are in the greatest danger. Enemy combatants usually possess organizational and martial skills that can subvert a conquering state's hold on newly acquired lands. Prisoner abuse represents a brutal though potentially effective strategy for eliminating those elements most willing and able to mount resistance against an occupier's rule. In wars of conquest ranging from the Balkans of the early twentieth century to Somalia's quest to reestablish a "Greater Somaliland," captured combatants have suffered immensely in wars of territorial annexation. When land is at stake, concerns over retaliation or the possible benefits from good conduct are overshadowed by the advantages to be gained through brutality. Prisoner abuse during the course of severe fighting is driven by shorter-term incentives to coerce the opponent or maximize resources, but violence against captives in wars of conquest exhibits much longer time horizons related to trying to dominate new possessions for generations to come.

The theoretical framework I put forward to explain the treatment of prisoners shares many similarities to studies on civilian victimization that emphasize the strategic use of violence.[46] The decision to abuse prisoners is a function of rational strategic calculations by captors, resulting from domestic and external incentives produced by regime type and the nature of the conflict. This stands in contrast to approaches that give priority to cultural factors or irrational animosities in accounting for wartime conduct. Emotion and hatreds may play a role in some cases, but they do not provide much leverage for understanding broader patterns in the treatment of prisoners across wars, and particularly within the same war or over time. Although sharing some affinities to key works in the civilian literature, my argument diverges on several counts. In particular, regime type proves to be a significant constraint on the resort to prisoner abuse, while democracy has been found either to have no effect or actually to heighten violence against civilians.[47] The difference for regime type is not due to stronger humanitarian norms governing noncombatants. Rather, it exists because the two key mechanisms restraining democracies in their abuse of prisoners—fears of retaliation and the strategic benefits from humane conduct—are frequently weaker in the case

[10]

of violence against civilians. While focusing primarily on abuses perpetrated against captured combatants, I put forward a theory and evidence that offer the promise of understanding the wider conduct of armed actors when wielding violence.

A few comments are also in order to specify the scope of the study and clarify what the book does and does not purport to accomplish. First, I do not claim to offer a comprehensive account of the abuse of prisoners across all forms of warfare. I confine myself to examining the causes of prisoner abuse during modern interstate wars. Violence against prisoners has also taken place during civil wars, counterinsurgency operations, and other conflicts involving nonstate actors. The wide-ranging variation in the treatment of prisoners during wars between states, in addition to the daunting task of amassing suitable data across a single class of conflict, led me to limit the book to this type of war. While the theory and evidence focus on interstate warfare, the concluding chapter expands on some of the implications of my argument for other types of armed conflict.

Second, I do not seek to explain every instance of prisoner abuse committed during a given war. War inevitably remains a dirty business. Even in conflicts considered humane by most measures, atrocities are still often committed. Allied treatment of German troops during the Second World War was generally commendable, yet soldiers on the ground took occasional liberties at the expense of Axis prisoners.[48] Even in wars where captors received high praise from human rights groups, such as the United States during the Persian Gulf War, allegations of abuse still surfaced.[49] My focus is on the policy and practices of states toward enemy prisoners rather than isolated acts committed by single soldiers or small units of troops. The latter would require a theory of the conduct of individual soldiers—a worthy topic of interest but deserving of a separate study.[50] Although more bounded, my concentration on the prisoner policies of belligerents more closely follows much of the larger literature on wartime conduct. Both the best and the worst historical episodes involving prisoner treatment more often than not involved active intervention by the government's civilian and military leadership.

WHY PRISONER ABUSE MATTERS

Uncovering the causes of prisoner abuse offers several insights that are of interest to both scholars and practitioners of international security. From a humanitarian standpoint the stakes are not small, since the number of prisoners captured during wars is often sizable. Deaths of civilians or soldiers in the heat of battle are horrific but neglect the full costs of war. Indeed, several current data-collection projects use only battle deaths when classifying whether or not a particular armed conflict qualifies as a war, with the fate of captured combatants playing little meaningful role.[51] Yet the suffering and deaths attributed to prisoner abuse often constitute a substantial proportion of wartime fatalities—almost one in three deaths of Soviet soldiers during the Second World War took place in captivity rather than in battle.[52] During the American Revolutionary War, by some estimates, between two and three times as many U.S. troops perished in captivity as died on the battlefield fighting English forces.[53] Figuring out where and why prisoners are abused is crucial for understanding the resort to extreme forms of violence and assessing the full costs of war.

The study of prisoner abuse is relevant for several other continuing debates. Examining regime type and the treatment of prisoners offers a further opportunity to evaluate the impact of domestic norms and institutions and the value of promoting democracy worldwide. The democratic peace has established that democracies are less likely to go to war against one another, but added to this is the further potential benefit that democracies may conduct themselves more humanely when they do end up fighting. I offer cautious support for the alleged distinctiveness of democracies, but I highlight some caveats. Democracies may be less prone to abusing prisoners on the whole, but under the right circumstances can turn on their captives if they believe the benefits outweigh the costs. Recent U.S. treatment of prisoners in Afghanistan and Iraq may be not aberrations but part of a long tradition of violence committed by democracies against captives. Alongside their often-vaunted humanitarian credentials, democratic regimes exhibit a darker side that should not be ignored.[54] Identifying potential limits in the willingness of democracies to restrain their behavior helps us to understand the overall impact of regime type on wartime conduct, especially when we think about the use of violence by different regimes in other types of conflicts.

The book also contributes to the large body of work on international laws and norms dealing with the use of force. Much of this research has focused on the development of particular rules, such as the distinction between civilians and combatants, limits on the destructiveness of military technologies, and the outright prohibition of certain weapons.[55] In light of the status of international rules governing the treatment of prisoners of war, I look at the flip side concerning the factors leading captors to transgress long-held norms. Why do belligerents violate international protections for prisoners, while at other times they uphold these norms with the utmost care? Other scholars have found international law can significantly shape wartime conduct,[56] but I show that international law

[12]

and norms offer few restraints against prisoner abuse in most circumstances. Yet this does not mean that treaties and humanitarian norms have no value. If norms or rules outlawing the use of violence against surrendering soldiers did not exist, studying violence against prisoners would in some ways make little sense—there would be nothing out of the ordinary in their suffering. In fact, the very way prisoner abuse is understood in this book is indebted to principles rooted in the laws of war. International law and norms also matter in the sense that actors often feel they need to justify their conduct (toward prisoners or otherwise) in legal and moral terms.[57] Other factors ultimately play a greater role in determining the treatment of prisoners, but international law and related values remain an inescapable element of contemporary warfare.

Lastly, prisoner abuse does not operate in isolation but can affect the general course of conflicts with enduring consequences. The treatment of enemy combatants and their eventual fate poses the danger of heightening animosities between already bitter rivals. The back-and-forth nature of the Korean War, where opposing armies marched up and down the Korean peninsula and the great powers of the United States and China clashed head-on, counts as one of the more intense conflicts of the twentieth century. Despite many deplorable facets from which to choose, one prominent historian of the war reserved particular disdain for the role played by prisoner issues:

> No aspect of the Korean War was more grotesque than the manner in which the struggle was allowed to continue for a further sixteen months after the last substantial territorial obstacle to an armistice had been removed by negotiation in February 1952. From that date until the end in July 1953, on-the-line men endured the miseries of summer heat and winter cold, were maimed by mines and killed by napalm, small arms, and high explosives, while at Panmunjom [the main site for negotiations] the combatants wrangled around one bitterly contentious issue: the post-armistice exchange of prisoners.[58]

The delay in ending hostilities only furthered the bloodshed; almost half of all U.S. casualties took place after the first armistice negotiations, where prisoner issues quickly became one of the central stumbling blocks.[59]

The abuse of prisoners also has the potential to spill over into other issue areas and cause further suffering both during and after war. One of the justifications put forward for Harry S. Truman's decision to drop the atomic bomb on Japan near the end of the Second World War was to respond to the brutal Japanese conduct toward U.S. prisoners.[60] In Europe during the same war, the first victims of the gas chambers at Auschwitz were not Jewish civilians but rather Soviet prisoners of war.[61] In many

[13]

respects, the orders and policies formulated by the German government toward Red Army prisoners served as the operational basis for the Final Solution.[62]

In more recent years, abuses perpetrated against soldiers significantly influenced the progress of several foreign crises. Images of beaten and mutilated corpses of U.S. servicemen dragged through the streets of Mogadishu in 1993 are widely viewed as pivotal in the reduction and eventual withdrawal of the U.S. military presence in Somalia.[63] While it is difficult to know for certain what would have happened if U.S. forces had remained, Somalia descended into even greater chaos and violence from which it is still struggling to escape. Similarly, in the early days of the Rwandan genocide, Hutu hardliners specifically targeted and ruthlessly murdered Belgian peacekeepers they had captured in an effort to push UN forces out of the country.[64] The gambit was largely successful, with remaining Belgian forces departing, followed shortly thereafter by most other foreign military personnel. Only a skeleton peacekeeping crew remained and could do little to prevent the unfolding humanitarian disaster. As the hardliners had hoped, they were left unencumbered to carry out massacres across the country, leading to the deaths of at least a half million Tutsis and moderate Hutus in just one hundred days.[65] The treatment of enemy combatants thus has implications for understanding the broader conduct of war and the resort to mass violence.

The next two chapters define prisoner abuse in greater detail and present a theory to explain the wide differences in the treatment of captured enemy combatants with a particular focus on regime type and the nature of the conflict. Chapters 3 through 5 then offer several empirical tests of the theory and competing explanations, beginning with a quantitative analysis of the determinants of prisoner abuse followed by a series of in-depth case studies. Finally, I conclude by discussing the theoretical and policy implications of my findings.

[1]

Repertoires of Violence against Prisoners

For many surrendering soldiers at the mercy of their captors, the question often becomes not whether they will be abused but what kinds of violence will be levied against them. The myriad forms of brutality connect to form a repertoire of violence inflicted upon the minds and bodies of captives. As the armed forces of Nazi Germany advanced rapidly in their 1941 eastern offensive, the feared *Einsatzgruppen* (task forces) followed behind, methodically killing thousands of captured Soviet soldiers, often alongside other groups of victims. As horrific as these early deaths were, they paled in comparison to the hundreds of thousands of Red Army captives who would perish from an explicit starvation campaign during the fall and winter of 1941, where death rates in some camps verged on 2 percent *per day*.[1] The fate of these prisoners parallels earlier conditions during the First Balkan War of 1912–13, where Ottoman soldiers held by Bulgaria on an island in the Tundzha River were reduced to eating grass and tree bark in a frantic attempt to survive.[2] Absent such blatant practices of inducing famine, the squalid disease-ridden confinement to the "floating hells" that were British prison ships during the American Revolutionary War of the late eighteenth century nevertheless left many captured fighters for American independence welcoming death.[3]

Prisoners who do not die in captivity have still suffered greatly in many other ways. Mutilation through such acts as amputation or castration, for the purpose of neutralizing combatants or to send a grim message to the adversary, has been common across varied cultures and periods. After fourteen thousand Bulgarian prisoners were captured at the Battle of Kleidion in 1014, Byzantine Emperor Basil II, later known as the "Bulgar Slayer," had ninety-nine out of every hundred captives

[15]

blinded and the rest left with only one eye. Shocked by the sight of his mangled army upon their return, Bulgarian Emperor Samuel reportedly died of a heart attack.[4] In the contemporary era, even as the worst excesses from the early days of the U.S.-led War on Terror may have subsided, the prospects for indefinite detention without trial at Guantanamo and other facilities continued to garner widespread international condemnation.

Beyond the type of abuse perpetrated, a full assessment of prisoner treatment can be further complicated by the fact that not all instances of violence may be under the complete control of government authorities. Disagreements persist over whether or not abuses against detainees at the Abu Ghraib prison in Iraq were due to "a few bad apples," as former president George W. Bush claimed, or rather part of a larger policy sanctioned by the administration.[5] While deliberate British mistreatment of captured American revolutionary troops was certainly harmful in many respects, neglect and exploitation by local prison administrators and guards often made the plight of captives even more desperate.[6]

Issues concerning the type, severity, and perpetrators of abuse can have fundamental consequences not only for the prospects faced by captured combatants but also for determining responsibility and guilt under international or domestic law. The extent of abuse, nature of the victims, and who exactly was in command and issued orders have proved crucial in tribunals ranging from the post-WWII Nuremberg Trials to those for conflicts in the former Yugoslavia, and have continued to figure prominently in charges more recently brought under the International Criminal Court (ICC).[7]

The varieties of violence evident in past episodes of prisoner abuse further reveal some of the obstacles to developing a better understanding of the full scope of prisoner treatment. Unlike with studies looking at the targeting of civilians, there is no widely accepted conceptual or operational definition of what should and should not be considered prisoner abuse. Who counts as a combatant? What types of actions are violations? Even if violations against prisoners do take place, how can their scope and severity be distinguished? How have the patterns of prisoner abuse varied over time?

DEFINING PRISONER ABUSE

For this book, prisoner abuse is defined as a military strategy enacted by political and military authorities that involves the intentional killing or harming, either directly or indirectly, of enemy combatants who have laid down their arms and surrendered. This definition contains four elements that merit further elaboration and that help to differentiate between those acts that are either included or excluded as prisoner abuse.

First, prisoners represent captured fighters, but this necessitates knowing which individuals should be considered combatants in the first place. International lawyers and just war theorists have spent a great deal of time and effort trying to precisely define the boundary separating combatants from noncombatants, or civilians.[8] Going back to the first modern international conventions of the nineteenth century, one of the core elements concerned creating a distinction between civilians trying to carry out their regular lives, on the one hand, and combatants engaging in military activities, on the other.[9] In practice, the line between the two groups is not always clear. A concerted push in some quarters even asserts that any meaningful distinction is no longer tenable because of deepening linkages between a country's war-making capabilities and its national economy, alongside the public's implicit consent (and sometimes outright support) even in nondemocratic regimes when entering into armed conflict.[10]

The boundary separating civilians and combatants has become further blurred with the rise of insurgencies, where guerrilla forces frequently hide among the local populace and rely on noncombatants for information, protection, and supplies.[11] Just as rebels seek to blend in among the surrounding population, a countercurrent has increasingly taken hold where many groups long considered civilians are relabeled as combatants. This trend is perhaps illustrated most starkly in the procedures developed under the Obama administration when compiling civilian and militant deaths from U.S. drone strikes. For accounting purposes, the government generally considers all males of military age in a strike zone as combatants except if intelligence afterward definitively proves their innocence.[12] While the United States has gone to great lengths to reduce risks to noncombatants from counterterrorism operations, frequent claims of low or nonexistent civilian deaths need to be treated with some caution, since many of the publically declared militant victims may have played little direct role in the insurgency. Yet arguments for this alleged soldier-civilian nexus across both conventional and irregular conflicts mask substantial differences in the degree to which combatants and noncombatants participate and actively contribute toward military activities of either government or rebel forces.

The 1977 Additional Protocol I (AP I) to the Geneva Conventions offers a baseline definition in which combatants "consist of all organized armed forces, groups and units which are under a command responsible to that Party for the conduct of its subordinates."[13] "Armed forces" are interpreted broadly to refer not only to individuals serving in a country's official national uniformed military but also members of irregular forces, such as guerrillas.[14] Civilians are distinguished from combatants in that they pose no direct threat of harm to enemy personnel or property. Civilians may give moral support to combatants through nonviolent demonstrations or provide food and other nonlethal supplies, but these activities do not on their own pose an immediate physical threat to the adversary and thus do not legitimately make those who engage in them equivalent to combatants.[15]

One additional group that does not directly belong to the armed forces but is sometimes still included under the combatant category is munitions workers.[16] It is a fair critique that those individuals making the tools necessary for armed forces to fight should be classified differently from those making what soldiers merely need to live. Nevertheless, munitions workers are excluded here for the purposes of defining and studying prisoner abuse. Munitions workers are frequently included alongside national armed forces to argue that they, unlike other civilians, represent legitimate targets during military operations like aerial bombing campaigns.[17] During the Second World War, factories employing local workers in occupied France were frequently bombed by Western Allied warplanes, many even piloted by members of the Free French Forces (FFL).[18] As regrettable as the deaths resulting from these bombing raids may have been, the factories and their workers were viewed as justifiable targets given their material contributions to the Nazi war effort.[19]

The concern with questions of prisoner abuse is not so much with general attacks against combatants during the heat of battle, but rather with the treatment of troops once they have laid down their arms and are deemed hors de combat. Munitions workers have, more often than not, been treated in a similar manner to civilians and laborers in other industries by occupying forces, though as a group with a particularly useful set of skills from which to profit.[20] The status of surrendering armed forces is usually a study in contrasts and almost always involves some form of captivity at least for a period of time. Civilians are sometimes also detained, but the narrower definition of combatants used here, which focuses only on those who are part of the armed forces while counting civilians as everyone else, more closely follows conventional thinking in international law.[21]

A final remark concerns the relationship between this definition of combatant and the legal term "prisoner of war" (POW). In order to be formally considered POWs, combatants must fulfill several criteria, such as being commanded by a leader responsible for his or her subordinates, wearing a fixed and recognizable emblem, carrying their arms openly, and acting in accordance with the laws of war.[22] Some combatants, especially guerrilla fighters, might not be granted POW status because they fail to meet one or more of these criteria, though even in such cases AP I sought to loosen some of the restrictions.[23] Similarly, mercenaries captured during the course of fighting are generally considered not to have the right to claim POW status.[24] Debate over the status of detained combatants from al-Qaeda and the Taliban, which arose shortly after the 9/11 terrorist attacks and invasion of Afghanistan, highlight many of the tensions over who should and should not qualify as a POW under international law. The U.S. administration of George W. Bush rejected claims that members of these groups were protected under the Geneva Conventions, instead categorizing detainees as "unlawful combatants."

On the other hand, international humanitarian law mandates that certain types of persons who accompany the armed forces but are not actual members, such as war correspondents or merchant marines, also be granted POW status. This means that not all combatants (understood broadly) might qualify for POW status, while at the same time not all POWs are combatants. Since this study is concerned with the treatment of captured combatants writ large, irrespective of their official status once detained, I use the terms "combatants," "prisoners," and "POWs" in the broader sense and clarify references to the narrower legal term where relevant.

Second, prisoner abuse refers to government policy and practices rather than isolated acts by individual soldiers or small troop units. During war it is not uncommon for some soldiers to take matters into their own hands and release their anger or frustrations on hapless enemy personnel.[25] Since enemy soldiers often find themselves surrendering not long after intense firefights when comrades from the captor's forces may have been killed moments before, the period immediately after capture can be extremely risky. The tendency of many German soldiers to discharge all of their ammunition before volunteering to surrender certainly did not help to alleviate summary killings on the battlefield.[26] As the psychologist and former army ranger Dave Grossman points out, "Revenge killing during a burst of rage has been a recurring theme throughout history."[27]

Although atrocities committed at the individual or small group levels are relevant for understanding the broader character of armed conflict, these types of violations are qualitatively and quantitatively different from most state-directed policies. Historian Max Hastings remarked that, to fully comprehend the behavior of U.S.-led and communist forces during the Korean War, "It remains important and valid to make some distinction between the random acts of individual UN troops and the systematic brutality of the North Koreans."[28] Furthermore, both the worst and best historical cases of prisoner treatment involved government authorities playing a leading hand in directing their forces to

[19]

perpetrate or refrain from violence against captured enemy combatants. The induction of prisoners by Japan into a vast slave labor force for intensive railway and other construction projects would not have been possible without centralized monitoring and management by higher-level Japanese military planners.[29] Likewise, the generally excellent treatment afforded to surrendering Iraqi forces in the 1991 Persian Gulf War would have been very difficult to achieve without specific directives and coordination by the U.S. leadership in the larger UN coalition.

Of particular importance, the causes of violence against prisoners instigated by small groups of troops on the ground will not necessarily be the same as abuses directed by the civilian and military leadership. Only forms of abuse flowing directly from government policy are considered cases of prisoner abuse for the purposes of this study.[30] Individual violations may be included, but only insofar as higher military or political authorities condone such actions and make little or no attempt to stop their reoccurrence. This means violations that may start out as isolated acts by individual soldiers can eventually transform into official policy and thus count as prisoner abuse. After enduring summary executions and being treated as common criminals over years of resistance during the Second World War, pockets of fighters from the French Forces of the Interior (FFI) sometimes began taking revenge on captured German troops as the tide turned after the Normandy landings. Nevertheless, it was only when the FFI leadership officially announced and carried out the execution of eighty German prisoners as reprisal killings that FFI violations would meet this criterion as an act of prisoner abuse.[31]

Third, prisoner abuse comprises a variety of violations beyond the immediate execution of prisoners. It bears emphasizing that even in the best of circumstances, experience in captivity can be traumatic, leading to a psychological condition commonly known as "barbed-wire disease" or "Stalag syndrome."[32] Although any form of violation is regretful, a hierarchy is evident in the repertoire of violence that makes certain abuses more salient than others when seeking to uncover the nature and scope of prisoner abuse. Over the course of the nineteenth and twentieth centuries, international treaties have granted an expanding number of rights for prisoners, ranging from protections against torture or execution to more minor provisions, such as providing postal services and facilities for recreation and intellectual activities, or respecting personal belongings. For instance, it is technically a contravention of the Third Geneva Convention of 1949 not to provide adequate equipment for prisoners to play sports or other games.[33] Notwithstanding the importance of intellectual or athletic pursuits, the definition of prisoner abuse here focuses on those violations bearing most directly on the core physical and mental well-being of prisoners. It is these latter forms of abuse that

[20]

are likely to bear most directly on the overall quality of life of combatants after laying down their arms.

Distinguishing what counts as a serious form of abuse from more minor acts thus proves to be essential. To determine the category of relevant abuses, Article 130 of the 1949 Third Geneva Convention outlines certain "grave breaches" occupying a separate position above other obligations toward prisoners. Violations falling into this category include execution, torture, inhumane living or working conditions, forcibly conscripting prisoners into the captor's armed forces, and denying proper judicial rights. While perpetrators are liable for penal sanctions when violating other provisions under the Geneva Conventions, grave breaches have come to occupy a privileged place and are treated as war crimes under international law.[34] Other more minor violations are, in turn, excluded from the definition of prisoner abuse.

Relying on the 1949 Geneva Conventions might appear to pose a problem of applying one particular set of rules and principles to earlier periods that may have been guided by different norms and expectations. The perceived conduct of belligerents toward prisoners in conflicts taking place in the first half of the twentieth century, such as the various wars in the Balkans, may be shed in an unfairly negative light as a result. Elements of each of these grave forms of abuse, however, are evident in prior treaties and documents. The 1949 Geneva Conventions were not drafted in a vacuum but built upon earlier agreements, such as the 1929 Geneva Convention on Prisoners of War as well as the older Hague Conventions from 1899 and 1907.[35] The customary basis for many of these norms governing prisoner treatment extend further back into the nineteenth century if not earlier, outlined in such documents as the 1880 Oxford Manual of the Laws and Customs of War, the 1874 Brussels Declaration, and the 1863 Lieber Code.[36] Rules prohibiting the most serious abuses against the body and mind of prisoners are not a recent phenomenon. A common set of expectations has developed around the treatment of prisoners, even if the adherence to such provisions has varied across many conflicts.

The list of acts considered as prisoner abuse also closely follows common interpretations of some of the worst episodes involving the treatment of prisoners both in the distant past and in more contemporary conflicts. The execution of prisoners that became commonplace during the Peloponnesian War between Athens and Sparta would come to bear a striking resemblance to the reciprocal killings that eventually dominated fighting between Nazi and Soviet forces on the eastern front.[37] The inclusion of torture shows that violations do not need to end with the captive's death to count as abuse. The use of waterboarding gained prominence more recently in U.S. interrogation of terrorist detainees, but

[21]

a similar practice then known as the "water cure" was employed by U.S. forces over a century earlier during the war against the Philippines.[38]

Indirect means of inflicting violence against captives can be just as damaging to their fortunes and lives. While some prisoners of Japan on the Pacific front during the Second World War were liable to be beheaded or subjected to medical experimentation, many others perished from a lack of adequate food or shelter often combined with grueling labor.[39] The harsh working conditions showed many parallels to the common employment of prisoners in salt mines or on galleys popularized in Roman times.[40] Even if not employed for economic gain, prisoners have been put in extremely hazardous situations, such as the use of Vietcong guerrillas as human mine detectors by several U.S. platoons during the war in Vietnam, which would frequently end in the captive's death.[41] Prisoner abuse can thus take many forms, but the commonality is a severe assault upon the body and mind of captives subjected to varieties of violence.

Fourth, intentions matter, meaning that prisoner abuse refers to practices that purposefully kill or harm prisoners. Abuses like execution or torture are fairly clear-cut in this regard, but others such as nutritional standards and living conditions are at times more ambiguous. Failing to provide adequate food, shelter, or medical care might not appear as reprehensible as the active shooting of captives. Denying these necessities, however, can in fact cause even worse suffering from malnourishment or disease than does execution, and often leads to similar final outcomes.[42] At the notorious Totskoe camp in Tsarist Russia, upwards of close to 70 percent of Austro-Hungarian prisoners died during the winter of 1915–16 from a typhus epidemic resulting from poor and neglected sanitation and medical facilities.[43]

The proper treatment of combatants involves both negative and positive requirements. Under international law captors are required to refrain from certain practices, like torture or willful killings, but also obligated to provide other services, such as adequate shelter and medical care. General living conditions can, of course, vary a great deal due to the local climate, as well as the economic situation facing the captor state. During both world wars, Germany found it increasingly difficult to care for prisoners due to a tightening naval blockade in the first instance and mounting aerial bombardment in the second. Yet it is also common for many states to cynically claim an inability to care for prisoner populations as a bargaining chip or in order to preserve their image. A general expectation is that captors put forth a good faith effort to care for their prisoners across all of the key dimensions listed above, or at the very least permit help from outside organizations like the International Committee of the Red Cross (ICRC) or other neutral powers. Prisoner abuse

TABLE 1.1 Varieties of prisoner abuse with historical examples

Type of Abuse	Violator	War	Year(s)	Description
Execution	England	Hundred Years' War	1415	Killing of French prisoners at Battle of Agincourt by the order of King Henry V.
Torture	France	Algerian War	1954–62	Harsh interrogation of Algerian fighters.
Living conditions	Great Britain	American Revolutionary War	1775–83	Poor housing, hygiene, and nutrition conditions on British prison ships holding American captives.
Working conditions	Roman Empire	Various conflicts	Early centuries BC/AD	Use of prisoners as hard labor in salt mines; gladiatorial combat; enslavement.
Forced military conscription	Germany	World War II	1941–45	Soviet "Hiwis" pressed into the German armed forces.
Denying judicial rights	United States	War on Terror	2001–present	Indefinite detention without charge or trial of many al-Qaeda and other terrorist suspects.

includes not only cases of deliberately harming captured combatants, but also those instances where the consequences of the captor's actions or inaction would cause foreseeable and avoidable harm to prisoners. Table 1.1 provides an overview of the main varieties of prisoner abuse along with several historical examples.

JUDGING PRISONER ABUSE IN PRACTICE

To reiterate, prisoner abuse is defined as a military strategy enacted by political and military authorities that involves the intentional killing or harming, either directly or indirectly, of enemy combatants who have laid down their arms and surrendered. Translating this general concept

[23]

into a practical measure for assessing the treatment of prisoners presents several challenges. The fog of war enshrouds not only the fighting on the ground but also the ability to observe and assess the treatment of captured combatants. The often chaotic nature of the battlefield, combined with desires of belligerents to conceal their own crimes while magnifying those of the enemy, turns even a straightforward accounting of the number of prisoners held into a daunting endeavor. Past conflicts still point to meaningful differences in the treatment of prisoners that merit some metric for distinguishing between the benevolence and brutality displayed by captors. Three issues in particular need to be addressed when deciding how to rank past instances of prisoner abuse: the types of conflict covered, which captors to include, and how to differentiate the overall level of violence inflicted upon prisoners.

Captives in Interstate Wars

Because the focus of the book is on the treatment of prisoners in wars between states, the data for assessing the patterns and determinants of prisoner abuse consist of interstate wars from the widely used Correlates of War (COW) project.[44] The time period of the study ranges from the end of the nineteenth century, starting with the Spanish-American War of 1898, to the 2003 interstate portion of the Iraq War. While references are sometimes still made to earlier conflicts, for the main analysis prior wars were excluded because of the lack of accessible and reliable data on prisoner treatment in many instances. Near the turn of the twentieth century a wider range and more comprehensive set of scholarly and other primary sources became available that allows for determining in a more comprehensive manner the ways prisoners were treated in a given war.

One of the benefits of selecting this time period is that it matches quite closely the development and codification of the laws of war. Admittedly, the first most commonly accepted international treaty dealing specifically with wartime conduct was negotiated much earlier in the 1864 Convention for the Amelioration of the Condition of the Wounded in Armies in the Field. As the title of the convention makes clear, however, it was fairly narrow in scope and dealt only tangentially with issues related to prisoners of war.[45] In contrast, the 1899 Hague Conventions are widely considered to represent the foundation of the modern laws of war. The Hague treaties provide the basic definition and principles for the treatment of prisoners, which have largely continued in a similar form to the present, though with further inclusion and elaboration of certain rights and responsibilities. The wars considered in this data set thus involve belligerents who at least had an understanding of the general prevailing international rights and obligations concerning prisoners, even if they did not subscribe to them. The greater availability and quality of information on prisoner treatment is likely a further beneficial side effect of the establishment of international laws during this period, providing a focal point for governments and nonstate actors to pay greater attention to, and document the care of, captives during wartime.

Beyond the fact that some of the most notorious instances of prisoner abuse (along with praises of humane treatment) took place in wars between states, a more pragmatic reason for limiting the main analysis to interstate wars is the difficulty of reliably measuring prisoner treatment in each individual case. Data are also generally of a higher quality for interstate wars compared to other conflict types, which allows for greater accuracy and confidence when evaluating each episode of prisoner treatment.

The list of wars examined here includes a few notable changes from the standard COW interstate war data set. As has become increasingly common in the quantitative conflict literature, several long multiactor wars are divided into a series of separate military confrontations to more accurately reflect the actual fighting and political relations between the relevant belligerents. World War I was separated into four individual conflicts, World War II into nine separate conflicts, and the 1990–91 Persian Gulf War into the Iraq-Kuwait and U.S. Coalition-Iraq conflicts.[46] The final data set contains seventy-nine wars in total, which are summarized in table A.4 in the appendix.

Each case of prisoner treatment is composed of a separate warring-directed-dyad. This means that in a given war there are two cases for any pair of opponents, where each is a potential violator or victim. For instance, in the 1982 Falklands War, one case examines British treatment of Argentinean prisoners while the other looks at Argentinean treatment of British prisoners. In wars involving more than two parties, there are two corresponding cases for each pair of opposing states.[47] In theory, this potentially entails an enormous number of cases given the myriad combinations of opponents in large conflicts such as the world wars or the Korean War. In reality, however, most wars involve only a handful of states that are relevant when assessing the treatment of prisoners.

Capable Captors

Genuine instances of prisoner treatment are limited solely to those belligerents deemed "capable captors." A state is considered a capable captor if it meets both of the following two criteria concerning autonomy and opportunity. First, a state must have the capacity for an independent prisoner policy. This is not really a concern in wars between only two states, but in conflicts involving large coalitions subordinate alliance partners often have little leeway in adopting military practices separate from their more powerful patrons. During the Korean War allied forces were nominally under a unified UN command, but the United States dominated all aspects of the planning and prosecution of the war, especially with regard to prisoners.[48] "Beneath a thin veneer of respect for the authority of the United Nations, Americans conducted the war as they saw fit."[49] Similarly, a host of countries technically contributed to the large coalition constructed under UN authority to counter Iraqi aggression in the Persian Gulf War. Yet the planning and care for surrendering Iraqi prisoners were primarily directed by the United States and Saudi Arabia, supplemented somewhat by Britain and France, with others members playing a minor role.[50]

By the same token, violations committed by smaller partners are more appropriately viewed as the responsibility of the larger countries controlling the military coalition. After the failed Dieppe Raid of August 1942 against a German-controlled port in Normandy, it was found that the Allied attackers had bound and blindfolded captured German troops, and orders to this effect were also recovered. While the attacking contingents were primarily composed of Canadian troops, the overall planning for the military operations and the specific orders were primarily made by the Combined Operations Headquarters of the British War Office.[51]

Prisoner treatment by states occupying such subordinate positions should not be treated as distinct episodes since their behavior toward captives is not independent, but largely determined by their overarching ally or allies. Only when belligerents possess separate operational control over prisoner treatment are they considered to have an independent prisoner policy, as in the case of U.S. and British forces during the Second World War.

Second, even if a state is deemed sufficiently autonomous in formulating and implementing prisoner policies, it must also have a sincere opportunity to either treat enemy combatants well or mistreat them. Most wars involve both sides capturing substantial, though not necessarily equal, numbers of soldiers from opposing forces. In cases of particularly one-sided fighting, however, it is not uncommon for the losing side to capture few if any prisoners from their superior adversary. During the Second World War Belgium was quickly overrun by Germany's armed forces, and records indicate no German prisoners were captured.[52] Saudi Arabia likewise easily pushed aside Yemeni defenses during their war in 1934, meaning Yemen had little if any opportunity to capture Saudi combatants.[53] In a similar manner, preoccupied with a more pressing two-front war in Europe, German forces stationed in the Far East and Pacific were overwhelmed after Japan's entry into the First World War on the side of the Entente powers. While Japan captured over four thousand

[26]

German prisoners during its limited military operations, an outmatched Germany was not able to capture a single Japanese soldier.[54]

Coding such belligerents as captors not engaging in prisoner abuse would equate states that never had a meaningful chance to harm enemy combatants with those captors, like the United States during the Persian Gulf War, that actually had an opportunity and actively chose to treat their captives decently. The latter are legitimate negative cases of prisoner abuse, since the state in question committed few if any violations against their prisoners. In contrast, the former are inappropriate, or at best irrelevant, for purposes of comparison, because resorting to abuse is impossible when no prisoners are held.[55] Investigating patterns of prisoner treatment is thus limited to cases of states that had both an independent prisoner policy and an opportunity to harm enemy combatants.

Of course, hypothetically speaking, if a country adopted a universal take-no-prisoners policy, then such a captor may perversely be considered incapable according to the second criterion. Yet even some of the worst abusers from the last century of warfare, such as Nazi Germany on the eastern front during the Second World War or China in the Korean War, took many surrendering soldiers into captivity. Furthermore, summary executions are considered violations of the laws of war and thus count as prisoner abuse by a capable captor.[56] The key is rather to exclude from consideration belligerents without the capacity (whether because of subordinate allied status or the absence of the chance) to engage in and be considered responsible for the mistreatment of prisoners in the first place.

Classifying Prisoner Abuse—Problems and Solutions

War remains a brutal business, and it is a frequent and unfortunate reality that all too many soldiers die in the heat of battle. Soldiers who raise their hands to surrender have removed themselves from the line of fire and the legitimate right to engage in violence. Captors are generally expected to care for their captives appropriately. This is why, as regrettable as the deaths that take place during combat may be, the mishandling or killing of prisoners is so often held in particular disdain. The Katyn massacre described in greater detail in chapter 5, which involved the systematic execution of thousands of Polish officers by the Soviet Union, is a case in point. Even more than seventy years later the massacre continues to trouble Russo-Polish relations, and the name remains a reference point throughout eastern Europe for other past Soviet crimes.[57]

Any wrongdoing deserves to be highlighted and condemned, but acknowledging and identifying substantial differences in abuses by certain countries or in particular wars is important for placing specific episodes in a broader historical context. For instance, the United States certainly committed many deprivations against North Korean and Chinese captives during the Korean War. These actions were far less extreme, however, than the systematic violence wrought by U.S. and other intervening forces in China fifty years earlier during the Boxer Rebellion when troops would go on "Boxer-hunting" expeditions, which frequently ended with summary executions.[58]

Despite notable contrasts in the treatment of captives across many past wars, wartime environments can make reliably determining the level of abuse across a wide range of conflicts extremely difficult. Confusion often reigns on the warfront, leading to an accumulation of battle dead, wounded soldiers, deserters, and prisoners that make it, in the words of one Austro-Hungarian official in charge of POW affairs during the First World War, "impossible to obtain even half-reliable statistics."[59] The sheer mass of prisoners, often numbering in the thousands or sometimes even millions, can make simply keeping track of names an ambitious task, much less ascertaining their treatment or ultimate fate. Actors like the ICRC offer themselves as neutral intermediaries to monitor and advocate for prisoners, but many captors have forbidden access to such groups out of mistrust of foreign influence or to conceal their own misdeeds.[60]

Propaganda is a further concern as belligerents have incentives to downplay their own crimes while exaggerating those of the adversary to heighten domestic or international support. During the 1919–20 war between the Bolshevik Russian regime and a newly independent Poland, both sides were accused of embellishing abuses committed by the opponent to steel the resolve of their soldiers and publics as well as influence international opinion.[61] One U.S. State Department official, tasked as a neutral envoy between Britain and Germany during the First World War, observing the charges and countercharges by both sides remarked that, "In order to stimulate the patriotism of the people, to create the proper atmosphere towards the enemy it is considered essential to attribute to him the faults of heartless cruelty, a lack of all humane principles, and to lay at his door the impossible of all crimes, including rape, massacre and murder."[62] Similarly, belligerents often wish to paint an overly rosy picture of their own treatment of prisoners to assuage domestic and foreign publics as well as to manipulate the beliefs of the adversary's populace. Belying the wretched conditions reported on prison ships in the American Revolutionary War, the British commissary for naval prisoners David Sproat had a dozen captured American officers sign a statement applauding their treatment "in wholesome clean ships . . . every man furnished with a cradle, bed, and sheets made of good Russia linen."[63]

Even if the twin obstacles of wartime environments and propaganda are overcome and it were possible to amass detailed information on the number of prisoners taken or deaths in captivity, this would still only reveal one aspect of the broader phenomenon of mistreatment. According to the more encompassing view of prisoner abuse used in this book, captives do not need to be killed in order to suffer greatly. Torture or other hardships caused by poor nutrition or dangerous labor conditions also count as brutal injustices. Many U.S. and British Commonwealth prisoners fortunate enough to survive their time in Japanese captivity during the Second World War would go on to suffer lifelong and sometimes debilitating ailments.[64] Any sort of continuous measure of prisoner deaths (for instance, total number of deaths, or deaths as a proportion of prisoners taken) not only presents severe practical challenges, but also obscures the full scale of violence that might have taken place against captives.

A categorical scale is instead more appropriate for differentiating between levels of prisoner abuse and allowing clearer comparisons across episodes. Reflecting similar hurdles to data collection involving wartime contexts, employing a categorical measure is in line with many other studies investigating the conduct of states or other warring parties during armed conflict.[65] Following the set of "grave breaches" outlined in the 1949 Geneva Conventions, the treatment of enemy prisoners for capable captors in each war is examined across six separate dimensions: execution, torture, denial of legal rights, compulsory military conscription, hazardous labor, and poor housing and nutrition conditions. Other than a few exceptions, for each type of abuse the captor's treatment is classified according to one of three levels: high, medium, or low.[66] The measure thus centers on determining a belligerent's overall treatment of an enemy's prisoners across the entire war, rather than gathering details on each and every instance of prisoner mistreatment over the course of the conflict. Although a full account of prisoner-related events would provide an extraordinary opportunity for investigating the dynamics of abuse, the realities of existing conflict data preclude such a collection effort across even a small number of cases.[67] Existing events-level conflict sources also are not without their own problems and can often introduce an exaggerated sense of confidence and precision to fluid and uncertain wartime contexts.[68] The present measure focusing on the conduct of capable captors across each war as a whole nonetheless provides a firmer basis for identifying broad distinctions in the behavior of belligerents toward prisoners across different categories of abuse and over time.

High-level cases involve state-sanctioned, widespread, and systematic mistreatment of prisoners along the given dimension of abuse. Although differences in the overall extent of violence may still certainly exist, cases included in this category generally involve captors who show little to no regard for the rights of prisoners falling into their hands. Not every prisoner is necessarily killed or horribly violated, but a general policy and expectation exist that captives will be treated in a brutal manner. Examples include North Vietnamese torture practices toward captured U.S. service members during the Vietnam War and the mass executions frequently carried out by both sides in the 1980–88 Iran-Iraq War.[69] Typifying such high-level abuses, a Carnegie Endowment report on the First and Second Balkan Wars from 1912–13 observed, "In the Balkans they kill their man. If he is made prisoner, disapprobation from very high quarters is sometimes incurred. 'What is the use of dragging this rubbish about?'"[70]

At the other extreme are low-level cases where prisoners are generally treated well and offenses for the relevant type of abuse are rare. In a corresponding manner to high-level cases, this does not necessarily mean violations never occur. Warfare unfortunately, but almost inevitably, entails a harsh reality for most participants, and the lot of prisoners is far from ideal even under favorable conditions. Low-level episodes are perhaps better thought of as the best-case scenario possible out of a range of poor options often facing surrendering soldiers. What distinguishes lower levels of abuse is that mistreatment or hardship is the unusual exception rather than the rule. One indication of the fairly decent treatment assured by U.S. Coalition forces during the Persian Gulf War was that many Iraqi troops flocked toward allied positions, such that mass surrenders actually slowed down Coalition military advances in many areas.[71] Other examples include the relatively humane treatment afforded by both Argentina and Britain to captured enemy combatants during the Falklands War of 1982.[72]

Between these two points lie medium-level cases, where abuses certainly take place to a much greater extent than in low-level instances but are overall less common or extensive compared to high-level abuse. This category may also include more frequent individual actions that are not explicitly supported by the state, but neither are firm steps taken by authorities to prevent further violations from taking place. Examples include several executions of Turkish captives by Italian forces during their 1911–12 war, as well as Finnish conduct toward captured Russian troops during the so-called Continuation War fought on the eastern front later in the Second World War.[73]

The conduct of captors is measured along the same high/medium/low scale for each type of abuse, except for the denial of legal rights and forced military conscription where a binary coding was deemed more suitable. In contrast to the greater degree of gradation in treatment across the other components, in both of these violations prisoners were either forced to serve or not in the captor's armed forces, or their legal rights were or were not infringed upon. Forced conscription, such as by North Korea toward captured South Korean troops during the Korean War, places prisoners directly back into the line of fire and is widely considered a sui generis violation of the laws of war.[74] Violators were thus automatically coded as engaging in high levels of abuse for this type of violation. Denying legal rights, such as Japan's decision through what became known as the Enemy Airmen's Act of 1942 to classify downed Allied pilots as "captured enemy flyers" rather than granting them official POW status, does not in and of itself cause direct physical harm to the prisoner.[75] Violators of legal rights were thus coded as engaging in medium levels of abuse for this dimension. Of course, if denial of legal rights subsequently resulted in torture, summary execution, or other relevant abuses, then the treatment on those other dimensions is reflected accordingly.

The individual component violations are then used to construct a single summary indicator for the level of prisoner abuse based on the following decision rule: the overall value of prisoner abuse is equal to the highest level of offense across the six dimensions. For instance, if a state engaged in high levels of abuse for execution but offered decent labor conditions, it is still considered to have engaged in high levels of abuse overall. This rule was adopted to hold captors to the stringent legal standards that prevailed, since any of these violations on their own constitutes a war crime punishable under international law.[76] Nevertheless, overall patterns in the treatment of captives do not change substantially when using alternative procedures for constructing the prisoner abuse summary indicator.[77]

Decisions on the classification of prisoner treatment in each case were based on an extensive reading of secondary historical resources supplemented by primary documents.[78] To minimize biases posed by relying on historical materials, multiple sources were employed for each war to the greatest extent possible, along with studies written well after the war ended or by individuals without close ties to the conflict in question.[79] Taken together, the amassed data represent the most comprehensive collection of information on prisoner treatment to date, thereby offering the opportunity to assess in a more systematic manner patterns in prisoner abuse over the last century of interstate warfare.

TRENDS IN PRISONER ABUSE

How common is it for prisoners to be abused once they surrender, or are they actually courteously cared for more often than we might think?

Although there are several ready examples of both brutal and honorable prisoner treatment, identifying overall trends in the conduct of captors has remained difficult in the absence of a common metric for abuse. With such a measure in place, general patterns in the treatment of prisoners across interstate wars from 1898 to 2003 begin to emerge more clearly. As will become evident, there is substantial variation in the treatment of prisoners by level of abuse, specific type of violation, and over time.

Table 1.2 summarizes the frequencies and corresponding percentages of cases falling into each level of abuse for the six dimensions of violations. The total number of cases included across each component sometimes differs, since for some types of violations or wars sufficient material was harder to locate than for others. For instance, information was generally more readily available for execution, while gathering definitive details on labor practices proved more challenging.

As we can see, the two extreme points for execution are almost equally likely: a little under one-third of all capable captors engaged in high levels of direct prisoner killing and a similar amount engaged in low levels of direct prisoner killing. Medium degrees of execution turn out to represent the most common outcome for prisoners, though the relative risks of capital punishment faced by surrendering soldiers is fairly evenly balanced across the three levels of abuse. The frequency of killings conducted by Somalia against captured Ethiopian soldiers during the 1977–78 Ogaden War might not be the norm, but the more benevolent conduct of India in safekeeping the lives of many Pakistani prisoners during the 1999 Kargil Conflict is not majority practice either.[80] The fact that prisoners in over two-thirds of the cases faced pronounced dangers of perishing directly at the hands of their captors points to the life-and-death nature of captivity across many conflicts.

A less even distribution is apparent when it comes to the torture of prisoners. Over 40 percent of captors choose not to engage in torture or sparingly resort to harsh interrogation practices. The relatively lower incidence of torture may be due to the greater time, training, and resources required to organize a concerted torture program. The infamous "Hanoi Hilton" of the North Vietnamese had a complex series of holding and interrogation rooms where captives could be interrogated, often for months on end.[81] Torture has also come to be seen as a particularly horrendous violation even compared to other crimes.[82] Any notion that conduct has been driven by a strong antitorture norm, however, is confronted by the fact that the next most common outcome is high levels of torture. Given the smaller propensity for captors to engage in medium amounts of torture, it appears that states more frequently choose to either systematically adopt or refrain from this method of torment. Should a captor choose to engage in torture, they appear more likely to do so in a

TABLE 1.2 Summary for each dimension of prisoner abuse in interstate wars, 1898–2003

Dimension and level of abuse	Frequency	Percentage
Execution		
High	83	31.92%
Medium	95	36.54%
Low	82	31.54%
Torture		
High	80	33.90%
Medium	53	22.46%
Low	103	43.64%
Denial of legal rights		
Yes	185	71.15%
No	75	28.85%
Forced conscription		
Yes	3	1.24%
No	239	98.76%
Hazardous labor		
High	25	16.34%
Medium	29	18.95%
Low	99	64.71%
Living conditions		
High	56	23.73%
Medium	89	37.71%
Low	91	38.56%

Notes: Capable captors only.
Denial of legal rights represents medium-level abuse.
Forced conscription represents high-level abuse.

comprehensive manner as was evident by both sides in the Iran-Iraq War, which led to the ICRC's exceptional decision to twice publically declare that the laws of war needed to be enforced in the conflict by the international community.[83]

The dire fortunes facing most prisoners are perhaps best summed up by the more than 70 percent incidence in which captives have their rights denied in some meaningful sense. The frequency with which legal rights are breached is perhaps not completely surprising, since this is the broadest category of abuse and is not completely divorced from many of the other types of violations.[84] By contrast, the rarity of forced military conscription shows that captors do not resort to all types of violations equally.[85] The reluctance of states to coerce enemy combatants into serving in their armed forces makes some sense. Given U.S. concerns during the Vietnam War of the rise in so-called fragging incidents, where American troops even targeted their own superiors, captors may have good reasons to be wary of placing weapons into the hands of erstwhile enemies.

Although direct use of prisoners in battle is uncommon, more frequent is their placement in hazardous labor conditions, such as mining or large construction projects. Around one-third of all cases involved the presence of labor conditions that reached medium or high levels of abuse. Compared to execution and torture, however, hazardous labor conditions reaching the maximum level of abuse are around half as common. The fact that over two-thirds of captors engage in only low-level abuses in this area suggests that labor has been less of a concern as an overall source of abuse. Some of the practicalities in putting captives to work may put a brake on some of the worst excesses for this dimension of violence. To effectively exploit prisoner labor, working conditions must meet at least modest levels of safety. Even Nazi Germany realized the need to improve conditions for Soviet prisoners somewhat if captive labor forces were to effectively contribute to the war effort for more than a minimal amount of time.[86] There still remain numerous instances, from Imperial Japan to Tsarist Russia, where captors sought to exploit prisoner labor to the greatest extent possible with little care for the well-being of their captives.

On the other hand, in well over half the cases, prisoners must cope with subpar housing, nutrition, and medical resources, which greatly heighten risks of dying from injuries, hunger, or disease. While many Ottoman prisoners were summarily executed by Bulgarian captors and their allies during the First Balkan War beginning in 1912, a large number of others suffered a far worse death through malnutrition and ultimately starvation as they languished in scantily equipped prison camps. Similarly, executions were not infrequent on the western front during the First World War, but as the conflict wore on British prisoners were far more likely to die in the sparse conditions of German camps than in the immediate war zone, which one British War Cabinet member likened to a policy of "slow assassination."[87] Although food and housing requirements are among the areas receiving the greatest attention under international humanitarian law, this has not necessarily translated into healthier or more comfortable living conditions for the vast majority of prisoners.

Looking at each dimension of violations separately reveals some interesting similarities and differences, but it is instructive to assess in a more

[34]

TABLE 1.3 Summary of overall prisoner abuse in interstate wars, 1898–2003

Level of abuse	Frequency	Percentage
High	102	37.50%
Medium	100	36.76%
Low	70	25.74%

Notes: Capable captors only.

comprehensive manner the general risks posed to prisoners across past wars. Table 1.3 reports the relative frequency and percentages of each level of abuse using the summary indicator for prisoner treatment, which is equal to the highest observed extent of violations by a captor across the six components of abuse. Brutality is by no means the only fate awaiting surrendering soldiers in captivity; in more than one in four instances captors behaved fairly humanely and treated prisoners more like guests (albeit under a watchful eye) than victims. The conduct of the United States during the Spanish-American War, Russia during the Russo-Japanese War, or Paraguay during the Chaco War shows that the decent treatment of prisoners is by no means a rarity over the last century of interstate warfare.

Despite numerous episodes where abuses were limited to relatively low levels, history shows this represents the least common strategy adopted by captors. Far more pervasive are medium or higher levels of abuse, which take place at almost identical frequencies. Seemingly irrational decisions, such as continuing to fight on against low odds, become more comprehensible when troops contemplating surrender may be alarmed by what likely awaits them upon capture. The fear of falling into the hands of the North Vietnamese even led several U.S. soldiers to take such extreme actions as calling down air strikes on their own positions during attacks, believing this offered a greater chance of survival than capitulating to the adversary.[88] The prevalence of high levels of abuse, followed in close succession by more modest yet still substantial mistreatment of prisoners, directs attention to the poor prospects faced by many troops finding themselves under enemy control. The distribution across the three categories indicates that no level of prisoner abuse clearly predominates. The fate awaiting many soldiers who surrender is oftentimes certainly harsh but must be considered alongside a significant minority of episodes where the conduct of captors remains more encouraging from a humanitarian standpoint.

Looked at together, the relative frequency of each type of violation and the overall level of abuse demonstrate substantial variation in the

[35]

treatment of prisoners across wars. To provide a better sense of possible temporal trends in the pervasiveness of prisoner abuse, figure 1.1 illustrates changes in the treatment of prisoners over time. The lines in the figure show the percentage of captors engaging in each level of overall abuse during separate twenty-year periods.[89] The final period from 1978 to 2003 covers a slightly longer range, since the time periods do not

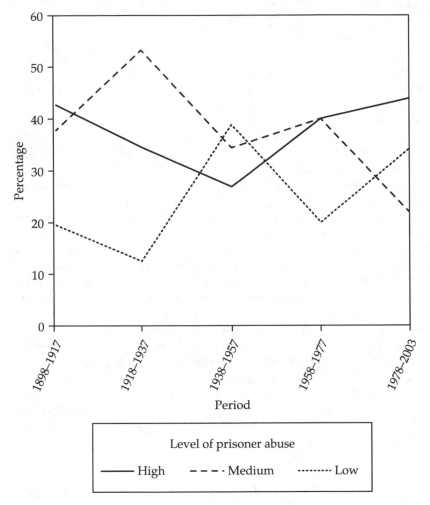

FIGURE 1.1 Trends in the levels of prisoner abuse over time in interstate wars, 1898–2003

Notes: Percentage of each level of prisoner abuse across twenty-year periods of interstate war onset for the years 1898–2003. Last period includes twenty-six years of war onset since the time frame does not divide into an equal number of years.

divide neatly into equal intervals. Figure 1.1 reveals some interesting patterns. Low-level abuses took place at a fairly modest relative frequency in the first period from 1898 to 1917, while high-level abuses were more common compared to the others during the same time frame (43 percent). This period most notably includes the First World War and the marked gap between low- and high-level abuses lends some credence to claims that these truly were the bad old days of warfare typified by brutality both on and off the battlefield.[90]

The subsequent interwar period saw low- and high-level abuses declining somewhat together. While instances at either extreme still occurred, such as the horrific treatment of Chinese captives by Japan in the Third Sino-Japanese War versus the fairly decent conditions for prisoners in the Chaco War, both levels of abuse were less prevalent compared to the earlier period. Mid-level violations, such as during the 1919 Hungarian-Allies War, were by far the most common category, making up over half of all episodes of abuse. This trend toward the mean perhaps reflects a degree of war weariness from the lengthy trench warfare of the First World War but also the smaller overall scale of conflicts at this time compared to the adjoining periods.

The next period, 1938–57, is the only time where lower forms of abuse predominated, which may be somewhat unexpected given both World War II and the Korean War broke out over this stretch. World War II was certainly characterized by almost unprecedented levels of brutality on the eastern front. The treatment of prisoners was on the whole much better in the western theater, though even here Nazi Germany engaged in more frequent and severe abuses against captured Allied troops. This was also a time when the distribution across each level of abuse was the most even, which is reflected in fairly comparable numbers of cases falling into each category of abuse.

Moving further into the second half of the twentieth century, the following period shows a general pattern of convergence in the relative frequency of the two more violent levels of conduct with lower-level abuse again becoming less pronounced. This was the heyday of several drawn-out insurgencies, particularly in Indochina. However, there were also numerous fairly quick wars, such as the Six Day War between Israel and several of its Arab neighbors, or the even shorter Football War between El Salvador and Honduras, where prisoners were for the most part spared the worst forms of violence.

If the prior period was characterized by some merging in the tendencies behind the two greater levels of abuse, the final span from 1978 to 2003 points toward a slight polarizing trend. Mid-level abuses declined to their lowest point of the periods studied, while both lower and higher levels of abuse rose relative to the prior interval. The last few decades

[37]

have witnessed many cases heralding the benevolent ideals espoused by many lawyers and just war theorists, such as U.S. conduct in the Persian Gulf War or the conflict in the Cenepa Valley between Peru and Ecuador in the mid-1990s. However, the most recent era also testifies to the persistent horrors of war where captives have been brutalized, whether on the battlefields separating Iran and Iraq or in the Nagorno-Karabakh region disputed between Armenia and Azerbaijan.

Except for the interwar period, no level of abuse appears to overshadow the others. Focusing solely on lower-level abuses seems to offer some promise for humanitarian proponents, since the relative frequency of these more benevolent cases of prisoner treatment shows some gradual, albeit halting, improvement over time. Counterbalancing this positive swing are the stubbornly high levels exhibited by the most severe forms of violence against prisoners. After dipping around the middle of the twentieth century, the propensity for captors to engage in the most deplorable types of abuse has continued to climb such that levels in the most recent era are actually slightly higher than in the first interval one hundred years earlier.

To be fair, episodes involving medium levels of abuse have shown a general decline, especially since the end of the interwar period. Combined with the modest rise of captors refusing to engage in significant prisoner violations, the average level of abuse demonstrates a small drop over time. It is nonetheless a stark reality that the twentieth century largely ended as it began, with the most common fate for captured soldiers being the infliction of systematic and extreme forms of violence. Although several prominent scholars have pointed to a general improvement across a wide range of metrics related to violence,[91] this uplifting current does not seem to have gained much traction for combatants literally caught in the midst of war. The general pattern over more than a century of interstate warfare indicates that the treatment of captured combatants is not becoming more humane—high levels of abuse regrettably persist. This is sobering news for those policymakers or activists hoping belligerents would have progressively embraced prevailing international norms of humane conduct and correspondingly placed a higher priority on respecting the health and well-being of prisoners falling into their hands.

With this picture of the trends involving prisoner treatment in place, left untouched thus far is what accounts for why captives are victimized in some conflicts but not others. The propensity of captors toward prisoner abuse reveals significant variation over more than a century of warfare but also within specific time periods. There appear to be no universal pressures pushing all, or even most, belligerents toward either purely cruel or completely compassionate conduct toward captives. The next chapter lays out the main set of factors captors often take into account when deciding how to care for surrendering troops and develops an explanation for why belligerents turn to the decent versus poor treatment of their prisoners.

[2]

The Captor's Dilemma

On a wet and dreary October day in 1415, during what would become known as the Battle of Agincourt, thousands of French men-at-arms suddenly found themselves prisoner to their English foes. Although heavily outnumbering the meager English forces led by King Henry V, two successive lines of French assaults had been repelled at horrific costs to the attackers. Many of the newly surrendered Frenchmen would have likely considered themselves the lucky ones. Custom in medieval times dictated that prisoners be ransomed—certainly an expensive proposition for the captive and his family but preferred circumstances to the heaps of their dead or dying brethren accumulating on the muddy battlefield in northern France.[1]

The relative comfort and security enjoyed by the captives would change in an instant. At the same time as the third French line appeared to be massing for a final charge, Henry V received reports of a raid on the English baggage train in the rear that had been left largely undefended. Fearing an impending attack from both sides and the menace of prisoners still in full armor who could easily pick up one of the many weapons strewn across the battlefield, Henry V ordered all captives be immediately executed.[2] Many of the English knights balked at their king's command, less out of any moral qualms or chivalric honor than from the monetary loss of killing such lucrative prizes.[3]

It was thus left to several hundred archers to carry out the gruesome work, and many prisoners were stabbed or cut down at close range, while others were burned alive in cottages where they had been taken for shelter just moments before. After the French assault failed to materialize and word came that the rear attack ended up being only a group of peasants seeking pillage under the direction of a local lord, the threat posed by the prisoners receded and the king spared those still alive. In recounting these events in his play titled after the English king, Shakespeare could not resist betraying a certain irony: "the king, most worthily, hath caused every soldier to cut his prisoner's throat. O, 'tis a gallant king!"[4] Gallant or not, the killings were largely viewed as justified, even by French scribes at the time, given the threat posed by the surrendering French soldiers to the English army.[5] While the exact number of prisoners killed is uncertain, the battle represented a turning point in the Hundred Years' War. In a single day a large share of the French regime's main nobles were dead or captured, opening the way for further conquests by Henry V, though these gains would not be capitalized upon by his successors.

Although taking place six centuries ago, the Agincourt episode highlights some of the enduring questions raised when trying to understand the varied fates that have awaited soldiers in captivity. Captors face a dilemma when deciding what to do with enemy combatants under their control.[6] The resort to abuse, on the one hand, or the offer of humane treatment to prisoners, on the other, can each entail substantial benefits as well as costs. No universal best practices are evident for captors, who have instead often needed to consider both the advantages and drawbacks of the range of prisoner policies available to them.

The lack of any clear guideposts has consequently meant that even if soldiers do not die in battle, their fortunes once taken captive remain far from certain. In some instances, the chivalric code of decency and mutual admiration between captor and captive appears to hold. During the Falklands War, both Argentinean and British prisoners were largely accorded professional courtesies and treated humanely despite the enmity felt between the adversaries.[7] Contrasting conduct is apparent in many other conflicts that reflect some of the worst excesses from the Middle Ages up to the present.[8] During one of the most vicious periods of the Second World War, of approximately ninety thousand German prisoners surrendering at the Battle of Stalingrad, less than five thousand survived to eventually return home.[9]

The prospects for some prisoners of war can at times take on a Hobbesian existence—solitary, poor, nasty, brutish, and short—while for other captives conditions can at times approach more normal levels of comfort. What accounts for these grim differences in the ways captor states choose to treat enemy prisoners? Why are the lives of some prisoners treated so cheaply, while other captured soldiers are accorded the highest care and respect? Differences in the abuse of prisoners over time, or even within the same war, are startling and beg for a more systematic explanation for both the humane treatment and mistreatment of captured combatants.

ASSESSING THE COSTS AND BENEFITS
OF PRISONER ABUSE

What might states have to gain from abusing prisoners? Conversely, what might be the advantages of treating prisoners well? Decisions over how to treat prisoners are far from automatic, as conduct both nasty and nice involves advantages and disadvantages to would-be tormentors or Samaritans. Before considering the causes of prisoner abuse, it is instructive to perform an accounting of some of the possible costs and benefits captor states take into account when developing policies of prisoner treatment along the continuum from diligent care to outright brutality.

Advantages of Abuse

A common presumption is that brutality is an ineffective strategy at best and often becomes detrimental to a belligerent's own interests.[10] Morality and expediency might fortuitously run in the same direction, and the lives of prisoners could be saved if only belligerents somehow realized their mistaken views. Unfortunately, a more sober reading of both recent and earlier conflicts indicates that captors willing to adopt a more vicious approach toward prisoners can reap sizable rewards. Although perpetrators may be deserving of disdain, as with Henry V for his actions at Agincourt, the pervasiveness of the repertoires of violence put forth in the previous chapter points to several substantial benefits that can flow from abusing captives.

Captured enemy combatants represent a potentially valuable source of intelligence regarding the adversary's armed forces and military plans. The use of torture is not simply limited to cruel jailers satisfying their sadistic desires, but rather often intimately tied to broader strategic considerations. Indeed, one of the most widely accepted definitions of torture specifies that a primary objective when inflicting this form of abuse on a person is "for such purposes as obtaining from him or a third person information or a confession."[11] Employing torture, and coercive interrogation techniques more generally, can be an attractive option for captors desperate for knowledge regarding the adversary's movements and motives.[12] The perceived value of torture has even become deeply ingrained in contemporary popular culture. Kiefer Sutherland's character Jack Bauer on the popular television show 24 brought into the mainstream depictions of torture as an effective, but also completely normal, practice when dealing with dangerous foes.[13]

Despite these widely held views, the few empirical studies of torture that exist indicate that coercive interrogation practices are relatively unproductive in securing either reliable or useful intelligence from suspects.[14]

In interviews, many retired interrogators remark that a combination of coaxing and deception often proved more useful than outright violence.[15] Even many captors who have employed torture acknowledge the downsides frequently accompanying the practice. Instructions in an interrogation manual from Imperial Japan's Kempeitai (secret police) cautions, "Care must be exercised when making use of rebukes, invectives or torture as it will result in his telling falsehoods and making a fool of you."[16]

The application of direct coercion is thus not the only way captors can gain intelligence, since holding out the promise of better food and living conditions can also be helpful. China used a mix of carrots in the form of extra rations and comforts, and sticks through a systematic policy of harsh interrogations to obtain information from U.S. prisoners during the Korean War.[17] Yet China's experience also shows the value that can sometimes be gained from torture regardless of the information's veracity; a common Chinese aim was to extract confessions from downed pilots admitting they engaged in bacteriological warfare or similar crimes for propaganda purposes.[18] Irrespective of the actual effectiveness of torture as an interrogation technique, what ultimately matters is the perceived utility of the practice among military and civilian leaders. Appraisals by many high-level decision makers remain stubbornly optimistic, helping to account for the continued popularity of torture both inside and outside of war.[19]

Along with their value as human intelligence, prisoners also present a ready pool of physical labor. Captive workers have rarely been used in the legendary Keynesian fashion of digging holes simply to fill them up again, but rather they augment the war-making capabilities of captor states. A historical study of the benefits of prisoners concludes, "As a worker who may legitimately play a positive role in the enemy's economy, his [i.e. the prisoner's] greatest historical impact may indeed be to benefit the enemy."[20] Modern international humanitarian law conventions actually allow captors to employ prisoners but strictly regulate the type of work allowed, labor conditions, and wages.[21] Even some of the harshest captors like Nazi Germany came to recognize that a minimum level of safety was necessary for *Arbeitskommandos* (labor camps) of prisoners to be productive over more than just the immediate term.[22]

Nevertheless, harsh conditions and dangerous tasks remained a reality for captives in many past conflicts. During times of crisis, of which war is one of the most obvious examples, it can often become expedient to exploit prisoners ruthlessly as a slave workforce. Japanese captors drove their prisoners relentlessly in the building of strategically important bridges and railways to cement control over much of southeast Asia during World War II.[23] During the First World War, Russia pressed thousands of prisoners into a crash program to construct the Murman railway

[43]

to circumvent the blockade imposed by the Central powers on its Baltic and Black Sea harbors. Of around seventy thousand prisoners employed on the railway, twenty-five thousand are thought to have died, while thirty-two thousand others suffered from disease and a series of other debilitating ailments.[24] What was important from Russia's point of view, of course, was that the railway was completed by December 1916.

Beyond the gains from the goods produced, the use of prisoners has the added advantage of freeing more domestic workers to join the military.[25] Belligerents can reallocate domestic labor to the war front while using prisoners to make up for any shortfalls in production. Although somewhat more fortunate than their compatriots laboring on the arctic rail lines, prisoners of Tsarist Russia would come to occupy a significant proportion of the work force in several crucial industrial sectors.[26] Although less common, prisoners can also provide an even more direct contribution to a country's military capacity through forcible conscription into the national armed forces. Germany enlisted approximately three hundred thousand Soviet prisoners, commonly known as *Hiwis*, often against their will, in order to bolster Wehrmacht forces for prolonged campaigns on the eastern front during World War II.[27] In both direct and indirect ways, the ruthless exploitation of prisoner labor can improve the fighting capacity of captor states on the battlefield.

A more socio-psychological logic tying prisoner abuse to increased military capacity centers on the belief that perpetrating atrocities against the enemy can be a good way to fortify the morale and courage of troops on the ground.[28] Officers in the First World War who issued orders to "take no prisoners" thought these would heighten the aggression of their soldiers and their performance in battle.[29] Some of the social benefits gained through violence may be especially attractive for armed groups trying to promote greater social cohesion among their members.[30] Of course, these dividends need to be balanced against likely psychological damages to individual perpetrators, which are especially crippling for those engaging in torture and similar brutalities.[31] The "festering secret" of detainee abuse had particularly pernicious consequences for U.S. service members returning from tours in Iraq.[32] Beyond the mental well-being of individual soldiers, the resulting dynamics can even undermine overall fighting effectiveness. The German armed forces recognized this too late as the almost constant brutalization of Soviet combatants and noncombatants in the east had the corrosive result of unraveling discipline within Wehrmacht ranks over time.[33]

Counterbalancing these more abusive tendencies has been a military code of conduct, or warrior's code, that places certain moral limits on the use of force against the enemy as a whole and prisoners in particular.[34] Embodying a certain timeless quality, historian Michael Ignatieff writes,

"While these codes vary from culture to culture, they seem to exist in all cultures, and their common features are among the oldest artifacts of human morality."[35] Many of the modern laws of war find their origins in the principles of chivalry derived from knightly combat, especially for the protections accorded to prisoners of war.[36] The placing of honor above all else even led historian John Keegan to declare, "There is no substitute for honour as a medium of enforcing decency on the battlefield, never has been, and never will be."[37]

In actual practice, however, principles of the warrior's code have remained malleable, where different understandings or appeals to honor employed to restrain wartime excesses can also enable them.[38] German military officers supporting a devastating *Endkampf* (final battle) as the First World War wore on focused on the importance of preserving their (and by extension, the German people's) honor despite the destruction and loss of life that would have ensued.[39] Likewise, comprehending what behavior counts as honorable is closely linked to the obverse of dishonor, which can have more vicious implications for wartime conduct. Japanese soldiers in the Second World War were taught to view surrender as the ultimate dishonor, which only added to their contempt toward enemy soldiers who laid down their arms.[40] Beyond the particular experiences of Imperial Germany or Japan, even Ignatieff acknowledges, "Such codes may have been honored as often in the breach as in the observance."[41] Although attachments to a warrior's code may frequently be used to justify a more humanitarian course of action, such a code in and of itself does not necessarily provide firm guidance over the costs and benefits involved in the choice to mistreat prisoners.

Even if a captor would in theory prefer to treat its prisoners well—whether out of a notion of honor or more instrumental motives—properly caring for captives is no small logistical undertaking. Food, shelter, medical facilities, and the necessity of large numbers of guards all mean fewer resources can be deployed to the war front or to civilians behind the lines of battle. The needs for housing and maintaining prisoners are often far from minor. For the 1916–17 fiscal year during World War I, Austria-Hungary devoted more of its war expenditures to taking care of its 1.8 million mostly Russian prisoners than it did on explosives for the army.[42] Given the importance of artillery during the war, especially for its ongoing campaign against Italy at the time, the costs of dealing with prisoners were substantial. In light of these concerns, it is not surprising that some captors may choose to mistreat prisoners through more seemingly benign practices, such as neglecting to provide adequate living conditions, in order to devote scarce resources to the military campaign or assuage disgruntled domestic publics facing shortages at home.

[45]

Drawbacks from Abuse

Balanced against the benefits from prisoner abuse are several sets of costs, which highlight the dilemma faced by captors. First, reciprocity always looms large when thinking about the side effects, unintended or otherwise, from choices over wartime conduct. Abusing prisoners almost certainly increases the likelihood the adversary will retaliate against the captor state's own soldiers. While reprisals have fallen out of favor in more recent iterations of international humanitarian law, earlier foundational documents such as the Lieber Coder expressly condoned reciprocating in kind against prisoners for the enemy's misdeeds.[43] Retaliation may be motivated out of a desire for revenge but also as a means to pressure the other side into ceasing its abusive behavior.[44]

In the broader historical context of war, however, retaliation can just as often lead to an escalating series of reprisals that in the end leaves prisoners from both sides worse off. The feelings of many Scottish troops during World War I perhaps best sum up the rationale for retribution, "Fritz [a derogatory term for German soldiers], they insisted, did not take any [prisoners], so why should we?"[45] The tendency for conduct during the Great War to degenerate toward the lowest common denominator led one ICRC official to lament, "Reciprocity, that implacable and unbending deity, [is] the only one to which, during this war, universal and vile homage has been paid."[46]

States thus often remain mindful of the responses their actions in wartime are likely to engender, which may deter them from engaging in abuses. Prisoners often serve a function similar to the exchange of hostages during earlier periods of warfare, ensuring each side would abide by agreed-upon limits to wartime conduct.[47] The degree to which a government is concerned with reciprocity will in large part be a function of how much they value the well-being of their own soldiers, which can vary a great deal. Although dangers from reciprocity may always be present between belligerents, the susceptibility of states to the costs of retaliation is not always equal. As will be explored in further detail below, factors that influence the relative sensitivity of belligerents to the suffering of casualties among their own troops will come to have deep implications for their concerns over reciprocal abuses and, in turn, their willingness to mistreat prisoners in the first place.

Second, abusing prisoners may also become militarily counterproductive. Although detractors of wartime violence often underestimate the benefits of abuse,[48] they do have a point regarding some of the liabilities that mistreating prisoners can incite on the battlefield. Knowing the gruesome fate awaiting them should they fall into the hands of an abusive captor, enemy soldiers may prefer to continue fighting rather than surrender. As a field report from a German Panzer Division stationed on the eastern front in World War II observed, "Numerous interrogations of soldiers of the Red Army have repeatedly confirmed that they are more afraid of falling prisoner than possible death on the battlefield."[49] Abusing prisoners, whatever the immediate advantages, may simply produce a sterner foe, making eventual victory all the more difficult.

In contrast, properly treating the enemy's combatants could actually be advantageous by making remaining soldiers more likely to surrender, thereby removing them from the frontlines.[50] Contrasting patterns in the willingness of soldiers fighting during the First World War to lay down their arms were in large part a function of how they expected to be cared for upon capture.[51] This may help account in part for the level of resources and attention some belligerents have devoted toward publicizing to enemy soldiers that they would be well treated should they choose to give themselves up.[52] Taking steps toward increasing the surrender propensity of the enemy can make good strategic sense, since surrenders drain the adversary of both the physical manpower and morale necessary to effectively wage war.[53]

Good treatment also has potential benefits from the point of view of the captor state's own soldiers. During its brutal war from 1979 to 1989 in Afghanistan, the Soviet Union came to recognize the military advantages stemming from an ICRC plan to transfer prisoners from both sides to a safe haven in a neutral third-party country. As one historian remarked, "it is possible that the Soviet authorities accepted the ICRC proposal because it would enhance the morale of their troops in Afghanistan if they knew that capture by the mujaheddin need not mean a long period of deprivation or summary execution."[54]

Soviet motives in this instance also bring to the fore the other main benefit to one's own soldiers from properly caring for enemy combatants. Reciprocity runs both ways, and just as abuses can result in a downward spiral of atrocious acts, positive treatment can cultivate a virtuous cycle of cooperative behavior even among opponents. Good behavior, or at least ensuring adequate restraints on the extent of abuses and deviations from accepted rules, can create a self-reinforcing process leading to relatively stable levels of cooperation even between warring parties.[55] The latter more benevolent dynamic is expressed in the belief among officials responsible for administering the U.S. prisoner of war system in Europe during World War II that fair and proper care of German prisoners was the best way to ensure the good treatment of U.S. prisoners in Nazi hands.[56] In a similar manner to reciprocity, certain attributes of the belligerents themselves or the conflict may make captors value to a greater (or lesser) extent the possible side benefits to be gained through humanely treating prisoners.

[47]

These various strategic interactions involving the adversary's armed forces on the battlefield would seem to provide compelling reasons for states to avoid harming their captives. However, abusing enemy combatants may present some further benefits for the perpetrator, especially in terms of the expectations and resolve of the captor state's own soldiers. Knowing the adversary is likely to retaliate against prior violations, soldiers from an abusive captor state may be similarly emboldened when facing enemy troops, deciding it is more worthwhile to continue fighting rather than surrender.[57] Part of Adolf Hitler's reasoning behind brutally mistreating Soviet prisoners was to make it almost certain Joseph Stalin would respond in kind. The Soviets' own vicious prisoner conduct in revenge consequently increased the likelihood that German troops would carry on the fight instead of allowing themselves to be captured.[58] The resulting equilibrium involved a much more brutal battlefront, but one with the benefit that the Third Reich's own soldiers remained motivated to continue to bear arms rather than risk almost certain suffering and death as captives.[59] The flip side of the earlier benevolent logic is that prisoner abuse can remain an indirect yet potent instrument (along with more traditional tools like repression or threats of court martial and similar punishments) to encourage one's own forces to continue fighting on the battlefield.[60]

A third downside that captors need to consider is the possible response by third parties and the international community to any violations committed. In wars that outwardly appear to involve fighting between only two states, such as the Russo-Japanese War or the later Falklands War between Argentina and Britain, anticipating the reactions of outside actors can inform the belligerents' decision making over all aspects of the conflict.[61] External actors have frequently inserted themselves in a variety of ways, from outright military intervention to serving as mediators, which can fundamentally transform the nature of ongoing conflicts.[62] Third parties do not necessarily need to actively interfere for their effects to be felt—expectations of intervention can often be sufficient to alter the behavior of warring parties on the ground. Expanding notions of humanitarianism over the course of the last century have meant that outside actors have become increasingly concerned with the fate of populations in other countries, especially in the midst of armed conflict.[63]

External actors have many tools at their disposal to pressure transgressors, which might lead belligerents to think twice before engaging in atrocities like prisoner abuse. At the most basic level, particularly egregious violators may soon themselves fighting more than one enemy as other countries choose to intervene militarily to stop further abuses. In response to ethnic cleansing and several large massacres in the Bosnian War, the North Atlantic Treaty Organization (NATO) began an air campaign in conjunction with UN forces to destroy Bosnian Serb military targets, contributing to the end of the conflict. Wartime conduct, and humanitarian concerns more generally, has become an increasingly cited justification for foreign military intervention.[64]

Third parties do not need to use overt military force to make their outrage felt. Economic sanctions can constrain the flow of goods into a country and impose significant economic hardship on violating governments (though unfortunately often also on their populations). Absent outright embargoes, violators may quickly find themselves excluded from economic opportunities available through preferential trade agreements or from development loans from international organizations like the World Bank.[65] Violators can also face diplomatic rebukes, as well as public condemnations from international institutions and nonstate actors for their conduct, which may hurt their image and interests on the world stage.[66]

The personal stakes for officials ordering or committing abuses have grown with the spread of war crimes tribunals beginning with the Nuremberg and Tokyo Trials after the conclusion of the Second World War. At Nuremberg Wilhelm Keitel, former head of Germany's Oberkommando der Wehrmacht (Armed Forces High Command), was found guilty on several counts including war crimes and crimes against humanity for the poor treatment and killing of prisoners of war and was subsequently sentenced to execution by hanging.[67] The rise of later ad hoc tribunals for conflicts in the former Yugoslavia and Rwanda, subsequently culminating in the International Criminal Court (ICC), has been frequently viewed as offering the potential for an end to impunity for violators.[68]

Coercion in its various forms is not the only way external actors can influence the conduct of armed forces during war. Governments, international organizations, and nongovernmental organizations (NGOs) also often use less confrontational tactics in an attempt to persuade violators to change their ways. One of the most notable success stories in fact involves the very origins of modern humanitarian principles during wartime. From its founding the ICRC played a pivotal role in influencing the world's powers to value the importance of humanitarian action, leading to the support of the international community for the rules of warfare regulated by the Geneva Conventions.[69] In seeking international legitimacy, conformity with existing rules, and esteem in the eyes of others, states can eventually become socialized into appropriate norms of conduct.[70] Taken together, third parties can place pressure upon belligerents—whether through more coercive or more persuasive policies—and raise the costs for engaging in abuses during wartime.

Although there is little doubt that international responses can have repercussions for armed actors, the real question is whether the threats or actions of third parties are sufficient to prevent or halt prisoner abuse. There are several reasons for suspecting that international reactions may not figure prominently in the cost-benefit calculations of captors when deciding how to treat their prisoners.

First, humanitarian norms have certainly spread widely, but they favor certain victimized groups over others, with prisoners of war remaining a lower priority compared to civilians and other specific noncombatant categories. This trend in discounting the needs of prisoners relative to other victimized groups is especially evident in the emerging norm of the responsibility to protect (R2P or RtoP). Grounded in various country-level and UN initiatives, R2P contains three main pillars: (1) countries are responsible for protecting their own populations from grave abuses; (2) the international community should help states meet this responsibility; and (3) if a state fails to protect its population, then the international community should intervene up to and including military force. In one of the first multilateral affirmations of R2P, the Outcome Document of the 2005 World Summit of the UN General Assembly declared in broad terms the "responsibility to protect *populations* from genocide, war crimes, ethnic cleansing and crimes against humanity and its implications" (emphasis added).[71]

The general term "populations" has come to largely denote civilians, even though captured combatants can be the target of genocide, ethnic cleansing, and similar crimes. Many prominent works outlining the origins and development of R2P focus primarily on the protection of civilians and pay little or no attention to the conditions of prisoners.[72] In later actions affirming R2P, such as the 2006 UN Security Resolution 1674 or in the operational mandates for recent peacekeeping operations, objectives continue to be largely framed in terms of protecting civilians.[73] The tenor of the contemporary discourse thus suggests that even in more active periods of humanitarian intervention, prisoners remain a largely hidden and forgotten victim relative to civilians, which leaves captors with substantially greater leeway in their treatment of captives.[74]

Second, even in the case of civilians, where outrage and the potential for action would seem ripest, the international community has been very inconsistent and unequal in its responses. Condemning atrocities may be frequent, but translating this shock into concerted policies to prevent mass killings has been much less forthcoming.[75] The intervention of Western military forces in Libya during the Arab Spring compared to the lack of a robust response at the outset to killing in the Syrian Civil War reinforces how outside actors take into account multiple factors other than the humanitarian merits of an episode of violence. Normative obligations are rarely enough on their own but often need to be buttressed by the material interests of outside powers to motivate intervention.[76] From

[50]

Tsarist Russia's numerous incursions against the Ottoman Empire to protect fellow Christians, to Vietnam's attack against the murderous Pol Pot regime in Cambodia, countries have frequently intervened in humanitarian disasters for unavowedly nonhumanitarian purposes.[77] Taking advantage of apathy or contending interests within the international community, regimes as varied as fascist and communist dictatorships and Western democracies have been able to rationalize noncompliant behavior in ways adequate enough to avoid any meaningful censure.[78] Alongside the poor prospects of outside intervention, the seemingly clear-cut prohibitions on the mistreatment of civilians and prisoners provide a great deal of room for violators to justify or excuse their actions on the world stage. This leeway may be closing somewhat in recent years as many international actors, in particular various UN bodies, place a greater emphasis on humanitarian concerns.[79] Yet throughout much of the twentieth century and earlier, belligerents could count on a relatively free rein in their wartime conduct.

Supposing outside actors actually choose to intervene, a third constraint is that the available policy tools to prevent or halt atrocities have a fairly rough track record. Military interventions, even those with explicit humanitarian goals, under many circumstances can lead to more rather than less killing.[80] Given the fate awaiting civilians, it is unlikely prisoners under enemy control would fare much better. Likewise, economic sanctions in response to human rights abuses, or naming-and-shaming campaigns condemning violators, often have little effect and can even be counterproductive.[81] Even seemingly innocuous steps like diplomatic sanctions to isolate a violator internationally can often have unintended negative consequences.[82] Taken together, the international community may have the potential to hold captors accountable for their actions toward prisoners. Yet both historically and in more recent times, international costs for prisoner abuse have been less consequential than those related more directly to the conflict, such as concerns over reciprocity and consequences for the course of fighting on the battlefield.

In sum, the countervailing costs and benefits thus create an inescapable dilemma for captors when contemplating how to treat prisoners from the opposing side. Each consideration is unlikely to be equally salient for all belligerents, or even for the same state across different situations. Different costs and benefits may also change and interact in complex ways for different captors in shaping their prisoner policies. Past wars demonstrate that no clear universal course of action exists for the treatment of captured combatants. In some cases states seem to emphasize the benefits to be gained from abuse, such as North Korea or Communist China during the Korean War, while in other conflicts, like the Spanish-American War, both sides tend to focus on the downsides of prisoner abuse and refrain from committing violations. The appraisal above suggests a fundamental tension between the costs and benefits of abuse, since acting either virtuously or viciously comes with its own risks and rewards.

INTERNATIONAL LAW AS A CONSTRAINT ON WARTIME CONDUCT

As I described in detail in the prior chapter, beginning concertedly with the 1899 Hague Conventions the international community of states negotiated several treaties laying out a wide range of obligations regulating the proper treatment of prisoners during war. The deeply engrained norm of *pacta sunt servanda*, that promises must be kept, has led to the view that international law fundamentally reshapes the preferences and behavior of states, leading them to overwhelmingly act in ways that comply with their legal obligations.[83] As such and despite some limits, international law is often seen as central to understanding patterns of wartime conduct.

From their very origins (whether in antiquity or more modern times), however, attempts to place legal limits have been under attack from detractors emphasizing the realities inherent to the rigors of warfare. The maxim of Roman politician and philosopher Cicero, "Silent enim leges inter arma" (Laws are silent in time of war), reflects the subservience of legal considerations when national security is at stake. Similar feelings have been evident among military officials. Acknowledging their technical existence, military scholar Carl von Clausewitz was equally skeptical of the relevance of legal rules: "Attached to force are certain self-imposed, imperceptible limitations hardly worth mentioning, known as international law and custom, but they scarcely weaken it."[84] Following in Clausewitz's footsteps, many contemporary realist scholars presume that in an anarchical system where no higher authority exists to enforce treaties, the ability of international law to influence conduct is nonexistent, or at best extremely limited.[85] Just as power is often crucial to the outcome of wars, so too are international agreements seen as largely a function of existing power and interests, possessing no independent effects of their own.[86]

In response to those praising the principle of *pacta sunt servanda*, critics point to the darker corollary of *rebus sic standibus* (things thus standing). The latter provides for terminating legal obligations in the event of changes in circumstances, which belligerents are especially prone to interpret in a flexible fashion to meet their strategic needs.[87] During the First World War, German civilian and military officials relied on precisely this concept to justify a variety of violations.[88] Hopes that captors will

[52]

abide by their legal commitments may be particularly low for prisoners compared to other aspects of wartime conduct. While compliance has actually been fairly impressive on questions like the use of chemical and biological weapons, the record of the laws of war for prisoner treatment has been much more disconcerting.[89] In the related area of civilian victimization, belligerents who ratify the prevailing laws of war appear just as prone to targeting noncombatants as those staying out of the international legal regime.[90] Simply put, when facing severe security threats countries may be especially loath to abide by treaties impinging upon their conduct, such as those concerning the use of torture. In such contexts proviolation groups, whether in official circles or the broader society, are well situated to ensure few limits are placed on the behavior of the government toward its enemies.[91]

In light of critics' contentions that international law is so weak and powerless, the codification and rapid spread of legal institutions over the last few decades is somewhat puzzling. With thousands of agreements across a wide range of issues including international security, state and nonstate actors appear to place a growing faith in the ability of treaties to help solve their problems. In many respects countries certainly seem to act *as if* they are taking international legal commitments seriously. If international law is indeed so inconsequential, it is not clear why states devote so much time and resources to negotiating these agreements in the first place.[92] Recognizing the value of being on the right side of the law, countries also often actively seek to justify their behavior in legal terms.

Even a country's rejection of an international agreement is not necessarily contrary to the influence of international law. Assuming skeptics are correct that the laws of war wield no influence, then there should be few reasons for states not to join such agreements, which would entail few, if any, costs. Yet countries have shown themselves to be extremely careful regarding the legal commitments they are, or are not, willing to make. Ronald Reagan explicitly refused to bring Additional Protocol I (AP I) to the U.S. Senate for consideration because the agreement's expansion of who counts as a combatant would potentially legitimate the status of guerrillas in the eyes of the law. Fights over the scope and design of the ICC during the formative stages of the Rome Statute similarly showed that negotiators realized that the final outcome would have significant implications for the future enforcement of wartime violations and related rules.[93]

There are several routes through which international law can affect the preferences and behavior of states inside and outside of war. Law possesses certain attributes, including generality, nonretroactivity, consistency, and coherence, that distinguish legal norms from other forms of social organization.[94] This unique pedigree creates a "compliance pull" where states obey the rules out of a sense of the laws' legitimacy, rather than simply as a result of possible sanctions from noncompliance.[95] Even countries that have not formally joined a treaty may feel a greater sense of obligation to follow the relevant underlying norms.[96] Toward this end, the 1949 Geneva Conventions were viewed as a crowning achievement for the norm of humanitarian protection of prisoners, which would have deep implications well beyond the actual members of the agreement.[97]

Beyond these more normative functions, international law can help to raise some of the costs of violating the protections of prisoners during war. The laws of war help to clarify which combatants are afforded POW status as well as the protections they are to be granted once in captivity. International law can thus strengthen the functioning of reciprocity between adversaries who will have a common understanding of the promises to which both sides have committed, which helps to reduce possible ambiguities and misunderstandings.[98] Clearer expectations, in turn, further help to deter belligerents from initiating any abuses, since the victimized states would likely see these violations for what they are. What this means, however, is that international law does not inherently serve as a constraint on wartime conduct, since violations of such "legal bright lines" may be more likely to face retaliation in kind than if the situation was more legally vague.[99] Yet by smoothing the dynamics of reciprocity, international law can sow the seeds of its own destruction, especially once a cycle of abuse is in full swing. As the Hague Conventions were slowly undermined during the First World War, U.S. Secretary of State Robert Lansing deplored that "every new breach begat another, which in turn begat others, until the standards of right sanctioned by treaties and usage, were torn to bits."[100] The clarity offered by international treaties also needs to be balanced against the imprecision and vagueness that often accompany legal provisions. The potential for taking advantage of loopholes has been especially acute in the case of prisoner treatment, where rules ranging from nutrition to repatriation have been exploited to the advantage of captors. Even when members of the same treaty, parties can have fundamental differences in the interpretation of their obligations under international law, as occurred to devastating effect through a series of clashes between Germany and her British and French adversaries during the First World War.[101]

Despite some limitations, clarifying legal expectations regarding appropriate wartime conduct can also heighten the strategic liabilities of prisoner abuse on the ground. International promises filter down and can shape the beliefs of troops on the battlefield, meaning that violators of shared legal standards should anticipate facing a sterner and more determined foe both in the near term and the longer run.[102] Lastly, clearer standards can provide a focal point for the beliefs of third-party actors to impose costs upon violators of the international rules governing prisoner treatment in ways that would be more difficult to achieve in their absence.[103] Committing to an international treaty raises the reputational stakes involved in any subsequent untoward behavior.[104] Even if outside actors do not intervene military or economically, breaching avowed international rules can harm the international image and trust previously enjoyed by the violator. In these various ways international law can raise the costs of engaging in prisoner abuse; the question nonetheless remains whether the laws of war can do so sufficiently to alter the conduct of states caught up in fighting on the battlefield.

Cultural Differences and the Barbaric Enemy

The account that stands out the most in the larger historical literature on prisoners centers on the extent of a cultural divide between opposing forces.[105] The sparse but generally fair conditions Napoleon provided for captured soldiers from other European powers while a general in the French Revolutionary Wars stood in stark contrast to his orders to execute all Muslim prisoners during the Battle of Acre against the Ottoman Empire over the same period.[106] Similar contempt for armed forces from opposing cultures was evident in the remarks by an Italian officer during his country's war against Ethiopia from 1895 to 1896: "A bit of Pizarro [referring to the Spanish conquistador of the Incan Empire] does not hurt; with some people terror works better than kindness."[107]

The flip side suggests that similar cultural backgrounds should be credited for breeding compassion among fellow belligerents. Across the many city-states of Ancient Greece, the *koina nomima* (common customs) mandated that prisoners be spared execution and instead properly cared for, while the same rules failed to apply in wars against non-Hellenic foes.[108] Similar restraint between adversaries sharing common cultural traits carried over into many modern conflicts as well. Fighting during the Chaco War between Bolivia and Paraguay from 1932 to 1935 certainly proved at times to be quite fierce. In spite of the high stakes involved, prisoners from both sides were often viewed as unfortunate brethren caught up in a nasty war beyond their control, and as a result were generally treated with decency and a good dose of sympathy.[109] Religious ties and a common sense of brotherhood are also cited as contributing to the lenient treatment Saudi Arabia accorded Yemeni prisoners during the war between the two Arab states in 1934.[110]

The general logic underlying the role of cultural differences exhibits many parallels with the so-called clash of civilizations thesis. According to this argument, civilizational differences, based primarily on religious values, have become the primary dividing lines between countries.[111] Reinforcing this dynamic in a broader manner, social identity theorists posit that processes of in-grouping and out-grouping are ubiquitous and part of a state's project in defining its identity. The unfortunate side effect of this identity formation is that competition with other countries becomes more intense and increasingly violent.[112] Research in this vein has tended to focus on the onset of conflict, but previous work by one of the foremost proponents of cultural arguments, Samuel Huntington, asserts that cultural differences have dire implications for wartime conduct as well: "Over the centuries, however, differences among civilizations have generated the most prolonged *and the most violent* conflicts" (emphasis added).[113]

Abuse against prisoners represents one of the more vivid manifestations of violence during war. Even in Europe, where many of the modern laws restraining wartime conduct originally developed, belligerents made clear distinctions between conflicts within the European family of states and those against external foes.[114] As one historian remarked, wars "against enemies that were considered 'uncivilized' and therefore, under the European code of conduct, could be fought with unrestrained ferocity," entailing grave consequences for captured enemy combatants.[115]

The benefits flowing from abuse may thus be weighed more heavily in wars between states from different cultures, given the absence of any perceived worth of members from the adversary. Lower levels of trust may further lead captors to believe the enemy will mistreat their prisoners irrespective of their own behavior—negating one of the main benefits coming from decent treatment. Although Germany had many motives guiding its conduct on the eastern front, Hitler's belief that the Bolsheviks would inevitably commit abuse themselves perhaps removed any second thoughts toward brutalizing Soviet prisoners during Operation Barbarossa.[116] This leads to the general expectation that warring states from different cultures are more likely to view each other as barbaric, emphasize the benefits of abuse over any costs, and become more willing to mistreat captured combatants compared to those adversaries who happen to share similar cultural traits.

Despite the compelling logic behind cultural approaches, evidence that civilizational differences are a key determinant of the likelihood and bloodiness of war is mixed on both counts. Some scholars have indeed found that civilizational differences increase the probability of conflict between states.[117] Other research has shown, in contrast, that civilization exerts little or no effect on conflict initiation.[118] Studies on the conduct of states once war has begun reveal similar lackluster results. Belligerents from different civilizations are no more likely to target civilians from the

[56]

opposing side than belligerents sharing the same civilizational background.[119] One alternative possibility is that cultural factors may be more salient among troops on the battlefield, leading to greater atrocities committed on the part of individuals or small groups of soldiers. Yet systematic policies of abuse, whether of prisoners or civilians, require the direction and consent of higher authorities, who are likely less brutalized by the fighting on the ground and thus less influenced by cultural forces.[120]

Several historians taking a broader view of patterns in the treatment of combatants nevertheless continue to grant a high status to cultural factors. One examination of a series of conflicts from World War II to the present concludes that prisoner abuse resulted in large part from "those persistent enemies of humanitarianism: mutual incomprehension of alien cultures, ideological fanaticism, and racial hatreds."[121] Reflecting on an even longer time frame involving the last two centuries of warfare, one prominent historian of international humanitarian law argued that "the circumstances most advantageous to observance of the law[s of war] were when armies of not dissimilar race, religion and general ethical notions (i.e. armies able to recognize in their foes 'people of their own kind') . . . faced and fought each other."[122]

If this perspective is correct, that cultural similarity acts as a restraint against atrocities, then it is not clear why in many civil wars between nearly culturally identical foes—where family members have often chosen to fight on opposing sides—the fighting can be so bitter and bloody.[123] Care must be taken when selecting cases to evaluate cultural arguments (or any others for that matter). For all of the wars where one country horribly abuses prisoners from a different racial or cultural group, many others do not fit this pattern. The fierce fighting characterizing the Pacific theater of World War II is often taken as the prototypical example showing how cultural differences and racial hatred led to shocking behavior by both Japanese and U.S. forces.[124] Yet during the same conflict, Japanese conduct toward peoples of Sinic origin, with whom they shared relatively more similar cultural traits, was equally brutal, if not more so, than the treatment of U.S. and British prisoners.[125] Furthermore, cultural differences did not prevent Japan from treating captured Russian and German soldiers in an exemplary fashion during earlier wars, such as the Russo-Japanese War and World War I.[126] Imperial Japanese forces certainly engaged in a brutal campaign against Chinese forces from the 1930s through early 1940s. Yet not far away, near Nomonhan in Mongolia, Japan generally treated captured Soviet soldiers fairly well, at least avoiding the worst excesses being committed simultaneously in battles further south.[127]

Perhaps it is not cultural differences in and of themselves that matter, but rather contrasting discourses of civilization and barbarism expressed by certain segments within a given country. Such discourses have been put forward to help explain the relative restraint exerted by U.S. forces toward Muslim civilians during the War on Terror compared to the extensive abuse against combatants from these same societies. The protection of "innocent" civilians may be justified by a civilizing principle of humanity, while the contrasting lack of regard for combatants is merited by the latter's depiction as a barbarian foe.[128]

Rhetoric concerning the barbarism and immorality of terrorists and other combatants was certainly widespread in many official U.S. pronouncements, but this is not equivalent to saying these beliefs caused U.S. behavior toward enemy combatants in the War on Terror or earlier conflicts. Fascist Italy and Nazi Germany were commonly described in similar barbaric terms in the midst of the Second World War, but this did not stop the United States from treating Axis prisoners quite well.[129] Similarly, during the Persian Gulf War in 1991, President George H. W. Bush deployed comparable language, likening Saddam Hussein to Hitler and Iraqi troops to his Nazi henchmen, yet the United States scrupulously ensured that Iraqi soldiers looking to surrender were protected upon entering captivity.[130]

Discourses of barbarism and the emphasis on the "otherness" of the enemy may sincerely reflect fundamental cultural divides between the belligerents. Barbaric rhetoric remains far more commonplace, however, than the actual abuse of prisoners during war. An alternative rationale for such extreme forms of rhetoric is that they serve as an instrumental device to mobilize public support behind the government during trying times that often demand great sacrifices from the citizenry.[131] When it comes to conduct during the actual war, however, cultural factors appear far less persuasive in accounting for patterns of prisoner abuse.

DEMOCRACY AND PRISONER TREATMENT

Although the merits of civilizational forces may be met with some skepticism, this does not imply that all internal attributes of belligerents are irrelevant for understanding patterns of prisoner treatment. Regime type has been shown to be a key factor explaining a wide range of foreign policies involving both war and peace. The characteristics distinguishing democracies from other regimes may lead them to act in a distinct manner when prosecuting their wars as well. Existing research on regime type and wartime conduct largely follows the democratic peace tradition by distinguishing between the role played by domestic norms and the role of institutions in explaining the distinctive behavior of democracies.[132] While the normative and institutional approaches are usually

[58]

viewed as complementary, recent scholarship on civilian victimization argues the two variants offer diverging predictions for the conduct of democracies during war.[133]

Domestic Norms as Limits on Abuse

Most scholars arguing that democracies fight their wars more humanely emphasize the particular liberal values inculcated in the political culture of democratic regimes.[134] Possessing norms propounding the virtues of nonviolence, democracies may be unwilling to "play rough" and employ more brutal counterinsurgency strategies.[135] Examining mass killings by states across interstate, civil, and colonial conflicts, Valentino et al. reason, "If democratic values promote tolerance, nonviolence, and respect for legal constraints, then democracies should wage their wars more humanely than other forms of government."[136] Such norms are not only embedded in the civilian leaders and their publics, but are also thought to diffuse into the military's thinking and practice, providing a frontline defense against potential abuses on the battlefield.[137] Along with conduct during war, normative arguments gain further support from numerous studies finding democracies are less willing to commit human rights abuses against their own citizens up to and including some of the most extreme forms of violence, such as genocide.[138]

Norms-based arguments have overwhelmingly focused on the treatment of civilians, but the same logic is consistent with properly caring for prisoners. If principles of tolerance, nonviolence, and respect for individual rights provide protections for enemy civilians, then the same should hold true for combatants. Normative arguments center on a broader process whereby states tend to translate their internal beliefs and practices externally into foreign affairs.[139] In democracies, domestic political culture centers on the fundamental equality of rights among individual citizens, which they are predisposed to apply with equal vigor in their external relations.[140] Translating Immanuel Kant's articles of perpetual peace to the battlefield, the tendency for democracies to project domestic norms of respect for individual rights necessitates complying with all aspects of the laws of war, in particular toward enemy combatants.[141] In his *Second Treatise of Government*, John Locke follows a similar logic in asserting that liberal principles of respect for individual rights mandate that states treat not only the adversary's civilians justly, but also their soldiers.[142] The norms promoted through domestic political culture, based on fostering a respect for individual rights and adherence to norms of tolerance and nonviolence, leads to the general expectation that democracies will treat enemy prisoners on the whole in a more humane manner.

[59]

The normative approach appears to offer a compelling explanation for the conduct of democracies during war, but several concerns need to be kept in mind. Returning to the democratic peace thesis from which many regime-type arguments draw their insights, democracies are generally only expected to externalize their norms of nonviolence when facing other democracies. When dealing with other regime types, a democratic state "may feel obliged to adapt to the harsher norms or international conduct of the latter, lest it be exploited or eliminated by the nondemocratic state that takes advantage of the inherent moderation of democracies."[143] Since democracies only tend to fight nondemocracies, by extension they may be expected to act in ways more similar to their autocratic counterparts. Prohibitions against violence are by no means absolute. Particularly when facing a violent adversary, democracies may find it entirely consistent with their values to respond forcefully in order to protect themselves.[144]

Even taken on their own terms, in numerous instances the domestic political culture distinctive to democracies appears to have offered few constraints on their conduct in times of armed conflict. Supposedly robust norms of nonviolence and respect for individual rights have not prevented democracies from waging wars of imperial conquest or engaging in covert actions to topple legitimately elected foreign governments.[145] Even in cases where democracies did not personally commit atrocities, they still frequently provided indirect support to perpetrators or stood by, allowing violence to continue unchecked.[146]

Democratic publics do not always reflect the liberal norms so often attributed to them and can in fact be quite bellicose, or at the very least indifferent to the suffering of outside groups.[147] Belying their supposedly pacific nature, democratic publics in many cases have been quite supportive of both aggressive territorial expansion and the use of brutal methods against civilians and combatants alike.[148] When facing threats to national security, democratic publics have also proved enthusiastic in supporting harsh methods against prisoners, ranging from coercive interrogation techniques to the denial of basic legal rights.[149] Indeed, in times of severe political conflict democracies often willingly heighten repression against their own citizens, meaning enemy combatants should expect to receive even less mercy.[150]

Reflecting this more ambivalent view on regime type and wartime violence, several recent studies find democracy exerts little or no restraining effect on the treatment of civilians inside or outside of armed conflict.[151] If the skeptics are correct and democracy does not reduce risks to the lives of unarmed civilians, then democratic norms are likely to exert even less restraint on the treatment of combatants who were directly engaging in battle up until their capture.

Domestic Institutions—Enabling Abuse?

The second main variant of regime-type arguments centers on democracies' institutional rather than norms-based characteristics. The logic focuses on the tendency for democratic leaders to be held more accountable by their publics than leaders of other regime types. War remains one of the most salient measures of a government's competence, and the tenure of democratic leaders may be especially sensitive to the rising costs of war and the prospects for defeat.[152] Although governments may benefit from an initial rally-round-the-flag effect from the opening use of force, public support often declines precipitously as the duration of the war lengthens and casualties mount.[153] The greater electoral vulnerability of democratic governments leads to the contention that democracies are both more selective in the wars they initiate and more likely to fight harder and more effectively once war begins.[154]

Fighting "hard" can refer to a wide range of behavior, such as devoting greater resources and energy to the war effort.[155] However, a more direct implication is that this increased enthusiasm may also translate into more violent conduct on the battlefield. The stringent demands placed upon democracies not only to win but also to minimize their own casualties might actually make them *more* likely to fight in nastier ways than nondemocratic belligerents.[156] Democracies have indeed been shown to be more willing in many situations to target civilians during war, and the motives behind this democratic bent toward atrocity are often rooted in domestic institutional pressures.[157] For democracies, strategies relying on extreme forms of violence may be part of an attempt to coerce the other side into giving up because of the greater human toll wrought by targeting noncombatants, or as a way to shift the risks and costs of fighting from their own troops and onto civilians from the opposing side. It follows that a similar logic may operate even more forcefully with enemy combatants, since they pose a greater threat to the belligerent's own citizens and soldiers. Institutional strains on democracies to win may lead them to emphasize the benefits of prisoner abuse over the costs, thus making them more prone toward mistreating captives under their control.

Institutional Constraints on Wartime Violence

Much of the existing research on wartime conduct portrays domestic normative and institutional imperatives as producing radically different expectations for the conduct of democracies during war.[158] Domestic norms of nonviolence (to the extent that they exist) restrain the worst forms of abuse, while institutional pressures push democracies toward ever-greater levels of violence in wartime. Looking more closely at the particular dynamics involved in the treatment of prisoners, however, shows democratic institutions should actually generate significant constraints on prisoner abuse. Although democracies may be expected to fight harder to win their wars, domestic institutional forces also command them to win quickly and cheaply in terms of casualties.[159] These pressures mean democracies will be especially concerned with two of the costs associated with abusing prisoners: fears of retaliation and the strategic liabilities from poor conduct.[160] The flip side is that good treatment can yield substantial advantages on both counts, which democracies should have a greater desire to capitalize upon. The logic of reciprocity is intimately tied to regime type because domestic institutional incentives raise the relative sensitivity of democratic regimes to retaliation, which directly affects the well-being of their own troops. In a similar manner, democratic regimes may also be more attracted to the benefits accrued through humanely treating enemy soldiers, irrespective of any normative appeals stemming from their political culture.

First on reciprocity, if democracies are indeed more sensitive to the fate of their soldiers because of greater accountability to their public, then the looming prospect of reprisals will make them less, rather than more, willing to mistreat enemy prisoners. Even if abusing enemy prisoners holds out the promise of substantial immediate gains, democracies may be more susceptible to the resulting costs than autocracies and think twice before turning to such harsh tactics. Mistreating enemy prisoners regularly results in retaliation in kind. Because of this, decent treatment can offer some insurance, however limited, against an adversary's use of even worse forms of violence against prisoners. Pressured by the public's demand to improve the safety of their soldiers in captivity, the British government devoted sizable resources during World War I to sending aid packages and arranging visits by international monitors to prisoner camps in Germany.[161] During the next great conflagration a few decades later, and contrary to his normal hardnosed character, Winston Churchill intervened on many occasions throughout World War II to safeguard the treatment of German and Italian prisoners under Allied control out of fear the Axis powers would retaliate against British and Commonwealth prisoners in their hands.[162]

Decent prisoner treatment on the part of democracies is by no means unique and shares many parallels with their tendency to adopt fairer military policies out of the need to obtain domestic support and legitimacy.[163] When democratic regimes have adopted practices that are not in the interests of their citizens, and especially their soldiers, they commonly suffered grave consequences as a result. Large-scale mutinies within the French army in 1917 almost led to the collapse of the western front in many locations and were largely credited to the growing discontent among soldiers toward the horrific death tolls from seemingly pointless frontal assaults on prepared German positions.[164] Turning specifically to prisoner abuse, some of the most vocal opponents within the Bush administration to the decision to reject the Geneva Conventions in the War on Terror came from those with close ties to the military, who shared fears of retaliation against U.S. service members captured by the adversary.[165]

Overall, the institutional pressures for democracies to win the wars they fight need to be counterbalanced by *how* their publics and domestic elites expect them to win. If prisoner abuse is liable to result in abuse in kind against prisoners held by the enemy, then institutional incentives may in fact run in the same direction as, rather than counter to, normative commitments toward individual rights and nonviolence. Of course, nondemocracies are not oblivious to the potential loss of their own soldiers on the battlefield or in captivity. All states to a certain degree care about the fate of their troops, since this will likely produce domestic ramifications and also affect their military capabilities if large numbers of soldiers are lost and cannot easily be replaced. Nevertheless, the lack of similar public accountability in autocracies means their leaders have less reason to worry over the possible domestic consequences of retaliatory abuses.

Stalin showed little sympathy for Soviet troops at the mercy of Nazi Germany. Those lucky enough to survive their time in German captivity were usually not welcomed home with open arms. During the war, he asserted that "In Hitler's camps there are no Russian prisoners of war, only Russian traitors, and we shall do away with them when the war is over."[166] Even after one of his own sons was captured, Stalin refused numerous German offers of exchange, and his offspring eventually died in captivity.[167] If the communist dictator showed so little regard for the well-being of his own family, it is unlikely that fears of retaliation against Soviet troops would have had much bearing on his decision making over how to treat Axis prisoners. Napoleon showed a similar lack of concern, declaring "I do not care a fig for the lives of a million men," suggesting that worries over the fate awaiting his soldiers upon capture was not a top priority.[168] In contrast, the domestic institutions generating greater accountability to the people make democracies relatively more sensitive than autocracies to the costs of reciprocity, and their conduct toward enemy soldiers should correspondingly be more lenient.

Second, democracies emphasize to a much greater extent the strategic benefits to be gained from treating enemy combatants in a humane manner. As noted earlier, acting "justly" is not always contrary to military effectiveness. All else being equal, treating enemy combatants decently should increase the propensity of those soldiers still on the battlefield to surrender. By caring for enemy prisoners properly, democracies can mitigate the risks of retaliation against their own soldiers and at the same time reduce the fighting force of their opponent by inducing greater numbers of surrenders.

Democracies possess certain comparative advantages over other regime types that make them especially attracted toward emphasizing these strategic benefits arising from humane conduct, instead of advantages gained from abuse. Surrendering can be an agonizing decision both on the minds of soldiers who may feel shame in letting down their comrades and country, and also for their bodies given the physical hardships that often accompany captivity. To encourage surrenders requires in large part convincing enemy soldiers that captors will assure their rights and protections as prisoners. Such assurances are by no means straightforward to make, nor are they likely to be simply taken by troops at face value—one scholar wagers that in the heat of battle a soldier looking to surrender has at best a 50 percent probability of being given quarter.[169]

Yet there are reasons to believe that the regime type of the adversary can affect not only individual beliefs about the likelihood of being taken alive but also subsequent conditions once in captivity. Because democracies generally treat their own citizens humanely, enemy soldiers are more likely to believe democratic promises of good conduct, and thus be more willing to lay down their arms to a democratic captor.[170] Individual beliefs were essential to the success of Allied promises of humane prisoner conduct in prompting Wehrmacht soldiers to surrender during the Second World War. German soldiers shared "the attitude that the British and the Americans were respectable law-abiding soldiers who would treat their captives according to international law."[171] As one soldier admitted, "Nobody exactly wants to get captured, but I and my comrades all expected humane treatment from the Americans."[172] Similar patterns held during the Great War two decades earlier, where soldiers from the Central powers gave themselves up at much higher rates to British and French forces compared to their Russian Entente ally who provided much harsher conditions for prisoners.[173]

Nondemocracies usually have a harder time convincing enemy combatants to surrender. Promises of humane prisoner treatment are unlikely to be seen as credible in the eyes of enemy soldiers—autocratic penchants to violate the rights of their own citizens mean enemy combatants may expect similar or even worse levels of violence directed toward them.[174] Similar attempts by dictatorships to encourage surrenders through promises of good treatment have usually come across as clumsy and met with reactions ranging from skepticism to outright derision.[175] Autocrats thus have fewer strategic incentives to treat prisoners humanely and all the more reason to weigh the benefits of abuse more heavily over those from good conduct.

Because of these democratic advantages, past episodes indeed show that democracies often devote significant resources not only to properly caring for captives but also to publicizing their prisoner policies to enemy soldiers. During the 1990–91 Persian Gulf War, the United States dropped millions of leaflets on Iraqi forces in the field encouraging them to surrender with promises of proper treatment.[176] U.S. planning expanded to educating their own soldiers of their obligations under international law to respect the rights of prisoners and the military advantages to be gained. Through a widespread dissemination campaign, the Geneva Conventions became the "Book Choice of the Month" for U.S. forces during the war.[177]

Of course, democratic institutional restraints on prisoner abuse may not always be enough to guarantee proper care for enemy combatants. Should the strategic benefits from good treatment seem minimal, the advantages of acting justly may lose out to the potential benefits of abuse. Furthermore, if concerns over retaliation weaken or disappear either because abuses by the adversary spiral out of control or because the adversary no longer possesses adequate numbers of prisoners to serve as a deterrent, then institutional incentives and any associated normative constraints may be insufficient to prevent democratic belligerents from resorting to prisoner abuse. The relative presence or absence of fears of reciprocity and sensitivity to strategic advantages from good treatment thus point to ways in which the domestic institutions of democracies may help explain instances of *both* benevolent and brutal conduct toward prisoners.

Attention to the constraints generated by domestic institutions may also help to explain the divergence between the humane conduct often accorded to prisoners, on the one hand, and the inclination of many democracies to victimize civilians evident in other studies.[178] Both institutionally driven incentives—fears of retaliation and the strategic benefits from good conduct—are less present in most cases involving civilians compared to enemy combatants. Publics may be wary that a government willing to kill foreign civilians will one day turn on its own people, but this concern does not appear to be terribly compelling. Past wars indicate that strategies of civilian victimization can actually be quite popular with publics, especially if they are seen as saving the lives of their own soldiers.[179] Concerns over reciprocity should still exist, but democracies often significantly reduce the risks to their own civilians by finding ways to wage conflicts far away from their homeland.[180] Soldiers are instead much more vulnerable, since they often have to fight on the ground and come into direct contact with enemy troops, irrespective of the location of the battlefront. Democracies may perhaps be able to reduce these dangers by relying more heavily on air or naval forces, but recent conflicts demonstrate that substantial ground forces are usually still required for effectively prosecuting wars.[181] Furthermore, beliefs over the benefits from targeting civilians have generally remained high, or at least higher than beliefs over the benefits of prisoner abuse, though debates over the merits of detainee policies during the War on Terror suggest the trend may be changing somewhat. The domestic institutions of democracies thus offer a compelling account not only for their generally humane treatment of prisoners during war, but also instances where democratic belligerents adopt more violent practices.

THE NATURE OF THE CONFLICT: WAR AIMS AND THE SEVERITY OF THE FIGHTING

Regime-type arguments place the emphasis on internal incentives but leave open motives resulting from the nature of conflict as factors in their own right. Armed conflicts differ across a wide range of dimensions, with implications for how vulnerable groups like captured combatants are likely to be treated. Two characteristics of the war itself—the types of aims sought through force of arms and the severity of the fighting—can greatly influence how states weigh the costs and benefits of prisoner abuse, irrespective of their domestic characteristics.

The Severity of Warfare

Conflicts vary greatly in terms of just how grim and harsh the combat between opposing forces ends up being. Some conflicts, like the aptly named Six Day War between Israel and a number of its Arab neighbors, involve lightning-quick maneuvers leading to outright victory for the superior power in a short period of time. Others, such as the static warfare defining much of the western front during the First World War, devolve into a series of seemingly unending battles between two increasingly exhausted opponents. A number of reinforcing factors make the latter types of wars characterized by fighting of higher severity more likely to result in prisoner abuse. When the quarrel becomes bogged down into a war of attrition, and as the conflict lengthens and the number of battle deaths rises, states may be more likely to abuse prisoners falling into their hands, as occurred in the trenches of western Europe.[182]

Belligerents in the midst of a hard-fought war are especially appreciative of a further benefit of prisoner abuse only briefly touched upon up to this point—the coercive potential available from mistreating captured enemy combatants. At its core, coercion involves manipulating the costs and benefits of the adversary for the purpose of changing its behavior.[183] Wars rarely finish with one side utterly exhausted and completely defeated; rather, they usually end through some form of negotiated settlement even if both sides still have resources to continue the campaign.[184] Fighting reveals information about the capabilities and resolve of the belligerents, particularly each side's relative ability to inflict and bear the painful costs of war.[185] Leaders often take into account not only their chances of winning and the potential spoils of victory but also the costs to themselves and their country. A warring party may pull out not because it no longer has the capability to fight but rather due to its unwillingness to absorb the continued costs from war. Employing massive amounts of violence against combatants presents a stark, yet potentially effective, means for imposing sufficient pain on an adversary.[186]

The allure of coercion may be present in many wars but should be particularly enticing to captors in protracted stalemates where achieving a definitive favorable outcome using traditional methods becomes remote. Bearing a close resemblance to the stagnant fighting in western Europe from 1914 through 1918, Eritrea and Ethiopia's conflict more than eight decades later also shared in the horrific treatment of prisoners, as each side tried to make the war as excruciating for the other side as possible.[187] Similar dynamics were also evident several millennia before when the supposedly robust cultural norms limiting violence within the Greek world came crashing down in an escalating series of prisoner massacres and other atrocities during the prolonged Peloponnesian War between Athens and Sparta.[188]

Beyond undermining the resolve of the enemy, prisoner abuse can significantly impact the material capabilities of the adversary over both the near and long term.[189] The capture of enemy troops already reduces the adversary's ability to wage war by removing these soldiers from combat. Whether prisoners are treated well or abused does not change this immediate impact on the manpower of the adversary. Employing violence against those prisoners, however, can produce several additional side effects on the enemy's power calculations. States are obviously concerned with the current war but also remain wary of possible future military threats.[190] This is especially true for rivals, who tend to get involved in more intense and protracted wars with each other to begin with, but who are also likely to meet the same opponent in armed conflict in the not too distant future.[191] If prisoners are instead executed or abused in other extreme ways, then the future military capacity of the victim state can be substantially weakened.

[67]

Even without the outright killing of prisoners, belligerents can use captives to manipulate their adversary to devastating effect. Captors are normally expected to return prisoners at the end of the conflict, which would allow former captives to once again contribute to their home state's fighting forces.[192] Yet there is no guarantee that prisoners will be returned in a timely manner, if at all. States recognize the strategic value of prisoners as an asset for bargaining with the enemy, which helps explain why negotiations over their return (either in exchanges during the war or repatriation afterward) are often long and arduous. One of the reasons Western powers delayed repatriating formerly allied Russian soldiers still held by a recently defeated Germany from the First World War was the fear they would strengthen the Bolshevik side in the unfolding Russian Civil War.[193] Russian prisoners languished in prison camps well after hostilities formally ceased, many dying in captivity when they could have returned, because of power politics between the Western victors and an emerging communist rival.

Belligerents caught in severe wars are also tempted to avail themselves of prisoner labor to the greatest extent possible through a logic of extraction. The high costs and personnel needed to properly care for prisoners often grate on captors, since these captured combatants directly contributed to the drawn-out fighting in the first place. Resources are especially scarce in conflicts of attrition, which often take on the quality of a total war where belligerents mobilize their entire societies and economies. Prisoners are often then viewed as a nettlesome problem diverting resources from more pressing needs on the war front. In such extreme conflicts captured enemy combatants are, instead, likely to be exploited to a similarly harsh degree with little regard for their safety and well-being. Some of the most ruthless episodes of hard prisoner labor, from the jungles of Japanese-controlled southeast Asia to the tundra of Siberia, took place in wars where captors were trying to maximize every resource possible.

The dilemma facing captors is that these coercive and extractive benefits of prisoner abuse need to be balanced against the potential costs. Belligerents trying to punish the adversary into submission have generally found this to be a not terribly effective strategy in past conflicts.[194] Modern nation-states have shown themselves to be fairly resilient against even extremely high levels of suffering, and attempts to coerce can just as soon harden the will of the enemy to resist.[195] Instead of weakening the other side, mistreating prisoners may end up creating a smaller but more resolute enemy fighting force. Nevertheless, victimizing vulnerable groups from the adversary has proven to be effective in some circumstances.[196] Whatever the precise balance of the pros and cons of prisoner abuse, during an entrenched conflict increasingly desperate states will often feel pressured into adopting any strategy that improves their chances of victory, however remote.[197] While good treatment can offer benefits of encouraging enemy surrenders, implementing humane policies in the midst of wars of attrition is likely to face daunting hurdles both on the battlefield and at home. Especially severe fighting often leads to the barbarization of warfare, brutalizing combatants and making it more likely they will commit atrocities rather than conduct themselves with restraint.[198] Affording decent treatment to enemy prisoners is likely to be met with derision and viewed as coddling foreign killers by the captor state's own population, which has had to bear hardships and make sacrifices toward the all-out war effort. Civilians of the captor state have themselves even become the perpetrators of abuse against enemy combatants, as took place toward prisoners on both sides during World War I where publics are often thought to serve as a constraint against violent impulses.[199] When finding themselves in such severe conflicts, belligerents will thus tend to calculate that the expected benefits of prisoner abuse outweigh the costs that may follow.

War Aims and the Centrality of Territory

States going to war have sought to achieve a wide range of objectives through force of arms.[200] Some aims generate greater incentives to abuse prisoners than others. Disputes over territory are particularly intractable and tend toward higher levels of conflict.[201] Taking territory or regaining lost lands represents a key source behind the origins of political extremism and subsequent perpetration of mass levels of violence across varied countries and contexts.[202] The desire not only to conquer, but also to continue to control, enemy territory also contains at its core the reasoning for captors to especially want to engage in prisoner abuse when land is at stake. One of the reasons civilians are so consistently targeted in wars of annexation is because they embody a potential "fifth column," which could foment rebellion against occupying powers.[203] If conquerors perceive civilians as threats, then enemy prisoners present a particularly menacing danger. Soldiers are usually of prime military age and have received at least a minimum level of combat training, making them a serious hazard for would-be conquerors.[204]

The problem of what to do with prisoners at war's end given their latent military power has vexed many captor states. Former prisoners have often played a pivotal role in the politics of both their captor and home states. After World War I, the Czech Legion influenced the course of the Russian Civil War by bolstering anti-Bolshevik forces.[205] Working from similar experiences but ending up at the opposite ideological spectrum, the communist takeover of Hungary in 1919, resulting in the Hungarian-Allies War later that year, was largely led by former prisoners who had absorbed radical Bolshevik teachings during their earlier captivity in Russia.[206]

The defining trait of wars of annexation is the aspiration of prospective conquerors to achieve permanent rule over the territory in question. Indefinitely holding enemy combatants in captivity is one option but would quickly become costly and divert resources from solidifying control over the civilian populace and exploiting freshly conquered lands. Furthermore, the danger of prisoners escaping and taking up arms would always exist. Rather than taking such chances, conquerors are highly inclined toward ruthlessly eliminating any future threat posed by enemy combatants.

The close ties between territorial motives and prisoner abuse demonstrate a remarkable consistency over time. After successfully taking over Jerusalem during the First Crusade in 1099, the victorious Christian army quickly dispatched all remaining captured Muslim soldiers to cement their hold over the Holy City, especially in the face of a counterattack by enemy Fatimid forces.[207] Both the sheer number and speed at which prisoners were killed led one observer to exclaim, "If you had been there, your feet would have been stained to the ankles in the blood of the slain."[208]

The propensity to see enemy combatants not only as unwanted elements but also as a direct challenge to conquering captors endured into the modern era of warfare. Despite the public pretext to protect minorities under the control of the Ottoman Empire, the brutalities meted out to surrendering Turkish soldiers by various Balkan allies reflected their desire to wipe out any resistance to extending their national borders.[209] Challenging any notion of common Balkan ties of respect and fraternity, former allies quickly turned on a displeased Bulgaria when coveting further territorial gains at its expense, and Bulgarian prisoners were correspondingly victimized with equal fury.[210]

The German campaign against Soviet Russia during World War II is often described as an ideological war driven by a sense of racial superiority, but the territorial dimension of the conflict should not be overlooked. The living space (*Lebensraum*) sought by the Nazi regime was to come primarily at the expense of Soviet territory. The German leadership also realized that the threat posed by all Soviet prisoners was not equal. In the lead-up to the invasion, Hitler issued to German armed forces the Commissar Order (Kommissarbefehl), which mandated the immediate execution on site of all commissars found within captured Soviet armed forces. The preamble justified the order as follows, "To show consideration of these elements [i.e., principles of humanity] or to act in accordance with international rules of war is wrong and endangers both our own security and the rapid pacification of conquered territory."[211] Territorial conflicts may certainly differ somewhat among each other in their intensity, in particular regarding the size of the land and the nature of the populations under dispute, and correspondingly in the strength of the incentives for abusing enemy combatants.[212] Yet overwhelmingly territory has been a central motive behind many of the worst cases of prisoner abuse across a wide range of captors and eras.

While annexationist desires have been central in many past instances of prisoner abuse, other expansive war aims, such as unconditional surrender or regime change, do not necessarily provide such clear incentives. The coercive potential of prisoner abuse provides one route toward forcing an adversary to surrender without preconditions. As noted earlier, however, extreme levels of violence can actually prove detrimental for achieving unconditional surrender, because enemy soldiers may prefer to continue fighting rather than laying down their arms. U.S. aims for unconditional surrender on both the European and Pacific fronts during the Second World War were followed by concerted attempts later in the conflict to employ good prisoner treatment to induce surrenders instead of heightening violations.[213]

A similar ambivalence in the resort to prisoner abuse is evident in wars involving regime change, where a belligerent needs to be mindful of the effect of the current conduct of the war on the stability and quality of the subsequent peace.[214] As with wars of territorial annexation, forcibly imposing regime change on a conquered society can lead to significant resistance, up to and including armed rebellion.[215] As with territorial annexation, former prisoners would be well placed for playing a potentially active role in any resulting armed insurgency against outside powers. Yet soldiers, and the military more generally, have at times demonstrated their usefulness as allies helping to stabilize the domestic situation after the overthrow of the prior government.[216] Committing abuses against prisoners risks undermining both the capability and willingness of the adversary's military to make a constructive contribution to any future regime. The experience of the United States in the aftermath of the 2003 invasion of Iraq offers a cautionary tale in this regard, where outright abuses along with poor planning left a core of disgruntled former Iraqi soldiers who would only help to fuel the insurgency that bedeviled U.S. forces for a decade to come.[217] As these cases show, incentives for mistreating captives are not necessarily absent when looking at other types of ambitious war aims, but the prospects for prisoner abuse are less clear compared to territorial motives.

Assessing the dilemma faced by captors points to a series of factors shaping how belligerents choose to weigh the costs and benefits for the range of prisoner policies available to them. The next chapter turns to using quantitative evidence to examine the treatment of captives across a large number of wars over the last century to evaluate which factors offer a more compelling account for the patterns of prisoner treatment.

[3]

Prisoners by the Numbers

Just as wars do not break out by accident, prisoner abuse is not some random occurrence in which captors suddenly and unwittingly engage during the course of armed conflict.[1] The previous chapter put forward a theory where belligerents weigh the various costs and benefits of prisoner abuse and make deliberate decisions over whether to treat enemy combatants falling under their control well or mistreat them. A set of domestic incentives centered on democracy combined with external factors related to the nature of conflict are put forward as having the greatest implications for understanding patterns of abuse during wars between states. Other factors, such as cultural differences, are instead thought to be less consequential for predicting the risks of deprivations against prisoners.

Assessing the persuasiveness of these competing explanations is less straightforward. Several cases readily come to mind that may appear to undermine the impact of particular factors on prisoner treatment. For instance, not all dictators engage in high levels of prisoner abuse, which is reflected in the fairly decent treatment of enemy combatants in the two wars fought among various Central American autocracies during the first decade of the twentieth century. Similarly, when it comes to culture, there are numerous instances where belligerents from different civilizational backgrounds engaged in low levels of prisoner abuse, as in the Kargil War between India and Pakistan, or both French and Thai captors during their fighting from 1940 to 1941. The particular choice of individual cases can, therefore, have an enormous bearing on what factors might appear to best explain prisoner treatment.[2]

To offer a more rigorous test, this chapter leverages the use of quantitative methods across a much larger number of cases to evaluate competing explanations for prisoner abuse. The evidence comes from the data set on the treatment of prisoners in interstate wars from 1898 to 2003, which was introduced in greater detail in chapter 1. Results provide strong support for democracy and the nature of the conflict as key determinants of prisoner abuse. Wars involving aims of territorial conquest, as well as those devolving into especially severe and drawn-out fighting, lead to higher levels of violence inflicted upon captives. Democracy instead has an overall constraining effect on the abuse of captured combatants. Further investigations into democratic conduct reveals some support for both normative and institutional accounts, but the weight of the evidence favors domestic institutional forces as playing a greater role in shaping decisions over the treatment of prisoners.

By contrast, common alternative explanations receive more fragile support. Belligerents possessing distinctive cultural identities are slightly more likely to mistreat each other's prisoners than those coming from similar backgrounds, though the effect is not significant. The general impact of mutual deterrence from each side holding captives from the enemy is similarly weak, while others like international law and norms either operate in unexpected directions or are conditioned by other factors. A logic of prisoner abuse does appear to exist, but one centered on the twin role played by a key set of incentives facing captors both at home and on the battlefield.

Prisoner Abuse in Interstate Wars—What the Evidence Says

Data covering a number of characteristics for each country and war were gathered in order to evaluate each of the main explanations for the determinants of prisoner treatment. The appendix at the end of the book offers further details on the specific coding rules for each measure. To test for the role of regime type, each country's level of democracy at the start of the war was coded.[3] For expectations related to the nature of the conflict, an indicator for war of attrition was included to reflect those conflicts that became bogged down into static or protracted fighting. The related dimension concerning war aims is represented by two separate measures. Wars where belligerents aspired to conquer and absorb territory from another state, such as the designs of Benito Mussolini's Italy on Ethiopia in the 1930s, are distinguished from those where the conquest of foreign lands was not a major objective. Similarly, conflicts involving other types of expansionist aims, such as regime change or unconditional surrender, were differentiated from those wars involving more limited pursuits.

As a measure for evaluating identity-type arguments, belligerents were coded for whether they came from different civilizational backgrounds, such as African, Eastern Orthodox, Hindu, Japanese, Latin American, Sinic, or Western European. To assess whether the presence of their own troops under enemy captivity would discourage captors from resorting to abuse, a deterrence variable was included for whether or not both belligerents were capable captors. International law was coded by a series of variables based on whether or not the captor, along with their adversary, had ratified the prevailing international treaty respecting prisoner rights by the start of the war. For the possible wider normative significance of the Geneva Conventions in shaping subsequent conduct, an indicator was included for wars starting after 1949, the year the conventions opened for ratification. A few other factors were also included that have been found to affect wartime conduct more broadly and might in turn influence the choices of captors concerning their care for captives: the relative material capabilities of the participants in the war, and whether the opposing side had engaged in prisoner abuse to see if reciprocal dynamics in the treatment of prisoners could also be at play.

As with the overall data on prisoner treatment, the unit of analysis remains the warring-directed-dyad, meaning there are two separate cases for each pair of opponents in a given war, where each is examined as a potential violator and victim. To reiterate, prisoner abuse is defined as a military strategy enacted by political and military authorities that involves the intentional killing or harming, either directly or indirectly, of enemy combatants who have laid down their arms and surrendered. When looking for cases of abuse only captors regarded as capable are included in the analysis—in other words, those with both the capability to formulate an independent prisoner policy and the opportunity to harm captives by actually having captured enemy combatants. Cases are then classified according to whether the captor engaged in low, medium, or high levels of abuse against prisoners from the relevant opponent during the course of the war. Reflecting the challenges inherent to collecting information in wartime contexts, prisoner abuse is measured in each case across the war as a whole, since events-level data are largely ruled out for even a small number of conflicts.

Figures 3.1 to 3.5 display results from a series of cross-tabulations showing the relationship between prisoner abuse and some of the main purported determinants for the treatment of captives: democracy, wars of attrition, territorial annexation, expansive war aims, and cultural differences. The figures report the percentage of capable captors engaging in each of the three levels of prisoner abuse across the categories for the factor of interest.

The figures offer some opening clues into the role of both regime type and the nature of the conflict in accounting for patterns of prisoner treatment. Figure 3.1 shows a clear negative relationship between democracy and the more brutal treatment of prisoners. Democracy is in no way a cure-all, since almost one-quarter of democratic belligerents resorted to high levels of prisoner abuse and not much separates democracies from their autocratic adversaries at medium levels of violence. Yet democratic propensities toward mistreatment are still much lower compared to autocratic belligerents where more than 40 percent engaged in the highest orders of violations against captured combatants. Democracies were thus around 75 percent less likely than nondemocratic captors to engage in high-level prisoner abuse in interstate wars, and this difference is statistically significant.[4] Decent treatment of Iraqi prisoners by the United States during the Persian Gulf War shows humane democratic conduct to be more of the rule than the exception. Although there exist instances

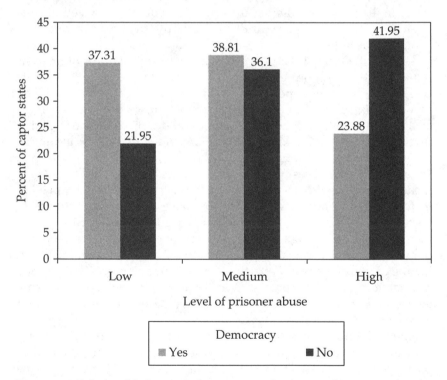

FIGURE 3.1 Relationship between democracy and prisoner abuse

Notes: Capable captors in all interstate wars, 1898–2003. Kendall's Tau-b = -0.173 Pr = 0.000. Percentages across each category for the independent variable may not sum to 100 due to rounding.

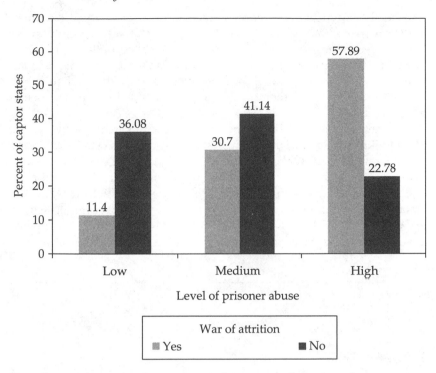

FIGURE 3.2 Relationship between war of attrition and prisoner abuse

Notes: Capable captors in all interstate wars, 1898–2003. Kendall's Tau-b = 0.357 Pr = 0.000. Percentages across each category for the independent variable may not sum to 100 due to rounding.

of decent care afforded to enemy combatants by autocrats, such as by Argentina's military junta during the Falklands War, the lack of similar institutional or normative constraints appears to make autocratic captors on the whole more callous toward their captives.

The next three figures examine various aspects concerning the nature of the conflict and point to stronger support for certain elements over others. As shown in figure 3.2, states finding themselves in wars of attrition turn to the highest levels of prisoner abuse well over half of the time. Those involved in less drawn-out fighting exhibit less violent tendencies, resorting to comparable conduct in a little more than 20 percent of cases, meaning attritional warfare is associated with more than 1.5 times greater odds of high-level abuses against prisoners. The reverse pattern is evident at the lower end of abuse, where only around 10 percent of belligerents entangled in wars of attrition exhibit significant restraint compared to more than one-third of states in less static conflicts. This difference is statistically significant and represents a decline of more than two times in the prospects that prisoners will be treated relatively decently in attritional versus nonattritional fighting. Troops locked in the trench warfare that defined much of the western front during the First World War thus had good reasons to fear for their lives not only during battle, but also should they find themselves behind barbed wire in an enemy prisoner camp.

The stakes generated by the nature of the conflict are even starker when looking at territorial objectives, which also show a statistically significant relationship with prisoner abuse. Figure 3.3 reveals that more than three-quarters of all conflicts where a captor's main objective is conquering sizable lands from the enemy are associated with the greatest amounts of brutality inflicted upon prisoners. Given that conflicts where real estate is not a key issue lead to high levels of abuse at a relatively lower rate of less than 30 percent, wars of territorial annexation are

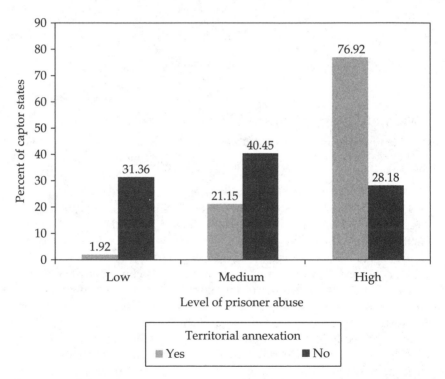

FIGURE 3.3 Relationship between territorial annexation and prisoner abuse

Notes: Capable captors in all interstate wars, 1898–2003. Kendall's Tau-b = 0.374 Pr = 0.000. Percentages across each category for the independent variable may not sum to 100 due to rounding.

almost twice as likely to witness high-level prisoner abuse. Nonterritorial wars are actually more likely to involve medium levels of prisoner abuse, but this is partly a reflection of the seemingly strong drive toward captors abusing captives at the extreme bounds of violence when fighting over territory. Consistent with the compelling relationship between conquest and abuse, in less than 2 percent of all cases of territorial annexation did captors limit themselves to lower levels in their mistreatment of prisoners, while the corresponding figure of decent treatment in nonterritorial conflicts was close to one-third of the cases. The rarity of humane conduct in the context of territorial wars is actually due to a single instance involving Pakistani treatment of Indian captives during the Second Kashmir War over the disputed lands of the same name.

Figure 3.4 shows, however, that not all types of wartime objectives lead to similar misfortune for captured enemy combatants. Conflicts

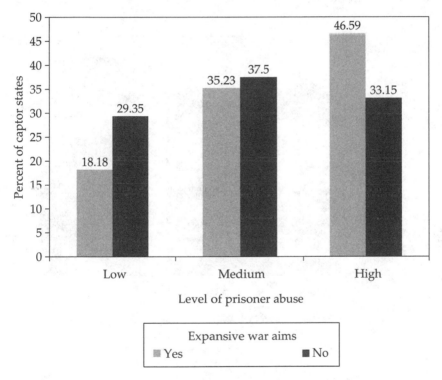

FIGURE 3.4 Relationship between expansive war aims and prisoner abuse

Notes: Capable captors in all interstate wars, 1898–2003. Expansive war aims include regime change and unconditional surrender. Kendall's Tau-b = 0.138 Pr = 0.133. Percentages across each category for the independent variable may not sum to 100 due to rounding.

involving other sorts of expansive war aims display over a 45 percent chance of degenerating into massive amounts of prisoner mistreatment. Yet given that around one-third of wars not involving objectives like regime change or unconditional surrender also lead to high levels of prisoner abuse, the difference for expansive war aims is not statistically significant. This suggests that wartime objectives do play a role in encouraging captors to engage in extreme transgressions toward their captives, but are most significant when the designs involve undermining the territorial integrity of the adversary.

The reality that not all factors are firmly associated with the extent of prisoner abuse is reinforced by the examination of cultural differences in figure 3.5. Cultural differences also raise the risk of high-level abuse, but the magnitude of the effect is smaller than for the other main determinants and is not statistically significant. When warring parties come from different cultural backgrounds the chances for captors resorting to the

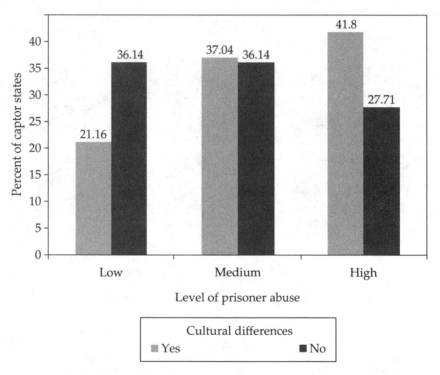

FIGURE 3.5 Relationship between cultural differences and prisoner abuse

Notes: Capable captors in all interstate wars, 1898–2003. Kendall's Tau-b = 0.159 Pr = 0.078. Percentages across each category for the independent variable may not sum to 100 due to rounding.

highest levels of violence against prisoners increase by about 50 percent. Cultural forces operate in the expected direction, but the cross-tabulations indicate that civilizational differences are not a crucial determinant of prisoner treatment. There are certainly many cases of culturally dissimilar foes treating enemy soldiers horribly, such as both the Greek and Turkish sides during the war over Cyprus, or the various belligerents in the Balkans after the end of the Cold War. These episodes need to be considered, however, in light of contrary cases where a culture clash did not inevitably lead to extreme violence toward captives, as during the Russo-Japanese War, or situations where a greater degree of cultural affinity failed to prevent prisoner brutality, as in the war between Saddam Hussein's Iraq and Revolutionary Iran.

The marked effects for regime type and the nature of the conflict on prisoner abuse continue to hold when estimating a multiple regression model, which includes the main determinants of interest alongside a number of other control variables. Table 3.1 reports the statistical significance for all of the variables, along with the substantive impact of each factor on the expected probability that a captor resorts to the highest levels of abuse against captured enemy combatants.[5] The second column, "Initial probability," shows the chances for high-level prisoner abuse when the relevant determinant takes on a lower value (zero for dichotomous variables, the 10th percentile for continuous variables, or medium for the level of abuse committed by the opponent), while all other variables are held constant at their average values. The third column then shows either the greater or lesser risks of extreme abuses against prisoners when the variable in question is changed to its higher value (1 for dichotomous variables, 90th percentile for continuous variables, and high-level abuses by the opponent). The fourth column then simply calculates the absolute rise or decline in the expected probability of prisoner abuse when the relevant variable is moved from its lower to higher value. For instance, the relevant value for democracy shows the absolute difference in the probability of high-level prisoner abuse when comparing an autocratic to a democratic captor state. To give a better sense of the relative magnitude of the difference in the resulting threat to prisoners, the fifth and final column then reports the percent change in the likelihood of high levels of abuse resulting from the altered value for each variable.[6]

The measures for both wars of attrition and goals of territorial conquest continue to be strong contributors toward greater violence inflicted upon captured combatants even when controlling for other variables. Belligerents struggling in wars of attrition were over 1.5 times more likely to commit extreme levels of prisoner abuse compared to countries participating in conflicts involving less sustained fighting. Even more noticeable, states

[81]

TABLE 3.1 Effects of independent variables on the probability of high levels of prisoner abuse

Variable	Initial probability	Probability after change in variable	Absolute change in probability	Percent change in probability
Democracy*	0.36	0.15	−0.21	−58
War of attrition*	0.19	0.48	0.29	153
Expansive war aims	0.29	0.32	0.03	11
Territorial annexation*	0.22	0.72	0.50	232
Cultural differences	0.25	0.32	0.08	31
Prisoner abuse by opponent*	0.28	0.63	0.35	122
Deterrence	0.52	0.28	−0.24	−46
Relative capabilities	0.29	0.31	0.02	6
Treaty ratification	0.29	0.37	0.09	30
Treaty ratification (opponent)	0.29	0.46	0.17	59
Joint treaty ratification	0.29	0.27	−0.01	−5
Post-1949 norms*	0.25	0.37	0.12	48

Notes: * Significant at 5 percent (95 percent confidence interval for absolute change in probability of high levels of prisoner abuse does not include zero). Baseline probability of prisoner abuse equals 0.30 where all independent variables are held constant at their means. Estimates for each independent variable are based on changing dichotomous variables from 0 to 1, continuous variables from their 10th to 90th percentiles, and *Prisoner abuse by opponent* from medium to high. Calculations for the absolute and percent changes in probability may sometimes differ due to the rounding for presentational purposes of the first two sets of probabilities based on the lower and higher values for each relevant independent variable.

seeking to annex territory from their adversary were almost 2.5 times more prone to treating enemy combatants horribly than countries without clear territorial motives. The distinct nature of territorial objectives is confirmed by the contrasting weak findings for other expansive war aims, which have minimal and insignificant effects on patterns of prisoner treatment. Except for the case of expansive war aims, the results for the nature of the conflict show some parallels to the civilian literature, where both attritional warfare and territorial annexation strongly increase the likelihood that noncombatants too will be targeted.[7]

Alongside external forces generated by the nature of the conflict, key internal attributes of warring parties also continue to matter a great deal.

Democracy reduces the likelihood of the worst levels of prisoner abuse by almost 60 percent, and the difference between the relatively humane democratic belligerents and the comparatively more vicious autocracies remains statistically significant. The general restraining effect of democracy evident in the analysis presents an intriguing contrast to existing quantitative research on civilian targeting. While some work indicates democracy acts as a similar constraint, other studies show regime type plays no role at all, and some even find that democracies can be more likely to target noncombatants.[8] The difference in results is unlikely to be due to any biases in the coding of prisoner abuse that would systematically find in favor of democratic humanitarianism. If anything, the initial procedures used for measuring the level of prisoner abuse represent a tougher test for democracy proponents, since the relatively greater openness and transparency of democratic regimes makes it such that any violence committed against enemy combatants is more likely to surface compared to the more closed nature of many autocratic regimes. This does not mean that democratic governments do not try to conceal offenses, but that these attempts are more likely to fail and any abuses liable to come to light. Continuing revelations regarding controversies over U.S. counterterrorism policies in both the Bush and Obama administrations are indicative of the challenges in concealing past transgressions in contrast to the relative paucity of information coming out of many autocratic countries. The constraints observed for democracies therefore probably represent an underestimate of the likely role played by domestic political factors in improving the lot for captured enemy combatants.[9]

Not all internal attributes, however, matter as much as others. Controlling for other factors, cultural differences only modestly heighten the dangers of abuse, and the variable remains weak statistically. Despite the common claim that cultural factors definitively shape wartime conduct, the minimal impact of civilizational differences on the treatment of prisoners is in line with many other quantitative studies showing that cultural forces offer little in accounting for the level of violence during armed conflicts.

Despite being championed by many lawyers and activists, international law and humanitarian norms also appear to provide few robust protections for prisoners. The effects for unilateral ratification by either the captor or victim state are actually positively related to higher levels of prisoner abuse. While this factor does not attain standard levels of significance, states may feel less bound by legal constraints if their adversary failed to commit as well.[10] Of potentially greater promise is when both sides have jointly ratified the prevailing treaty protecting prisoners, developing a common commitment and understanding of their obligations, which should help reduce the propensity toward abuse. Yet the effect is miniscule and far from significant, suggesting that committing to international legal instruments (at least on their own) does little to limit the worst excesses of war.

Separate analyses looking into some of the specific compliance-inducing mechanisms attributed to international law also do not find much support, at least with regard to prisoner treatment.[11] Joint ratification may not necessarily have a direct effect, but might rather be conditional on the adversary's conduct where reciprocity should be expected to operate much more forcefully when both sides have a clearer understanding of what counts as appropriate behavior. Although some past work has found support for this dynamic, the data here show no conditional relationship between joint ratification and reciprocity on prisoner conduct among the belligerents.[12] Looking instead at the role of third parties, the prospect of punishment by the international community or other outside actors for violating international humanitarian law also does not appear to figure prominently in the decision making of captors. Those belligerents who are more vulnerable to coercion and potential costs imposed by external actors are no less likely to engage in prisoner abuse than captors who are relatively immune from outside pressures.[13] While international law appears to have little overall influence in shaping the treatment of prisoners, there is one exception related to the regime type of the ratifier that will be discussed in greater detail below when looking to understand what precisely appears to motivate the conduct of democracies.

More troubling is that the era after the emergence of the 1949 Geneva Conventions—when norms promoting the decent treatment of captured combatants should have been ascendant—is on the whole associated with worse levels of violence against prisoners. Consistent with the rise in high levels of abuse over several later periods observed in chapter 1, states fighting in wars after 1949 were almost 50 percent more likely to resort to extreme brutalities against prisoners, and the difference is significant. Growing support for humanitarian norms should not immediately be interpreted as directly causing deteriorating conditions for captives, since the variable may be reflecting other developments that also changed over time. Nevertheless, the temporal differences confirm that the conduct of war has not generally become more humane in recent years, at least with regard to prisoners.[14] International norms might be better understood as a response to previous wartime conduct, rather than serving an autonomous function in influencing the behavior of belligerents.

Table 3.1 shows that a number of other factors generally thought to influence wartime conduct have little impact on prisoner treatment. When both sides are capable captors holding enemy combatants, a deterrence dynamic does seem to come into play as the risk of committing high levels of abuse appears to decline somewhat. Yet the mutual hostages logic generated in such circumstances is not sufficient to guarantee the safety of a country's own troops held by the adversary, since the effect for deterrence is not statistically significant. Many countries would clearly prefer to avoid the position faced by Belgium or Norway when German forces overran and easily captured many of both defenders' armed forces during the early phases of the Second World War. Nevertheless, capturing Wehrmacht soldiers did not prevent Nazi Germany from committing significant abuses against Allied captives, especially on the eastern front, as prisoners simply became a further bargaining chip and source of friction between opposing sides.

The results are also mixed for the other remaining control variables concerning the likelihood of prisoner abuse. Material power seems to have little bearing in accounting for patterns of violence. Captors possessing greater relative capabilities are somewhat more like to engage in violence; the coefficient is slightly positive in most models but far from achieving statistical significance. Material power has instead been shown to be a much greater predictor of violence against civilians,[15] but in the case of captured combatants abuse appears to be neither a tool of the powerful nor a weapon of the weak. Although concerted campaigns of civilian victimization often require substantial technological capacities, such as the massive bombing campaigns of Axis cities during the Second World War, violence against prisoners often involves fewer capital-intensive means. Of course, more powerful countries may have a greater ability to abuse prisoners. Yet more pragmatically, military superiority means stronger captors may have less need to mistreat captives and at the same time have greater resources at their disposal to adequately care for prisoners falling into their hands. A captor's relative abilities and incentives to mistreat prisoners may ultimately pull in opposite directions, meaning that material power overall has little discernable impact overall on how prisoners will be treated.

Unlike material capabilities, retaliation figures more prominently in the decision making of belligerents over how to treat enemy combatants. When the adversary flagrantly engages in abuse against a country's own soldiers, captors are more than twice as likely to act in a similarly atrocious manner toward prisoners under their control. The flip side is that reciprocal dynamics can facilitate decent conduct among adversaries who consciously choose to limit their abuses. Yet from a more negative standpoint, once violence commences such dynamics can reinforce one another and lead to a downward spiral of depravities among belligerents.[16]

To sum up so far, a quantitative analysis of the determinants of prisoner abuse in interstate wars since the turn of the twentieth century gives strong support for the argument that democracy and the nature of the conflict shape the prospects (good or bad) that captured combatants are likely to face once in captivity, or if they even make it to captivity in the first place. Democratic regimes are significantly less likely to resort to high levels of prisoner abuse, though warfare over the last century shows that democracies by no means always treat enemy combatants in a humane fashion. Despite these domestic constraints, attritional fighting greatly heightens the risks prisoners encounter, whether as a form of coercion or to extract greater resources necessary for the intensifying war effort. When territory is at stake, the hopes for prisoners are even direr, though the same cannot be said for other types of expansive war aims. On the other hand, commonly cited alternative factors offer less leverage in understanding patterns of prisoner treatment; cultural differences, general dynamics of deterrence, and international law are all insignificant, while humanitarian norms turn out to push in the opposite direction, being associated with higher levels of violence. The findings generally hold up to a wide range of robustness checks, which are described in greater detail in the appendix to the book.

DEMOCRACY AND PRISONER TREATMENT: A CLOSER STATISTICAL LOOK

The collective results point to some interesting similarities, but also differences, in the determinants of abuse against prisoners compared to prior research looking into the causes of violence directed toward civilians. Wars of attrition, aims of territorial conquest, and reciprocity all tend to enable greater mistreatment directed against both groups of victims. On the other hand, cultural factors and international law have little impact in each instance. Some contrasts are evident for other factors—material capability is a less consequential predictor of violence involving prisoners, while post–World War II humanitarian norms sometimes diverge in both direction and significance depending on whether the victim is a civilian or a captured combatant. However, one of the most noticeable reversals concerns regime type, where democracies are on average significantly less likely to resort to prisoner abuse, but have been shown either to have little effect on or to actually heighten the dangers posed to noncombatants.[17]

These contrasting findings highlight the need to consider the possibility that the determinants of wartime conduct may not be the same across all types of violence or victims, and by extension that it is important to examine prisoner abuse on its own terms. While democracy acts as a restraint upon the worst levels of prisoner abuse, what is less clear from the analysis up until this point is *why* democratic belligerents tend to act more humanely in their treatment of enemy combatants. Attention to the particular political culture of democratic systems emphasizes the role of liberal values, such as nonviolence and the promotion of individual rights, in explaining the devotion of democracies to benevolent wartime conduct. By comparison, an institutionally driven account instead focuses on how the greater accountability of democratic governments to their publics increases the sensitivity of democracies toward fears of retaliation and the strategic benefits that can be gained from the kinder care for prisoners, such as inducing enemy soldiers to prefer surrendering over continuing to fight. On its face, the observation that democracies are simply less likely to abuse enemy combatants overall could be explained by either the normative or institutional approach.[18]

Exploring some of the specifics dynamics involved in choices over prisoner treatment offers a chance to start thinking more concertedly about the motives driving democratic conduct during wartime. Although the data set looks at belligerents' treatment of captives across each war as a whole due to the obstacles involved in adequately collecting events-level measures within each conflict, it still remains possible to investigate in greater detail the timing and extent of the violence that was perpetrated. Identifying which country begins abusing prisoners, along with the subsequent conduct by both sides, has the dual benefit of further testing the general democracy finding, as well as offering an opportunity to potentially distinguish between the normative and institutional explanations for prisoner treatment. Looking at some of these more fine-grained measures, table 3.2 displays the percentage of democratic and nondemocratic captors that have engaged in various forms of initiation, retaliation, and escalation of violence against captured enemy combatants.[19]

TABLE 3.2 Democracy and prisoner abuse: first movers, retaliation, and escalation

Outcome	Percent of democratic captors	Percent of nondemocratic captors
First violator*	33	57
Retaliate*	74	93
Retaliate against high-level abuse	83	94
Escalate*	13	25
Retaliatory escalation*	0	11

Notes: * Difference between democracies and nondemocracies significant at 5 percent.

The first row presents the relative propensity of democracies versus autocracies to strike first in mistreating prisoners under their control. To concentrate on more sizable abuses, a captor is considered the first violator if it is the initial actor in the pairing of warring states to engage in medium or high levels of prisoner abuse.[20] For instance, in the Persian Gulf War, Iraq is considered the first violator given the brutality it meted out to soldiers falling into its hands, while the United States would not since it engaged in few violations and comported itself fairly well toward captives during this conflict. Alternatively, records generally indicate Nazi Germany was the first to mistreat prisoners in the early days of its successful blitzkrieg offensive against France in 1940, even though each side took liberties with surrendering troops.[21]

Both normative and institutional explanations would expect democracies to be less willing to initiate the first violation. From a political culture standpoint, attachment to norms of nonviolence means democracies should refrain from committing abuses in general, and by extension be less likely to instigate violence in the first place. The more pronounced fear of reprisals against their own troops due to greater institutional constraints similarly implies that democratic regimes should be less likely to initiate prisoner abuse out of fears over retaliation. A negative relationship between democracy and first violators thus does not distinguish between normative and institutional explanations but is helpful in providing a further testable implication for the overall democracy finding. The results show that just one-third of all democratic belligerents are the first to engage in substantial abuses against prisoners. Democracies sometimes launch the opening salvo against enemy combatants, as occurred with the U.S. invasion of Afghanistan in 2011. Yet more often than not, it is nondemocracies that open the doors to abuse with well over half of all autocratic captors becoming the first violator; the difference between the two regime types is also statistically significant.[22]

While the identity of first violators is consistent with both normative and institutional stories, other elements in the decision making over prisoner abuse offer a better chance to differentiate between the two accounts. Domestic institutions generate incentives for democracies to limit any retaliatory longings even when the adversary has already begun abusing prisoners. Democratic belligerents often fear that any response in kind against prisoners they hold could lead to even worse atrocities perpetrated by the enemy, along with undermining the strategic benefits to be gained from their own continued good behavior. In the Persian Gulf War Saddam Hussein paraded on television soldiers from the U.S. Coalition who were clearly beaten, to the anger of many, yet the desire to employ promises of humane treatment to encourage the surrender of Iraqi troops overrode any inkling for retaliation. On the other hand, if the enemy is already engaging in extreme levels of abuse, then one of the main institutional incentives is weakened for democracies contemplating how to respond. Although the strategic benefits of good conduct may still remain, the desire to avoid further retaliatory violence against the democracy's own troops is less relevant, since the enemy is already engaging in high levels of abuse. An institutional approach thus expects democratic captors to be comparatively less constrained in retaliating when dealing with opponents already committing higher levels of prisoner abuse.

Turning to the role of political culture, the expectations for normative forces are more ambiguous. If domestic norms of nonviolence are truly the primary drivers for democratic captors, then the decisions of these regimes over how to treat prisoners should in many ways be independent of the enemy's behavior. Whether or not the opponent initiates abuses should not in and of itself affect a democratic belligerent's normative commitments, suggesting a certain constancy in the conduct of democracies in the modern era.[23] In the face of especially horrific violence inflicted by the enemy against prisoners, these restraining principles might be expected to weaken somewhat, but on balance domestic political culture should still limit any retaliatory impulses felt by democratic states. Borrowing insights from the democratic peace, a different line of thinking suggests domestic norms may have little effect on democracies' wartime conduct when facing autocratic opponents. If foes cannot be trusted because of their autocratic attributes, then democracies might then choose to put aside their own liberal norms when fighting.[24] Particularly after becoming the target of violence, even democratic countries with deeply entrenched liberal values may be expected to respond in kind.[25] Importantly, however, this more ferocious picture of domestic norms and war making suggests democracies should act no differently from autocrats when retaliating against any level of prior abuse, while the prior institutional account limits this expectation to only when reciprocating against the highest levels of violence. Taken together, these contradictory interpretations pose a problem for a normative approach in generating clear expectations regarding the patterns of violations that democracies do end up committing.

The next two rows in table 3.2 examine the rate of retaliation of democracies and nondemocracies under different contexts. With a similar concern over more substantial levels of abuse, a country is considered a retaliator if (after being the initial victim of prisoner abuse) it is also subsequently found to have engaged in medium or high levels of violence against captured combatants.[26] The third row then restricts the set of cases to see whether states whose prisoners were subjected to the highest levels of prisoner abuse replied with at least moderate amounts of violence against prisoners under their control.

The results confirm one of the results from the earlier general analysis—reciprocity figures prominently in wartime conduct. Regimes of both democratic and autocratic stripes show a strong propensity toward responding in kind to violations committed by the adversary, meaning that if prisoners from one belligerent are mistreated, abuse is likely to follow for those from the other side. Nonetheless, when looking at overall rates of retaliation in the second row, democracies are less willing to retaliate against abuses committed by the enemy, while over 90 percent of autocratic captors reply with some form of violence of their own against prisoners. Looking at the third row, where captors are deciding how to respond to an enemy that has already engaged in the highest levels of abuse, reveals some of the limits in the extent to which democracies are reluctant to retaliate. Democracies are still somewhat less likely to exact retribution in the face of high-level abuse than nondemocracies, but the difference is no longer statistically significant. While far from approaching the horrors wrought upon U.S. service members in the Pacific, the liberties sometimes taken by the United States in the capture and treatment of Japanese prisoners illustrates that vengeance is not completely contradictory to democratic inclinations. The differentiated findings on retaliation also offer greater support for an institutional explanation for democratic wartime conduct. When it comes to retaliation across different scenarios, normative accounts are rather inconclusive or assume a consistency in behavior (either constrained or unconstrained depending on the specific variant). By contrast, both democracies' general reluctance to retaliate and the narrowing in the difference between democracies and autocracies when facing higher levels of abuse are more consistent with institutionally driven incentives.

A further point of differentiation between institutional and normative accounts concerns the related question of escalation in the violence perpetrated against prisoners. It is one thing for a belligerent to retaliate in a tit-for-tat fashion to a wrong committed by the adversary; it is quite another for a state to up the ante and commit graver abuses during the war. Although reciprocal dynamics are certainly important, they are far from symmetrical where each side only engages in equal levels of violence against prisoners. History is replete with instances where one side engaged in far worse abuses against captives than their adversary—from Italy during its conquest of Ethiopia, to China and North Korea during the Korean War.

A normative approach is indeterminate on the question of escalation in a similar manner to the prior discussion of retaliation. In one sense, prisoner abuse is fundamentally inconsistent with internal democratic norms of nonviolence and respect for individual rights, though the relative retaliatory propensities of democracies already started to call this assumption into question. On the other hand, democracies have been prone toward "imprudent vehemence" when dealing with autocratic governments and often exhibited a crusading zeal in many of their past conflicts.[27] Normative constraints on the use of violence may be correspondingly weakened, and democracies might actually be more likely to escalate the level of violence against prisoners.[28]

By comparison, a nonescalatory dynamic is largely consistent with an institutional explanation. By limiting themselves to similar or lower levels of abuses compared to their opponent, democracies can increase the likelihood through reciprocity opponents will not choose to resort to even higher levels of violence against the troops of democratic belligerents. Furthermore, engaging in some level of abuse reduces the strategic advantages gained through good conduct, but any advantages still remaining will be greater if the democracy does not escalate.[29] So even though the United States retaliated against many Japanese atrocities in the Pacific, U.S. forces did not escalate the level of violence, which allowed them to maintain some strategic advantages on the battlefield. The relative propensity of different regime types toward escalation is thus in many ways more consistent with an institutional explanation, but less evident from a normative perspective.

To assess the relationship between the relative extent of prisoner abuse and democracy, a captor is considered to have escalated if it committed greater levels of violence against captives during the war than its adversary. For instance, Japan was found to have escalated its abuse of Chinese prisoners during the Second Sino-Japanese War from the interwar period. Linking together retaliation and escalation, a country is also regarded as engaging in retaliatory escalation if it commits an even higher level of abuse in response to an enemy that committed the first violation. The fourth and fifth rows of table 3.2 show that escalation is less frequent overall as captors often engage in equal or lower levels of prisoner abuse than their opponent. The results also confirm that democracies are less likely to turn to either form of escalation than autocracies. In fact, there are no cases in which a democratic belligerent engaged in retaliatory escalation after being the initial victim of prisoner abuse. The findings continue to be more consistent with institutionally driven incentives for democracies to diminish the overall amount of abuse inflicted upon captives, while normative appeals remain unclear or in the opposite than expected direction. This closer look into dynamics involving the initiation, retaliation, and escalation of violence against prisoners provides more support for institutional over normative accounts of democratic conduct during wartime.

A further strategy to help differentiate between the two approaches is to examine how much democracies differ from autocracies in their treatment of prisoners depending on the presence or absence of other determinants of wartime conduct. Similar to before, to the extent that a normative account generates firm expectations, the general assumption is that domestic political culture should lead democracies to treat enemy combatants on the whole in similar ways even if the broader context of the conflict changes. By contrast, an institutional explanation expects democratic conduct to differ if other elements lead to changes in the incentives facing democracies, particularly related to concerns over reciprocity and the strategic benefits from good conduct. Table 3.3 reports the effect of democracy on changing the probability of high-level abuses compared to autocracies for different values across several of the other main causes of prisoner mistreatment.

In the area of deterrence, democracies are 20 percent less likely to engage in extreme levels of prisoner abuse when both sides have captured enemy combatants. Democratic constraints in cases where both captors are capable are compatible with both normative commitments to nonviolence and institutional incentives to avoid retaliation or escalation by the adversary against troops from the democracy. The second column deals with situations where the adversary does not hold prisoners and illustrates some of the limits to decent democratic conduct. Although the absolute size of the effect is slightly larger, the difference in the behavior of democracies and autocracies is no longer statistically significant in instances where deterrence is absent. The lack of democratic constraints in

TABLE 3.3 Conditional effects of democracy on the probability of high levels of prisoner abuse

Conditional on . . .	Yes	No
Deterrence	−0.20*	−0.28
War of attrition	−0.36	−0.10
Territorial annexation	0.32*	−0.20*
Expansive war aims	−0.35*	−0.11
Treaty ratification	−0.26*	−0.07
Post-1949 norms	−0.27*	−0.16
Initiator	−0.10	−0.24*

Notes: * Significant at 5 percent.
Each value represents the effect of democracy on the absolute change in the probability of high levels of prisoner abuse conditional on the presence or absence of the relevant explanatory variable, where all other variables are held constant at their means.

these situations is problematic for normative accounts. If anything, the effect of regime type should be even clearer in such one-sided circumstances, where the adversary is largely defenseless and democratic norms of mercy and benevolence should face few obstacles in coming to the fore. By contrast, this same nonfinding is fairly consistent with an institutional explanation. When the opponent is not a capable captor one of the primary institutional incentives for good conduct—fear of retaliation—is removed, and the treatment of prisoners by democracies should be expected to converge toward that of autocratic belligerents. Across many conflicts from the Second World War to the Persian Gulf War democracies have loudly proclaimed their attachment to humanitarian norms. Yet when faced with few immediate worries of retaliation, as occurred in the early phases of the U.S. invasion of Afghanistan, democracies have shown themselves to be willing to let those more charitable values slide.

Shifting to the role played by the nature of the conflict on the effects of regime type similarly reveals greater, though not complete, support for institutions as the main force guiding the wartime conduct of democracies. Prior work has found that domestic institutional imperatives to win quickly and limit their own casualties make democracies much more likely to target civilians during wars of attrition.[30] When dealing with prisoners, however, democracy actually has the opposite constraining effect on the resort to abuse, though again the contrast from autocracies is not statistically significant. The difference in the conditional effect of wars of attrition continues to suggest that the incentives and behavior of democracies during wartime may differ in important ways across various issue areas. While institutional incentives may certainly encourage democracies to employ strategies to shorten the war, the benefits of prisoner abuse are far from clear in this regard. In wars of attrition, like the multitude of confrontations across several continents that together made up the Second World War, many more of a country's soldiers are likely to be captured, or at risk of being caught, so democracies will likely remain concerned with the danger of retaliation. Furthermore, some of the largest propaganda campaigns designed by democracies to encourage enemy surrenders were deployed during the two world wars, both frequently characterized by high levels of attritional warfare.[31]

War aims provide a much more definitive window into the behavior of democracies under different strategic contexts. Democratic belligerents continue to abide by their more restrained preferences in the treatment of prisoners when territory is not a key aim of the war. However, democracies are actually *more* likely than autocracies to engage in the highest levels of prisoner abuse when seeking to annex territory from the adversary, and the effect is statistically significant. As a somewhat surprising finding, this poses problems for a normative approach, which would generally assume that few conditions exist where democracies would exhibit a greater propensity to engage in atrocities compared to the more violent and intolerant political culture espoused by most nondemocracies.

The enabling effect for democracy can instead be more straightforwardly incorporated into institutional accounts by reconsidering the role of domestic preferences and the strategic merits of different prisoner policies depending on the aims sought through conflict. Democratic publics are by no means always pacific and have sometimes been enthusiastic supporters of wars of conquest and the brutalities oftentimes accompanying these sorts of conflicts.[32] Good treatment can still bring benefits like encouraging enemy surrenders, but these positive side effects may be outweighed by desires to rid conquered territories of all elements of resistance with enemy combatants as an especially palpable threat. To be fair, democratic wars of territorial annexation are relatively rare, so this relationship may be a function of a small number of positive cases. Democracies have generally sought to settle most territorial disputes peacefully, but the findings here suggest that when they do get involved in wars over territory those conflicts are in danger of becoming especially gruesome.[33] Of the many wars between Israel and its Middle East neighbors, Israeli treatment of prisoners took on its most violent character during the initial Palestine War of 1948, where aims of territorial conquest were most salient.[34] Democratic Turkey similarly possessed few qualms in its treatment of prisoners and demonstrated a willingness to engage in extreme forms of abuses in its bid to take over large portions of the island of Cyprus during its 1974 war against Greece.[35]

Expansive war aims operate differently than territorial ambitions and show some interesting conditional effects that were not apparent in the original statistical analysis looking only at the overall determinants of prisoner treatment. Although little separates democracies and autocracies in nonexpansive wars, when more far-reaching objectives are sought democracies turn out to be significantly less likely to commit the highest levels of prisoner abuse. The startling difference in the effect of regime type when pursuing territorial versus other expansive war aims again should be considered in terms of the relative strategic incentives facing democratic captors in each context. Regime change or unconditional surrender may generate a strong push for democracies toward favoring decent treatment, especially in the latter case where encouraging enemy soldiers to lay down their arms directly contributes to the objective of forcing the adversary to give up completely. Consistent with institutional expectations, democratic belligerents appear to tailor their prisoner policies to a large extent depending on the anticipated strategic benefits and costs, rather than simply conforming as closely as possible to normative attachments of nonviolence.

The impact of democracy on prisoner treatment also sometimes differs depending on the role of international law or global humanitarian norms. Although the earlier analysis on the general causes of prisoner treatment found little that was conclusive regarding the overall effect of international law or norms, democracies may be more receptive to these constraining forces on their policies and conduct.[36] Table 3.3 shows that democracies that have ratified the prevailing laws of war are significantly less likely to abuse prisoners; the effect of regime type for nonratifiers is also negative but does not achieve statistical significance. This supports prior work arguing that the centrality of the rule of law in their domestic political culture also makes democracies more rule-bound in their external relations, including armed conflict.[37] However, the decent conduct of democratic ratifiers is also in line with more institutional approaches, where domestic accountability makes democracies more vulnerable to punishment by domestic audiences if leaders fail to uphold their international commitments.[38] The positive relationship between regime type and international law is thus potentially consistent with either normative mechanisms emphasizing attachment to the rule of law or institutional mechanisms focused on public accountability to abide by commitments.[39]

Potentially more supportive of normative explanations for democratic conduct is the greater constraining role played by post-1949 humanitarian norms in democracies. While democracies fighting in wars taking place before 1949 were somewhat less likely to target prisoners, the effect of regime type is strongest in both substantive and statistical terms in the post-1949 period.[40] The seemingly greater kindness exhibited by democracies over time offers some support for domestic normative forces, since principles of nonviolence and individual rights share many similarities with the international norms promoting protections for prisoners during war that gained more widespread currency during this era. Yet the post-1949 improvement in the conduct of democracies may still be consistent with institutional mechanisms to the extent that the public's aversion to casualties involving their own soldiers (and consequent fears over retaliation) has solidified in recent years.[41] Irrespective of the precise motives underlying more recent humane democratic conduct, the temporal effects go some way toward accounting for the recent polarization of prisoner treatment with more of the extreme cases of violence perpetrated by autocracies, while democracies appear increasingly likely to limit themselves to lower levels of abuse against captives.

The conduct of the countries starting wars, compared to those initially on the defensive, provides another opportunity to test some of the implications of institutional approaches to prisoner treatment. Public accountability is generally thought to make democratic leaders more risk averse because they are in greater danger of being removed from office if their side loses the war.[42] Democracies should thus exhibit greater caution when deciding to go to war and tend to select conflicts where they are especially likely to emerge victorious.[43] These institutional forces leading democracies to choose wars they are favored to win suggest that democratic belligerents may also be less likely to need to engage in prisoner abuse in the wars they initiate compared to conflicts where they are on the receiving end of the first offensives. Unlike other evidence in support of an institutional explanation for democratic conduct, democracies do not appear much better at picking easier fights that could result in less need for prisoner abuse. Instead, democracies actually appear less likely to engage in high levels of prisoner abuse in conflicts in which they are the original targets.[44] Democratic targets may perhaps be less willing to employ abuse out of particularly high fears of retaliation, since many of their soldiers may have already been captured in the initial enemy offensive, as happened to a large portion of British forces during the fall of France to Nazi Germany during the early phases of the Second World War.

Taken together, this closer examination of regime type and prisoner treatment provides stronger, though not perfect, support for the importance of domestic institutions over principles ingrained in a country's political culture. Normative commitments may have played a more substantive role in the recent era, but the weight of the evidence suggests institutional incentives rooted in higher sensitivity toward retaliation and the strategic merits of different prisoner policies influence the behavior of democracies during war. Rather than institutional factors pushing democracies toward violence, as frequently claimed in past research on the targeting of civilians, domestic structural incentives appear to generally act as a force for restraint in the case of prisoners. Yet under certain circumstances, the results suggest that democracies can be just as or even more likely to resort to violence against prisoners. The statistical analyses carried out in this chapter established several promising findings regarding the causes of prisoner abuse but cannot conclusively determine the motivations behind democracies' decisions over how to treat their captives. The correlations gleaned from the quantitative data are suggestive of the impact of democracy on wartime conduct but do not establish in a more definitive manner the precise logic underlying democratic treatment of captured enemy combatants.

The more in-depth and fine-grained evidence available from historical case studies serves as a basis to more directly assess the relative importance of institutional versus normative factors in the conduct of democracies. The rich data and varying contexts surrounding the behavior of the main democratic belligerents during the Second World War offer a particularly fruitful opportunity in this regard. The goal of conducting such case studies is not chiefly to establish once again that a relationship exists between democracy and more humane levels of prisoner treatment; this was the purpose of the preceding quantitative analysis. Rather, the main objective of the case-study evidence that follows is to investigate the degree to which such causal-process observations are more consistent with institutional forces rather than normative mechanisms promoting democratic wartime conduct.[45]

[4]

World War II, Democracies, and the (Mis)Treatment of Prisoners

A prisoner of war is a man who tries to kill you and fails, and then asks you not to kill him.

—Winston Churchill

I'll tell you, pal, if there is ever another war, get on the side that America isn't, then get captured by the Americans—you'll have it made.

—Wilhelm Sauerbrei, former German POW from the Second World War

Based on Winston Churchill's notoriously gruff and severe demeanor, it might be entirely reasonable to surmise, based on the former British prime minister's blunt definition of POWs, that the newly captured soldier's request would more often than not be rebuffed. Yet as the reflections from a German captive show, the United States along with its British ally generally treated their prisoners in an exemplary fashion during the Second World War. This reinforces one of the main findings from the statistical analysis presented in the previous chapter demonstrating the overall tendency for democracies to be less willing to resort to extreme abuses against prisoners falling into their hands. Far less clear are the precise reasons guiding the general restraints exhibited by democracies in their conduct. An institutional perspective received somewhat greater support than normative accounts, though the findings were by no means conclusive. This chapter delves more deeply into the role of democracy by directly evaluating the relative strength of normative and institutional explanations for patterns of prisoner abuse by democracies. Of course, other factors including cultural or racial differences, war aims, and leadership personalities, among others, affect particular episodes of prisoner treatment by democratic and nondemocratic belligerents alike, though perhaps to varying degrees. While accepting that a host of other factors may help to shape prisoner policies, the more specific purpose in what follows is to assess the influence of normative versus institutional forces in limiting or contributing to prisoner abuse by democratic captors.

This chapter explores the relationship between democracy and the treatment of captives by focusing on what is often considered the prototypical example of proper prisoner care: the treatment of captured Axis combatants by the United States and Great Britain during the Second World War, in particular with regard to the western theater. A number of military historians have heaped praise upon the Western democracies for their conduct, going so far as to declare that their practices reached "the pinnacle of the historic development of prisoner protection."[1] A wide range of evidence from this case study reveals, however, that the motives behind the democratic belligerents' humane practices were more pragmatic than principled. In particular, benevolent conduct on the part of the Western democracies toward their captives largely stemmed from the two key domestic institutional incentives: fears of retaliation from engaging in abuse, and the strategic advantages of good conduct.[2] Normative concerns played at best a subservient role in democratic decision making over what to do with Axis prisoners. While the decent treatment afforded to many captives is certainly admirable, a broader analysis of the conduct of the Western powers over the course of the Second World War, along with a number of other conflicts, demonstrates some of the limits to democracy. Most revealing, when institutional incentives waned or were absent, democratic captors' behavior correspondingly worsened. In these hardened circumstances, normative appeals to democratic political culture offered few protections behind which increasingly vulnerable prisoner populations could hide. The institutional constraints at the heart of one of the greatest instances of humane prisoner treatment thus simultaneously also portended a darker side to the conduct of democracies.

DEMOCRACIES AND THEIR PRISONERS IN THE SECOND WORLD WAR

The Second World War was unprecedented in its scope and brutality, with the best records indicating that more than forty million people perished over the course of five long years of conflict.[3] Tens of millions of troops from countries around the world were mobilized, either drafted or as volunteers, to fight on distant and often bloody battlefields. With so many soldiers on the frontlines, the risks were high of either dying in combat or surrendering and becoming a POW. Laying down one's arms brought its own hardships, which ranged from the worst-case scenario of death during captivity to the better situation of imprisonment until the end of the war except for those fortunate enough to take part in occasional prisoner exchanges. Table 4.1 summarizes the estimated numbers of prisoners taken and their relative death rates in captivity for several of the main belligerents from the war.

All sides captured large though varying numbers of enemy combatants, but what is truly startling is the wide range of the overall death rates across captor states. Even these numbers are likely an understatement of the true extent of prisoner abuse, since they generally only include casualties that happened once a soldier reached the prison camps rather than those who were summarily executed upon capture. The available data suggest the fortunes for prisoners falling into the hands of an autocratic belligerent were usually terrifying. The likelihood a prisoner would survive their time in captivity was little better than half—on average, around 46 percent died with the worst being German treatment of Russian prisoners where around 58 percent (over three million total) perished after surrendering.[4] There are also some impressive differences in conduct among the autocracies, in particular between German treatment of prisoners on the eastern versus western fronts. Consistent with the importance of the nature of the conflict, one of the biggest differences concerned

TABLE 4.1 Statistics of prisoners captured and death rates for the major powers in World War II

Captor State	Prisoner State	Number of Prisoners	Death Rate in Captivity
Germany	Soviet Union	5,700,000	58%
Soviet Union	Germany	3,155,000	36%
Japan	U.S./U.K.	76,000	25–33%
U.S./U.K.	Japan	50,000	< 1%
Soviet Union	Japan	600,000	10%
Germany	U.S./U.K.	240,000	4%
U.S./U.K.	Germany	1,000,000	< 1%

Notes: Figures in the third column represent estimates for the total number of enemy combatants captured during the war. Surrenders that occurred after the war ended were excluded when possible. Figures were based on the following sources, Bartov 2001, 153; Ferguson 2004, 163–86; Forster 1986, 21; Hata 1996, 263; Morrow 2001, 984; Overy 1997, 355; Vance 2006, 458–72. Italy was also one of the other major belligerents during this war, but precise figures on prisoner death rates in Italian prison camps unfortunately could not be located. Figures for Soviet prisoners of Japan were not included because Japan was not considered a capable captor in this warring-directed-dyad.

the relative aims sought through war on each side of the continent. Germany's brutal war in the east was centered upon conquering vast tracks of Soviet and other neighboring lands to achieve the living space (Lebensraum) long sought by the Nazi leadership. By contrast, German ambitions were more modest in the west and consequently accompanied by better, though far from humane, treatment of captured enemy combatants. Racial and ideological factors likely played some role as well, though they should not be exaggerated or thought to offer a monocausal explanation for German patterns of prisoner abuse. For instance, while the Nazi government brutalized large numbers of Poles in the east as well as Jewish populations as part of the Final Solution, soldiers captured from these and other minority groups in the west were generally accorded comparable treatment to their Anglo-Saxon compatriots.[5]

Despite some disparities across fronts, and in line with regime type expectations, Germany's policies toward western prisoners as a whole still remained harsh in numerous respects. In 1942, Adolf Hitler issued the so-called Commando Order (Kommandobefehl), which mandated that Allied prisoners be summarily executed if they were engaged in missions German authorities deemed to be of an irregular or subversive nature, irrespective of the fact that these soldiers still qualified as prisoners deserving of all regular rights and protections under international law.[6] Although not universal, summary executions became more common, such as the infamous Malmédy Massacre and related slaughters that later led to the prosecution of seventy-four German soldiers for war crimes.[7] German captors also became more prone to severely punishing escape attempts as a sharp warning to others, even though these actions contravened existing legal norms.[8]

In contrast, those soldiers surrendering to the democratic powers generally fared much better, with only around 1 percent dying in captivity. With hundreds of thousands of Axis troops falling into Allied hands as the war wore on—a number later turning into millions—the sheer logistical difficulties of feeding and clothing the growing masses in captivity mounted. In the week ending May 5, 1945, just days before the official German capitulation ending the war in Europe, the U.S. Army alone was distributing 1,751,513 food rations daily to enemy prisoners.[9] The extent to which resources were allocated to prisoner care is reflected by the fact that rations destined for prisoners made up 30 percent of the total food allotments issued by the U.S. armed forces, including those for their own troops and allies on the continent.[10]

Many Axis soldiers who first surrendered to U.S. or British forces were eventually transferred to camps in the United States proper or overseas territories of the British Empire and dominions. With greater space and resources, the comforts of prison life in these camps were in many ways superior to those for even regular civilians in Europe. Many German prisoners would even come to describe their time in captivity in the United States as "wonderful years" and "the experience of their lives."[11]

Praises of this magnitude should not overshadow the reality that U.S. and British abuses still occurred, especially on the Pacific front against Japan. Many scholars have pointed to the role played by race in the treatment of enemy combatants in the Pacific war.[12] As the relative death rates of German and Japanese prisoners at the hands of the United States reported in table 4.1 above makes clear, however, there were ultimately as many similarities as differences in U.S. prisoner policies across both fronts. Cultural approaches thus do not account for these parallels in prisoner treatment despite the stark difference in racial rhetoric across each theater. Although some differences were evident, abuses in both instances were generally initiated by individual or small groups of soldiers rather than reflecting official policy or orders from the highest-level authorities.[13] For instance, the worst incident in a prison camp on the U.S. homeland occurred when a deranged guard at a camp in Utah opened fire with a machine gun on tents housing German prisoners, killing nine and wounding another nineteen.[14] Importantly, the guard was quickly punished, since U.S. authorities wanted to make sure such acts were roundly condemned and not viewed by the enemy as sanctioned government practices.

Events of this sort were certainly regrettable but pale in comparison to abuses committed by autocratic belligerents, where it was not uncommon for Germany to execute hundreds of Russian prisoners on the spot.[15] Russia later accomplished its own equally horrific revenge against German troops as the Red Army reversed its prior battlefield defeats and pushed forward against Wehrmacht positions on the eastern front. Japan similarly engaged in systematic brutality against prisoners through a stark menu of abuses that included summary executions, starvation diets, grueling labor, and medical experimentation. In light of the harsh fighting conditions, along with the cruelty inflicted in captivity by many of the other captors during the war, the relatively more benevolent conduct by the Western powers is all the more impressive and provides a relatively tough test for the constraints of democracy on prisoner treatment.

What appears to have influenced the decisions of the United States and Great Britain to restrain themselves when dealing with enemy combatants? A normative approach leads to the expectation that democratic leaders were influenced by prevailing domestic norms of tolerance, limits against violence, and a general respect for individual rights. If this were the case, then the evidence should point to leaders frequently referring to these domestic principles when deciding what to do with prisoners under their control.[16] On the other hand, an institutional account instead emphasizes the importance of concerns over reciprocity and how good conduct could improve their side's chances to win the war in a timelier and less costly fashion. As will become evident, the historical record offers greater support for the importance of institutional incentives over normative commitments.

Democratic Concerns over Retaliation

Through a series of rapid offensives, Nazi Germany quickly cemented control over much of the European continent by the end of June 1940. An uneasy yet mutually beneficial equilibrium in prisoner affairs came to develop on the western front between Germany and Italy on the one hand and Britain (later joined by the United States) on the other. Decisive victories early on by the Axis powers brought with them large numbers of prisoners, leaving the Western Allies acutely worried over the risks of retaliation given they held a much smaller collection of enemy captives at the time. Even as the tide of the war later turned in the Allies' favor, and with it swelling prisoner ranks, the democratic powers remained extremely sensitive to the effects their treatment of Axis prisoners would have on the corresponding fate of Allied soldiers in enemy hands.

Worries within both the public and the military over the treatment of American prisoners once behind enemy lines became a major issue for the U.S. government throughout the war. Rationalizing the decent conduct toward German prisoners, Brigadier General R. W. Berry of the War Department General Staff stated plainly this policy meant "our boys over there were better treated as prisoners than they otherwise would have been."[17] Archibald Lerch, U.S. provost marshal general and the main military official in charge of the POW system in the United States proper, stressed the stakes involved by declaring, "Any non-adherence by this government [to the 1929 Geneva Convention] probably would result in instant retaliation against American prisoners held in Germany."[18] Reinforcing the point, Lerch continued by saying, "The War Department has an abundance of evidence which leads it to believe that our treatment of German prisoners of war has had a direct effect in securing better treatment of American prisoners in Germany."[19]

U.S. officials were clearly aware of the twin role played by reciprocity in guiding their conduct toward German prisoners. In the first place, good treatment was more likely to be met in kind by German authorities, or at the very least limit any abuses committed against Allied prisoners. This was possible not only through direct actions taken by Germany to care for U.S. prisoners, but also by making it easier for relief agencies to gain access to and operate in German camps. The role of external agencies grew in importance, especially later in the war as German infrastructure was devastated and supplies became much scarcer. One official from the American Red Cross noted that good U.S. conduct "has rendered a great service in enabling us to demand many things in hard-pressed, blockaded enemy countries which we might not otherwise have been able to obtain for our prisoners."[20]

The darker side of reciprocity was a discernable fear among policymakers that abuses committed in U.S. camps would result in swift retaliation against American prisoners held by the Axis powers. The result was that U.S. authorities often interpreted obligations under the prevailing 1929 Geneva Convention in as strict a manner as possible to ensure Axis prisoners would be treated according to the highest standards. The generous level of care even led to periodic outcries in the American media that enemy prisoners were receiving better treatment than regular U.S. soldiers in the field or citizens at home.[21] Beyond the particular level of care, groups including labor unions protested against the use of prisoner labor, which they felt crowded out work for U.S. civilians and depressed overall wages.[22] Part of the government's effort was thus devoted to convincing skeptical segments within domestic society that humane prisoner policies were in line with international obligations and necessary for the public's broader concern over the safety of their own troops overseas.[23] Government policies generally found a fairly sympathetic audience. Surveys of newspapers during the early war years showed the center of gravity in public opinion was clearly toward restraint when possible abuses against Axis prisoners were being contemplated in government circles. At the height of what became known at the Shackling Crisis, where prisoners were being manacled for long hours each day, some Allied leaders were receiving letters from concerned citizens at a rate of eight to one in opposition to retaliation.[24]

Although consistent across different government agencies as well as nongovernmental organizations, public pronouncements provide only indirect, and potentially uncertain, evidence of the importance of reciprocity in guiding the conduct of the democratic allies toward captured enemy combatants. Perhaps officials were in actuality primarily motivated by normative considerations but chose to couch their policies in terms of reciprocity for public consumption. Even in this case, however, it is not clear why direct normative appeals would not be just as convincing, or even more so, to domestic and Allied audiences if norms of nonviolence and individual rights were truly the driving force behind prisoner treatment.

In contrast to statements intended for public consumption, "harder" sources, like internal government reports or meetings, involve fewer reasons for actors to dissemble their true beliefs, are more difficult to manipulate or conceal after the fact, and thus offer a much firmer basis for

[104]

evaluating the preferences of political elites.[25] In particular, private discussions among government officials provide a clearer window into the motivations underlying the conduct of democracies during war. One incident in particular highlights the relative role of normative versus institutional factors in internal British discussions on prisoner treatment during the early years of the war. With Germany's quick defeat of France in just six weeks from May to June 1940, Britain lost its foothold on the continent after the remnants of the British Expeditionary Force escaped at Dunkirk. While an air war continued to rage between the two sides, the main site for ground operations became North Africa, where Britain used its colonial holdings as a launching point to challenge German and Italian dominance in the region. During the nascent North African campaign, Britain was able to maintain its positions and frequently took modest numbers of Axis prisoners, whom it treated according to a decent standard of care. However, this policy would quickly be tested.

In early 1941, Britain began receiving reports that Italy was ordering its soldiers to execute all captured members of the Free French Forces (FFL) during battles in Libya and the surrounding area. The FFL were composed of remnants of the defeated French armed forces, which were not loyal to the German-backed French Vichy regime and thus nominally allied to Britain. When faced with this situation at a meeting with his Chiefs of Staff (COS) Committee, Churchill reportedly proposed at first that Britain should send one thousand Italian troops to the FFL for what he termed "working capital."[26] The initial thinking was that giving the French the capability to either threaten retaliation or actually commit abuses in kind against Italian captives would deter any future executions of captured FFL troops.

Whatever the initial merits of this plan, it does not provide much support for the view espoused by the normative approach that democracies tend to externalize domestic norms of nonviolence and respect for individual rights when dealing with foreign adversaries. Even the very words Churchill chose to use indicate Axis prisoners were perceived less as individual persons deserving of rights and respects, and more as a commodity to be dealt with as Britain saw fit.

This was in many ways consistent with earlier opinions expressed by Churchill regarding the status of enemy prisoners. Before becoming prime minister in May 1940, Churchill served as first lord of the Admiralty for the opening months of the war. During his tenure he set forth the following policy to the military branch in an internal memorandum from October 15, 1939:

> it is our policy to capture and hold as prisoner the largest number of able-bodied enemy aliens capable of military service whom we can catch

[105]

upon the seas. We must accumulate a *substantial stock* of German prisoners in case we may need to inflict reprisals because of German barbarity to our own prisoners of war. This will probably not be necessary; but I took great pains in the last war [referring to World War I] to catch as many as possible because the Germans always behave much better when you have more of their men in your hands than they have of yours. *And after all we want to help them to behave better* [emphasis added].[27]

Besides betraying a rather patronizing view of the German leadership, Churchill consistently displayed a very instrumental approach to enemy prisoners as assets to be exploited rather than individuals inherently entitled to respect. In his time heading the navy, he even considered plans to employ German prisoners as de facto human shields to protect British hospital ships from attacks during naval operations in Narvik, Norway.[28] In this context Churchill appears to have been less worried about possible retaliation, since the British navy had the upper hand at sea and there were few British naval prisoners at the time. Once he became prime minister not long after, however, Churchill needed to take into account the impact of prisoner abuse on the armed forces as a whole, and in particular public pressures over the safety of British troops now in enemy captivity.

Despite personal views on the relative worth (or lack thereof) of enemy prisoners, it is important to note the British prime minister would come to lean heavily in the direction of restraint when dealing with prisoners. The reluctance of engaging in abuses either directly or by proxy through allies appears driven less by norms-based convictions but more by reasons related to concerns over retaliation as expected by an institutional account. Although Churchill was tempted to exact some revenge against Italy over the FFL executions, there was a palpable fear among the members of the COS Committee that any violation would result in retaliation against the more than fifty thousand British prisoners already held by the Axis powers.[29] Continued good conduct by Britain toward prisoners in this case appears to have been more the result of instrumental considerations over the safety of British troops already held behind enemy lines rather than any inherent concern for the rights of Axis prisoners as an end in itself.

Over the course of the war Churchill personally intervened on numerous occasions to ensure that the treatment of enemy prisoners remained at the highest levels possible.[30] In personal correspondence, Churchill later revealed that his interventions were primarily driven by fears of "a general counter-massacre of prisoners" that could be sparked all too easily by any British abuses.[31] Concerns over initiating the first violation or responding too rashly in kind were thus a function of prospective fears of retaliation and escalation rather than an idealistic desire to remain consistent with domestic normative principles.

The pressures of reciprocity meant that both of the major democratic allies also preferred maintaining direct control over captives rather than transferring them to third parties, who may not have had similar desires for diligent prisoner care.[32] A source of friction throughout the war involved cooperation between Britain and the United States on the one hand and the residual French forces of the FFL on the other. A complete explanation for the conduct of nonstate actors like the FFL toward prisoners is beyond the scope of this study. Many elements nevertheless remain consistent with the overall logic of reciprocity presented above. As the case of the Italian-led executions makes clear, Axis captors systematically subjected captured members of the FFL to high levels of abuse. Levels of violence on an even greater scale were directed toward their fellow countrymen participating in the French resistance in Occupied and Vichy France.[33] Given that French fighters were already facing extreme hardships once captured, there were few qualms about responding in kind against any Axis prisoners falling into their grasp. As a sign of the poor conditions in FFL-controlled camps, many Italian prisoners sought to escape not with the aim of returning to their own lines, but rather to gain entry to U.S. facilities where captives generally fared much better![34]

Whatever the precise reasons for the FFL's abuse of prisoners, the prospect of transferring captured Axis soldiers to the FFL remained a constant worry for Britain and the United States. British and U.S. prisoners were treated much better on the whole, but both democratic belligerents realized the safety of their troops would be jeopardized if they were seen as handing off captives to the FFL to be treated as the latter saw fit. Prisoner transfers often involved a difficult trade-off between military expediency and the risk of retaliation. Whether it was in North Africa or later in France proper after the Normandy invasion, transferring prisoners was seen as an attractive option to U.S. and British leaders by relieving the burden on already limited resources.[35] Several proposed transfers of prisoners to FFL camps were dismissed during high-level U.S.-U.K. meetings, however, because of fears of possible retaliation against Allied servicemen held by the Axis powers. Some later transfers eventually took place, especially when huge numbers of German prisoners fell into Allied hands after D-Day and subsequent offensives, but U.S. and British leaders incorporated explicit guarantees over treatment alongside stringent monitoring requirements. Through collective pressure the two main democratic belligerents were moderately successful in improving the conduct of FFL captors, though when possible both powers still showed an overall preference to personally maintain control over enemy combatants they captured.[36]

Despite their best efforts, good conduct by the United States and Britain could not provide a surefire guarantee that their own troops would be treated accordingly. In part this was because Nazi Germany was less sensitive to the potential costs of retaliation since the government was not subject to the same degree of domestic pressures as its democratic counterparts. As the war gradually shifted in the Allies' favor, Germany became increasingly willing to abuse prisoners, especially those attempting to escape. Escalating abuses were intended to serve as an example to other prisoners along with troops still in the field, but also to deter millions of foreign workers essential to the German war effort from any thought of resistance.[37] Although never approaching the horrific treatment of prisoners on the eastern front, as noted earlier German treatment of U.S. and British prisoners was punctuated by several episodes of extreme violence.

The ways in which the Western Allies chose to respond to German provocations offers further support for the role of reciprocity and an institutional account of democratic wartime conduct. Both the United States and Britain generally refrained from retaliating against German abuses, but the reasons for this restraint were more a function of the fear that any retaliation would simply result in an escalating cycle of violence between the captors. For instance, reports surfaced in spring 1944 that fifty prisoners were executed on Hitler's direct command through the infamous Sagan Order, after they along with others had attempted to escape from the German camp Stalag Luft III. Britain seriously considered reprisal executions but rejected the idea as counterproductive to the safety of remaining British soldiers in German custody.[38] In a similar manner, the United States decided to refrain from retaliating in kind against German abuses later in the war out of concern that this would only endanger those U.S. prisoners still in German captivity.[39]

In personal correspondence between the two elected leaders, Churchill and Franklin D. Roosevelt recognized that as the tide was turning against Germany, their adversary had fewer and fewer reasons to continue caring for Allied prisoners and could instead become desperate enough to inflict whatever damage it could on Allied troops.[40] Rather than threaten to reciprocate with violence against Axis troops in captivity, both leaders preferred to issue direct warnings to German officials who would personally be held responsible for any abuses against Allied prisoners and liable for war crimes once the war was over. As they asserted in a joint statement, "Any person guilty of maltreating or allowing any Allied prisoner of war to be maltreated, whether in the battle zone, on the lines of communication, in a camp, hospital, prison or elsewhere, will be ruthlessly pursued and brought to punishment."[41] The added danger of personal indictment in war crimes trials after the war contributed to deterring more extreme levels of German abuse against Allied prisoners.[42]

Concerns over reciprocity thus appear to have constrained the willingness of the democratic belligerents to initiate prisoner abuse, or even to retaliate against abuses committed by their German adversary. Reciprocity-related motives were driven largely by the greater sensitivity of British and U.S. leaders to preserving in any way possible the safety of their own troops, which they believed depended on maintaining proper treatment of Axis prisoners in return. In contrast, the available documentary record dealing with both public and private communications suggests that normative considerations were for the most part absent from the decision-making process, or at best secondary to the attention devoted to retaliatory dynamics.

The Strategic Benefits of Good Conduct

Beyond the risks of retaliation, a further institutional restraint on the conduct of the democratic powers was the belief that humane conduct provided additional strategic rewards both on and off the battlefield. Properly treating prisoners can increase the propensity of those enemy combatants still fighting to surrender, calculating they are better off laying down their arms than continuing to risk death in battle. The greater domestic accountability to win wars quickly and with fewer casualties also makes democracies more motivated to capitalize on these strategic gains.[43] While the logic of strategic benefits differs from reciprocity incentives, both mechanisms share the assumption that democracies' predisposition toward humane conduct is more a means to achieving instrumental objectives, rather than an end itself to remain consistent with domestic political values as presumed by normative accounts.

Given the dilemma facing captors, refraining from abuse presents certain trade-offs. The coercive potential of prisoner abuse is forsaken along with other possible dividends, including an exploitable pool of slave labor, devoting fewer resources to properly caring for prisoners, or using torture during interrogations to obtain intelligence. Against these drawbacks, the Western Allies during the Second World War consistently stressed the benefits to be gained from good treatment.

Even if it turned out that good prisoner treatment produced few tangible gains, what ultimately matters for explaining democratic conduct is that the Western powers *believed* such conduct would be effective. Faith in the value of humane treatment is evident in the beliefs of those officials most directly involved in implementing prisoner policies on the ground. An assistant judge advocate involved in POW camp affairs, U.S. Lieutenant Newton Margulies, remarked that it was "eminently more sensible, and really more clever, to win our war with butter and beefsteaks instead of bullets and bombs."[44]

[109]

Similar sentiments were evident when the U.S. House of Representatives convened a special committee to investigate the overall Allied war effort. After receiving testimony from all branches of the armed forces, the State Department, and several other agencies, the committee concluded as follows regarding the contribution of prisoner policies toward winning the war:

> Commanders abroad have stated that reports reaching German soldiers to the effect that we are treating prisoners fairly, in spite of what their officers told them, were a great factor in breaking down the morale of German troops and making them willing, even eager, to surrender. So pronounced was this effect that General Eisenhower had safe-conduct passes dropped by the millions over enemy lines, promising treatment in accordance with the provisions of the Geneva Convention. *Had these promises not been true, and believed, victory would have been slower and harder, and a far greater number of Americans killed* [emphasis added].[45]

It is also important to note that the committee was well aware of both the strategic and reciprocal benefits gained through good conduct. Referring to the fewer number of U.S. soldiers killed as a result of humane treatment, they explicitly included not only those lives saved on the battlefield by shortening the war, but also those spared behind barbed wire in enemy POW camps.[46]

Capitalizing on the strategic benefits of prisoner treatment was apparent not only in the public statements of Allied officials, but also in the military plans developed by the democratic powers. The use of propaganda, and informational warfare more generally, to communicate democratic preferences and policies to enemy soldiers became an integral component of the Western Allies' overall approach to fighting the war. The joint U.S.-U.K. Psychological Warfare Division (PWD) viewed its mission as "to destroy the fighting morale of our enemy both at home and on the front."[47] Although "morale" is a rather nebulous concept, it is instructive that a later survey of PWD officials found a large number described their specific primary objective as "To induce surrender."[48]

In order to achieve this aim, the Allies devoted significant resources to disseminating propaganda materials to the enemy. In the period between the Normandy landings of June 1944 and Germany's defeat in May 1945, the United States and Britain dropped approximately six billion leaflets on German positions in western Europe alone.[49] As the war went on, the Allies were increasingly successful in finding their targets and communicating information directly to German soldiers on the ground. Surveys of German POWs later found that over 80 percent had been exposed to Allied leaflets.[50] The actual messages contained in these materials further point to the importance of humane prisoner conduct. A content analysis of leaflets found that promises of good treatment for prisoners was the most prevalent theme.[51]

Given the importance of expectations over treatment once a prisoner, it is perhaps not surprising that the *Passierschein* (safe-conduct pass) became widely viewed as the most successful propaganda tool from the entire war, since it capitalized more than any other on vows of humane conduct toward surrendering soldiers.[52] The leaflet did not focus on any other issue, such as the strategic situation on the ground or the moral depravity of the Nazi regime. Instead, the pass concentrated on a simple message of good treatment. The text of one of the most popular variants of the leaflet read:

Safe Conduct

The German soldier who carries this safe conduct is using it as a sign of his genuine wish to give himself up. He is to be disarmed, to be well looked after, to receive food and medical attention as required, and to be removed from the danger zone as soon as possible.

Signed—Dwight Eisenhower, Supreme Commander,
Allied Expeditionary Force

The final design went through several revisions based on information gleaned from German prisoners questioned over what aspects of the leaflet they found to be more or less convincing.[53] In addition to the personal signature of General Eisenhower, the overall design of the pass was intended to look official not only to signify the seriousness of the commitment but also to give German soldiers a sense that they had the authority to surrender. The leaflet contained the government seals of both the United States and Great Britain and was usually printed on high-quality paper using superior inks and in color. As one historian remarked, "From a rather crude beginning, the Allied surrender leaflet ended the war looking like a cross between gilt-edge bonds and a college diploma."[54] The leaflet was viewed as doubly effective because it articulated in clear terms the Allied promise of humane conduct but also provided a concrete tool for enemy combatants to actually surrender. Government reports from the war showed that German soldiers would carry the pass with them, oftentimes waving it over their heads, to demonstrate their good faith when laying down their arms.[55]

Was all this effort in the careful design of leaflets, along with the enormous scale of their distribution, actually successful in encouraging greater numbers of surrenders than would have otherwise been the case? Propaganda operations began in earnest from mid-1944 onward and were indeed followed by increasing levels of surrenders.[56] However, it is problematic to automatically conclude that propaganda directly led to rising capitulations, especially given the prominent role played by significant Allied military advances during this same period. A rigorous examination of the merits of Allied propaganda unfortunately faces several challenges. There was no equivalent to the massive *United States Strategic Bombing Survey* evaluating the effectiveness of air power during the war.[57] Even if more detailed data existed, a compounding problem is that psychological warfare was never intended to be deployed separate from military force.[58] As one historian of the period comments, "it is difficult to discern where the demoralization induced by battlefield defeats left off and where the demoralization induced by propaganda in support of military operations began."[59] There is thus the danger of circular reasoning concerning the relationship between promoting surrenders and battlefield success.

Although it is difficult to isolate the precise independent effect of propaganda, several signs point to promises of good conduct playing a contributing role in encouraging the capitulation of enemy troops. A series of surveys of German POWs from December 1944 to February 1945, a key period involving continued Allied offensives and Wehrmacht counterattacks, found respondents remembered leaflets focusing on promises of good treatment more than any other theme.[60] By comparison, messages emphasizing the inevitability of the Allied victory or appeals attacking Nazi ideology appeared to have little impact. German prisoners were also likely to placed faith in Allied promises of proper prisoner treatment; other surveys showed between 82 and 90 percent of captives believed they would be treated according to the regulations of the 1929 Geneva Conventions.[61]

Care must be taken in drawing any firm conclusions from these surveys given the potential desire of respondents to please their captors out of fear or other motives, as well as the fact that those deciding to surrender were probably more likely to remember and believe Allied commitments than soldiers choosing to fight to the bitter end. However, if respondents were purely motivated by giving answers pleasing to their captors, other choices such as the attacks on Nazi doctrines would in many respects appear even more attractive given the ideologically charged nature of the conflict. The high level of trust exhibited by prisoners to promises of the Western powers is also impressive given the German government went to considerable lengths to counter Allied propaganda as well as punish those looking to surrender.[62] Furthermore, if soldiers had the opportunity to vote with their feet they appeared to have overwhelmingly preferred giving themselves up to U.S. and British forces rather than to the Western Allies' more brutal Soviet partner. In the closing months of the war around one million German soldiers fled westward into the hands of the democratic powers instead of leaving themselves at the mercy of the advancing Red Army.[63] Despite the initial deployment of significant numbers of German troops to both fronts, the final tally of prisoners held at the end of the war was a ratio of 4:1 in favor of the Western powers.[64] This might be indicative more of fears toward the Soviet Union than beliefs in the benevolence of the Western powers, but the point remains that prisoners' words were ultimately more consistent with their deeds regarding the relative prospects of decent prisoner treatment.

It bears emphasizing that, irrespective of the actual effectiveness of promises of humane treatment, what ultimately matters from the point of view of an institutional explanation for wartime conduct is that democratic leaders believed there were strategic benefits to be gained. As one U.S. general asserted, "German prisoners in America write thousands of letters to their families in Germany telling of the treatment that they are accorded. This is America's greatest propaganda and is having a decided influence on the course of the war."[65] The fact that the German government also believed in the power of these messages, evidenced by vigorously seeking to counter such propaganda, points to the substantial role played by concerns over strategic benefits from good conduct.

While much of this discussion so far has focused on the Western theater, the potential for accruing strategic advantages from humane treatment was noticeable even in the much harsher climate prevailing on the Pacific front. There is little doubt U.S. treatment of Japanese prisoners, especially in the early portions of the war, was below the standards afforded to Axis prisoners in the European theater. Atrocities on the battlefield were more common as the Pacific War descended at times into brutal combat.[66] Part of the reason for the poorer conduct by the democratic powers is actually in many ways consistent with an institutional explanation. Japanese treatment of U.S., British, and Commonwealth prisoners was oftentimes ruthless. Prisoners were made to perform hard labor in unsanitary conditions often on meager food rations, which led to almost one-third of prisoners dying in captivity.[67] In light of the fact that Japan was already committing high levels of violence, constraints relating to fears of retaliation and escalation were weaker compared to the situation that prevailed on the Western front where German and Italian abuse was more moderate.

The forces resulting from reciprocity thus make the Pacific War a relatively hard case when arguing for the merits of strategic advantages. The United States and Britain did indeed engage at times in significant levels of violence against Japanese prisoners, though the abuse was not nearly as systematic or extreme as that committed by their adversary.[68]

Nevertheless, Allied conduct remained relatively more forgiving than their opponent's and, if anything, gradually improved rather than worsened as the war progressed. One of the reasons was that military benefits from good conduct were in many ways even greater with Japanese soldiers than for any other prisoner group during the war. Japan's bushido tradition, which demanded soldiers fight to the death and viewed surrender as the ultimate dishonor, is often credited with making Japanese troops extremely reluctant to give themselves up.[69] Soldiers facing the prospect of surrender would often instead prefer death in battle or even ritual suicide (*seppuku*). As the Japanese Armed Forces' *Field Service Code* plainly stated, "Never live to experience shame as a prisoner."[70] The number of prisoners in the Pacific theater usually amounted to only a few thousand and was much lower than in Europe.[71]

This no-surrender preference made the use of Allied propaganda more difficult than in the German case. However, these same tendencies ironically translated into immense benefits to the Allies for those Japanese troops that did end up being captured. First, Japanese prisoners received little training on how to conduct themselves once caught, since surrender was never discussed as a viable option. Japanese captives were thus much less "security-conscious" than their German counterparts and often willingly shared valuable military intelligence.[72] Second, the feelings of dishonor brought on by surrender made many Japanese prisoners feel in essence dead and separated from their home country. Several prisoners were "reborn" under Allied captivity and actively collaborated with their captors by writing and designing propaganda leaflets or even directing U.S. pilots on combat missions over Japan![73] While the strategic benefits from good conduct in the case of Germany often manifested more in the form of growing numbers of surrenders, in the Pacific theater prisoner intelligence became a prized commodity. Importantly, this intelligence was often made available and gained through decent treatment rather than through torture or other coercive interrogation techniques.

A parallel pattern thus developed in both the beliefs of Allied officials and actual military policy. In personal correspondence, General Douglas MacArthur, supreme commander of Allied forces in the Southwest Pacific Area (SWPA), recognized that abusing prisoners was counterproductive to the overall war effort and in particular harmed the propaganda efforts of the Allies to induce Japanese surrenders, which meant a loss of potentially valuable intelligence.[74] Along with the use of propaganda along similar lines as in the Western theater, the U.S. Army developed a concerted campaign to make its own troops more mindful of the benefits of surrender and overcome the tendency of some soldiers to retaliate against Japanese abuses.[75] This education program highlighted the intelligence value of Japanese prisoners but also pointed out that committing atrocities would only strengthen the resolve of enemy soldiers to continue fighting.[76] While difficulties remain in determining the exact effectiveness of such efforts, beliefs concerning strategic benefits nevertheless played a significant role in shaping the prisoner policies of the United States on the Pacific front as well.

WWII and the Darker Side of Democratic Conduct

Institutional incentives heightening sensitivity to retaliation and strategic benefits help account for the overall benevolent treatment of prisoners by the democratic powers that has so often been celebrated. By extension, however, in the absence of those same constraints conduct toward prisoners may be not be quite so humane, revealing instead a darker side to democracy.[77] During the war and in its immediate aftermath, both the United States and Britain carried out various levels of abuse, calling into question any claims that democracies are always committed to humanitarian ideals. As several episodes examined in greater detail below illustrate, when institutional and normative forces operated in opposing directions, instrumental incentives more often than not prevailed to the detriment of those groups that were most vulnerable.

Postwar Treatment of Axis Prisoners in Europe

Although questions surrounding prisoner abuse generally focus on conduct during wartime, the situation facing Axis prisoners after Victory Day presents an even clearer test of normative versus institutional explanations, since each offers radically different expectations for democratic conduct. A normative approach presumes that the democracies would continue to treat enemy prisoners in a humane manner. If anything, treatment might even be expected to improve. Security concerns during the war, along with fears over what defeat might mean for the survival of democratic societies, are some of the reasons that democracies might use to rationalize less than ideal treatment of prisoners for the greater good of defending their core values. Once the war ends the enemy no longer poses the same threat, and democracies should hew even more closely to domestically rooted humanitarian principles and improve their treatment of prisoners.

In contrast, from an institutional perspective one of the primary motives restraining prisoner abuse—the fear of retaliation—largely disappears once the war is over. This is especially true in cases where one side achieves total victory, as in the European endgame of 1945. Previously benevolent captors will not necessarily suddenly turn vicious, but triumph does mean democracies have fewer reasons to uphold rigorous standards of prisoner care. The normative and institutional approaches, therefore, point to very different predictions regarding the conduct of the democratic belligerents at the end of the Second World War.

After defeating their Nazi foe, the Allies were in complete command of German territory and quickly liberated many of their own prisoners while rounding up millions of Wehrmacht troops as part of the terms of unconditional surrender. One prominent writer, James Bacque, charged that the Western Allies, led by U.S. General Eisenhower, went so far as to engage in a campaign of genocidal proportions to exterminate German prisoners in revenge for crimes committed by the Nazi regime. While only a few thousand German prisoners were thought to have died in U.S. and British custody during the war, Bacque argued that General Eisenhower personally orchestrated the deaths of between eight hundred thousand and one million German soldiers after the Second World War ended.[78]

Bacque's research has been roundly challenged on a number of fronts and is even contrary to the official report from the German-sponsored Maschke Commission. He has been criticized for his selective use of historical sources, the interpretation of the available evidence, and the dramatic conclusions he then draws. The general scholarly consensus is that no methodical plan was put in place by the democratic powers to rid the world of German soldiers.[79] The upper estimate puts the deaths of German prisoners in captivity after the war ended at around fifty-six thousand—certainly an unfortunately large number, but a fraction of the total alleged by Bacque.[80] This figure implies a death rate of just over 1 percent and is certainly higher than the rates prevailing under Allied captivity during the war, but not necessarily too far off in absolute terms from earlier trends.[81]

What is relevant here is not so much the claim that the democratic powers engaged in a massive campaign of prisoner killings, but rather whether or not their conduct changed in meaningful ways after hostilities ceased. The rise in death rates, while still modest compared to those on the eastern front or by Japan in the Pacific, is at least suggestive that the Allies expended less effort to ensure the needs of German soldiers after the war. The democratic victors certainly faced significant challenges with the sudden influx of millions of German soldiers, many sick and malnourished, all of which took place in the midst of the widespread devastation of Germany and surrounding countries from years of warfare. There is some contention that the harsher conditions experienced by German prisoners may also have simply been the unintended result of competing Allied preoccupations of caring for millions of additional displaced civilians.[82] Although postwar conditions in Europe presented obstacles for the treatment of German prisoners, there is little doubt the Allies implemented several measures that made the prospects for surrendering soldiers even more arduous.[83] This was especially evident with German POWs held in the continental United States, where food rations were cut and work details heightened even though these camps did not face similar resource shortages as those in Europe.[84]

Taking advantage of the disappearance of the Third Reich as a functioning government, the Allies argued that the 1929 Geneva Convention governing prisoners no longer applied. Subverting the letter and spirit of the laws of war, the democratic powers refused to grant official prisoner of war status to German soldiers surrendering after May 5, 1945, and stripped this status from German prisoners already held in Europe up to that point. Surrendering German soldiers were instead designated "Disarmed Enemy Forces" by the United States, or "Surrendered Enemy Personnel" by Britain, losing all the protections provided for under the Geneva regime. If democratic norms of respect for individual rights, or more broadly the sanctity of the rule of law, had any impact on the conduct of Western Allies during the war, their commitment appears to have greatly diminished at war's end.

The disappearance of any fears of reciprocity provides a more convincing explanation for the sudden change in Allied practices. Referring partly to Bacque's charges, one historian argues more generally that,

> while there is no real evidence to suggest that a deliberate "death camp" policy was being pursued by SHAEF (Supreme Headquarters, Allied Expeditionary Force), the absence of possible retaliation meant that less effort was put into finding ways of procuring scarce food and shelter than would otherwise have been the case, and that consequently tens of thousands of prisoners died of hunger and disease who might have been saved.[85]

Across a number of dimensions the treatment afforded German soldiers in the postwar period was inferior to that provided during the course of hostilities. The ICRC was accorded significantly less access to monitoring the conditions of prisoners and recording complaints compared to the much more open policy that had prevailed in wartime.[86] During the war over a dozen German captives were court-martialed and condemned to death by the U.S. Army for murdering fellow prisoners while in captivity, but none of the sentences was initially carried out. The hesitation to execute foreign citizens turned out to be due less to any moral concerns than to the fear of reprisals by Germany. It is indicative that once the war was over, the accused were promptly sent to the gallows.[87]

One of the biggest problems was the refusal to promptly repatriate prisoners to their home countries at the end of the war, as mandated under Article 75 of the 1929 Geneva Convention. Some have suggested that Allied reluctance to send enemy troops home was partly driven by normative concerns over the latter's health and safety upon returning to societies ravaged by war.[88] Yet the Western Allies had strong practical reasons for delaying the repatriation of certain enemy combatants, especially given their value as labor for much-needed reconstruction efforts. The newly reconstituted French Republic was particularly demanding that German soldiers help rebuild destroyed infrastructure across France. French policy also had a punitive element to exact a certain amount of vengeance against their erstwhile occupiers. The United States and Britain were content to meet French needs with some of their existing stocks of prisoners.[89] The willingness of U.S. and British authorities to transfer prisoners to the French with less regard for their well-being stood in sharp contrast to their attitude during the war, when both were especially fearful of Axis reprisals.[90]

Unlike in wartime, prisoners were often forced to perform dangerous work, in complete contradiction to existing international agreements. One of the most hazardous duties was mine clearing, and an ICRC report found that by the fall of 1945 around two thousand Germans were dying per month carrying out this task.[91] When pressing needs were present and no threat of retaliation against their own soldiers existed, the humanitarian norms of Western Allies appeared to have had little restraining effect. The final repatriation of Axis prisoners originating in the West did not conclude until 1948, around three years after the end of the war, though the Western Allies' effort was at least better than that of the Soviet Union, where the last German prisoners did not return home until the mid-1950s. Nevertheless, the treatment of prisoners by the democratic powers converged more closely with that of its communist partner compared to each side's more disparate practices during the earlier active hostilities.

The willingness of the United States and Britain to eschew previous commitments to international law even led to some rather paradoxical situations, such as continuing to hold prisoners from countries that became formal allies. When the war began, fascist Italy was one of the main Axis adversaries of the major democratic powers, first Britain and France followed later by the United States. Throughout the summer of 1943, the Western Allies made steady advances across Sicily and started initial operations against the Italian mainland. By the fall of that same year Italy was defeated, Benito Mussolini had fallen from power, and new prime minister Pietro Badoglio signed an armistice with the Allies. One of the main stipulations was that Italian forces would switch over to fight for the Allied cause. Upon receiving word of the armistice, German forces quickly occupied much of the Italian peninsula, though the Italian government became a nominal partner in the U.S. and British coalition against Germany and Japan.

One key problem confronting the democratic powers, however, was what to do with the approximately 450,000 Italian soldiers captured during earlier Allied campaigns in North Africa and the Mediterranean.[92] In negotiations leading up to the armistice, the Allies told the Badoglio government that Italian prisoners would be repatriated so long as Allied captives under Italian authority were promptly returned as well. The conditional nature of the proposal reflected the common concerns of reciprocity expressed by U.S. and British leaders throughout the war. The Italian government would eventually prove unable to uphold its end of the agreement, though not from a lack of trying. In occupying much of the Italian mainland, Germany quickly took over most POW camps and in short order shipped Allied captives out of Italy to areas under firmer German command.[93]

Heightened German control over thousands of additional Allied prisoners was far from a welcome development for the democratic powers, but one favorable side effect was that these new events provided more flexibility when dealing with the Italian prisoners in their hands. The 1929 Geneva Convention never really envisioned the scenario of one state switching sides midway through a war, which meant no explicit provisions outlined how to deal with Italian prisoners. By that point many of these captives had been transported to the United States, or to the United Kingdom or its dominions, and became important contributors to their wartime economies. There were thus strong incentives to put aside arguments that these prisoners should be liberated and instead to maintain them in a similar indentured status. As one U.S. military official commented, "We felt it absolutely necessary from the military standpoint to keep these people [i.e., Italian prisoners] and get useful labor out of them."[94] By the end of 1944, Italian prisoners on U.S. soil had provided over ten million worker-days of labor, freeing up U.S. soldiers for deployment overseas.[95] In essence, the fifty thousand Italian prisoners on the continental United States, along with hundreds of thousands in North Africa and the British dominions, allowed the democratic belligerents to substitute an equivalent number of their own troops directly toward the war effort.[96]

To be fair, in comparison with the fate later met by many of their German counterparts, the actual conditions and restrictions for Italian prisoners improved somewhat after 1943 as they were viewed as less of a threat to national security.[97] It was still not lost on Italian prisoners that they remained confined to camps despite the fact that their countrymen lucky enough to have avoided capture were now fighting alongside their democratic captors or had been able to return to their homes. Taken

[119]

together, the evidence of Allied treatment of both defeated Germany and their newfound Italian ally provides further support for an institutional approach, which suggests the democratic powers were more willing to bend legal norms and discount humanitarian concerns once the threat of reciprocity receded. In the postwar environment, they also recognized the advantages to be gained from mistreating their prisoners, or at least not adequately caring for their needs, and were more than happy to reap those benefits.

The Forcible Repatriation of Soviet Prisoners

The Second World War generated enormous movements in populations; by some estimates up to thirty million people were displaced, including civilian refugees, workers coerced into enemy fields and factories, and of course huge numbers of prisoners.[98] Many Soviet prisoners fortunate enough to survive the brutal conditions in German captivity during the war would eventually see their luck run out, due in no small part to conscious decisions taken by the democratic powers.

Many of these captives, along with millions of uprooted Russian civilians, did not want to return to live under Joseph Stalin's rule. Between 250,000 and one million prisoners either volunteered or were coerced into joining the German armed forces, and they feared they would subsequently be punished as fascist collaborators.[99] Only four months after the June 1944 Normandy invasion began, the Western Allies already held twenty-eight thousand Russian soldiers caught fighting in German uniform, a number that would only continue to grow.[100]

Even regular prisoners worried for their safety. Under Soviet military law, it was considered a serious offense for soldiers to surrender without having first been wounded or receiving explicit permission from a superior.[101] Stalin further issued Order No. 270 in August 1941 requiring military units to fight to the last man, that any soldier attempting to surrender or desert be shot, and that families of these "malicious deserters" be arrested and punished.[102] Reinforcing this point when speaking to a foreign reporter, Stalin stated, "In Hitler's camps there are no Russian prisoners of war, only Russian traitors, and we shall do away with them when the war is over."[103] The fate awaiting many Russian prisoners was thus well known should they eventually go back to their homeland.

With prisoners of all nationalities scattered across Germany and former Nazi-occupied territories, the Western powers faced the formidable challenge of how to handle millions of Russian soldiers and civilians falling into their hands. According to normative expectations, those prisoners refusing to return home would likely not be forced to do so by a democratic captor. Sending individuals back to a country where they were at grave risk of execution or extreme forms of violence and deprivation contradicted long-standing principles of asylum.[104] The 1929 Geneva Convention regulating POWs contained no explicit provision outlawing forced repatriation since this, as with the earlier discussion of the ambiguous status of Italian prisoners, was not a scenario originally foreseen by negotiators. However, compelling prisoners to return against their wishes could be interpreted as contradicting the core precept of the convention, as outlined in Article 2, that prisoners "shall at all times be humanely treated and protected, particularly against acts of violence," and "measures of reprisal against them are forbidden." In terms of precedent, bilateral treaties negotiated in the aftermath of the First World War, several signed even by the Bolshevik Russian government, stated that prisoners could only be returned to their home country on a voluntary basis.[105]

The steps taken by the democratic powers would turn out to be completely at odds with normative expectations. The United States and Britain showed little reluctance in forcibly transferring Russian prisoners back to the Soviet Union. The policy was codified in a specific private agreement negotiated at the Yalta Conference in February 1945.[106] The accord was not made public until March 1946, after the bulk of repatriations had already been carried out. The dissident Russian writer Aleksandr Solzhenitsyn described these orders, and later Western attempts to downplay their complicity, as the "last secret" of the war.[107] Article 1 of the Yalta Repatriation Agreement stated:

All Soviet citizens liberated by the forces operating under United States command . . . will, without delay after their liberation, be separated from enemy prisoners of war and will be maintained separately from them in camps or points of concentration until they have been handed over.[108]

The agreement did not contain any explicit provision authorizing forced repatriation, but there was also no reference to the 1929 Geneva Convention and little doubt that prisoners would be returned irrespective of their wishes, and by any means necessary.[109] The terms were in many ways a continuation of existing policy at the time, since both Western powers had already committed to forced repatriation well before the conference. Britain quietly began returning captured Russian prisoners as early as the summer of 1944.[110] Future British prime minister Harold Macmillan, at the time resident minister at SHAEF, gave an official order in November 1944 stating in blunt terms, "All Soviet citizens, irrespective of the situation in which they are found or of their past history, should be turned over as soon as possible to the Soviet authorities for the latter to *dispose of as they wish*" (emphasis added).[111] The United States took similar steps not long after their British allies.[112]

The policy of forced repatriation targeted Russian prisoners, while purposefully excluding other nationalities. In the SHAEF *Handbook of July 7, 1945, Amended through 20 September 1945*, the section dealing with prisoners and displaced persons read as follows:

No United Nations national, stateless person, national of a neutral state or persons persecuted because of race, religion, or activity in favor of the United Nations will be compelled to return to his domicile except for a criminal offence. *Liberated Soviet citizens uncovered after 11 February 1945* [the date of the Yalta Agreement] *are excluded from this policy* [emphasis added].[113]

Unlike the slow return of German prisoners employed on reconstruction projects across Europe, the United States alone transferred over two million Russian soldiers and civilians to the Soviet Union in a few short months from May through September 1945.[114] At the height of repatriation operations more than fifty thousand Russians were shipped daily from Western-controlled zones to impatient Soviet authorities.[115]

The Western powers even needed to resort to brute force on several occasions to compel Russian prisoners to return home.[116] A rash of suicides ensued across several Allied camps as many Russian prisoners panicked over the prospects of going back to the Soviet Union.[117] Learning from these experiences, Western authorities turned to duplicity to convince prisoners to be transferred. In one instance at a camp in Lienz, Austria, British officials announced to over two thousand Cossack officers and several hundred other interned elites that they were invited to attend a conference. This raised some suspicion among the largely anti-Bolshevik captives, but a lieutenant gave his "word of honor as a British officer" that they would be safe. The prisoners were then herded onto trucks and transported to awaiting Soviet forces. As one Cossack officer later remarked, "The NKVD or the Gestapo would have slain us with truncheons, the British did it with their word of honor."[118]

The fate awaiting many repatriated soldiers was in little doubt. Less than two years later, in January 1947, the Soviet government found the Cossack leaders from the Lienz camp guilty of treason, among other crimes, and sentenced them to death.[119] For regular troops execution was also feared, especially if they had been caught in German uniform. However, it was not uncommon for many Russian soldiers, whose sole crime was to have fallen into German captivity, to be condemned to serve between fifteen and twenty-five years in a Soviet labor camp, which effectively became a death sentence.[120]

The prospects for repatriated Soviet soldiers were thus daunting at best. Recognizing the threat often facing persons who escaped or otherwise found themselves outside of their homeland, U.S. Secretary of State George C. Marshall testified in congressional hearings several years after the war, "It is the fixed policy of the United States Government to oppose any forced repatriation of displaced persons."[121] However, during the war Marshall was the U.S. Army's chief of staff and instrumental in coordinating the forced return of Russian soldiers. Why then did the democratic powers act completely at odds with their own humanitarian principles, and through their actions directly contribute to the deaths of so many Russian prisoners?

One answer offered by some scholars is that democratic leaders were naïve, and blind trust in their wartime communist ally led them to be deceived.[122] This view does not stand up to scrutiny when looking both at internal documents of the Western powers and the statements by Soviet authorities regarding their motives. Rather, the decision was purposeful, with the Western powers having a good idea of the fate awaiting repatriated Russian prisoners.

Part of the motivation for the democracies appears to have been prioritizing unity and an unwillingness to upset their Soviet ally, which could have complicated negotiations over other more pressing issues, such as the future of Germany and other European countries.[123] For the Soviet Union, the return of all prisoners served several ends beyond simply enforcing domestic military law and punishing defectors. Years of war with Germany, much of it fought on Soviet soil, exacted an enormous toll. There was consequently a pressing need for labor, and returning Soviet prisoners offered a ready pool of workers.[124] Perhaps even more important was the potential loss in both international and domestic prestige if hundreds of thousands of citizens were seen to actively reject the Soviet system to instead live in the West. For these reasons, as early as August 23, 1944, the Soviet government issued a formal request to its Western allies for all Russian prisoners to be returned "at the earliest opportunity."[125]

As with other aspects involving the wartime conduct of the Western allies, reciprocity also proved paramount. A more immediate impetus for the democratic powers had less to do with Soviet demands and more with anxiety over the fate of their own soldiers who had fallen under communist control. Because many prisoner camps were located in eastern parts of Germany and other occupied areas, British authorities estimated in September 1944 that upwards of two-thirds of British and Commonwealth captives would likely be liberated by the Red Army.[126] As the war neared its end, around sixty thousand U.S. troops who had originally been captured by the Axis powers fell under Soviet control.[127] Both Churchill and Roosevelt worried that Stalin would delay the return of Western prisoners as a bargaining chip in postwar negotiations.[128] Roosevelt expressed his concern over the pressures emanating from "the intense interest of the

[123]

American public in the welfare of our ex-prisoners of war."[129] Similar demands from the British public even led Churchill to write directly to Stalin pleading with the Soviet leader to personally intervene to ensure all British prisoners were returned promptly. The prime minister added, "There is no subject on which the British nation is more sensitive than on the fate of our prisoners in German hands and their speedy deliverance from captivity and restoration to their own country."[130]

In light of the intense desire for the return of their own soldiers under Soviet custody, the fate of Red Army prisoners was given little consideration by the democratic powers.[131] Some officials, such as Joseph Grew, U.S. undersecretary of state, expressed concern over the moral implications of forcibly repatriating millions of Russian prisoners and civilians. Grew's position nonetheless remained the minority view within the higher echelons of both democratic governments. Secretary of State Edward Stettinius refused to entertain Grew's unease, fearing that raising any humanitarian issues would cause "serious delays in the release of our prisoners of war unless we reach prompt agreement on this question [i.e., the repatriation of Russian prisoners]."[132] National publics in the democracies offered few constraints that might change the minds of authorities—in addition to wanting the return of their own soldiers, there was little sympathy for the Russian prisoners, especially those who had fought in German uniform.[133]

The United States and Great Britain were thus quick to transfer Russian prisoners back to the Soviet Union once the war ended. Despite having only recently regained its full sovereignty, France even allowed Soviet agents to carry out manhunts for Russian citizens on its territory.[134] The timing of the Western powers' decision also reflects the change from Germany to the Soviet Union as the main threat from the standpoint of reciprocity. Many Russian prisoners were captured well before the end of the war, but except for a few they largely remained in Western-controlled camps for months before they were eventually repatriated. Although a few U.S. and British prisoners began falling into Soviet custody as the Red Army advanced, the bulk of Western captives remained under German control until almost the very end of the war. Both democratic powers feared that widespread repatriations of anti-Bolshevik Russian prisoners or those who had fought in the Wehrmacht would result in swift retaliation by the Third Reich against Western prisoners. As General John R. Deane, the U.S. military attaché in Moscow and the main U.S. official to sign the Yalta Repatriation Agreement, commented:

> To avoid reprisals by Germany against our own men held as prisoners of war by the Germans we took the position that we would have to hold those

Russians found in German uniform until the end of the war, when the danger of reprisals had been removed by victory.[135]

Concerns over retaliation, first by Germany and subsequently by Soviet Russia, played a crucial role in shaping the decision and timing of the Western Allies to forcibly repatriate Russian prisoners. The democratic powers were well aware of the humanitarian implications of their policy. They appeared more than willing to trade the lives of millions of Soviet soldiers and civilians in order to ensure the safety of several thousand of their own troops. In a somewhat morbid reference, U.S. Army historians gave the top-secret documentary record for their country's repatriation of Soviet citizens the code name Operation Keelhaul. Keelhaul refers to an old method of naval punishment, which involved dragging a bound individual from bow to stern underneath a ship.[136] As one historian concluded, "The West's humanitarian concern appears, in retrospect, to have been restricted to Westerners."[137]

Some defenders contend that the democratic powers eventually realized the error of their ways and by 1947 the United States allegedly refused to engage in any further forced repatriations.[138] Yet by then the damage had already been done to millions of Russian soldiers. Furthermore, the democracies had little reason not to now claim the moral high ground as East-West tensions steadily grew and their own prisoners had been returned, thereby reducing concerns over retaliation. It may be unreasonable to expect democratic governments to always uphold in their foreign affairs the norms preached at home, since some exceptions will inevitably occur. What seems more problematic for a normative perspective was the ease with which the democratic powers were willing to abandon Soviet prisoners and civilians in their care.

From Soldiers to Civilians

Differences in Allied treatment of enemy combatants and civilians offer further insight into the greater role played by institutional over normative forces in shaping democratic wartime conduct. In contrast to the generally decent treatment of surrendering troops during World War II, civilians were not nearly so fortunate. As the war progressed the Western Allies conducted an increasingly intense series of aerial bombing campaigns against German cities. Allied air power during the war is estimated to have killed 305,000 civilians, wounded 780,000 more, and made 7.5 million homeless.[139] Similar discrepancies between the treatment of prisoners and noncombatants were evident on the Pacific front with the systematic firebombing of Japanese cities, culminating in the dropping of the atomic bombs on Hiroshima and Nagasaki.[140]

[125]

Why were civilians brutally targeted by the democratic powers, while prisoners were largely spared the worst excesses of violence? The motives underlying the conduct of the United States and Britain toward German, and later Japanese, civilians suggest that democratic norms had little restraining effect.[141] This did not appear to be the case before the war, or in its early stages, when the democratic powers often couched civilian bombing predominantly as a moral problem. After news broke in September 1937 that Japan was attacking Chinese cities from the air, the Western Powers were quick to lead a League of Nations resolution condemning Japanese actions. Roosevelt later publically spoke out against Japanese atrocities in moral terms, saying:

> without warning or justification of any kind, civilians, including vast numbers of women and children, are being ruthlessly murdered with bombs from the air. . . . Innocent peoples, innocent nations, are being cruelly sacrificed to a greed for power and supremacy which is devoid of all sense of justice and humane considerations.[142]

Referring to both the bombings in China and the Spanish Civil War, the U.S. State Department issued a formal statement, stressing that "Such acts are in violation of the most elementary principles of those standards of humane conduct which have been developed as an essential part of modern civilization."[143] Nevertheless, once the democratic powers were at war, the moral condemnations reserved for others appeared to exert little impact on their own behavior.

The conduct of the democratic allies toward civilians largely goes against the prescriptions of a normative approach, but what of institutional expectations? When examined in a closer light, both of the two main institutional restraints operating in the case of prisoner treatment were much weaker or largely absent for the use of violence against civilians. First, the demands of reciprocity provided few incentives for either British or American forces to avoid targeting noncombatants.[144] Britain was initially a victim of a concerted German air campaign, commonly known as the "Blitz," to destroy British industrial capacity but also to terrorize its populace into submission.[145] British authorities thus had little to lose by responding in kind given the enemy was already targeting its own civilians systematically. Of course, the United States did not face similar bombings, since its homeland was well beyond the range of the German Luftwaffe. However, after Germany lost the battle over the skies of England by May 1941, it lacked any real capability to target Allied civilians in any systematic large-scale manner. The democratic belligerents could thus have fewer worries about the risks of retaliation against their own civilians when planning bombing runs against German cities, which increased the chances such campaigns would become more frequent and intense.

One interesting issue is why abuses against civilians and prisoners did not become more interdependent and closely linked over the course of the war.[146] Even if civilians of the democracies were safe from attack, threats of violence against their troops held by the Axis countries might have given their leaders pause before conducting the massive bombing campaigns that followed. There were occasional steps in this direction, such as sometimes placing camps holding Allied prisoners near cities or key industrial installations to deter attacks.[147] The Nazi leadership also later encouraged local populations to take their anger out on downed airmen, leading to several lynchings. Yet in Europe, more egregious attempts to punish Western captives for bombings conducted by their countrymen were generally not followed through.

Part of the reason likely had something to do with the particular structure of German prisoner affairs in the Western theater. While Nazi paramilitary organizations like the SS (Schutzstaffel) played a greater role in the war in Eastern Europe, in the West authority over captured enemy combatants ultimately fell to the German Armed Forces High Command (Oberkommando der Wehrmacht/OKW). The more hardcore political units within the Third Reich thus had less ability to influence the treatment of prisoners in the West.[148] Given the military background and mandate of the OKW, its leaders were much more concerned with the repercussions that punishment would have on German prisoners held by the Allies. Military leaders could not stop all violence against captives, but they engaged in delaying tactics and other strategies to prevent the implementation of the worst attempts at abuse.[149] In the case of bombing Japanese cities, fears over further retaliation were less relevant, since Japan was already engaging in horrific levels of prisoner abuse such that it could not get much worse.[150] Concerns over reciprocity thus did not figure prominently for the democracies when deciding how to treat civilians compared to prisoners.

Second, the democratic powers had a much stronger perception that greater strategic benefits would flow from attacking rather than protecting civilians. Drawing on the vision of air power theorists from the interwar period, both the U.S. and British armed forces would come to develop elaborate notions of the potential for bombers to revolutionize warfare by taking the fight directly to the most vital targets of the enemy's society.[151] This thinking was indebted to the views of one of the most famous proponents of air power, Italian general Giulio Douhet, who saw the bomber as the ultimate offensive weapon and explicitly recommended targeting civilian populations as one of the surest ways to achieve victory in war.[152]

[127]

The incentives and resulting conduct of the democratic belligerents were quite similar in the case of U.S. bombing of Japanese cities in the Pacific theater. Many scholars have argued that the large-scale use of incendiary bombs to target Japanese cities, such as the Tokyo firebombing that resulted in the deaths of between eighty thousand and one hundred thousand civilians in a single night, was driven by the racial demonization of Japan by U.S. forces, while "civilized" German civilians were spared the worst horrors.[153] However, many German urban areas were attacked using similar tactics, such as the bombing of Dresden, which killed an estimated forty thousand civilians. This suggests Allied air strategy was more similar than different in both theaters and cannot be explained primarily as a function of racial differences between the two main enemies of the Western powers during the Second World War.[154]

Beliefs about the strategic benefits of indiscriminate bombing to undermine the economic capacity and civilian morale of the enemy to continue fighting, whether in Germany or Japan, can therefore be seen at the very least as a permissive cause of civilian targeting. Attention to these benefits made it much more likely that the democratic powers would target civilians, in contrast to their incentives to protect prisoners in order to encourage further surrenders.

Both democratic institutional incentives involving concerns over reciprocity and the strategic benefits from good conduct were largely absent in the case of civilians, which help to account for differences in their treatment relative to prisoners during the Second World War. In contrast, normative principles might be expected to operate even more strongly in the case of protecting civilians, as they represent in purest terms the defenseless and innocent compared to soldiers on the ground. Nevertheless, in a similar manner to the previous episodes dealing with postwar prisoner treatment and forced repatriation of Russian soldiers, when institutional incentives diverge from normative prescriptions it appears all too frequently that democracies choose to shed their humanitarian principles. Rather than being deeply embedded in the very fabric of democratic domestic political cultures, normative ideals are willingly sacrificed when it suits the interests of democratic belligerents.

When Democracies Go Bad: Other Instances of High-Level Prisoner Abuse

An in-depth analysis of prisoner treatment during the Second World War offers a more somber picture of the seeming virtues of democratic behavior during wartime. Far from displaying any inherent benevolence, more calculated institutional concerns over retaliation and strategic benefits were the main drivers behind decent democratic treatment toward their prisoners. This pattern in the conduct of democracies is further apparent in instances beyond the case at hand. A brief investigation of other wars shows that democracies tend to resort to higher levels of prisoner abuse and act more like their autocrat counterparts in situations where these key institutional constraints are lacking or point in the direction of condoning brutalities.

The Boxer Rebellion

When fighting enemies already committing high levels of prisoner abuse, democratic belligerents likely face fewer incentives not to respond with similar viciousness. During the 1900–1901 Boxer Rebellion, the United States, Britain, and France all sent troops as part of a relief expedition to save Western missionaries and other civilians threatened by rising violence in China. Boxer fighters resorted to horrible levels of abuse against Western civilians and soldiers alike. Torture was a common fate for those from the Relief Expedition who were captured, usually ending with their execution.[155] Decapitation and mutilation were also frequently committed by Chinese soldiers, and in several instances commanders actually offered rewards to their troops if they brought back the severed heads of foreign soldiers.[156] Facing the prospect of surrender, many Western soldiers preferred committing suicide rather than face the trials of Chinese captivity, a choice all the more unusual given their cultural background.[157]

Encountering such high levels of prisoner abuse, the Western powers more often than not responded in kind. Facing an ideologically driven foe whose movement was largely based around anti-Western principles, there was also little strategic benefit to be gained from good conduct. For instance, the Western Legation, which was under siege in the Legation Quarter of Beijing, preferred to bayonet captured Chinese prisoners in order to save bullets for the continued defense of their embattled position.[158] British and U.S. forces sometimes sought to keep Chinese prisoners alive for labor purposes, yet in many battles U.S. commanders issued orders to give no quarter.[159] As the war wore on and the Relief Expedition gained the upper hand, U.S. soldiers developed the colloquial term of "Boxer-hunting" for scouting missions tasked with mopping up the remnant Chinese forces.[160]

The Western powers defined their conduct by a harsh reciprocity—they believed there was little reason to hold back given the violence already being perpetrated by their adversary. When direct evidence was found of atrocities committed by Chinese troops, such as the possession of severed heads, Western captors often "responded by killing every enemy without mercy."[161] With a grim cycle of retaliation ruling the day, another scholar concluded that "there was little to choose between Chinese and foreign brutality in the summer of 1900."[162]

The Vietnam War

Although not displaying any systematic conditional relationship in the quantitative analysis from the prior chapter, the severity of the fighting can also sometimes heighten incentives for prisoner abuse, even in the case of democracies. The U.S. intervention in Vietnam from 1965 to 1973 gradually devolved into a long and drawn-out counterinsurgency, taking on many attributes of attritional warfare.[163] U.S. treatment of North Vietnamese and Vietcong prisoners correspondingly became increasingly harsh as the fighting wore on. U.S. armed forces on the ground in Vietnam developed a general pattern of brutality, which was implicitly sanctioned and sometimes actively encouraged by high-ranking military officials.[164] Vietcong prisoners were viewed as particularly stubborn and "during interrogation they were threatened, abused and tortured in what appears to have been an officially condoned policy of extracting intelligence by violence."[165] In an attempt to disrupt the Vietcong's vast command, control, and communication network, the U.S. government instituted Operation Phoenix in 1967 to target leaders through infiltration, interrogation, and often execution.[166] While primarily focused on the civilian leadership, the program had implications for prisoner abuse by using harsh interrogations to identify Vietcong suspects who were then captured and likewise often tortured or killed.[167] Counterinsurgency operations in Vietnam were thus typified by high levels of prisoner abuse.

The Balkan Wars of the Early Twentieth Century

In other cases democratic constraints on abuse against enemy combatants can be overcome by competing incentives, especially related to the aims sought through war. In the Second Balkan War beginning June 1913, after initially taking the offensive Bulgaria would eventually become the prey of its previous Orthodox allies, Serbia and Greece, over the territorial spoils of their conflict earlier that year against the Ottoman Empire. By the end of the war, Romania and even the Ottoman Empire itself joined the Greco-Serbian side to conquer land at Bulgaria's expense. Atrocities were common on the battlefield with few prisoners taken.[168] Democratic Greece conducted itself in just as extreme a manner toward captives as its more autocratic allies. A variety of factors certainly contributed to the horrors inflicted during the war, but the desire to annex territory from the adversary was a key cause of the high levels of prisoner abuse. The patterns of violence mirrored those of the First Balkan War lasting from October 1912 to June 1913; the only difference was that the primary victim changed from Ottoman to Bulgarian in the subsequent conflict. In such wars of conquest, far from acting as a constraint through liberal norms of nonviolence, democratic publics can goad their governments into ever-greater levels of brutality in the quest for national glory.[169] In both wars, aggressors sought to kill enemy troops in order to clear the way for a more assured occupation of newly conquered territory. Greece would turn out to be just as influenced by territorial desires as its allies and issued explicit orders to its soldiers to this effect.[170]

This chapter has shown that democratic belligerents can be capable of impressive acts of humanity, but also equal deeds of brutality, toward captured enemy combatants. Under the right conditions, institutional forces arising from fears of retaliation and the strategic benefits of good conduct lead democracies to prioritize the proper treatment of prisoners. Yet as the brief overview of other instances of democratic conduct shows, the nature of the conflict can sometimes overwhelm these institutional constraints and push belligerents toward ever-greater levels of violence. Desires to conquer foreign lands, in particular, have figured prominently in many past instances of severe prisoner abuse. Understanding more precisely how territorial motives lead to the terrorizing of captives is the question that will be the focus of the following chapter.

[5]

Territorial Conquest and the Katyn
Massacre in Perspective

> They took us to a small wood. They took away rings, my watch,
> belts, knives. What will they do to us?
> > —Final entry in the diary of a Polish officer
> > held prisoner by the Soviet Union

In early April 1940 Soviet forces executed over twenty thousand Polish military officers and other elites across several sites. These killings became collectively known as the Katyn massacre, or Katyn Forest massacre, one of the most notorious atrocities from the Second World War. That the killings stand out is all the more telling given the sheer number and extent of crimes committed during a period marked by such intense violence. The Soviet Union carried out many other extreme acts before, during, and after the war, but the targeted and systematic nature of the mass executions along with later secrecy over the slaughter led to a unique renown for the Katyn casualties. As one scholar concludes, "Katyn, despite accounting for only a minuscule percentage of the total number of Stalin's victims, was among the worst excesses."[1]

Differences were papered over during the Cold War with Poland entrenched behind the Iron Curtain, but the massacre would come to significantly strain relations between successive Polish and Soviet (and later post-communist Russian) governments. Amends haltingly began to be made in earnest during the post–Cold War era, though not without great controversy and acrimony at times on both sides concerning the precise details and motives behind the deaths. Significant progress was nonetheless achieved such that in 2010, seventy years after the killings, then prime minister Vladimir Putin became the first Soviet or Russian leader to commemorate the anniversary of the massacre side by side with Polish officials. Yet just three days later a plane carrying Poland's president, Lech Kaczyński, and many other of the country's elites crashed just miles from the Katyn Forest grave sites, killing all ninety-seven people on board. Although ruled an accident, the loss of so many of the country's elites was viewed as a "Second Katyn," reopening memories of old wounds that have yet to fully heal.[2] Aleksander Kwaśniewski, a former Polish president not on the plane, summed up the feelings of many concerning the Katyn Forest: "It is a damned place. . . . It sends shivers down my spine."[3]

One of the biggest ironies is that the murders at Katyn and related sites might never have come to light if not for Nazi Germany's invasion and brutal occupation of large parts of the Soviet Union. In April 1943 Nazi officials announced that they had uncovered mass graves where many of the victims had been buried. So horrific was the discovery that even Joseph Goebbels, the Third Reich's minister of propaganda and ardent fascist, wrote in his personal diary "Polish mass graves have been found near Smolensk. . . . Gruesome aberrations of the human soul were thus revealed."[4] Hoping to use the discovery to fracture the coalition between Poland, the Western allies, and the Soviet Union, Germany invited an independent commission led by the ICRC to inspect the site. In what became known at the "Katyn Lie," Soviet authorities would deny the charges, even after later condemning many of Joseph Stalin's other crimes, alleging instead that it was actually German forces who had killed the Polish prisoners.[5]

When finally taking official responsibility for the executions almost fifty years later in an April 1990 statement, Soviet authorities acknowledged that the Katyn massacre "represents one of the most heinous crimes of Stalinism."[6] The many depravities committed by Stalin's Russia along with other communist regimes are well documented.[7] From this perspective, the murder of thousands of Polish prisoners in the forests of Katyn and other locations may simply represent one more regrettable, though all too common, example of the murderous predilections resulting from communism that was further compounded by long-running cultural animosities.

Yet attributing the Katyn massacre to the particularities of communist doctrine risks disregarding important underlying causes of the decision to liquidate so many captives in such a short period of time. Rather than ideological motivations, the killings were motivated by the Soviet Union's desire to permanently annex long-sought-after Polish territories. The method of violence employed, the timing of the killings, and the selection of which captives to kill and which to spare all suggest that concerns over conquest largely drove this extreme prisoner abuse. When territorial motives were less present, Soviet conduct toward captives improved significantly, even if the lot for prisoners remained far from ideal. The Katyn massacre remains one of the most horrific crimes of the twentieth century, but its origins are rooted more in territorial ambitions than in the ideology or individual personalities of the perpetrators.

The impulses linking territorial conquest to the abuse of prisoners have just as much to do with what belligerents expect to happen well after the fighting has stopped as with the events taking place during the conflict proper. This stands in contrast to the incentives resulting from regime type, which center on more immediate fears of retaliation or what steps could be taken to help win the war in the near term. States annexing territory from an adversary and finding themselves with large numbers of captured enemy combatants instead have much longer time horizons to take into account. Beyond figuring out to how grab large swaths of land at other countries' expense in the first place, triumphant belligerents also need to consider how they will occupy and hold on to their newfound spoils well into the future. Existing peoples in these dominions represent a potentially valuable resource to be exploited, which many victorious occupiers have indeed done to great effect.[8] Yet native populations, often hostile to their new foreign masters, can also become a source of opposition that has often frustrated the ambitions of many conquering powers. These "fifth columns" contain the seeds of rebellion that can ultimately coalesce into a resistance movement threatening an occupier's very rule over its extended territories.

Not all segments of the native population are equal in their ability or willingness to mount a concerted challenge to an occupier's authority and control. Civilians living in conquered areas have frequently been victimized precisely to undermine any future resistance on their parts.[9] Yet if civilians are viewed as "fifth columns," then captured enemy combatants might be more appropriately counted as sixth, seventh, or eighth columns combined. In comparison to the wider civilian populace, combatants are often of prime fighting age, possessing at least a very minimum and often extremely advanced training in military operations and the use of weapons. These skills and attributes make captured combatants an especially salient threat to the occupying power, since they have a greater potential not only to fight but, more importantly, to organize and lead a domestic insurgency.

Just as with prisoner abuse more generally, employing violence against captured combatants to preventatively eliminate future resistance is not a strategy without hazards. Abuse may engender further hostility from surviving elements from the enemy, only fueling grievances against the occupier. States with more modest territorial ambitions may thus be less likely to assume the risks and expend the resources necessary to conduct a widespread program of prisoner abuse. Enemy combatants also do not pose a similar degree of threat when seeking more limited forms of occupation, as in French plans over parts of the former Ottoman Empire during the 1919–21 Franco-Turkish War. French abuses of Turkish prisoners certainly occurred but were not extensive or widespread compared to earlier episodes of territorial annexation in the Balkans or the later conquests in the period leading into the Second World War.[10] The preventive incentives for prisoner abuse may thus vary a great deal depending on the strengths of desires for conquest, as well as the size and nature of the enemy territory to be annexed.

Nevertheless, for belligerents eager to establish absolute command over fresh conquests, prisoner abuse often represents the most direct route to achieving their goals. As was shown in the earlier quantitative analysis from chapter 3, wars involving territorial annexation are much more likely to involve the most severe and systematic violence against enemy combatants. The prospects for prisoners in wars of territorial annexation should thus be especially poor, as conquerors appear attracted to the benefits of abuse while discounting the potential downsides. This prior statistical relationship is still only suggestive of the territorial logic connecting conquest to the abuse of captives. When examining particular historical episodes in greater depth, the record should show that would-be occupiers sought to target enemy combatants in their custody specifically because these groups presented the greatest threat to their plans of consolidating control over new conquests.

The general territorial logic also provides several additional observable implications beyond the overall level of violence inflicted upon captured combatants. Just as differences exist within the wider enemy population, so too the threat posed by various groups of prisoners will not be equal. Most combatants may possess a minimum level of military skills, but enemy officers present an especially clear and present danger. Even in countries with large standing armies, the quality of troops can vary widely. This is especially the case when states are actually confronted with full-scale war; forces can become stretched thin, and the military may need to rely increasingly on reservists or hastily trained recruits. In contrast, officers not only tend to receive more extensive military training and have greater combat experience than most regular soldiers or reservists, but they also possess valuable leadership talents necessary to coordinate resistance movements. It follows that those segments of the prisoner population perceived as most threatening to a conquering captor should also be most at risk of serious abuse. All enemy combatants might suffer severely during wars of conquest, but the worst levels of violence will be reserved for groups like officers given their skills and corresponding threat. One further implication is that those prisoners from the targeted groups deemed to be most capable are likely the first to be eliminated.

The explicit targeting of the officer corps contradicts the usual thinking about the relative treatment of different ranks of prisoners. The laws of war set up an explicit hierarchy governing the rights and protections of prisoners of war based on rank, reaffirmed in later treaties up to the present day. Unlike regular soldiers, officers were not required to do any physical labor even though they were still allowed to collect their regular higher pay.[11] These legal privileges have historically translated into superior treatment for officers while in captivity, though with some exceptions.[12] During the First World War, Tsarist Russia ensured that captured German and Austro-Hungarian officers lived in relative comfort, while the masses of other ranks were often deprived even of many of the basic necessities to survive.[13] Yet in the context of a captor seeking to annex territory, the privileged position of officers and other elite combatants may quickly turn into a liability.

A territorial logic of prisoner abuse also provides expectations regarding when violence against captives is most likely to take place. If control over the annexed territory appears assured, then the abuse of captured combatants should follow in fairly short order. Since part of the motivation is to destroy future possible threats, then conquering captors have every incentive to enact any overall plans of prisoner abuse as soon as possible. On the other hand, if the conqueror's tenure over the newly gained territory becomes precarious because of possible incursions due to other outside challengers, then the captor state may actually have less incentive to engage in prisoner abuse. Far from being a danger, captured troops from the conquered territory may present a valuable ally against a new common threat. Outside threats may lead occupiers to hold on to surviving enemy combatants in reserve, or even deploy them in battle against mutual enemies. Disputed territories have often changed hands on numerous occasions, and antagonists at one point may turn into welcome partners at others.[14] Poland offers a particularly vivid example in this regard, as the country and its people were the victims of an almost unending series of external aggressors over the course of the last several centuries.[15] The most recent dismemberment and annexation of Poland early on during the Second World War through Soviet and Nazi complicity also presents a useful test case of the territorial logic and additional implications for understanding the sources of prisoner abuse. When we look at the full set of patterns in the bloodshed wrought by the Soviet Union upon Polish prisoners, the territorial dynamics underlying the conflict offer the most convincing explanation.

Poland, the Soviet Union, and the Katyn Forest Massacre

The Second World War was in many ways harder on the Polish people than almost any other nationality. Caught between Nazi Germany on one side and the Soviet Union on the other, the Polish state was occupied by the two great powers and became a key battleground on the eastern front. Poland lost upwards of 20 percent of its prewar population by the end of the conflict.[16] Despite the extreme hardships felt by most Poles, certain groups suffered to a much greater extent than others. Polish combatants who were captured during the course of hostilities were a particularly vulnerable group, but not all prisoners were treated in an equal fashion.

This section lays out in greater detail the treatment of Polish prisoners of war, and in particular the systematic execution in the spring of 1940 of around twenty-two thousand Polish officers and related elites by Soviet forces in what has become known as the Katyn Forest massacre. After capture the officers had initially been sequestered for more concerted interrogation in several special camps near the towns of Kozelsk, Ostashkov, and Starobelsk,[17] as well as a number of smaller facilities located across modern-day Russia, Ukraine, and Belarus. The imprisonment of the Polish officers would eventually culminate in the execution of nearly every single inmate. The massacre is named after the Katyn Forest, though this site only contained mass graves for the Kozelsk victims. It emerged as a common reference for the entire Soviet massacre of Polish POWs because Katyn was the only site to be exhumed during the Second World War, becoming the most well-known mass grave from the conflict.

Background to the War: Soviet Territorial Motives

Poland and Russia's interactions have been rancorous during much of their history, punctuated by occasional intervals of grudging friendship. From the late seventeenth century up to the end of the Cold War, Poland was largely dominated by its larger and more powerful eastern neighbor, except for a few brief spans of time.[18] During the eighteenth century Russia, alongside Prussia and Austria-Hungary, profited from three successive partitions of Polish territory to the point where Poland ceased to exist as an independent state. The Russian regime, whether in its tsarist or later communist forms, thus possessed a long-standing interest in Polish territory.

One of the exceptions to Russian dominance occurred following the First World War when Poland regained sovereign statehood. Taking advantage of internal weakness after the Bolshevik Revolution and ongoing Russian Civil War, an independent and rejuvenated Poland turned

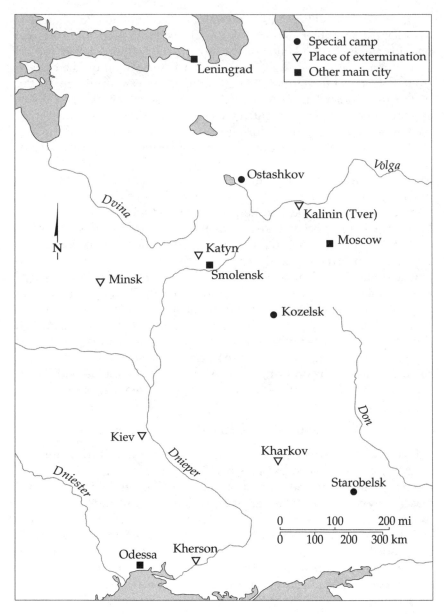

FIGURE 5.1 Map of Soviet special camps for Polish POWs and locations of prisoner executions

the tables and successfully fought a war against its disheveled neighbor from 1919 to 1920. After Polish forces drove back a Russian advance that had reached all the way to the outskirts of the capital of Warsaw, the Bolshevik government sued for peace. The two sides concluded a formal peace treaty, the Peace of Riga, in March 1921 through which Poland secured large tracts of Russian territory in what is now western Belarus and Ukraine. The gains were later ratified in 1923 with some reluctance by the Allied Conference of Ambassadors, which was established by the victorious powers after the end of the First World War and the Versailles Peace Treaty.[19] Forfeiting these vast expanses of territory became a great source of grievance for Soviet Russia and contributed to the derisive depiction of Poland by Vyacheslav Molotov, who later became Stalin's foreign minister, as "the monstrous bastard of the Peace of Versailles."[20]

During the interwar period, the Soviet Union harbored strong desires to reabsorb the territories now found within the eastern regions of a much-enlarged Poland. The events leading up to the Second World War provided the Soviet Union with a prime opportunity to retake the lost lands, while at the same time ensuring a more permanent solution to what they viewed as their Polish problem. The foreign ministers of Russia and Nazi Germany, Molotov and Joachim von Ribbentrop, signed a nonaggression pact on August 23, 1939. Article 2 of the agreement stipulated that should either partner enter into war against a third party, the other country would not come to the aid of the adversary.[21] The agreement is widely accepted as having sealed the fate for a German attack against Poland. One military historian described in a succinct manner the situation facing a country that had enjoyed its return to independence for a mere two decades: "Poland was now doomed."[22]

The publically released pact contained no specific provisions concerning German or Soviet interests in Poland. This was saved for a secret supplementary protocol, which divided eastern Europe into separate German and Soviet spheres of influence. Article 2 of the protocol explicitly outlined each country's share of Polish territory, though it left to a later date the final decision of whether to maintain a rump Polish state.[23] The Soviet Union thus entered into collusion with Nazi Germany to gain territorial spoils at the expense of a soon-to-be-defeated Poland.

The war officially began just over a week after the nonaggression pact was signed with Germany's invasion of Poland on September 1, 1939. Britain and France responded by declaring war on Germany, though they provided few resources or concrete support to a Poland that quickly found itself on the defensive. Stalin waited until Polish forces were sufficiently ground down by the German advance before invading Poland's eastern border just over two weeks later on September 17. In one of the many peculiarities that would take place throughout the wider war, neither

Poland nor the Soviet Union formally declared war on one another. The Soviets used a humanitarian pretext to justify its military actions, arguing it was only intervening to protect Ukrainian and Belarusian minorities from the dangers resulting from the collapse of the Polish state.[24] For its part, the Polish government was already under siege from German forces and saw the Soviet occupation as an almost foregone conclusion. Wanting to avoid any further bloodshed, Polish military and political leaders did not take any concerted steps to defend eastern portions of their country against the Soviet advance.[25] Pockets of resistance by Polish forces continued on both fronts, but the war was essentially over by the end of September. According to some estimates the Soviet Union suffered around eight hundred battle deaths during the fighting, while Polish forces lost around five thousand troops, though this would represent a fraction of the number of Polish combatants who would eventually die in captivity.[26]

The day after the war ended Germany and the Soviet Union reaffirmed their entente and consolidated their territorial gains with the September 28 Friendship Treaty. The agreement included a few revisions of the initial division of spoils presaged in the August 23 secret protocol, but the overall partition of Poland was put into effect with a German-controlled western region and Soviet-controlled eastern zone made up primarily of lands commonly referred to by Poles as the Kresy Wschodnie (Eastern Borderlands).[27] With the conclusion of the treaty the Soviets gained 52 percent of interwar Poland, composed of around seventy-eight thousand square miles of land, and 38 percent of its population, totaling more than thirteen million persons.[28] Germany took over large tracts of central Poland and their overwhelmingly Polish residents, yet Soviet claims that its conquered lands were largely composed of Slavic peoples and thus inhabited by few if any Poles are not credible. Demographic estimates based on Polish records suggest almost 40 percent of residents in the Soviet-controlled region at the time were ethnic Poles, amounting to over five million people.[29] Figures from the most recent census in 1931 showed that Poles represented the largest and most widespread minority group across various parts of the newly conquered lands.[30] Soviet expectations of resistance were thus likely to be quite high given the Polish population's historically strong sense of national identity coupled with their country's recent loss of independence.

Reflecting these concerns over possible defiance, and in a similar manner to the earlier August nonaggression pact, Molotov and Ribbentrop negotiated an additional secret protocol to the Friendship Treaty, which stated in part:

> Neither party will allow on its territory any Polish agitation that affects the territory of the other country. *Both shall liquidate such agitation on their*

[140]

territories in embryo and shall inform each other about expedient measures to accomplish this [emphasis added].[31]

The exact scope and extent of active German-Soviet collaboration in the suppression of Polish resistance remains an extremely contested issue.[32] The secret protocol nonetheless indicates that both countries were acutely aware of the threat posed by any Polish struggle against their respective rule and had already devised a strategy for dealing with this menace. How then did the territorial motives of the Soviet Union influence their decision making over how to treat captured Polish combatants? The Soviets would eventually identify Polish prisoners of war, and especially officers, as particularly dangerous groups deserving of a brutal, yet extremely efficient, solution.

The General Treatment of Polish Prisoners

From their first advances across the border into a besieged Poland, Soviet forces did not exhibit much kindness or sympathy in their treatment of captured enemy combatants. The high levels of prisoner abuse that resulted are largely consistent with what would be expected given the Soviet Union's territorial motives in eastern Poland. Polish armed forces were viewed as a general threat, and abuses like torture or execution of prisoners, whether or not they had put up any initial resistance, were a common phenomenon throughout the combat phase of the conflict.[33] During the few brief weeks of the war, between 1,000 and 2,500 Polish prisoners were summarily executed on the battlefield.[34] In one of the more gruesome episodes, General Józef Olszyna-Wilczyński, Polish commander of the Grodno military district, ordered his men to stand down in the face of advancing Red Army columns to avoid needless bloodshed. Foreshadowing the fate to befall other military elites, during his retreat Olszyna-Wilczyński was stopped by Soviet forces, roughly pulled from his car, thrown against a barn door, and shot on the spot.[35]

As callous as those early deaths were, most prisoners were not immediate executed and instead entered into some form of Soviet custody. While the precise number of captives is difficult to determine given the chaotic conditions prevailing in the country at the time, most estimates suggest around 250,000 Polish soldiers became prisoners of war to the Soviet Union.[36] Since the bulk of the Polish forces had been deployed to meet the earlier German offensive in the west, it follows that a far greater number of the close to seven hundred thousand troops found themselves under German control.[37] Not all Polish combatants fell into the hands of German or Soviet invaders, however, and many were successful in escaping to various neighboring countries. Around forty thousand soldiers were able to cross over to Hungary, while another thirty thousand went to Romania. About fifteen thousand more troops escaped to Latvia and Lithuania, though their relief would be short-lived as most were captured less than a year later when the Soviet Union eventually annexed the Baltic states in June 1940. Finally, 47,000 Polish soldiers, which included 9,200 officers, took various routes in secret to reach Allied-controlled territories like France and those in the Middle East.[38] Many of these officers and soldiers formed the core of Polish units who later fought under the command of the Western Allies throughout the rest of the war. Somewhat ironically, the contributions of these escapees to the Western powers would indirectly help the Soviet Union once it had partnered with the United States and Britain against a common Axis foe. However, in the autumn of 1939 the Soviet leadership was more concerned with the capability of Polish troops to undermine their country's control over eastern Poland than they were with Germany's invasion that would come several years later.

For the quarter million or so Polish soldiers who were unable to escape, the war was over, but their deprivations had just begun. Some were fortunate enough to be sent home early on, though this was primarily reserved for soldiers of Ukrainian or Belarusian origin.[39] The decision to do this was taken at the highest level of the Soviet government in a politburo meeting on October 2, 1939.[40] These other groups were largely viewed as less threatening to Soviet control over the recently acquired territories compared to the much more nationalistic ethnic Poles, who would continue to endure captivity for some time. While sparing some prisoners, the politburo meeting also ordered the creation of specific labor camps, as well as sites dedicated to separating and holding officers and other high-ranking Polish officials. As was the case throughout much of the war on the eastern front, the Soviet Union refused to allow the ICRC access to Polish soldiers or holding sites, which meant prisoners could not benefit in any way from the organization's oversight.[41]

Not long after capture, most prisoners were led on forced marches over vast distances to reach large temporary way stations and then on another arduous journey to their final destinations.[42] Since the war ended in late September, the weather became increasingly harsh, especially for those being sent to more distant locations in the Soviet interior. The further lack of adequate food and shelter meant large numbers died even before arriving at their intended prison camp. Although conditions often improved once prisoners got to more permanent facilities, the level of treatment for most Polish prisoners was far below generally accepted standards. After formally incorporating all conquered parts of Poland into the Soviet Union, the central government passed a decree on November 29, 1939, that all soldiers and civilians in these newly administered areas were now classified as Soviet citizens.[43] This was then used as a pretext to forcibly conscript over 210,000 persons into the Red Army, many of whom were former Polish combatants.[44]

Many of those not directly inducted into the military were instead organized into vast labor camps located in remote regions of the Soviet Union. Alongside many civilians, it is estimated that between one and one and a half million Poles were deported over the course of successive waves to various camps in the Soviet Union.[45] The grueling work, harsh living conditions, and paucity of appropriate food and shelter turned many of the labor camps into death sentences for prisoners. Rates of mortality across camps differed significantly, with some of the most extreme being those located in the far north and northeastern Komi and Kolyma regions of the Arctic, where around 75 percent of Polish deportees died in the years 1940–41.[46]

Forcibly removed from their homes to often faraway places, large swaths of Polish society were victimized through the use of mass deportations and labor camps as part of the broader Soviet policy of securing newly annexed territories. Upper estimates suggest that over 10 percent of the Polish citizenry was displaced or punished in some way by Soviet occupiers.[47] Territorial motives clearly played a major role in the overall use of violence by Soviet authorities in Poland. However, the general level of brutality hides important variation in the extent to which different segments of the populace were targeted. Approximately one-quarter of those who were deported, which included both civilians and former regular combatants, died over the course of years of grim living conditions and arduous labor.[48] Despite the horrific death rate suffered by deportees, this still pales in comparison to the eventual execution of over 95 percent of the Polish officers held in the lead-up to the Katyn massacre. The Polish civilian and general veteran populations certainly represented a potential threat to continued Soviet rule, since the possibility always existed that certain groups could coalesce and rebel against Soviet authority. The key issue for the Soviet Union remained the degree of threat posed by different elements of Polish society. The deportation of upwards of 1.5 million citizens was already an enormous endeavor in its own right, which involved Soviet authorities expending huge amounts of resources.[49] Ridding annexed eastern Poland of its remaining indigenous population representing over ten million more persons was thus not a feasible option.

The decision for the Soviet leadership essentially came down to how best to allocate the scarce resources available to its coercive machinery. Polish officers, who possessed a high level of both military and leadership skills, posed the most palpable threat. The Katyn massacre was thus a shortcut to suppressing the overall likelihood of a widespread rebellion in Soviet-held Polish territories. Surveying the choices facing the Soviet Union after its conquest, one scholar remarked that, "Short of destroying the entire population, a well-nigh impossible task, the next best method of reducing Poland for good was to remove all those in a position of leadership, military or intellectual."[50]

Prisoner Abuse Taken to the Extreme: The Fate of Polish Officers in the Special Camps and Related Prisons

The precise motives guiding the decision of Stalin and his inner circle to commit the Katyn massacre may unfortunately never be established with complete certainty. No documents are known to survive detailing Stalin's inner thinking or the private discussions among the top Soviet leadership that culminated in the final orders for the mass executions that followed.[51] Nevertheless, the available record reveals that the massacre was intimately connected to the long-term territorial ambitions of the Soviet Union in eastern Poland. Although Soviet authorities victimized nearly every segment of Poland's society, the most brutal and widespread tactics were reserved for those groups viewed as most endangering their hold on Polish territory. Officers were to find out that they were at the top of this list. As one prominent historian of the war in Europe's east concludes, "The death of Poland's military cadres was part of a calculated strategy to rid the occupied areas of any elements capable of raising the flag of national resurgence against the Soviet invader."[52]

Even though direct proof of Soviet intentions may be lacking, several pieces of evidence point to the crucial role played by territorial motives. Unlike in earlier wars during this period, the Soviet Union entrusted the running of the prisoner program to the NKVD (Narodnyy Komissariat Vnutrennikh Del, or People's Commissariat for Internal Affairs), rather than the Red Army.[53] This decision went against usual custom and further contradicted prevailing principles of international humanitarian law where prisoners were to be under the rules and regulations of the armed forces of the detaining power.[54] As the internal security apparatus and home to the Soviet secret police, the NKVD represented the main arm of domestic political repression. It already possessed a good deal of experience in extrajudicial killings and administered the notorious Gulag labor camps for domestic political prisoners and other individuals unfortunate enough to meet the wrath of the central government.[55] Delegating authority to the NKVD indicates that the treatment of Polish prisoners was viewed more as a problem of internal security to the stability of a now enlarged Soviet Union, rather than simply a matter of warfare involving an opposing state.

[144]

Lavrenty Beria, head of the NKVD and later a key player in the Katyn massacre, quickly formed a specific department within the organization, called the Administration for Prisoner-of-War Affairs, that was tasked with managing the Polish detention facilities.[56] With the NKVD structure in place, the objectives of these facilities went beyond the simple custody and care of captured enemy combatants, which was the traditional purpose of most POW camps. NKVD captors instead formulated an intense program of interrogation and indoctrination to identify individual prisoners who might be amenable to the communist cause, on the one hand, and to weed out and eliminate threatening elements, on the other. Polish officers became a key target of this program across the special camps that were set up expressly for the initial purposes of inquisition, and eventually used for elimination.

The turmoil ensuing from the fighting, as hundreds of thousands of Polish troops fled or surrendered in a haphazard fashion, meant that most of the early camps contained prisoners spread across all ranks. From the beginning, however, Polish officers were treated differently from regular enlisted soldiers. The NKVD gave explicit orders early on that officers should be identified and segregated from the general prisoner population.[57] Red Army commanders were forbidden from releasing any captured officers and further instructed to specifically seek out higher-ranking enemy combatants attempting to evade Soviet capture.[58] The sorting of captured Polish military and security elites from other ranks was largely concluded in less than two months. A top-secret NKVD report from November 19, 1939, detailed the number and placement of officers, along with other high-ranking police and gendarmes officials, in three specially designated camps, while junior officers and the rest of the rank and file were distributed across various other facilities.[59]

These camps were in or near the towns of Kozelsk, Starobelsk, and Ostashkov, which are located in contemporary Russia or Ukraine. Kozelsk and Starobelsk were designated primarily as camps for officers, while Ostashkov became a residual facility for remaining categories of prisoners; alongside soldiers the camp included officers from the police, border and prison guards, and a number of civil and judicial officials.[60] The emphasis on police and related officials at the Ostashkov camp may have illustrated a certain degree of projection on the part of Soviet authorities, overestimating the role of these individuals in running the former Polish state.[61] A number of additional officers and officials were also held in various smaller NKVD prisons in western portions of Belorussia and Ukraine. The decision by the Soviets to isolate officers was thus made early on and reflects the special attention devoted to this particular group of enemy combatants.

[145]

Unlike the sparse conditions that prevailed in more than two dozen regular prisoner camps and hundreds of other labor camps for Poles, the special camps for officers were relatively more comfortable though in no way sumptuous.[62] Work was still expected but was usually less arduous and often limited to building and maintaining camp facilities. The main purpose of segregating the officers from the rest of the prisoner population was to conduct a concerted screening process to identify candidates who might be sympathetic to the Soviet Union.[63] Irrespective of the initial feelings of the officers toward Soviet authorities, all prisoners were subject to an intensive indoctrination campaign to convince them to join the communist cause.[64]

Reflecting the paranoia that had already enveloped the Soviet Union during earlier domestic purges from the 1930s, camp officials were extremely sensitive to any hint of opposition to Soviet authority emanating from the prisoners. For instance, in late November 1939 a special NKVD team was sent to Starobelsk to deal with a secret "anti-Soviet organization," which turned out to be a request by a group of prisoners to contact the local American consulate regarding the possibility of joining the Polish army-in-exile that had by then formed in France.[65] In many respects, however, Soviet captors would ultimately be justified in their concerns over the beliefs of the prisoners from the special camps. Compared to most other countries that would be annexed or occupied during the Second World War by various powers, collaboration with outside authorities did not develop along a similarly large scale in Poland.[66] Polish officers in general remained fiercely patriotic to their former home country and often derided what they viewed as clumsy Soviet attempts at indoctrination. As one indication of these feelings, Soviet authorities later conducted an investigation in March 1940 of officers held at Starobelsk asking where they would prefer to be sent should the prisoners eventually be released. Feedback showed around half of the respondents wished to go back to former Polish territories even though they were under German or Soviet military control, while most of the rest wanted to be transported to a neutral country. Only sixty-four respondents, just over 1 percent of all prisoners held at the camp, indicated any desire to remain in the Soviet Union proper.[67]

The refusal by the vast majority of Polish officers to toe the communist line, up to and including the outright rejection of the Soviet Union, became a sore point for NKVD officials and the Soviet leadership more generally. Polish officers at the three special camps and other prisons were aware that the interviews were related to some form of selection criteria, though none knew their answers could become a matter of life and death. Interrogations revealed that the vast majority of prisoners had little sympathy for the communist cause and would likely oppose Soviet rule if given the chance. By their words and deeds, the Polish officers demonstrated to their captors that they represented a long-term threat to continued Soviet control over eastern Poland. While other Polish civilians and prisoners certainly suffered under Soviet rule, the threat posed by Polish officers meant they were destined to be almost completely eradicated.

The internal discussions and exact steps leading up to the final order to liquidate the special camps have either been destroyed or survive still hidden in archives from the Soviet era.[68] On December 3, 1939, the politburo ratified an NKVD bid to formally arrest all Polish officers in the three special camps as suspected counterrevolutionaries, putting them completely under the purview of the Soviet penal system rather than the laws of war.[69] Based on the recommendations of NKVD chief Beria, on March 5, 1940, the politburo issued the ultimate order to empty the special camps and examine the files for each Polish prisoner, which would eventually lead to the killing of almost every single captive.[70] The process that unwound involved the highest levels of secrecy; only Stalin, Beria, and a small inner circle of officials were privy to the discussions proposing the execution order in the first place, though it would later be distributed to other top members of the communist elite.

Even after the order had been authorized, just a dozen officials took part in the main planning, while it is estimated that those implementing the directives involved at most two hundred individuals.[71] Indicative of the special importance attached to the mission, the actual killings were entrusted to a small group of elite executioners, such as Vasili M. Blokhin for the Ostashkov prisoners, who had been instrumental in the Great Purges and other executions committed earlier or around the same time inside the Soviet Union. Those closely involved in formulating and carrying out the killings were subsequently bestowed some of the most prestigious honors, including the Order of the Red Banner and Order of Lenin, the latter being the highest award possible in the Soviet Union.[72] Even the guards at the special camps were incentivized with extra pay for ensuring no prisoners escaped during the initial emptying of the camps, after which the captives were transported to the locations where they would ultimately be murdered.

Beginning in early April, prisoners from the three special camps were moved to nearby facilities where they would eventually be killed: those in Kozelsk were moved 150 miles northwest to the city of Smolensk, Starobelsk prisoners 150 miles northwest to Kharkov, and Ostashkov captives east just over 100 miles to the town of Kalinin (now Tver). Most were subsequently shot, with the Koselsk prisoners killed and buried in the Katyn Forest close to Smolensk, from which the massacre gets its name. There have been various estimates of the exact number of prisoners killed across all of the various sites. Part of the difficulty is that even many NKVD records tabulating the total number of victims at various points in time contain numerous inaccuracies and contradictions. Table 5.1 below provides the best available figures for the number of prisoners killed and those spared for each of the three special camps.[73] Across these camps alone almost fifteen thousand officers and other high-ranking officials were killed.

Because of the paucity of records, details on the composition and fate of various captured combatants and other Polish prisoners housed at several NKVD prisons in western Ukraine and Belorussia is less well established. Along with the original politburo decree, Beria issued a separate order a few weeks later on March 22 to "clear out" these detention centers and transport the prisoners to more central NKVD locations in Kharkov, Kherson, Kiev, and Minsk, where they were likely killed.[74] It is now broadly believed that 7,305 out of 10,685 Poles originally held at these facilities were executed in a similar manner to prisoners from the three special camps.[75] The remaining inmates from these other NKVD prisons did not fare much better, since many were subsequently sent to labor camps or received similar harsh punishments. Unlike the special camps, determining the exact identity and makeup of the victims and survivors from these prisons is much more difficult. These facilities contained a wider array of Polish detainees, including some officers like at the special camps, but also an assortment of land and factory owners, spies, alleged insurgents, and a significant number of refugees.[76]

Taken together, the most widely accepted figures suggest NKVD forces systematically killed at least 21,768 Polish prisoners from early April through late May 1940. Those executed included 10 generals, 300 colonels and lieutenant colonels, 500 majors, 2,500 captains, and 5,000

TABLE 5.1 Death and survival statistics at the three Soviet special camps for Polish prisoners, April–May 1940

POW Camp	Mass Graves	Number Executed	Number Surviving	Percent Executed
Kozelsk	Katyn (near Smolensk)	4,410	205	95.6%
Starobelsk	Kharkov	3,739	78	98.0%
Ostashkov	Kalinin (now Tver)	6,314	112	98.3%
Total		14,463	395	97.3%

Notes: Figures are based on Cienciala, Lebedeva, and Materski 2007, 122–36, 205, 529 n.329; Sanford 2005, 94, 115. Does not include an additional 7,305 captives from several other NKVD prisons in western Ukraine and Belorussia who were also killed around the same time.

lieutenants and second lieutenants.[77] The Katyn massacre destroyed around half of the Polish Army's prewar officer corps along with a large portion of the former state's domestic security apparatus.[78] Furthermore, around half of the officers were composed of reserve forces drawn from some of the most elite segments of Polish society. As a result, in addition to their capacity as officers, Poland lost a further three hundred doctors, two hundred lawyers, three hundred engineers, twenty-one university professors, and a host of other professionals.[79] Along with the destruction of Poland's military leadership, the annexed country also lost the "flower of the Polish intelligentsia," which both individually and collectively would have likely posed a stern challenge to the Soviet Union's continued hold over the conquered territory.[80]

What is perhaps most astonishing is how few prisoners survived. The executions of captives from the three special camps resulted in the deaths of almost every Polish officer in Soviet custody at Kozelsk, Ostashkov, and Starobelsk at the time, 97 percent in all. In the more mysterious circumstances surrounding captives at the other NKVD detention facilities, estimates suggest death rates nearing 70 percent with likely an even greater proportion perishing among the officer contingents. Compared to the violence wrought on Polish civilians and the larger POW population, the Katyn massacre took prisoner abuse to an almost unheard-of level of ruthlessness. Even Japan and Germany, not exactly known as the most humane captors during the Second World War, did not achieve similar levels of carnage when looking at the different groups of prisoners falling under their control.

The Territorial Logic behind the Katyn Massacre

Why was the final order given to annihilate almost the entire Polish officer corps in Soviet hands? The text of the March 5, 1940, memorandum from Beria requesting Stalin to authorize the executions offers several indications of the territorial motives underlying the decision-making calculus of the Soviet leadership. In the opening paragraphs, Beria justifies his preferred outcome for the Polish prisoners as follows:

> Prisoners-of-war officers and police in the camps are attempting to continue their c-r [counter-revolutionary] work and are conducting anti-Soviet agitation. Each one of them is just waiting to be released in order to be able to enter actively into the battle against Soviet power.[81]

He goes on to note that NKVD officials had also uncovered a number of insurgent organizations in the western portions of Ukraine and

Belorussia, two of the main areas of Poland annexed by the Soviet Union the year prior. In all cases Beria charged that former Polish military officers or members of the police were instrumental to the planning and operation of these organizations.

After describing the specific number and distribution of prisoners across the special camps and other prisons, Beria concludes by recommending the prisoners be dealt with "using the special procedure, apply to them the supreme punishment, [execution by] shooting."[82] The document also definitively establishes that the highest echelons of the Soviet leadership both possessed knowledge of the massacre that was soon to unfold and played a direct hand in its authorization. Plainly marked on the memorandum were the signatures of Stalin, Foreign Minister Molotov, and other members of the politburo.

The memorandum thus reflects a deliberate policy of the Soviet leadership to eliminate the major sources of likely future resistance within the former Polish territory. Alongside the mass deportations and abuses of other soldiers and civilians, "The main aim of Soviet policy during 1939–1941 was to destroy Polish political, social and cultural influence entirely, and to disperse the Polish population throughout the USSR, where it could be controlled effectively."[83] A cornerstone of this policy would be the destruction of the Polish officer corps and related elements, in other words those who possessed the greatest capabilities and willingness to oppose from within Soviet power in the region.

Beria's discussion of counterrevolutionary threats, whether real or perceived, perhaps could have been a pretext for other motives to kill Polish officers, several of which will be examined in greater detail below. Taking into account later developments in Poland, however, the orders were a brutal, but in many ways foreseeable, strategy given their desire to consolidate power and hold on to the annexed territories. The Soviet Union only ended up enjoying their spoils of conquest for a little over a year after the Katyn massacre. Nazi Germany's offensive the following summer of 1941 would see the entire area of interwar Poland relinquished to the Third Reich for much of the remainder of the war. Yet by 1942, domestic resistance had consolidated into the formation of the Armia Krajowa, or Home Army, which became the primary indigenous opponent to German rule over Poland. At its height the Home Army fielded around four hundred thousand members, but its strength was widely believed to be rooted in a core of former Polish military officers. For instance, Stefan Rowecki, a former Polish Army officer, headed one of the precursors, the Związek Walki Zbrojnej (Union of Armed Struggle), and would later command the entire Home Army.[84] These officers coordinated all aspects of the Home Army's fighting force and turned it into one of the most formidable national resistance movements of the entire war.[85] Although the Soviet Union never faced the full force of Polish resistance, later events show the Soviet leadership appears to have been justified in its distress over the threat posed by the officers in their custody.

Examining other elements of the killings yields additional insights into the territorial motives behind Soviet decision making. First, the timing of the massacre in the spring of 1940 is interesting in that the Soviet leadership waited more than four months after it had completed the capture and separation of the vast majority of the Polish officers before commencing the executions. Part of the delay appears to have been balancing the future threat posed by the officers against the potential gains from using these captives as a bargaining chip and resource to be exploited in the wider European war. Beginning in late November 1939, the Soviet Union found itself in the small but hard-fought Winter War against neighboring Finland. There has been some thinking that the special camps were liquidated to make way for large numbers of Finnish prisoners.[86] Consistent with this line of thinking, Grigory Korytov, head of the Special Section in the Ostashkov camp, noted the following in a report from early March 1940 to his NKVD superiors: "it is rumored that in March we must basically clear out the camps and prepare to receive the Finns."[87] In this light, the Katyn massacre was merely a pragmatic and ultimately ad hoc solution to a housing shortage for the wider enemy prisoner population rather than a systematic plan to consolidate recently won territorial prizes.

This contention does not stand up well when looking at the overall course of the Finnish war. Contrary to Soviet expectations the Finns put forward a resolute defense, which translated into the Red Army capturing only around eight hundred prisoners throughout the entire war while suffering significant losses to their own forces.[88] The number of Finnish troops captured does not represent even one-quarter of the total prisoner population at the smallest of the three special camps, Starobelsk. The Katyn massacre also took place several weeks after the war with Finland formally ended on March 12, 1940. Space constraints would no longer seem to be an issue, since it was unlikely that more Finnish prisoners would be falling into Soviet hands. Unlike many of the captives from the defeated powers who languished in Soviet camps for years after the formal termination of the Second World War, all Finnish prisoners were promptly repatriated within three months once the fighting was called to a halt.[89]

The Polish prisoners did appear to figure prominently in Russian decision making during the Winter War, though not for the reasons initially thought. After war broke out with the invasion of Poland, the Soviet Union was accused of the international crime of aggression and expelled

[151]

from the League of Nations in December 1939. In early February of the following year, Britain and France put forward a proposal to send an intervention force to help their democratic Finnish counterpart.[90] There was some discussion about whether or not the Polish government-in-exile in London would contribute troops to the mission to thwart the Soviet Union, since the latter was one of the occupiers of the Polish homeland. Some historians have conjectured that Stalin kept the Polish officers in reserve as a source of leverage, should any military contributions to the expeditionary force on the part of the Polish administration in London ever take place.[91]

In the end the Western powers were unable to provide any significant aid to the Finns because of a variety of obstacles. Although the Red Army continued to suffer far greater casualties on the battlefield, Soviet material superiority ground down the Finnish forces, and by late February Finland had opened armistice negotiations with their adversary. Peace with Finland appeared more than likely by the start of March 1940. The possibility of any definitive Western intervention dwindled, and with it the usefulness of the special categories of Polish captives under Soviet control. Far from the threat of war, it appears more likely that the expected termination of the conflict with Finland helped seal the fate of the Polish prisoners at Kozelsk, Starobelsk, Ostashkov, and the other NKVD prisons. The Soviet leadership during this period also firmly believed a war against Germany was in no way imminent, since German attention was largely oriented westward in what the communist regime hoped would be a long and drawn-out war of mutual destruction between the fascist and capitalist forces. The need for a Polish ally was correspondingly perceived to be quite small at the time, which could allow Soviet desires to dispose of the Polish officers to come to full fruition.[92]

When turning to the details of the executions themselves, several aspects point to the particular importance Soviet leaders placed on destroying the capacity for future Polish resistance. In the sequence in which prisoners were selected, the first batches sent off to their deaths generally included the highest-ranking officers, in particular a select number of generals, as well as those individuals the NKVD diagnosed as possessing a particularly strong aptitude for leadership.[93] Removing the main leaders early on made the later executions easier to implement but also ensured that the most threatening elements were terminated at the soonest possible moment. Although the survival rate was extremely small across all prisoners within the special camps, those groups with particularly high levels of technical expertise were eliminated to the last person. For instance, Soviet authorities made certain to round up all officers from the Polish Institute of Gas Warfare, and every single staff member was executed.[94]

To eliminate or at least reduce later possible sources of grievances, the Katyn massacre was carefully coordinated with targeted deportations of other likely hostile elements. Soviet authorities had acceded to requests from officers in the special camps that they be allowed to correspond with their families, which was generally not the case with other prisoners. But the seemingly humanitarian gesture of permitting mail between the prisoners and their loved ones also contained a more nefarious motive—to gather the names, addresses, and other details of those closest to the interned officers.[95] Armed with this information, and in conjunction with the killings of prisoners from the special camps, the NKVD purposefully planned the mass deportation of the officers' families from their homes in Soviet-controlled areas of Poland. Three days before the March 5, 1940, execution order, the politburo issued a directive to the NKVD for plans to assemble the approximately twenty-five thousand families of the inmates.[96] By mid-April 1940, in the midst of the ongoing killings of the Polish prisoners, the family members were swept up and deported to collective farms and other facilities to perform hard labor in the Kazakh interior of the Soviet Union. Because the families mainly comprised women and children, the grueling work and harsh conditions killed a large though ultimately unknown number.[97] The aim was not only to punish those families of Polish officers but also to further remove any later sources of organized resentment against the Soviet Union that could coalesce into opposition to communist rule over the conquered territory.[98] The decision to liquidate the special camps, therefore, had much broader ramifications that would eventually embrace a number of groups beyond the original prisoners.

Although much of the discussion up until this point has centered on the officer contingents from the special camps, at Ostashkov and many of the smaller prisons in Western Ukraine and Belorussia the prisoners were high-ranking policemen, border guards, and other officials. Disposing of all these victims meant the Soviet Union was able to destroy not only the military leadership, but also almost the entire security and coercive apparatus of the former Polish government.[99] This had the effect of undermining the capability of any aspiring Polish state to reconstitute itself at a later date, but also eliminated almost every individual in Soviet custody at the time with the ability to meaningfully organize and lead a resistance force. The documentary evidence, along with the patterns and timing of the killings themselves, suggest the Soviet Union was primarily driven to this highly ruthless, yet targeted, strategy of prisoner abuse because of its long-term objective to assert complete control over recently conquered Polish lands.

Alongside the mass of prisoners killed in the special camps, a small number were not executed. Why were a select few spared? The vast

[153]

majority who were eliminated had been deemed enemies of the Soviet Union in one form or another. The exact criteria for those who were lucky enough to be saved are not known with certainty, though it is generally assumed they fell into one of three categories: professed communists; those thought to be more susceptible to further indoctrination; and those with some aspect of their background that aroused sympathy from their NKVD interrogators.[100] As the executions concluded by the middle of May 1940, the remaining officers from the three camps were sent to the Pavlishchev Bor facility at the Yukhnov camp before ending up in the Gryazovets camp.[101] Ironically, many were initially disappointed, since they assumed their compatriots had already returned home while they were being held back for some unknown reason. They would later find out that they were largely saved to become the core of a procommunist Polish Army under the command of the Soviet Union. In the end, however, the indoctrination program was an overall failure, since even among those specifically selected for further education only around a dozen ended up approved by Soviet authorities as genuine communists.[102]

Despite the few who managed to avoid execution, the objective of Soviet conduct toward the prisoners was clear—to destroy the Polish officer corps and all related elements under Soviet control. Although having immediate consequences for the Polish officers and their families, the Katyn massacre is better seen as part of a long-term Soviet plan to destroy any meaningful indigenous Polish influence within the newly absorbed territories.[103] Looking even more broadly, the massacres had an additional benefit of ensuring that any Polish rump state that might have somehow arisen out of the German-controlled areas was deprived of effective military leadership and would thus be as weak as possible.[104] In one way or another, Soviet territorial ambitions in Poland had dire implications for the general Polish prisoner population but would produce an especially brutal end for captured Polish officers.

ALTERNATIVE EXPLANATIONS FOR THE KATYN MASSACRE

Several alternative accounts have sometimes been put forward to explain the Katyn massacre. First, looking at another general factor used to explain many past patterns of prisoner abuse, cultural differences appear to figure prominently in the Soviet-Polish case. Animosities between Russia, whether in its Orthodox tsarist or communist incarnations, and its Catholic Polish neighbor were deep-seated. The clash of identity and ideals between the two countries could presumably explain the desire of Soviet Russia to rid itself of its culturally dissimilar foe once and for all. The cultural argument is consistent with the overall high level of abuse the Soviets unleashed on both Polish combatants and civilians. Cultural factors are less convincing, however, when trying to account for variations in the degree to which different groups of essentially ethnically similar Poles were targeted. If the motive was to destroy members of an opposing society, why were officers targeted more than regular soldiers or civilians, and especially to a much greater extent than even other Polish elites?

The cultural argument also does not account very well for why a later group of Polish officers first interned in the Baltic states did *not* end up being executed. As noted earlier, as many as fifteen thousand Polish soldiers had managed to initially escape to Lithuania and Latvia. Polish prisoners in both countries were later arrested after the Soviet Union annexed the Baltic states in June 1940.[105] It might be expected that these incoming prisoners would meet a similar fate as their earlier brethren from the special camps. By the time the new shipments of Polish officers had been detained in camps inside the Soviet Union, however, the broader strategic situation in Europe had changed drastically.

Over the course of May and June of that year, Germany achieved surprisingly rapid victories over many of the countries in Western Europe, including a crushing defeat of France in just six weeks. The hopes of the Soviet leadership that the fascist and capitalist powers would exhaust each other in a war of attrition appeared to be dashed.[106] The successes enjoyed by the Third Reich in the summer of 1940 greatly heighted the menace posed to the Soviet Union by its accomplice in the earlier dismemberment of Poland. With no ready counterweight on the horizon in the west, Germany potentially threatened the very survival of the Soviet Union, as well as Stalin's ability to hold on to annexed territories in eastern Poland.

One of the predicaments following from Soviet ambitions in Poland was that the newly gained territories provided many benefits in terms of greater land and resources, but also some disadvantages to its strategic position. The prior Soviet borders presented a more formidable set of natural barriers, which had been bolstered during the interwar period by a series of fortifications. In contrast, the new boundaries incorporating various portions of Poland were relatively lacking in both sorts of protection. Logistics and transportation also became more problematic, since Soviet forces now had to cope with two different railway gauges across the Russian and Polish areas. In particular, the disappearance of Poland removed what was often historically seen as a useful buffer against incursions by other great powers.[107]

Nevertheless, from the Soviet point of view, any drawbacks resulting from the 1939 partition have to be counterbalanced by the costs of potentially doing nothing in the face of German designs on Polish lands. Buffer states like Poland during this period were especially at risk of dismemberment, as surrounding great powers feared that rivals would take over and exploit the intervening territory at their expense.[108] Better for the Soviet Union to cooperate with Germany over the division of spoils than risk losing an even greater share of Poland to the Third Reich. Stalin also did not hold much trust in the Polish government to actually serve as a viable buffer against any Nazi attack, and even vetoed German suggestions to reserve a rump Polish state.[109]

Whatever the precise strategic merits in acquiring Polish territory, the Soviet Union nonetheless quickly found itself immediately opposite German forces and vulnerable to a surprise attack—an event that would later come to fruition with devastating repercussions. The resources and effort devoted to incorporating the newly conquered Polish lands were compounded by the generally accepted poor military planning by the Soviet leadership in the years leading up to the German invasion.[110] One Red Army officer expressed his skepticism over the wisdom of annexing Poland, judging that the operation "was not such a good move from the military point of view."[111]

Greater proximity to Nazi Germany combined with Wehrmacht successes in western Europe drastically changed the strategic situation facing the Soviet Union by the early summer of 1940, and correspondingly its conduct toward Polish prisoners. Just a few months earlier the Katyn prisoners were viewed as expendable, but as the German threat grew the Soviet Union preferred to hold on to those Polish officers taken from the Baltic countries should they be needed to help repel a future Wehrmacht offensive.[112] By November 1940, over half a year before the eventual German invasion, Beria discussed with Stalin the possibility of organizing the remaining Polish officers and soldiers into military units to operate alongside the Red Army. Although still preferring to select officers who demonstrated procommunist leanings, he concluded, "As a result of the work carried out, it has been established that the great majority of POWs can be undoubtedly utilized for organizing a Polish military unit."[113]

Considering NKVD records from the time listed 18,297 Polish prisoners in their custody, many of whom were officers of various ranks, this stands in stark contrast to the handful deemed sufficiently trustworthy to be spared from execution earlier that same year. If the German armies had indeed become bogged down in western Europe and in their weakened state posed much less of a threat, as the Soviets had initially hoped, the treatment of the later Polish prisoners would almost certainly have been much more brutal. It is more than likely the remaining Polish officers would have been branded as counterrevolutionaries and sacrificed to Soviet territorial ambitions in manner similar to their predecessors. Motives driven by cultural differences do not provide a convincing

[156]

explanation for the very different treatment accorded to the various sets of Polish officers over time. The shift of the prisoners in the eyes of Soviet authorities, from liabilities to be eradicated to assets that could be employed, is more consistent with the Soviet Union's changing hold over the conquered territories in light of the growing German peril to its west.

Second, perhaps Soviet abuse of the Poles was rooted in a particular historical hatred of its neighbor far greater in magnitude than that reserved for any other adversary, irrespective of the Polish people's specific cultural attributes. The resort to arms rarely takes place in isolation from past events or expectations of future military confrontations. Conflicts involving adversaries with a long-standing rivalry are likely to be more frequent and intense than those between states without a similar acrimonious history.[114] Past wars often fundamentally transform the beliefs and decision making of leaders, especially when faced with renewed crises and conflicts.[115] Related to this point is the contention that the Katyn massacre was retribution for the Soviet Union's humiliating defeat twenty years earlier during the 1919–20 Russo-Polish War.[116] Grievances from the earlier war certainly loomed large within the Soviet leadership, but if the thirst for vengeance drove Soviet actions it is again not clear why the later group of Polish officers taken from the Baltic states were not also executed. In the opinion of Stalin and the politburo, these prisoners should have been just as guilty as the Katyn victims for the humiliating outcome endured by the Soviet Union in the prior war. Furthermore, one of the main survivors of the massacre, Zygmunt Berling, who would later become the commander of the Soviet-sponsored Polish People's Army, had fought valiantly against Red Army forces and distinguished himself during the previous conflict between the two countries.[117]

Some defenders of Soviet actions claim the brutality unleashed at the Katyn massacre was a direct response to Polish conduct during the 1919–20 war. A large number of Russian prisoners died in Polish captivity during the war, and several Russian officials and historians have sought to portray these events collectively as a sort of "anti-Katyn" to demonstrate that Poland had been guilty of comparable levels of prisoner abuse.[118] On the same day that Putin became the first Russian leader to commemorate the massacre with his Polish counterparts, he later claimed the Soviet leadership was primarily motivated by retribution for earlier Polish wartime conduct, stating "It is my personal opinion that Stalin felt personally responsible for this tragedy, and carried out the executions (of Poles in 1940) out of a sense of revenge."[119]

Historical records show this is a difficult case to make. It is true that upwards of 20 percent of Russian prisoners did not survive their time in Poland's camps during the war. Nevertheless, this was more a function of neglect rather than a calculated strategy on the part of the Polish government, compounded by the already sick and weakened condition of many Russian prisoners upon entering captivity.[120] Furthermore, Polish prisoners in Russian hands did not fare much better during the conflict, which casts doubt on the notion that Katyn was largely committed in retaliation for earlier one-sided killings committed by Poland.[121] At best, both sides were guilty of abuse during the earlier conflict, and the Soviet Union did not possess a monopoly on prisoner-related grievances.

Placing Russo-Polish relations in the broader context of twentieth-century warfare reveals similarly weak support for the role of past conflicts and conduct on the decision of captors to resort to prisoner abuse. Building on the main model of prisoner treatment outlined previously in chapter 3, table 5.2 reports the effects of different measures of prior military competition and armed conflict on the likelihood a captor engages in the highest levels of prisoner abuse. The first rivalry measure comes from the work of Diehl and Goertz, which identifies rivals based on the frequency, intensity, and linkages between their past military interactions and thus expectations of future conflict.[122] The results show that belligerents who are rivals are around 8 percent more likely to engage in

TABLE 5.2 Rivalry, revenge, and prisoner abuse in interstate wars, 1898–2003

Variable	Change in probability of high-level abuse
Rivalry	
Rivals (Diehl & Goertz)	0.08†
Rivals (Thompson)	−0.01
Prior war and outcomes	
Fought prior war	0.03
Won prior war	0.06
Drew prior war	0.03
Lost prior war	0.02
Prior war and prisoner abuse	
Low abuse	−0.21*
Medium abuse	0.13
High abuse	0.02

Notes: * Significant at 5 percent; † Significant at 10 percent.
Each value represents the effect of the variable on the absolute change in the probability of high levels of prisoner abuse, holding other related variables at 0 (in the case of the models including prior war outcome or prior prisoner abuse) and all other variables at their means.

high levels of prisoner abuse compared to warring parties who do not share a similar conflictual history, and the effect is statistically significant at the 10 percent level. While the result is suggestive that rivalry can directly lead to prisoner abuse, the effect is relatively modest compared to annexationist war aims with an absolute rise of more than 50 percentage points in the risk of extreme prisoner abuse, which was established in the prior statistical analysis. Moreover, the finding for rivals is not robust, since another commonly used indicator of rivalry by Thompson has no significant impact on prisoner abuse and is actually slightly negative.[123] Even though such explicitly activated feelings and a sense of animosity might be expected to have the greatest impact on wartime conduct, the evidence suggests that the presence of such a rivalry has little bearing on how antagonists treat each others' captives during war.

In a similar manner, the experiences and lessons of past wars may have enormous repercussions on national interests and other areas of foreign policy but do not seem to affect the treatment of prisoners all that much. Countries that fought a war at some point in the previous twenty-five years against their opponent are slightly more prone to abuse prisoners, but the rise of 3 percent is negligible. Whether the prior war was won, lost, or settled by a draw also does not appear to have much impact. In fact, a country being defeated in the most recent war—the outcome that should especially fuel the fires of revenge as in the Russo-Polish case—has the weakest effect on the subsequent treatment of enemy combatants.

On the other hand, the actual conduct in the prior conflict does have some more lasting consequences, but only at the lower end of abuse. Interestingly, a captor whose troops were well treated by the adversary in their prior war is likely to show greater restraint in a later conflict, with a decline of 21 percent in the probability of resorting to high levels of prisoner abuse. This extension of reciprocity across conflicts suggests one possible pathway through which humanitarian impulses can diffuse over time even among belligerents. Yet harsher treatment of prisoners by the adversary in past wars does not translate into a greater desire to seek retribution later. Prior medium and high levels of abuse committed by the enemy are both positively associated with a captor subsequently engaging in greater abuse, but neither is significant and the effect for prior high-level violence is especially small at only 2 percent. In light of the strong results for reciprocity from the earlier main quantitative analysis, retaliatory impulses thus seem to be limited to the present war itself rather than carrying over into later conflicts. The collective results from table 5.2 indicate that motives embedded in feelings of rivalry and revenge have little influence on the resort to abuse, and even if there are some effects they pale in comparison to the incentives generated by territorial conquest.

[159]

A third alternative is somewhat related to territorial issues but instead emphasizes Soviet concerns to please Germany after their mutual dismemberment of Poland and demonstrate its trustworthiness as a partner.[124] Because the Wehrmacht was the first to attack Poland, followed only some weeks later by Red Army forces, Germany ended up taking almost three times as many prisoners as the Soviet Union, around seven hundred thousand in all.[125] Germany directly incorporated large portions of Poland into the Third Reich in a manner similar to the Soviet Union, though it also installed an occupying administration over the remaining territory, which it called the General Government (Generalgouvernement). Although never reaching the same degree of targeted mass killings of Polish prisoner as at Katyn, Nazi occupiers followed a similar territorial pattern of committing very high levels of abuse against Polish prisoners as well as civilians.[126] Since Poland was one of the eventual central sites for the Final Solution, German conduct toward prisoners remained extremely harsh.[127] Mass arrests, executions, and widespread use of hard labor became staples of Nazi rule over Poland both to extract as many resources as possible and to cement control.[128]

Both conquerors also engaged in a certain degree of cooperation, including prisoner exchanges and a modest amount of intelligence sharing. The Katyn massacre appears perfectly in line with requirements under the second secret protocol of the German-Soviet Friendship Treaty, which called for both parties to eliminate possible sources of agitation within their respective Polish territories.[129] Indeed, around the same time the Soviet executions were taking place in the Katyn Forest and nearby towns, Germany was engaging in its own massive repression of Polish elites. In the spring and early summer of 1940 German authorities initiated AB-Aktion (Außerordentliche Befriedungsaktion), a large-scale program targeting the Polish intelligentsia along with some members of the military, which resulted in the execution of over six thousand people with tens of thousands of others sent to concentration camps.[130] The fact that the respective Nazi and Soviet operations coincided so closely has given rise to claims the actions were coordinated as part of a larger fascist-communist effort to destroy Poland.[131] While new evidence may still come to light showing active collaboration, the biggest problem with this argument is that the NKVD took every step possible to conceal the massacre from German authorities. It seems strange that the Soviet Union would try to cover up the crime and not report anything to the partner it was supposedly so eager to impress.

The lack of concern over the reactions of outside parties, German or otherwise, would continue in a different way as the war widened and ground on. After German revelations of the discovery of the Katyn mass graves in April 1943, only Poland's government-in-exile expressed much outrage. Although expatriate Polish leaders formally sided with the anti-Axis coalition, the democratic powers were unwilling to take any concrete actions as evidence of Soviet responsibility began to mount. Displaying a similar pragmatism to that shown in their own prisoner affairs discussed in the previous chapter, British and U.S. leaders valued their Soviet military ally above all else, even at the expense of the Polish victims. Indicating what was to come, Winston Churchill stated plainly in a meeting with the Polish general Władysław Anders the year before, "No good could come of antagonizing the Russians."[132] Franklin D. Roosevelt went so far as to suppress a report by a U.S. diplomat condemning the Soviet Union for the massacre, and even reassigned the official to American Samoa for the remainder of the war where he could cause less trouble from the American standpoint.[133] Documents declassified in 2012 by the U.S. National Archives definitively show that both of the major Western Allies were aware of Soviet culpability but actively covered up the origins of the massacre so as not to upset their ally. In a May 1943 letter to Churchill, Britain's ambassador to Poland's government-in-exile, Owen O'Malley, wrote, "We have in fact perforce used the good name of England like the murderers used the conifers to cover up a massacre."[134] It was only in the face of growing East-West tensions after the war ended that the Western powers expressed greater interest in uncovering the truth about Katyn.[135]

Finally, perhaps it was the Soviet Union's ardent attachment to communist ideology that led the leadership to destroy the Polish officer corps. An enormous body of literature points to the widespread use of violence internally by communist regimes as part of an ideologically driven project to consolidate power and hasten radical changes to their societies.[136] Several quantitative studies of repression and mass murder confirm that communist regimes are much more likely to commit extreme levels of violence.[137] The previous century is unfortunately full of episodes where millions died at the hands of communist rulers, from Stalin's Great Purges to Mao Zedong's Great Leap Forward. If these regimes could be so cruel to their own citizens, then it follows that they probably would act in similar ways toward the populations of their foreign enemies.

In the realm of prisoners of war, communist regimes have taken certain notable steps that could be indicative of a greater likelihood to harm captured combatants. One of the avowed reasons for why the Soviets refused to ratify the 1929 Geneva Convention on Prisoners was that it represented a bourgeois institution that reinforced class hierarchies by according greater privileges to officers over regular enlisted soldiers.[138] Despite widespread participation in the later 1949 Geneva Conventions, most communist states entered a reservation to Article 85 of the Third Convention relating to prisoners, which provides that prisoners charged with crimes committed prior to their capture maintained protection under the laws of war even if they were subsequently found guilty.[139] Communist signatories instead interpreted their reservation to mean that even enemy soldiers suspected of alleged crimes could be denied POW status, which in turn allowed captors to treat these prisoners with much greater latitude.

Several cases certainly seem to reflect a communist tendency toward abuse, since both North Korean and Vietnamese care for captives during their wars with the United States was far from humane.[140] Examining the full set of interstate wars from the last century indicates, however, that the relationship between communism and prisoner abuse is much less straightforward. Using the same baseline model for the determinants of prisoner treatment introduced in chapter 3, table 5.3 reports the effect of different types of communist regimes on the probability a captor resorts to high levels of abuse.[141]

Contrary to their behavior toward internal opponents, communist regimes are on the whole only slightly more prone to engage in higher levels of prisoner abuse than governments of other ideological orientations, but the rise of 8 percent fails to be statistically significant. Focusing only on the Soviet system reveals that Russian communist captors were actually slightly *less* likely to abuse captives, while holding everything else constant. But perhaps the negative Soviet finding is glossing over more brutal prisoner abuse during the period when Stalin reigned supreme. After all, many commentators from both the East and West hold Stalin personally responsible for the most heinous crimes committed during the history of the Soviet Union, including the Katyn massacre.[142] When Soviet authorities finally admitted responsibility for the Katyn massacre in 1990, they laid the blame firmly at Stalin's feet.[143]

Irrespective of the precise role of Stalin in wider communist history, the seeming restraints on prisoner abuse were actually even *stronger* during

TABLE 5.3 Communist regimes and prisoner abuse in interstate wars, 1898–2003

Type of communist regime	Change in probability of high-level abuse
Communist (all)	0.08
Soviet	−0.11
Stalinist	−0.23†
Non-Soviet	0.21†

Notes: † Significant at 10 percent.
Each value represents the effect of the relevant type of communist regime on the absolute change in the probability of high levels of prisoner abuse, holding democracy at 0 (nondemocracy) and all other variables at their means.

wars when Stalin firmly controlled the Soviet Union, though the effect is only significant at the 10 percent level. The result for the Stalinist period is particularly surprising: even though he represented one of the most murderous leaders in history, these predilections for extreme levels of violence did not automatically carry over to the general treatment of prisoners during war. On the other hand, non-Soviet communist regimes, which include several Asian countries, Cuba, and a number of other regimes, were slightly more likely to go after enemy combatants, though again the effect is fairly modest statistically. What the results show is that communist ideology does not appear to have a clear and systematic impact on how captors from these regimes choose to treat their prisoners.

Even if the ideals that began with Marx and Engels are not the strongest predictor of prisoner abuse overall, perhaps communism played a more important role specifically in the Polish case. The targeting of Poland's officer corps, who were likely more removed from the Polish proletariat, might explain the particular pattern of abuse in the Polish case as a way for the Soviet Union to guard against the larger menace of "bourgeois contagion."[144] Writing about a future war with a capitalist state, which Poland would have certainly been from the Soviet point of view, one prominent Soviet legal scholar at the time argued ordinary enemy combatants would be welcomed as common brothers in arms. The attitude toward captured officers was quite different and potentially foreshadows the eventual fate of the elite Polish military contingents:

> The situation would not be at all the same were officers taken prisoners, however. Obviously, it could not be expected that officers, who in the majority of cases do not belong to the proletariat, would be converted to communism by mere theoretical instruction. Hence the officers would always be considered by the Soviet authorities as class enemies.[145]

The elimination of the Polish officer corps also bore some eerie resemblances to the Great Purges a few years earlier in the Soviet Union, where one of the groups most targeted were high-ranking officials from the country's own armed forces. Although most of the prisoners at the Kozelsk and Starobelsk camps were officers and might indeed fall under the bourgeoisie moniker, the vast majority of the inmates at Ostashkov were policemen, prison guards, and other individuals who could not credibly be accused of being comparable societal elites. Despite their more working-class background, they were sought after with the same ferocity as officers from the armed forces. The collective punishment of the prisoners from the special camps seems more consistent with an attempt to dismantle the coercive apparatus of the Polish state rather than undermine the bourgeois class per se. On the other hand, two survivors

[163]

from Katyn were princely aristocrats who would reasonably be more deserving of the label of class enemies than many of the eventual victims.[146] In contrast to those officers who were spared, Soviet authorities were also known throughout this period to liquidate avowedly Polish communists found to be too independent-minded.[147] Soviet decisions on who lived or died appeared to be a function more of which individuals posed the greatest threat to their continued rule over Polish territory rather than based on purely ideological grounds.

After examining a number of alternative explanations, none performs as well as the territorial motive in accounting for the various aspects relating to the Soviet decision to commit the Katyn massacre. The underlying motive for the killings was preventative in nature, to stamp out any future rebellion in newly conquered Polish lands. Polish officers were selected for a particularly brutal punishment because they represented the most salient threat out of the entire Polish population to the Soviets' territorial interests.

TERRITORIAL WAR AIMS AND SOVIET PRISONER
ABUSE IN COMPARATIVE PERSPECTIVE

Despite the infamy attached to the killings of Polish officers in spring 1940, the role played by territorial motives becomes even clearer when considering the Katyn massacre in light of the treatment of prisoners by the Soviet Union in other conflicts around the same time. At first thought, there might appear to be little to compare other than a series of unending depravities and suffering for those prisoners unlucky enough to fall into Soviet hands. Even though the Soviet Union was certainly extremely brutal at home, the previous section showed Communist Russia was not inherently disposed toward treating captured enemy combatants in similar ways. Soviet conduct during its several wars of the interwar period and in the years of the Second World War demonstrated a remarkable range of behavior toward prisoners. While there are certainly instances of horrific violence outside of Poland, Soviet captors exhibited impressive restraint during wars against such disparate adversaries as China and Finland. As with the fate of the officers at Katyn, the motives pursued by the Red Army during the conflict would have an enormous bearing on how prisoners would be treated.

Soviet Conduct toward Prisoners during
Wars of Territorial Conquest

After Tsarist Russia's defeat and collapse during the First World War, large portions of the former Russian Empire either broke away to gain independence or were taken over by other states. Throughout the inter-war period, the new Soviet regime harbored revisionist aims to regain lost tracts of land in eastern Europe as part of its larger grand strategy. The lands of eastern Poland became only one of a series of territorial annexations by the Soviet Union around this time. The Baltic states of Estonia, Latvia, and Lithuania came to realize they stood little chance of defeating their larger Soviet foe and offered little resistance to the eventual Russian advance. Romania similarly acquiesced to Soviet demands over Bessarabia and Northern Bukovina in an effort to forestall the loss of their entire country. Incidentally, Soviet incursions into the lands of its Balkan neighbor eventually created a revisionist Romania of its own that later allied with Nazi Germany in part to regain lost territory.

Although these additional cases of conquest did not strictly take place during separate interstate wars (though they did unfold in the context of the wider Second World War), the treatment of captured combatants in these conflicts is still relevant for assessing the role of territorial motives. Each represents an additional episode of Soviet annexation and provides an opportunity to examine whether territorial motives had a similar effect on Soviet conduct toward enemy combatants. Stalin and the Soviet leadership perceived their aims in all of these territories in a similar manner to the Polish question.[148] All were also explicitly included in the secret German-Soviet protocol from August 1939, outlining each side's spheres of interest in eastern Europe.[149]

In the case of the Baltic states, Soviet policy was initially more restrained compared to what was happening in Poland. At the same time as Soviet forces were occupying eastern Poland in the fall of 1939, governments from the Baltic countries were instead forced into signing trade agreements and mutual assistance pacts with the Soviet Union. The agreements included provisions for the stationing of Soviet garrisons within each country. The expressed purpose of the troop presence was to protect Baltic lands from outside threats, but they also proved beneficial from the Soviet perspective in facilitating full occupation at a later date.[150]

This precarious arrangement lasted less than a year. The Soviet Union took advantage of the diversion of the world's attention on Nazi Germany's victories in western Europe to invade the Baltic states in June 1940. Soviet actions indicated "Moscow's principal aim was now the reinforcement of the Soviet 'security system' following the pattern of territorial annexation."[151] The administrative and coercive apparatuses of each of the Baltic states were replaced with Soviet officials. Elections were held later the next month, but voters were only allowed to choose from a list of candidates from each country's Communist Party and handpicked by Soviet authorities.[152] Without much surprise, the new "People's Parliaments" then voted unanimously to incorporate their countries into the Soviet Union, thereby ending each country's brief spell of independence gained near the end of the First World War.

Soviet annexation in the Baltic states took place with little armed resistance compared to Poland, but patterns in the treatment of combatants and civilians were remarkably similar. From June through July 1940 alone, around twenty-five thousand "undesirables" were sent from the three countries to labor camps in the Soviet Union.[153] All told, approximately thirty-five thousand Latvians, sixty thousand Estonians, and seventy-five thousand Lithuanians were executed or deported during the Soviet annexations of the three countries.[154] Many of the most targeted victims were members of the various Baltic national armed forces, who were viewed as particularly undesirable given their potential threat to Soviet rule.

The officer corps in the Baltic states suffered a brutal fate similar to their Polish counterparts even if the killings did not garner the same level of subsequent attention. After the full incorporation of the Baltic states into the Soviet Union, each of the national armed forces was subsumed under the Red Army. Command of the new Soviet constituent forces, however, was taken over by Soviet commissars to ensure that most Estonian, Latvian, and Lithuanian military officers retained no significant leadership role. Native officers were then shipped off to the Soviet Union under the pretense that they were to receive "additional training." The vast majority received no such instruction, but were rather summarily executed or sent to labor camps for eventual liquidation.[155] The Baltic deportations paralleled closely the Katyn massacre as both pointed to a common policy of removing potential future leaders of resistance within the indigenous population of conquered countries.[156] Just as in Poland, Baltic officers were viewed as a particularly salient threat to Soviet control over the newly gained territories and consequently targeted using equally brutal tactics.

Less evidence is available regarding Soviet treatment of enemy combatants in the Romanian lands of Bessarabia and Northern Bukovina. The Soviet Union launched similar allegations that Bessarabia had been "stolen" by Romania in the aftermath of Russia's defeat during the First World War. Demands for Northern Bukovina were more of a surprise, since comparable claims were not evident from previous Russian regimes.[157] Nevertheless, both were absorbed by the Soviet Union starting in late June 1940 in a sequence of events resembling what took place in the Baltic countries.[158] Soviet policies toward all segments of society in Bessarabia and Northern Bukovina, including the armed forces, showed corresponding brutalities to those enacted in Polish territories.[159] Furthermore, while supportive for the overall territorial argument, the outcome of the Bessarabian and Northern Bukovinian cases is more problematic from a cultural perspective. Unlike the Baltic states, which were culturally distinct from the Soviet Union, the annexed Romanian lands shared many similarities with their Soviet conquerors. The fact that combatants in both areas were likewise abused suggests that cultural affinities did not play a determining role in these episodes.

Instead, when the Soviet Union possessed territorial aims in other countries during this period, prisoners in these lands more often than not suffered greatly. As with Poland and the Katyn massacre, the reasons for this abuse appear to have been rooted in eliminating potential future threats to the Soviet Union's continued hold on newly incorporated territories.

Soviet Conduct toward Prisoners during Wars with Less Clear Aims of Territorial Conquest

All of the cases discussed up to this point involved extremely high levels of violence inflicted upon prisoners, suggesting Stalin's Russia deserves its place as one of the most ruthless regimes of the twentieth century. When turning to conflicts during the period where the Soviet Union did not seek large-scale territorial annexation, however, the record of Soviet conduct toward captives is more mixed.

The Winter War against Finland is particularly useful for assessing the impact of territorial motives on prisoner abuse. Real estate certainly played a role in the conflict, but it was more a function of Soviet unease over the proximity of the Finnish border at around twenty miles from Leningrad, one of the communist country's largest and most strategically important cities.[160] The Soviet Union feared Finland could be used as a launching point for an attack against Leningrad by Germany, Britain, or France, with or without consent from the Finnish government.[161] The Soviets in fact offered to exchange a much larger parcel of Russian territory for the Finnish areas adjacent to the Leningrad environs. Soviet aims in this war were more modest and primarily based on occupying a nearby slice of land as a buffer zone rather than seeking a major or near complete annexation of Finland. As Stalin personally remarked in a private meeting with other Soviet officials on the more limited aims in a possible war against its neighbor, "We have no desire for Finland's territory. But Finland should be a state that is friendly to the Soviet Union."[162]

The two sides were unable to come to an agreement, and fighting broke out near the end of November 1939. Nevertheless, the disputed land was sparsely populated, and its inhabitants were for the most part not of Finnish origin, but rather predominantly from the Karelia people who were ethnically distinct from both Russians and Finns. Concerns over the dangers of potential "fifth columns" were correspondingly weaker. The motive to abuse captured combatants to ensure territorial conquest was thus less present in this case and was reflected in the lower levels of violence against prisoners during the war. The conflict also poses a further problem for cultural accounts, which would expect much higher levels of abuse against captives given the differences between the opponents. With the absence of strong territorial objectives, Finnish prisoners were instead on the whole treated fairly well.[163]

As with the Winter War, the Soviet conflict with Nazi Germany from 1941 to 1945 also involved culturally dissimilar foes but was associated with extremely high levels of prisoner abuse perpetrated by all parties involved.[164] The Soviet Union was on the defensive for much of the war and did not initially seek to aggrandize itself at Germany's expense unlike in the Polish, Baltic, and Romanian cases. Territory was instead a central issue for the Nazi leadership and its aims of Lebensraum, and help to explain the ferocity with which Germany eliminated many captured Soviet combatants. While territory would eventually present itself as an objective on the Soviet side as well, reciprocity appears to have been a much greater factor in this conflict from the communist leadership's standpoint. The ferocity of Soviet treatment of German prisoners once the war turned in its favor was partially motivated out of revenge for earlier abuses committed by the Third Reich when it had previously held the upper hand.[165] The German case thus does not necessarily undermine the role of territory in explaining prisoner abuse, but rather demonstrates that other factors can sometimes contribute in substantial ways to a captor state's prisoner policies.

Soviet Russia was also involved in several earlier conflicts during the interwar period against various Asian adversaries. None of these conflicts involved far-reaching territorial aims on the part of the Soviet Union, and as expected, levels of prisoner abuse were minimal compared to the later treatment of Polish prisoners or those from other nearby annexed territories during the Second World War. The pattern of prisoner treatment in these conflicts further questions the merits of racial or cultural factors, since in all cases Soviet troops were pitted against a culturally distinct enemy but did not resort to high levels of abuse. In the Sino-Soviet War of 1929, Russian forces limited themselves to relatively low levels of abuse against Chinese soldiers.[166] When entering into hostilities with China the Soviet Union sought the more modest aim of ensuring its continued stake in the Manchurian Chinese Eastern Railway rather than taking over the surrounding areas or beyond. Wanting to maintain good relations with the Chinese populace to further their narrower objectives in the region, the Soviets calculated that good conduct toward enemy combatants would reduce the threat of escalation and make a stable postwar environment more likely.[167]

[168]

Along similar lines, the fighting against Japan at Changkufeng in 1938 and then the following year at Nomonhan essentially involved border skirmishes that escalated into wars. Japan was the initiator of both conflicts, leaving the Red Army largely on the defensive, yet in neither instance were large swaths of territory at stake.[168] In both cases the Soviets refrained from instigating abuses that came anywhere near to those committed against Polish prisoners not long afterward.[169] When territorial annexation did not figure as a primary wartime objective, Soviet proclivities to commit high levels of prisoner abuse were greatly weakened.

The analysis from this chapter demonstrated that the Katyn massacre resulted primarily from Soviet territorial ambitions rather than cultural differences, the captor state's communist ideology, or other common alternative explanations. The threat posed by Polish officers to the Soviet Union's long-term absorption of lands acquired through the Molotov-Ribbentrop Pact meant these prisoners, along with other security elites, would be liquidated to reduce the strength of any future resistance movement. Although most Polish prisoners were treated harshly, the massacre shows that those segments of the armed forces most threatening to Soviet rule were dealt with in the most definitive manner possible. By killing almost every single officer and other high-ranking member of the Polish security apparatus under their control at the time, Soviet authorities sought to ensure that those with the greatest capability to organize and rise up against their occupiers would not be around to do so. Yet despite the ruthless reputation garnered by Stalin's Russia in its policies at home, the country was not always so brutal in its conduct toward external enemies. In the absence of a strong appetite for new territorial conquests, the Soviet Union was normally much more restrained in its treatment of captured enemy combatants, and in some cases even cared for its captives relatively humanely. Incentives generated by the nature of the war aims thus played a key role in patterns of prisoner abuse even for a country as exceptionally callous as the Soviet Union during the Stalinist era.

[169]

CONCLUSION

Explaining the Treatment of
Prisoners during War

Give heed to my cry,
For I am brought very low;
Deliver me from my persecutors,
For they are too strong for me.
Bring my soul out of prison,
So that I may give thanks to Your name.

—Excerpt from Psalm 142:6–7

We need to look forward as opposed to looking backwards.

—U.S. president-elect Barack Obama on the question of
authorizing an inquiry into allegations of CIA
torture and other programs from the
George W. Bush administration

I began this book by pointing to the puzzling and often divergent ordeals confronting many soldiers once they lay down their arms and surrender to the enemy. The fate facing captives proves to be fickle, as some have been dealt with in a humane manner, while many others suffered greatly at the hands of their captors. Even captives who started out in humane conditions could later see their fortunes fall, turning from patron to prey. These contrasting experiences formed the basis for the main research question I have addressed: what explains such wide-ranging differences in the treatment of prisoners during war?

My argument centered on two factors to explain how warring states weigh the various costs and benefits of the prisoner policies available to them. First, a country's regime type generates several internal incentives shaping how a captor chooses to treat its captives. One version credits the unique attributes embodied in the political culture of democracies,

[170]

where norms of nonviolence and individual rights govern their wartime conduct. Just as democracies treat their own citizens more humanely compared to the more repressive tactics employed by autocratic regimes, so too will democratic belligerents act with the same regard toward captured enemy combatants. One drawback to normative arguments is the difficulty in accounting for the many instances where democracies have deviated, often markedly, from their humanitarian precepts. The alternative account I have developed here instead focused on the motives produced by the particular domestic institutions of democratic governments. The greater accountability of democracies to their citizens leads them to exhibit an acute sensitivity to the dangers of retaliation, along with a heightened appreciation for the strategic benefits that can proceed from good conduct. These institutional pressures make democratic belligerents exert greater restraint in their treatment of prisoners in order to lower dangers for their own soldiers in captivity, as well as to capitalize on some of the accompanying military advantages like encouraging enemy troops to surrender. Importantly, however, when these institutional incentives are slight, then democracies demonstrate a readiness to commit violence against their captives, with normative appeals offering few limitations on their behavior.

Second, the nature of the conflict produces a set of external incentives guiding wartime conduct. Especially severe fighting that devolves into attritional warfare makes the outlook for prisoners quite dire. Desperate to find some way to break through the stagnant state of the bloodshed, captors are apt to abuse prisoners as a way of further intensifying the agony of combat to coerce their adversary into submission. When up against such all-encompassing contests, belligerents are also attracted to the potential of exploiting prisoners to the harshest extent possible to maximize resources devoted to the war effort. Similarly, the goals states intend to achieve through battle inform how they perceive the utility or threat posed by enemy combatants. When territory forms the core of sought-after spoils of war, extreme levels of prisoner abuse often quickly follow. Captured soldiers represent one of the biggest perils to an occupier's long-term control over newly acquired lands. In order to squelch any possibility of resistance, conquerors often hold firm convictions to eliminate those groups with the greatest ability to incite rebellion, with captured enemy combatants often the first and most readily available victims.

I investigated the question and argument using several complementary pieces of both quantitative and qualitative evidence. Based on a data set on the treatment of prisoners during all interstate wars from 1898 to 2003, I presented a statistical analysis in chapter 3 that examined a host of factors commonly thought to influence the likelihood of prisoner abuse. The results provided strong support for the overall argument.

[171]

Democracies were on the whole less likely to engage in the worst forms of abuse against captured enemy combatants. Upon closer examination, however, democratic restraints toward prisoners were not absolute but rather conditional upon specific dynamics of abuse or other factors related to the war. The nature of the conflict also proved instrumental in knowing when prisoners were in the greatest danger of encountering violence. Captors caught in wars of attrition were especially likely to employ brutality against enemy soldiers falling into their grasp. Wars of territorial annexation had an even stronger effect, where conquerors demonstrated a keen desire to target enemy combatants when given the chance. Other wartime objectives did not offer as clear a picture, as expansive war aims like regime change or unconditional surrender had a much weaker impact on prisoner treatment.

In contrast to the findings in favor of the main argument, commonly cited alternative factors received much less support. Despite its prominence in the existing prisoner literature, the presence of a cultural divide between belligerents based on their prior civilizational background did not systematically raise the likelihood enemy combatants would be victimized. The deterrent effect produced from holding enemy combatants appeared to make captors think twice about engaging in abuse but did not significantly alter the general dynamics of prisoner treatment. Retaliatory impulses, on the other hand, were much more discernable, as belligerents who abused prisoners were likely to see similar treatment in response against their own captured troops. Furthermore, international laws and norms prohibiting the mistreatment of captives did not figure prominently in the overall treatment of prisoners but did offer some possible positive steps for the behavior of democracies.

Building on the aggregate findings from the quantitative analysis, the remaining chapters consisted of in-depth case studies to examine how the logic underlying the argument operated in practice. Chapter 4 probed the sources of democratic conduct by examining the policies of Great Britain and the United States during the Second World War, cases often considered preeminent examples of humane treatment toward prisoners during armed conflict. Delving into the historical record surrounding the war showed that normative concerns of humanitarianism and nonviolence played a minimal role in the decision making of the democracies. Rather, democratic belligerents were primarily motivated by concerns over the dangers posed by retaliation, along with the strategic benefits obtained through decent treatment. When these institutional incentives weakened, such as the situation involving Axis POWs once the fighting ended, the forced repatriation of Soviet combatants, or the targeting of civilians, then democracies engaged in increasingly callous behavior.

Extending the analysis to other conflicts involving democratic belligerents confirmed that when faced with contending imperatives normative appeals were insufficient to rein in the sometimes harsh conduct of democratic captors toward their prisoners.

Chapter 5 examined why wars of territorial conquest often produce some of the most heinous levels of violence against captured combatants. The centerpiece of the chapter was the Katyn massacre involving the execution of several large groups of Polish prisoners of war by the Soviet Union. The massacre is notable not only for the controversy it later generated, but also because it is often considered to exemplify the brutalities of the Stalinist era and the depravity of communist regimes more generally. The details of the planning and implementation of the killings indicate that Soviet motives more closely follow a territorial rationale rather than ideological motivations or other interpretations. The massacre was primarily driven by the Soviet Union's desire to undermine the emergence of future rebellion in newly acquired Polish lands. Selected for execution were those captured officers and elites most capable of organizing later resistance, while more moderate though still painful levels of abuse were reserved for rank-and-file prisoners and other groups. I catalogued the timing and locations of the executions, as well as why many later Polish prisoners avoided a similar fate, in order to demonstrate the overriding role played by territory in Soviet decision making. I then examined the Katyn massacre within the broader set of wars fought by the Soviet Union during this period to further establish that the harshest forms of abuse generally took place when territory was on the line, while in other instances prisoners were spared some of the worst excesses. The body of evidence using multiple methods suggests that key attributes of the belligerents themselves and the nature of the conflict go a long way toward understanding when and at what levels prisoner abuse is perpetrated during warfare.

Relevance to the Study of Wartime Conduct and Contemporary Armed Conflict

Each of the main contributors to prisoner abuse—the severity of the fighting, territorial ambitions, and democracy—is not simply a product of wars from a bygone era that have since faded or disappeared from relevance. Rather, all remain readily apparent and central for thinking about the conditions under which prisoners are likely to be treated properly or unfavorably. The main findings thus have several implications for the broader study of political violence and wartime conduct in both the contemporary era and when looking ahead.

The Severity of the Fighting

The impact of the severity of the fighting confirms other research showing that events on the ground feed back and influence choices over how
to treat vulnerable groups during wartime. Just as armed forces may shift
attacks onto civilians when facing setbacks on the battlefield, so too do
captured combatants become ready targets for coercion when belligerents
face trying circumstances.[1] The world has fortunately avoided for more
than a half century the sort of drawn-out, all-embracing conflicts typified
by the two world wars. Recent work shows that the probability of a soldier dying in battle—one of the general metrics for the intensity of
warfare—has declined at a fairly consistent basis since the beginning of
the twentieth century.[2] If wars are becoming less severe on the whole
(even if not disappearing outright), then one of the main contributors to
wartime violence may be diminishing as well, which offers some hopeful
news for troops worried over captivity in current or future conflicts. On
the other hand, other research argues that the number of battle deaths has
shown no clear downward trend, suggesting this component of the nature of the conflict has not improved, but neither has it gotten any worse.[3]

According to the data used in the analysis for this book, the chances of
a war devolving into attritional fighting has remained relatively flat from
the end of the nineteenth century through the early years of the
twenty-first century.[4] Some recent conflicts have certainly been rapid and
decisive, such as the success of Operation Desert Storm when Iraqi military forces were dismantled in a matter of days with tens of thousands of
prisoners flocking to the positions of the U.S.-led coalition. Other episodes indicate, however, that wars of attrition will continue to be a hazard for the current era and beyond. The heavy fighting along a fortified
front that characterized the 1998–2000 war between Ethiopia and Eritrea
was in many ways reminiscent of the trenches stretching up and down
much of western Europe during the First World War. During the fighting
between the two countries in the Horn of Africa, tens of thousands of
troops died in hopeless frontal assaults, while prisoners from both sides
were horribly abused.[5]

Even if standard wars of attrition do eventually subside, the growing
attention to guerrilla warfare points to several similar dynamics that result in more severe conflicts overall.[6] Avoidance of set-piece battles, reliance on the local population, and the difficulty of locating dispersed and
often autonomous groups of enemy forces all mean that civilians have
been particularly victimized in such drawn-out irregular conflicts.[7] Yet
one of the lessons from the Vietnam War is that guerrillas are also extremely vulnerable once in captivity.[8] Given the greater challenges to
gathering intelligence on insurgent adversaries, captors may be much

more willing to turn to harsh interrogation techniques against detainees in an attempt to gain important information. Compounded by attempts by incumbent powers to delegitimize guerrilla tactics, much less recognize the status of guerrillas as official combatants, conduct toward these enemy armed forces upon capture can be quite poor. Whether on the conventional battlefield or in newly emerging irregular theaters of operations, the severity of the conflict is likely to continue to figure prominently in how captured enemy combatants are treated.

Territorial War Aims

Of the two elements associated with the nature of the conflict, territorial war aims were the single most important factor related to heightened levels of prisoner abuse. Similar to the targeting of civilians in annexationist wars, when territory was at stake the prospects for enemy soldiers were especially bleak. Yet the persistence of territory as a source of misery for prisoners may potentially be slowly dying out. The value placed on possessing and acquiring territory may be gradually giving way to newer more fluid forms of authority and sovereignty.[9] Fragmentation in fundamental processes of economic production along with the growing importance of knowledge-intensive industries for a country's wealth and vitality have also substantially reduced the traditional benefits associated with territorial conquest.[10] While in the past territorial ambitions may have been a key driver in the victimization of prisoners during war, from these perspectives desires for conquest could become less consequential in the future.

Unfortunately, in many respects territory remains a valued and contested prize in times of both war and peace, even as notions of boundaries and space may be changing.[11] The number of ongoing territorial disputes, in which two or more states lay claim to the same piece of land, has not declined significantly since the early part of the twentieth century.[12] If anything, the post–Cold War period witnessed an upsurge in new quarrels over land compared to prior decades, with many recently independent countries seeking to extend their boundaries. The creation of South Sudan as a newly sovereign state, resulting from a decades-long civil war, in certain ways simply replaced prior internal struggles with international strife against the Khartoum government ruling the remainder of Sudan. The conflict between the respective Sudans centers on the control of lucrative oil deposits, and the two sides came to blows on numerous occasions early on. Should the tensions eventually escalate to war where territory would likely be a main culprit and objective, conditions would likely be hazardous for combatants captured by either opponent.

[175]

Although not escalating to a full-blown war, the conflict between Russia and Georgia in 2008 over the breakaway Russian-sponsored areas of South Ossetia and Abkhazia similarly shows that territorial aims are likely to persist in one form or another for the foreseeable future.[13] Georgia has not been the sole victim of Russian expansion in the postcommunist region. Ukraine lost the Crimean peninsula to its eastern neighbor in March 2014 shortly after protests brought down the pro-Moscow government of President Viktor Yanukovych. While the annexation took place with few shots fired, concerns remain about possible designs by the Kremlin over lands in eastern Ukraine that also contain sizable ethnic Russian populations. With several locations of the Katyn massacre close by, including the Starobelsk (now Starobilsk) special POW camp and execution sites in Kherson and Kharkov (now Kharkiv), any escalation in hostilities between the two sides would be all the more ominous. States have often sought to settle their territorial disputes without military force, but the presence of conflicting claims over parcels of land poses a danger of wars breaking out that would be extremely grave for any resulting prisoners.

Democracy and Regime Type

The overall pattern of democratic restraint in the treatment of prisoners seemingly provides one of the more hopeful implications for the future of warfare. Many policymakers have grabbed hold of the democratic peace thesis to promote the spread of democracy around the world as a way to ensure not only greater rights and freedoms for citizens at home, but also peace and security abroad.[14] Decent conduct toward prisoners also provides more systematic evidence in favor of the conjecture that one of the ways in which democracies are more successful at fighting wars is their greater ability to induce enemy soldiers to surrender.[15] Expanding the community of democratic states not only may make wars less likely, but also means those conflicts that do break out will be relatively more humane.

The relevance of the regime type finding nonetheless needs to be further scrutinized in light of continued critiques of the democratic peace and the broader purported distinctiveness of democracies. In particular, a growing body of research questions the rigid distinction commonly put forth between democracies and dictatorships in their foreign policymaking.[16] Rather than a singular autocratic penchant for violence, dictatorships have demonstrated some extraordinary diversity in their willingness to use force, with some tyrants behaving in ways remarkably similar to democracies.[17] The mixed findings for communist regimes and prisoner abuse discussed in chapter 5 suggest that dictatorships should not be automatically thrown together. Sharing certain parallels to the argument in this book concerning democracies, some of the main points put forward to differentiate among autocracies involve the degree of accountability to domestic elites as well as the relative civilian or military background of those actors and their leaders.[18] Although not subject to the will of the mass public, certain types of dictatorships (especially those constrained by civilian-oriented elites) differ little from democracies in their caution over going to war, as well as their success once the fighting has started.[19]

Along similar lines, dictators may differ systematically in their actual conduct during wartime with certain more benevolent autocrats humanely treating prisoners in ways reminiscent of democratic belligerents. The available evidence, however, suggests that when it comes to wielding violence both on and off the battlefield, democracies appear to remain distinct in their wartime conduct. Irrespective of the particular categorization of dictatorships, additional analysis shows that autocratic captors are on the whole more likely to commit grave levels of abuse against prisoners during interstate wars compared to democratic belligerents.[20] Accountability to the wider public rather than a narrow set of domestic elites, or only to leaders themselves, thus appears to distinguish democracies from dictatorships in their conduct, at least toward enemy combatants. More work remains to be done to determine the precise ways in which domestic institutions and preferences, whether democratic or autocratic, shape the behavior of states before, during, and after war. In particular, future research needs to take seriously the possibility that the role of domestic politics can vary depending on the stage of the conflict or the particular arena of conduct.

Even if democracies do set themselves apart in their more restrained behavior toward prisoners, the promise of democracy still needs to be tempered somewhat. The commitment of democracies to humanitarian principles protecting the rights of prisoners appears tepid at best, though there are some grounds for optimism. Democracies have generally proven to be more humane toward prisoners in wars taking place after the advent of the 1949 Geneva Conventions, though it is not completely clear if this is due to the normative sway of humanitarian norms or other unrelated factors. Similarly, international law may not have a consistent overall effect, but democratic ratifiers do appear more likely to uphold their legal commitments toward the rights of prisoners. Of course, getting democracies to join the prevailing laws of war can sometimes be challenging. Some of the strongest holdouts to recent treaties regulating warfare, such as the 1977 Additional Protocols to the Geneva Conventions or the Rome Statute establishing the ICC, are leading democracies like the United States and Israel, who are unfortunately also among those most likely to be involved in future armed conflicts.[21]

Despite some of the possible mitigating effects of international legal or normative forces, the weight of the evidence shows that domestic institutional imperatives are the main drivers behind instances of benevolent democratic conduct. When concerns over retaliation are pronounced and the strategic benefits from good conduct are there for the taking, democratic belligerents can demonstrate amazing care for enemy prisoners even in the heat of battle.[22] Yet the same pragmatism guiding democratic decision making also suggests that, when these institutional incentives are absent, democracies exhibit an aptitude or even enthusiasm for engaging in extreme levels of abuse.

The tension between democracy and the rights of potential victims is also in line with recent research on repression and political violence. Faced with serious threats, democracies often willingly shed their humanitarian facade and turn to coercive practices, even if the manner and motives behind their violations may differ in numerous respects from autocratic regimes.[23] The uncomfortable reality of democratic abuse raises further questions about whether democracies possess their own particular logic of violence once they take a more brutal tack. The greater sensitivity of democratic leaders to public accountability and external retaliation can help explain not only *when* they will turn to abuse but also *how* those violations will be carried out.

The relationship between democracy and torture continues to be tightly contested, pitting liberal values of individual rights against protecting the government and populace from attack.[24] Democratic states like Britain, France, and the United States have been at the forefront of developing so-called clean techniques, which can still be excruciating for victims but leave few observable marks.[25] The use of electricity, water, and stress positions, among others, has allowed the application of extreme levels of pain while minimizing possible monitoring by domestic opponents, external enemies, or the international community. The increased use of solitary confinement by countries like the United States, both domestically and in armed conflicts, shows a similar desire by democracies to take advantage of grayer areas in the law.[26] Democracies have demonstrated a propensity to engage in subtler and more indirect violations, across issues as wide-ranging as trade protectionism and the targeting of civilians, in an attempt to evade detection and minimize possible negative repercussions.[27] While I have concentrated on the gravest breaches of prisoner treatment, more attention is needed to investigate possible ways in which democracies may seek to substitute more obscure forms of abuse or couch their violations in less flagrant terms. A more fine-grained approach to democratic wartime conduct would contribute to recent calls to disaggregate the study of political violence both across and within countries, over time, and especially among different types of activities.[28]

[178]

MAKING THE THEORY TRAVEL: PRISONER ABUSE
IN OTHER TYPES OF ARMED CONFLICT

Although I have in this book concentrated on the treatment of prisoners during conflicts between states, my argument and evidence offer a number of extensions to prisoner abuse in other forms of warfare. Contemplating how the dynamics of wartime conduct may differ across various types of armed conflict is particularly instructive, since interstate wars have become less frequent in recent decades, even if claims of their impending demise may be overstated.[29] Conflicts of different sorts have also become interrelated in many ways—developments in one zone of combat can spill over into others, and one type of conflict can later morph into another. Both of the insurgencies that raged throughout much of the last decade, first in Afghanistan and then Iraq, owed their origins to conventional interstate conflicts initiated by the United States. Similarly, the continuing rivalry between India and Pakistan over the disputed Kashmir region witnessed the outbreak of hostilities between their national armies in the Kargil district in 1999, but also fighting led by Pakistani insurgents that has ebbed and flowed over the years. The argument put forward for understanding patterns in the treatment of prisoners during interstate wars can also help inform conduct in other circumstances where groups resort to armed force.

Colonial Wars

Although less common over the last few decades, colonial wars were a mainstay throughout earlier centuries when great powers aspired to secure far-flung areas through the use of force.[30] Colonial wars inevitably involved some form of control over a foreign people, whether this simply meant acquiring land to extract natural and human resources or more ambitious plans like sending settlers to populate new holdings. Territory was almost always a goal to some extent in such conflicts, suggesting that prisoners were likely to be brutally treated in a manner similar to conventional interstate wars of conquest.

Colonial wars often involved belligerents of different races, but the American Revolutionary War showed that even when opponents came from the same cultural background conduct in these conflicts could be fierce. English forces viewed their opponents from the thirteen colonies as bandits, refusing to consider those captured as prisoners of war deserving of any protections.[31] Branding the colonial opposition as "rebels" was part of a general attempt to delegitimize the revolutionary cause. Policies of poor prisoner treatment served as a clear warning to enemy troops of the fate awaiting them and also signaled to other European nations that

Britain interpreted the fighting as internal to discourage any foreign involvement.[32] Anger over the thought of losing lucrative colonies led English forces to take a harsh approach in order to, as one captain put it, "scourge the rebellion with rods of iron," with particular brutalities befalling captured combatants.[33] Some limits were eventually achieved, especially as royal forces feared retaliation, but the horrific conditions on British prison ships testified to the terrible reality for prisoners during the war.[34]

Unlike the usual tendency of democratic states to settle their territorial disputes peacefully, the peak of colonial activity in the latter half of the nineteenth century showed that democracies were just as avid colonizers as other types of regimes. Even past colonies like the United States were, in turn, often merciless when fighting their own wars of imperial expansion. On the American continent, the United States prosecuted a series of conflicts against Native American tribes as the government expanded to the south and west. During these wars prisoners were often horribly treated, while those lucky enough to survive often languished on poorly equipped reservations.[35] Later, during war in the Philippines from 1899 to 1902, U.S. forces often relied on torture and summary executions as tools to cow the Filipino population into submission.[36]

U.S. forces were not alone in the ill-treatment of captives in colonial wars. Referring in part to Britain's increasingly harsh tactics in prosecuting the Maori Wars in present-day New Zealand, one historian remarked:

> A feeling among European armies that imperial wars were not governed by the laws or customs of European wars, particularly where prisoners were involved, together with a simple tendency to retaliate in kind when atrocities occurred, all too often set in motion an escalating spiral of abuse against POWs and civilian prisoners.[37]

The propensity of democracies to engage in colonial wars, along with their equally brutal treatment of prisoners, might at first seem puzzling given the attention to their constraints during interstate wars. When looking at both institutional mechanisms underlying democratic conduct and other contributing factors, the poor behavior of democracies in colonial wars is not quite so surprising. The frequent atrocities committed by democratic colonizers continue to call into question the supposed force of domestic liberal norms of humane conduct.[38] Furthermore, the restraints associated with democratic institutions probably exerted less pull in the colonial context. Any strategic benefits from good treatment would have appeared slight when compared to the advantages promised by coercing enemy populations into acquiescence. Expectations over reciprocity might also be expected to be substantially weaker, especially if compounded by prevailing cultural attitudes in democratic states and other powers at the time that colonized peoples could not be trusted. Consistent with the enabling function of democracy in conventional interstate wars of conquest, the record of colonial warfare thus suggests that democratic norms and institutions provided few protections to those soldiers from foreign lands who were captured.

Civil Wars

In many ways civil wars present an even tougher case for proper prisoner care than interstate conflicts. This is especially manifest in the relative energies states have devoted to creating rules regulating each type of warfare. In contrast to the extensive system of laws governing wars between states, legal prohibitions against prisoner abuse in civil wars are relatively sparse, suggesting governments prefer greater latitude when fighting against domestic enemies. In the 1949 Geneva Conventions, Common Article 3 offers the sole provision dealing with conflicts deemed to be "not of an international character." Common Article 3 calls for limiting certain types of violence, but compared to the rest of the conventions the provisions are not nearly as extensive or precise. It was only in 1977 with Additional Protocol II (AP II) that an agreement was negotiated to deal specifically with civil wars and similar conflicts. AP II was certainly a step forward in expanding proscriptions against abuse but remains fairly limited. Its interstate war sibling from the same year, Additional Protocol I (AP I), extended several protections under the Geneva Conventions and includes over one hundred separate articles detailing various obligations and restraints involving wars between states.[39] By comparison, AP II contains only one-quarter as many provisions, and several do not carry nearly as much force to equivalents under AP I. For instance, AP II does not accord any special status to prisoners of war compared to the extensive treatment of prisoner issues in the first protocol.[40] Even though the evidence shows that international law has little sustained impact on the behavior of belligerents toward captured combatants, the lack of clear rules or expectations for the treatment of prisoners in civil wars poses an even greater obstacle to proper conduct.

A further related problem for civil wars is that, unlike interstate conflicts, one side is often not a formally recognized member of the international community. Rebel groups usually have little official international standing and cannot even take such small steps of assurance as ratifying the prevailing laws of war.[41] Because of rebel groups' frequent lack of external legitimacy, governments may perceive that reciprocity is unlikely to hold when fighting against such opponents even if rebels were willing to limit their own conduct. In a similar way to colonial wars, expectations of reciprocity are apt to be weaker in civil wars, and a further incentive toward restraint for incumbent forces disappears. Rebels may also see little reason not to engage in brutality, since often one of the very reasons many groups initially take up arms is to combat repressive ruling regimes. It follows that a government willing to engage in abuses during peacetime is not likely to shrink back when confronted with internal rebellion, further negating the possibility for mutual cooperation.

Despite these dangers, there exists substantial variation in the treatment of prisoners during civil wars across history. In a similar manner to interstate warfare, in some civil wars prisoners are indeed horribly abused. The 1936–39 Spanish Civil War fought between Republican and Nationalist factions was typified by the systematic execution and torture of prisoners by both sides.[42] The war in Syria, erupting after the regime cracked down on protests in 2011 associated with the Arab Spring, brought about mutual recriminations and atrocities.[43] On the other hand, during Eritrea's struggle for independence, the Eritrean People's Liberation Front (EPLF) provided fairly decent care to surrendering Ethiopian troops.[44] EPLF actions are even more impressive given the fact that rebel prisoners were often not accorded the same respect when they fell to the Ethiopian government. Similar restraint was also evident hundreds of years earlier in England during the fifteenth-century Wars of the Roses and the later English Civil Wars of the seventeenth century. In the first instance, combatants from both the contending Lancaster and York houses were frequently treated well, although abuses still occurred. This more restrained conduct was mirrored almost two hundred years later even during the acrimonious battles between Royalist forces loyal to King Charles I and their Parliamentarian opponents.[45]

Several of the main causes of prisoner abuse in conflicts between states have ready corollaries when looking instead at civil wars. The severity of the fighting offers perhaps the closest similarity, since the logic of coercion or extraction may also hold for internal conflicts degenerating into attritional warfare. While belligerents in earlier civil wars in England demonstrated impressive restraint in their conduct during the initial periods of fighting, as the wars wore on the treatment of prisoners declined markedly.[46] More intense periods of combat still showed that not all enemy combatants were viewed as equally deserving of abuse; at the 1461 Battle of Towton the exclamation by the Yorkist King Edward IV and the earl of Warwick, "Spare the commons! Kill the lords!" bore a remarkable resemblance to Soviet feelings toward Polish prisoners almost five hundred years later.[47]

Territorial aims offer a similar expectation of greater levels of prisoner abuse. Rather than necessarily adding new lands as in the case of interstate conflicts, for civil wars the related objective more often involves one group trying to secede from the existing state. Looking more closely at past episodes suggests that the relationship between territory and prisoner abuse might not be quite so clear-cut in civil wars. After all, the EPLF was seeking to secede and create its own independent country at the expense of Ethiopia, but the former chose to treat its prisoners about as well as could be expected given the circumstances. Although it certainly contained a territorial element, the Spanish Civil War was rooted more in ideological differences between the two sides, yet this was more than enough for both parties to inflict violence against prisoners. The war in Spain also cautions against the hope that enemies sharing a common cultural heritage should be inherently more willing to show empathy toward their adversary. The fighting and patterns of abuse in the more recent Syrian Civil War reinforce the ambiguity of culture as an explanation for wartime conduct. While the Assad government has engaged in enormous amounts of repression especially as allegations of widespread and systematic torture surface, some of the most gruesome examples of prisoner killings have taken place *among* the various rebel groups ostensibly opposing the regime.[48] Differences between groups can be constructed on any one of a host of dimensions, and ideological clashes appear to have the potential to be just as deadly for prisoners as animosities based on race or ethnicity.[49]

The role of regime type also provides a parallel expectation that democracies should be less likely to commit prisoner abuse, at least as applied to incumbent governments. However, both of the institutional mechanisms related to fears of retaliation and the strategic benefits of good conduct may not operate to the same extent for democracies fighting internal wars. Indeed, the restrictions on civil liberties and other repressive steps taken by democracies facing security threats at home suggest that democratic incumbents may feel similarly justified in ignoring the rights of rebel prisoners.[50]

Although pressures toward abuse are formidable in many cases, civil wars might also provide certain incentives to care for prisoners that may not be found to the same extent in interstate wars. One motive in particular is the potential to lure members of the adversary over to one's own side, which is more likely to be successful through decent treatment and persuading enemy combatants of the righteousness of the captor's cause. Large-scale abuses may provide some immediate tactical gains but are unlikely to be effective in gaining new adherents among the victims. The restraint showed to many prisoners in the English Civil Wars was driven in large part by encouraging defections, with some soldiers switching between Royalist and Parliamentarian sides several times over the course of the war. After the fighting in Cirencester in 1643 subsided, only 16 of approximately 1,100 Parliamentarian survivors failed to change their allegiance and fight under the Royalist flag.[51] As one historian of the period remarked, "Prisoners were not 'the enemy'; they were a resource to be utilized either for recruiting or exchange (as well as being a highly public signifier of victory)."[52]

Such shifting loyalties may seem quaint in more modern times. The growing strength of nationalism over the course of the nineteenth and twentieth centuries has in many ways made it much more difficult to convince enemy combatants from an opposing state to switch sides in the context of interstate war. Some groups of prisoners have defected to the opposing state, such as Vlasov's Army composed of anticommunist Russian contingents who fought alongside Nazi Germany during the Second World War, but such examples are relatively rare. Although identities are far from fluid in civil wars, opportunities may still exist to bring enemy combatants over to one's cause. For instance, the EPLF benefited from their decent treatment of captured Ethiopian soldiers by convincing many prisoners to join the rebels' ranks and fight against their previous leaders.[53]

The prominence of civil wars in the current era, with their stark differences in the treatment of prisoners, suggests the need for a more systematic examination of the causes of prisoner abuse akin to this book's focus on interstate wars. As with the study of prisoner abuse more generally, data limitations remain daunting and beg for more concerted collection efforts that go beyond anecdotal evidence. Such an endeavor would also help to explore how incentives toward treating enemy combatants well or mistreating them may operate differently across civil versus international conflicts.

The War on Terror

Perhaps no issue related to prisoner rights has garnered greater attention in recent years than U.S. treatment of terrorist suspects and other insurgents as part of the War on Terror. The conflict began with an almost wholesale rejection of universal legal obligations for the humane treatment of enemy combatants. Just days after the 9/11 attacks Vice President Dick Cheney said that, in fighting terrorist organizations,

We also have to work, though, sort of the dark side, if you will. We've got to spend time in the shadows in the intelligence world. A lot of what needs to be done here will have to be done quietly, without any discussion, using sources and methods that are available to our intelligence agencies, if we're going to be successful. That's the world these folks operate in, and so it's going to be vital for us to use any means at our disposal, basically, to achieve our objective.[54]

The vice president's comments were foreboding of what was to come: the United States would need to set aside domestic and international rules when dealing with a terrorist adversary.

These sentiments were later confirmed when the White House under President George W. Bush publically declared that combatants from neither the Taliban nor al-Qaeda would be granted POW status under the Geneva Conventions, though some allowances would be made.[55] U.S. conduct toward detainees suggests that promises of decent treatment, however half-hearted, were not met across various dimensions of abuse. Human rights groups charged that the United States engaged in a systematic campaign of torture to extract from prisoners intelligence on the organization and activities of terrorist networks.[56] Coercive practices on the part of U.S. officials were compounded by the rendition of suspects to third-party countries known to use more permissive interrogation techniques.[57]

A fuller accounting of U.S. conduct in the War on Terror continues to emerge on an almost constant basis as new information about the government's actions comes to light.[58] The available evidence suggests that the democratic restraints normally operating in interstate wars may have little effect in conflicts like the War on Terror. To the extent that normative principles could play a role, commitments to individual rights and nonviolence are particularly challenging when the very legitimacy of the enemy is called into question. One theme that has continually surfaced in internal correspondence among U.S. policymakers in the years after the terrorist attacks is a common perception of facing a completely new sort of threat and enemy. As Alberto Gonzales, former attorney general and at the time White House counsel, declared in a confidential memorandum to the president, "the war against terrorism is a new kind of war . . . this new paradigm renders obsolete Geneva's strict limitations on questioning enemy prisoners and renders quaint some of its provisions."[59] Traditional democratic principles could consequently be more easily abandoned when dealing with such a severe threat to the United States and its people.

Debates over the legitimacy of the enemy also have implications for the strength of institutional restraints. Concerns over reciprocity are ultimately a function not only of the actual conduct of the adversary, but also of expectations about how the enemy will behave. When perceiving a foe as entirely illegitimate, it follows that they will likely be viewed as either unwilling or unable to act in a humane manner. The massive terrorist attacks against U.S. civilians strongly suggested any U.S. soldiers would be treated just as brutally upon capture. Continuing his justification for rejecting the Geneva Conventions, Gonzales bluntly asserted that any fears of retaliation against U.S. prisoners because of their government's policies were ridiculous: "terrorists will not follow GPW [Geneva POW Convention] rules in any event."[60] Several other officials still pointed to the danger posed to U.S. soldiers in the field if the administration rejected established international laws. Reflecting upon his extensive past military experience, then secretary of state Colin Powell countered that the administration's approach would "reverse over a century of U.S. policy and practice in supporting the Geneva Conventions and undermine the protection of the law of war for our troops, both in this specific conflict and in general."[61] Given the U.S. administration's final decision to set aside the conventions, Powell's opinion stood out as the minority view.

Expectations over the nature and legitimacy of the enemy also influence calculations over the relative strategic costs and benefits of abusing insurgent prisoners. The amorphous nature of terrorist organizations like al-Qaeda, along with the reliance on small groups for carrying out attacks, puts a much higher premium on obtaining actionable intelligence from those suspects that are captured. Vice President Cheney and others argued that only through the use of harsh interrogation methods could the United States extract from prisoners the necessary information to uncover terrorist networks and prevent future attacks against U.S. civilians and soldiers.[62] Unlike the military advantages accruing from humane conduct in interstate wars, many officials believed torture and other abuses were essential for effectively fighting terrorist foes.[63] The discovery and eventual killing of al-Qaeda leader Osama bin Laden in May 2011 renewed debates over the role played by earlier interrogations employing torture for obtaining vital details that helped lead to his whereabouts.[64] In his memoirs Jose Rodriguez, the former top official behind the CIA's Counterterrorism Center who was intimately involved in interrogation practices, argued that "I am confident, beyond any doubt, that these [enhanced interrogation] techniques . . . shielded the people of the United States from harm and led to the capture of Usama bin Ladin."[65]

Countering these claims, a lengthy investigation conducted by the Senate Intelligence Committee found no evidence that "enhanced interrogation techniques" had revealed plans for terrorist attacks or helped in the capture or killing of al-Qaeda leaders.[66] The stakes were raised even further two years later when in a follow-up report the same committee charged that the CIA actively misled government officials and the public regarding the effectiveness of its interrogation practices. With dubious benefits, harsher prisoner treatment in the aftermath of the 9/11 attacks has likely contributed to other problems in prosecuting the broader war. Compared to the earlier Persian Gulf War when Saddam Hussein's forces capitulated in droves, U.S. forces were much less successful at encouraging enemy surrenders in the 2003 invasion of Iraq.[67] Furthermore, while the United States has not faced direct sanctions for its conduct, reports on the difficulties of obtaining cooperation in counterterrorism operations from other countries are prevalent.[68] Yet, as in earlier periods, in many quarters the perceived benefits of prisoner abuse remain high.

Irrespective of the merits of the interrogation program and other abuses, responsibility for wartime conduct does not wholly reside with the political or military elites. In the post-9/11 context domestic actors did not provide a significant brake on government policies. Mass attitudes tend to be fairly supportive of repressive policies when facing threats to national security.[69] The public has been especially willing to condone the use of outright torture against suspects captured from irregular armed forces like terrorists, and general support for coercive interrogation techniques actually increased over the course of the decade after the 9/11 attacks.[70] Neither of the institutional mechanisms appeared to offer much restraint against U.S. abuse of prisoners. Taken together, it is perhaps not surprising that the treatment of captured terrorist suspects has been well below that seen in many interstate wars involving democracies.

The advent of the Obama presidency brought lofty promises to make fundamental changes to detainee policies. Yet the realities of prosecuting the War on Terror have resulted in just as much continuity as change between the two administrations.[71] Early on Barack Obama issued an executive order revoking the widespread use of some of the more excessive interrogation techniques from the previous government, hastened the closure of secret CIA prisons worldwide known as "black sites," and made increasing efforts to try terror suspects in civilian courts along with greater legal guarantees under military tribunals. Following on from one of the opening quotes to this chapter, however, the administration has sought to downplay prior abuses, effectively granting immunity to CIA agents previously alleged to have engaged in torture.[72] Other practices continue largely unabated, in particular the indefinite detention of hundreds of prisoners at Guantanamo Bay and other locations.

Partisan politics have certainly played their role in preventing the closing of the notorious U.S. facility in Cuba, but many supporters and detractors of the president believe that indefinitely holding on to the prisoners is justified by the relentless menace posed by terrorist networks. Although lacking the decisive end to the lives of Polish prisoners at Katyn, seemingly unending captivity serves a similar purpose by stopping those with the willingness and skills to threaten the United States. A leaked 2009 Pentagon report, which argued that one in seven of the detainees released from Guantanamo was later found to have engaged in terrorism or other militant activities, suggests these fears may have been warranted, though the findings are not without detractors.[73] Although indefinite detention may lack concrete signs of extreme violence, the practice remains controversial with many outspoken international and domestic critics.[74] This is especially indicative by its effects on detainees, with suicides and mass hunger strikes becoming increasingly prevalent at Guantanamo.[75]

Even as Obama may have curbed some of the more disproportionate tactics from his predecessor, other contentious practices that have grown under his presidency bear indelible marks from the fallout over earlier allegations of prisoner abuse. Belying the usual praises for the openness and transparency of democratic systems, the U.S. administration has placed a high priority upon maintaining secrecy at all costs. The lesson appeared to be taken from earlier events is that scandals over controversial counterterrorism measures only arise if the relevant information comes out in the open. Taking this guidance to the extreme, the administration has prosecuted more government whistle-blowers than all previous U.S. presidents combined. As one further irony, the only CIA operative who has gone to prison over the torture that took place in the War on Terror was not one of the interrogators engaging in such abuses, but rather an official who disclosed information regarding some of those involved in the program.[76] The explosion in targeted killings of insurgents and suspected terrorists through drone strikes under Obama's watch can also be better understood when considered in light of the country's previous experiences with prisoner abuse. Although garnering other criticisms, drone strikes promised a more definitive end to enemies of the United States, and avoided many of the vexing legal and practical issues raised by bringing additional detainees into U.S. custody.[77] Whether directly or indirectly, questions over the treatment of enemy combatants have remained at the core of policymaking across a host of issues related to counterterrorism operations.

Placing prisoner abuse in its proper historical context reveals both the political origins and consequences of how belligerents have decided to deal with prisoners during war. The violence frequently wrought upon captives shows that the prospects for troops who are captured are often grim. Yet the proper care offered to many other prisoners suggests all is not lost; humanitarian standards can prevail even in wartime. If benign conduct can promise to bring about strategic advantages to captors, then the tensions so often depicted between morality and military expediency may be exaggerated.[78] Yet normative principles are usually unable on their own to prevent abuse against prisoners. Only by fostering the conditions that make it in the self-interest of captors to protect their captives will proper treatment be more likely to prevail. Looking over the entirety of past conflicts nonetheless shows that the road into and out of captivity will likely remain perilous for many prisoners for some time to come.

[188]

APPENDIX

Codebook and a Statistical Analysis
of Prisoner Abuse

This appendix goes into further detail regarding the data and some of the empirical results presented in the preceding chapters. Data used in the statistical analysis are drawn from both original collection efforts as well as preexisting sources. The analysis covers all interstate wars from 1898 to 2003, using a modified version of the COW data set with several larger wars broken down into separate conflicts to more appropriately capture the actual fighting on the ground.[1] A full list of the interstate wars used is presented in table A.4 at the end of the appendix.

Dependent Variable—Prisoner Abuse

Prisoner abuse is defined as a military strategy enacted by political and military authorities that involves the intentional killing or harming, either directly or indirectly, of enemy combatants who have laid down their arms and surrendered. The unit of analysis is the warring-directed-dyad, meaning there are two separate observations for each pair of opposing states, where each is considered a potential violator or victim. To be included in the data set a belligerent must be considered a capable captor, which requires fulfilling both of the following criteria: having an independent prisoner policy by not being subservient to a larger wartime ally; having actually captured enemy combatants from the relevant adversary during the war.

Because of the difficulties in obtaining individual event or annual data across a sufficiently large number of cases, a single value for the level of prisoner treatment is measured for each observation. Coding was based on a wide variety of primary and secondary sources. Following the set of "grave breaches" outlined in the 1949 Geneva Conventions, six different dimensions of violations were first measured: execution, torture, denial of legal rights, compulsory military conscription, hazardous labor, and poor living conditions. Each captor's treatment was then classified on an ordinal scale as exhibiting high (2), medium (1), or low (0) levels of abuse against prisoners.[2] High-level cases involve the widespread and systematic mistreatment of prisoners along the given dimension of abuse. By contrast, in low-level cases prisoners are treated well on the whole, and offenses for the relevant type of abuse are rare. Medium-level cases involve greater abuse than in low-level instances, but violations are less frequent or extensive compared to high-level abuses. This middle category also includes cases involving more common individual acts of abuse not officially supported by the government but where authorities have not taken significant steps to prevent further violations from taking place. A summary indicator of the overall level of abuse for each observation is then constructed, which equals the highest level of offense across the six dimensions, given that any of these violations on their own is considered a war crime under international law. A more detailed discussion of the conceptual and measurement issues involved in prisoner abuse is provided in chapter 1.

INDEPENDENT VARIABLES

Democracy   The coding of each country's regime type is based on the Polity IV data set. Polity creates a measure for the level of democracy or autocracy in a country by combining information concerning the regulation and competitiveness of political participation, the competitiveness and openness of executive recruitment, and constraints on the chief executive.[3] These components are then used to construct a scale for regime type that ranges from -10 to +10, where higher values indicate a greater level of democracy. Employing a dichotomous indicator, a country is considered a democracy if it scored 7 or above on the Polity index at the beginning of the war, and not a democracy otherwise. The Polity index is not without its detractors, who criticize the measure on a number of conceptual and methodological grounds.[4] Nevertheless, it should be stressed that the Polity index remains one of the most widely used measures for democracy across both international relations and comparative politics, and for wartime conduct in particular.[5]

War of Attrition   This is one of the measures for the nature of the conflict based on prior work from Downes on civilian victimization and is supplemented with original coding for wars not included in earlier work.[6] This metric equals 1 for wars that become bogged down in static or protracted fighting, such as the trench warfare typifying much of the western front during the First World War, and 0 otherwise.

Expansive War Aims   This is another measure for the nature of the conflict that also draws on the prior work of Downes along with some additional personal coding. This metric equals 1 if the country sought as a war aim either regime change or the enemy's unconditional surrender, and 0 otherwise. Examples include U.S. aims to overthrow Saddam Hussein during the 2003 Iraq War, or U.S. demands for the complete capitulation of Japanese forces during the Second World War.

Territorial Annexation   This is the third and final main measure for the nature of the conflict, which is also based on prior work from Downes in addition to personal coding. This metric equals 1 if the country was seeking to conquer and permanently take over territory from the enemy state, and 0 otherwise. Notable instances include German designs over Soviet territory during the Second World War and Italy's conquest of Ethiopia during their war from 1935 to 1936.

Cultural Differences   There are many challenges to creating satisfactory measures for identity and images of the enemy.[7] Following other quantitative studies of armed conflict that draw on Huntington's clash of civilizations thesis, the cultural differences variable looks at the ex ante civilizational identity of each warring party.[8] Although somewhat crude, the measure captures key cleavages between different societies: Western, Latin American, Hindu, Orthodox, Islamic, African, Sinic, Buddhist, Japanese, and a residual Other category. The variable equals 1 if a given pair of adversaries comes from different civilizations or both are coded as Other, and 0 if they are from the same civilization.

Prisoner Abuse by Opponent   In order to account for the likely effects of reciprocity, this variable is equal to the level of prisoner abuse committed by the opponent in a given warring-directed-dyad and follows the same scale as the dependent variable: high (2), medium (1), or low (0) levels. The value for states whose opponent is not considered a capable captor is coded 0 for this variable.[9]

Deterrence   This dichotomous measure equals 1 if both countries in a pairing are considered capable captors, such as each side in the Iran-Iraq

War, and coded as 0 if a country faces an adversary that is not a capable captor by failing to capture enemy prisoners, as occurred with Germany against Belgium during the Second World War.

Relative Capabilities This equals the percentage of the total capabilities of all belligerents in the war controlled by the relevant country. Capabilities are measured using the COW composite index of national capabilities, which are then adjusted for distance to the main battlefront using the loss function originally developed by Bueno de Mesquita.[10]

Treaty Ratification This is one of the measures for assessing the effects of international law, which focuses on unilateral ratification decisions. This metric equals 1 if the country ratified the prevailing international treaty respecting the rights of prisoners by the start of the war, and 0 otherwise. Data on treaty ratification come from several sources.[11] The relevant treaty for each time period was as follows: from 1899 to 1907 the 1899 Hague Convention; from 1907 to 1929 either the 1899 or the 1907 Hague Convention, since the later version did not substantially build upon obligations from the original convention;[12] from 1929 to 1949 the 1929 Geneva Convention; and from 1949 to the present the 1949 Third Geneva Convention.[13]

Treaty Ratification (Opponent) This is an equivalent unilateral ratification measure that equals 1 if the opponent ratified the prevailing treaty protecting prisoners by the start of the war, and 0 otherwise.

Joint Treaty Ratification To assess the combined commitment decisions of the belligerents, this variable equals 1 if both states in a pairing ratified the relevant treaty, and 0 otherwise. Note that this variable is essentially an interaction term between the two prior unilateral ratification measures. One of the reasons why the prior measure for the opponent's ratification decision was added was so that all constitutive terms are included in the analysis.[14]

Post-1949 Norms This variable is intended to determine whether the 1949 Geneva Conventions ushered in a new era of humanitarian norms emphasizing the proper treatment of prisoners compared to earlier periods. The variable equals 1 for wars that began after 1949, and 0 for conflicts starting before that time.

Table A.1 summarizes the descriptive statistics for the prisoner abuse dependent variable and the explanatory variables used in the main statistical analysis.

Appendix

TABLE A.1 Summary statistics for main variables used in the analysis

Variable	Observations	Mean	Standard Deviation	Minimum	Maximum
Prisoner abuse	272	1.118	0.788	0	2
Democracy	272	0.246	0.432	0	1
War of attrition	272	0.419	0.494	0	1
Expansive war aims	272	0.324	0.469	0	1
Territorial annexation	272	0.191	0.394	0	1
Cultural differences	272	0.695	0.461	0	1
Prisoner abuse by opponent	271	1.048	0.813	0	2
Deterrence	271	0.915	0.279	0	1
Relative capabilities	272	0.312	0.290	0.002	0.988
Treaty ratification	272	0.739	0.440	0	1
Treaty ratification (opponent)	272	0.750	0.434	0	1
Joint treaty ratification	272	0.654	0.476	0	1
Post-1949 norms	272	0.397	0.490	0	1

Notes: Capable captors only.

DESCRIPTION OF SUPPLEMENTARY INDEPENDENT VARIABLES

A number of additional analyses were reported in the main text investigating other possible determinants of prisoner abuse, in particular those discussed in chapter 5. While the complete set of regression results from models including these and additional variables are not presented below, full details are included in accompanying online materials to the book.

Rivalry   Wars rarely take place in a vacuum, but are often related to past conflicts and disagreements between the belligerents. States can vary greatly in the nature and intensity of their earlier disputes with adversaries, which in turn shape expectations of future militarized competition. Two separate dichotomous measures are used to identify states in a warring-directed-dyad that are classified as rivals. The first rivalry variable comes from the work of Diehl and Goertz who rely on the Militarized Interstate Dispute (MID) data set, which covers cases of conflict involving the threat, display, or use of force between states.[15] According to Diehl and Goertz, a pair of states is generally considered rivals if they engaged in three or more MIDs that took place within ten to fifteen years of each other. Dyads that experienced less than two disputes were considered isolated conflicts rather than genuine rivalries. Rivalries were also typically deemed to have terminated ten to fifteen years after the end of their last dispute. Because of the focus of Diehl and Goertz on the interconnectedness of conflicts, the frequency and duration criteria were not hard-and-fast rules compared to earlier versions of their rivalry data. After constructing narratives for each potential rivalry, some cases with more than three disputes were nonetheless coded as isolated conflicts, while disputes taking place more than fifteen years apart were sometimes ruled as part of the same rivalry.[16] *Rivals (Diehl & Goertz)* equals 1 if states in a warring-directed-dyad are rivals according to their framework, and 0 otherwise. Rather than relying on objective indicators from prior militarized behavior, an alternative measure by Thompson delves into diplomatic history to include only those states that perceived and spoke of each other in terms of rivals.[17] *Rivals (Thompson)* thus equals 1 if states in a warring-directed-dyad viewed each other as rivals, and 0 otherwise. To ensure the relevant war being fought was not included in the measure, both rivalry variables were lagged one year.

Prior War and Outcomes   Formative events like past wars can weigh heavily on leaders and their states, fundamentally shaping their perceptions and foreign policies for years afterward.[18] *Fought prior war* is a dichotomous variable that equals 1 if countries in a warring-directed-dyad fought a war in the prior twenty-five years based on the COW list of interstate wars, and 0 otherwise.[19] To evaluate whether the particular wartime outcome from the prior twenty-five-year period affected a belligerent's conduct, three separate dichotomous variables were created for whether a captor won, lost, or drew the most recent interstate war against the other country in the warring-directed-dyad. All three variables are coded 0 if the states in the warring-directed-dyad did not fight a war in the previous twenty-five years. Data on war outcomes were drawn from COW as well as several additional sources that have identified concerns with the COW coding for certain wars.[20]

Prior Prisoner Abuse   To investigate instead whether the particular conduct by the adversary in the prior war affects how a captor decides to treat prisoners, three dichotomous indicators were created for whether the enemy engaged in low, medium, or high levels of abuse in the most recent war from the earlier twenty-five-year period. As with the war outcomes measures, all three variables are coded 0 if the states in the warring-directed-dyad did not fight a war in the previous twenty-five years. Noncapable captors were coded 1 for the low-level abuse measure, but the results do not change substantially if the few relevant observations are instead coded 0.[21] The main results from the rivalry, prior war, and prior abuse models are presented in table 5.2 from chapter 5.

Communist Regimes   A series of variables were constructed to evaluate various suppositions discussed in chapter 5 concerning the relationship between communism and prisoner abuse. Coding for communist regimes was based on the classification system developed by Karnai and supplemented by individual country histories where necessary.[22] *Communist (all)* is a variable that equals 1 if a country's regime is considered communist, and 0 otherwise. Differentiating between communist regimes, *Soviet Russia* equals 1 for observations where the captor state was Russia during wars taking place once the Bolsheviks came to power in 1917 until the fall of the Soviet Union in 1991, and 0 otherwise. To determine whether Joseph Stalin's reign was punctuated by extreme forms of violence against not only his own citizens but also enemy combatants, *Stalinist Russia* equals 1 for Russian captors for the years where Stalin ruled the country, from 1922 with his appointment as general secretary until his death in 1953, and 0 otherwise.[23] Lastly, to assess whether communist countries other than the Soviet Union display different patterns of prisoner treatment, *Non-Soviet* is a dichotomous variable that equals 1 for communist countries in the data set that are not the Soviet Union, such as China, Hungary, Vietnam, and North Korea, and 0 otherwise. The main effects from the various communist variables are presented in table 5.3 from chapter 5.

PRISONER ABUSE: A QUANTITATIVE ANALYSIS

Because the prisoner abuse dependent variable is ordinal, table A.2 presents the ordered logit regression results from the primary model for the determinants of prisoner abuse, which includes the measures for regime type, the nature of the conflict, and a number of the other main factors that could also affect the treatment of captives. The findings confirm that democracies are less likely to engage in prisoner abuse, and the coefficient for regime type is statistically significant. The nature of the conflict also continues to matter a great deal, as wars of attrition and territorial annexation both increase prisoner abuse, while expansive war aims have little effect. Other common explanations, such as cultural differences, deterrence, material capabilities, and international law, have little consistent effect on patterns of prisoner treatment. On the other hand, prisoner abuse by the opponent significantly increases the likelihood of similar conduct by belligerents, while wars after 1949 are actually associated with greater levels of prisoner mistreatment. Given the difficulties of interpreting coefficients when using categorical dependent variables, the output from this model was then used to estimate the substantive effects for the determinants of prisoner abuse reported in table 3.1 in chapter 3.

A number of robustness checks were also conducted using the model from table A.2 as the baseline. The model was rerun using alternative summary indicators for prisoner abuse, including the lowest value across the six component violations, the average value, the median value, and a dichotomous measure to distinguish high-level abuses from all other cases. The models were also reestimated using both capable and noncapable captors to ensure that any potential biases from limiting the results to capable captors were not somehow driving the results.[24]

Other studies have found that the particular measure used for democracy can affect findings regarding regime type.[25] Different cutoff points of 6 and 8 on the Polity index were employed to distinguish democracies from nondemocracies, as well as alternative measures for democracy.[26] Similarly, in place of the dichotomous war of attrition variable for the severity of the fighting, alternative measures involving battle deaths and the duration of the war were substituted.[27]

The war of attrition measure, along with the variable for prisoner abuse by opponent, may raise some concerns over endogeneity, since the dependent variable measuring a country's own abuses may affect the values for both of these independent variables. As a check to ensure endogeneity was not unduly affecting the results, instruments were created for the attrition and opponent abuse variables respectively, and the model was reestimated using two-stage least squares in each instance. While the size of the coefficients for each variable is reduced somewhat, they remain statistically significant and in the same direction.

Finally, a number of additional tests were conducted to ensure that the results were not simply a function of particular countries or wars. Included were specific variables for noteworthy captors like the United States and Nazi Germany, as well as prominent conflicts such as both the First and Second World Wars. Only the coefficient for the First World War turns out to be statistically significant, which offers some support for contentions that the Great War brought about a new era of brutality on the modern battlefield.[28]

In general, the main set of findings continues to hold across most of the alternative model specifications.[29] While not reported here due to space constraints, the full set of results is discussed in greater detail in supplementary online materials.

Table A.3 displays results from the full set of models used to estimate possible effects for democracy on prisoner treatment that are conditional on the values of other explanatory variables. The models incorporate a

TABLE A.2 Regression analysis for determinants of
prisoner abuse in interstate wars, 1898–2003

	(1) Main Model
Democracy	−1.187*
	(0.477)
War of attrition	1.394**
	(0.341)
Expansive war aims	0.147
	(0.352)
Territorial annexation	2.309**
	(0.575)
Cultural differences	0.378
	(0.230)
Prisoner abuse by opponent	1.504**
	(0.472)
Deterrence	−1.027
	(0.643)
Relative capabilities	0.0842
	(0.523)
Treaty ratification	0.403
	(0.587)
Treaty ratification (opponent)	0.780
	(0.601)
Joint treaty ratification	−1.218+
	(0.687)
Post-1949 norms	0.589*
	(0.268)
First cutpoint (τ_1)	0.240
	(0.621)
Second cutpoint (τ_2)	2.902**
	(0.693)
Observations	271
Pseudo R-squared	0.298
Log likelihood	−206.6
Chi-squared	74.45
Number of wars	77

Notes: Robust standard errors in parentheses (clustered by war).
+ p < .1; * p < .05; ** p < .01.
Ordered logit estimation. Capable captors only.

TABLE A.3 Regression analysis for democracy interactions and prisoner abuse in interstate wars, 1898–2003

	Democracy × Deterrence	Democracy × Attrition	Democracy × Territory	Democracy × Expansive aims	Democracy × Treaty	Democracy × Norms	Democracy × Initiator
Democracy	-1.405	-0.783	-1.523**	-0.614	-0.522	-1.056	-1.537**
	(1.350)	(0.529)	(0.490)	(0.430)	(0.745)	(0.785)	(0.537)
War of attrition	1.394**	1.607**	1.426**	1.613**	1.434**	1.393**	1.398**
	(0.341)	(0.514)	(0.348)	(0.461)	(0.359)	(0.345)	(0.344)
Expansive war aims	0.141	0.281	0.0889	0.563	0.123	0.128	0.256
	(0.348)	(0.351)	(0.356)	(0.376)	(0.352)	(0.348)	(0.340)
Territorial annexation	2.307**	2.356**	1.743**	2.412**	2.249**	2.311**	2.365**
	(0.573)	(0.606)	(0.559)	(0.620)	(0.565)	(0.571)	(0.600)
Cultural differences	0.378	0.382+	0.409	0.386+	0.368	0.401+	0.343
	(0.230)	(0.224)	(0.254)	(0.227)	(0.231)	(0.243)	(0.233)
Prisoner abuse by opponent	1.503**	1.502**	1.568**	1.474**	1.491**	1.493**	1.541**
	(0.472)	(0.478)	(0.467)	(0.479)	(0.467)	(0.476)	(0.510)
Deterrence	-1.077+	-0.974	-1.152+	-0.928	-1.005	-1.037	-1.090+
	(0.631)	(0.644)	(0.663)	(0.653)	(0.648)	(0.633)	(0.650)
Relative capabilities	0.0977	0.0980	0.215	-0.0812	0.104	0.114	-0.143
	(0.522)	(0.548)	(0.554)	(0.586)	(0.521)	(0.521)	(0.565)
Treaty ratification	0.408	0.346	0.738	0.462	0.614	0.393	0.469
	(0.585)	(0.609)	(0.657)	(0.604)	(0.600)	(0.596)	(0.553)

	(1)	(2)	(3)	(4)	(5)	(6)	(7)
Treaty ratification (opponent)	0.795	0.646	1.029	0.603	0.643	0.743	0.823
	(0.598)	(0.620)	(0.698)	(0.598)	(0.598)	(0.639)	(0.540)
Joint treaty ratification	-1.237+	-1.063	-1.582*	-1.177+	-1.075	-1.173	-1.326*
	(0.679)	(0.681)	(0.792)	(0.679)	(0.690)	(0.731)	(0.668)
Post-1949	0.596*	0.560*	0.577*	0.533+	0.610*	0.664	0.554*
	(0.271)	(0.280)	(0.269)	(0.288)	(0.267)	(0.405)	(0.277)
Democracy × Deterrence	0.237						
	(1.416)						
Democracy × Attrition		-0.945					
		(1.129)					
Democracy × Territorial Annexation			16.61**				
			(1.022)				
Democracy × Expansive war aims				-1.678			
				(1.185)			
Democracy × Treaty ratification					-0.933		
					(0.971)		
Democracy × Norms						-0.305	
						(1.081)	
Initiator						0.0814	
						(0.521)	

(Continued)

TABLE A.3 (*Continued*)

	Democracy × Deterrence	Democracy × Attrition	Democracy × Territory	Democracy × Expansive aims	Democracy × Treaty	Democracy × Norms	Democracy × Initiator
Democracy × Initiator							1.067
							(0.758)
First cutpoint (τ_1)	0.202	0.362	0.322	0.362	0.398	0.262	0.185
	(0.606)	(0.655)	(0.656)	(0.602)	(0.638)	(0.629)	(0.614)
Second cutpoint (τ_2)	2.863**	3.037**	3.038**	3.090**	3.081**	2.923**	2.873**
	(0.676)	(0.740)	(0.734)	(0.693)	(0.689)	(0.691)	(0.714)
Observations	271	271	271	271	271	271	271
Pseudo R-squared	0.298	0.301	0.316	0.308	0.301	0.298	0.304
Log likelihood	−206.6	−205.5	−201.2	−203.6	−205.7	−206.5	−204.6
Chi-squared	74.84	75.47	73.47	74.34	76.90	79.85	74.77
Number of wars	77	77	77	77	77	77	77

Notes: Robust standard errors in parentheses (clustered by war).
+ p < .1; * p < .05; ** p < .01.
Ordered logit estimation. Capable captors only.

TABLE A.4 List of interstate wars, 1898–2003

War Name	Start Year	End Year
Spanish-American	1898	1898
Boxer Rebellion	1900	1900
Sino-Russian	1900	1900
Russo-Japanese	1904	1905
Third Central American	1906	1906
Fourth Central American	1907	1907
Second Spanish-Moroccan	1909	1910
Italo-Turkish	1911	1912
First Balkan	1912	1913
Second Balkan	1913	1913
WWI.a (Western Allies-Central Powers)	1914	1918
WWI.b (Russia-Central Powers)	1914	1917
WWI.c (Romania-Central Powers)	1914	1917
WWI.d (Serbia-Central Powers)	1914	1918
Estonian War of Liberation	1918	1920
Latvian War of Independence	1918	1920
Russo-Polish	1919	1920
Hungarian-Allies	1919	1919
Second Greco-Turkish	1919	1922
Franco-Turkish	1919	1921
Lithuanian-Polish	1920	1920
Sino-Soviet (Manchurian)	1929	1929
Second Sino-Japanese	1931	1933
Chaco	1932	1935
Saudi-Yemeni	1934	1934
Conquest of Ethiopia	1935	1936
Third Sino-Japanese	1937	1945
Changkufeng	1938	1938
Nomonhan	1939	1939
WWII.a (Poland)	1939	1939
WWII.b (Norway)	1940	1940
WWII.c (France)	1940	1940
WWII.d (Germany-Western Allies)	1941	1945

(*Continued*)

[201]

War Name	Start Year	End Year
WWII.e (Greece)	1941	1941
WWII.f (German-Yugoslav)	1941	1941
WWII.g (Eastern Front)	1941	1945
WWII.h (Pacific War)	1941	1945
WWII.i (Soviet-Japanese)	1945	1945
Winter War/Russo-Finnish	1939	1940
Franco-Thai	1940	1941
First Kashmir	1947	1949
Palestine	1948	1949
Korean	1950	1953
Off-Shore Islands	1954	1955
Sinai	1956	1956
Russo-Hungarian	1956	1956
Ifni	1957	1958
Taiwan Straits	1958	1958
Assam (Sino-Indian)	1962	1962
Vietnam	1965	1975
Second Kashmir	1965	1965
Six Day	1967	1967
Second Laotian War Phase 2	1968	1973
War of Attrition (Israeli-Egyptian)	1969	1970
Football	1969	1969
War of the Communist Coalition	1970	1971
Bangladesh	1971	1971
Yom Kippur	1973	1973
Turco-Cypriot	1974	1974
War over Angola	1975	1976
Ethopian-Somali (Ogaden)	1977	1978
Vietnamese-Cambodian	1977	1979
Ugandan-Tanzanian	1978	1979
First Sino-Vietnamese	1979	1979
Iran-Iraq	1980	1988

War Name	Start Year	End Year
Falklands	1982	1982
War over Lebanon	1982	1982
Chad-Libya (Aouzou Strip)	1986	1987
Second Sino-Vietnamese	1987	1987
Persian Gulf.a (Iraq-Kuwait)	1990	1990
Persian Gulf.b (U.S. Coalition-Iraq)	1991	1991
War of Bosnian Independence	1992	1995
Azeri-Armenian (Nagorno-Karabakh)	1993	1994
Cenepa Valley	1995	1995
Badme Border War (Ethiopia-Eritrea)	1998	2000
Kosovo	1999	1999
Kargil	1999	1999
Invasion of Afghanistan	2001	2001
Invasion of Iraq	2003	2003

series of interaction terms between regime type and the relevant independent variable of interest, while including the same baseline set of other determinants of prisoner abuse. Interpreting the results from interaction models is problematic because neither the constitutive nor interaction terms represent unconditional marginal effects. Since the relationship between regime type and the conditioning variable depends on the value of both the lower-order and interaction terms, calculating marginal effects using substantively meaningful values is normally recommended.[30] Fortunately, this is relatively straightforward in the models presented in table A.3, since all of the relevant explanatory variables are dichotomous. The substantive effects for the difference between democracies and autocracies in resorting to prisoner abuse conditional on the particular context for each independent variable were generated from the results of these models. The results are then reported in table 3.3 in chapter 3.

Notes

Introduction

Dostoyevsky epigraph: While widely cited and usually associated with Dostoyevsky's book *The House of the Dead*, the exact source and origins of this quote remain obscure. Nevertheless, many others have reiterated the general theme of linking the treatment of prisoners to the surrounding society. For instance, from Nelson Mandela, "It is said that no one truly knows a nation until one has been inside its jails. A nation should not be judged by how it treats its highest citizens, but its lowest ones," quoted in Smith 2009.

1. Barton 1993, 34; Harris 1985, 56.

2. Quoted in Carnegie Endowment 1993, 215.

3. Hassig 1988, 37–39, 115–21.

4. Bartov 2001, 107.

5. Reiter and Stam 2002, 68.

6. Montesquieu (1748) 1989, 247.

7. Walzer 2000, 46.

8. Excerpt from Article 15 of Instructions for the Government of Armies of the United States in the Field (Lieber Code), April 24, 1863. The full text for this and other historical legal documents, as well as related international treaties, can be found at Avalon Project 2008; ICRC 2014.

9. Bedjaoui 1992, 292; Ishay 2008, 41–42.

10. M. Keen 1965, 156. Of course, the need to meet the demanded ransom could often bankrupt prisoners and their families, though the monetary hardship would likely have been preferable to the alternative of failing to pay (Prestwich 1999, 104–6).

11. Vance 2006, 323. Although not for strictly monetary reasons, one theory posits that the prime motivation behind wars involving Native American Iroquois tribes eventually became to capture prisoners in order to replenish dwindling populations due to prior conflicts and disease. However, this did not stop the Iroquois and many other Native American captors from also frequently engaging in torture and similar abuses against some prisoners (Lee 2011, 155).

12. Spaight 1911, 265. The timing of Spaight's comments was somewhat unfortunate, taking place just a few years before the First World War, which became

[205]

known for many brutalities, including misery for soldiers both on and off the battlefield.

13. R. Posner 2002, S325.

14. Poe and Tate 1994.

15. Roland 1996, 165.

16. Horne 2006, 195–97.

17. Blainey 1988; Levy 1989.

18. Van Evera 1999, 3.

19. Goemans 2000b; Reiter 2009.

20. Gartner 1998.

21. Sarkees and Wayman 2010, 1–2.

22. D. Keen 2005, 4.

23. Balcells 2010; Downes 2008; Hultman 2007; Kalyvas 2006; Valentino 2004; Valentino, Huth, and Balch-Lindsay 2004; Valentino, Huth, and Croco 2006.

24. Harff 2003; Midlarsky 2005; Straus 2007.

25. Bloom 2005; Pape 2003. Though see below on several books investigating the specific case of detainees in the War on Terror.

26. Rachamimov 2002, 31.

27. Morina 2004, 323–25.

28. Best 1994, 135.

29. Dower 1986; Hull 2005; Morrow 2007. One exception is Legro's (1995) study of the conduct by the major powers during the Second World War across the areas of submarine warfare, strategic bombing, and chemical weapons, though he does not directly deal with the treatment of prisoners.

30. Carlson 1998; R. Doyle 1994; Kochavi 2005; MacKenzie 2004.

31. Hull 2014; H. Jones 2011; A. Kramer 2007; Rachamimov 2002; Speed 1990.

32. Forsythe 2011; Goldsmith 2009; Mayer 2009.

33. This is reflected in sometimes eerily similar titles: Carvin 2010; R. Doyle 2010; Springer 2010.

34. Bravin 2013; Lightcap 2011; McCoy 2006; Rejali 2007.

35. Downes 2006, 157 n.43. For example, there is no equivalent for prisoner deaths as of yet to large-N data collection efforts on the targeting of civilians, such as the one-sided violence data set (Eck and Hultman 2007). Those that do cover combatants only focus on battle deaths rather than those of prisoners in captivity (Lacina and Gleditsch 2005, 147–52).

36. Clausewitz 1984, 76.

37. Baudendistel 2006, 234–35; Beaumont 1996, 280; A. Kramer 2007, 2–3.

38. Dower 1986, 11.

39. Fazal and Greene, forthcoming.

40. Kier 1997, 28.

41. Legro 1995, 27–28.

42. Hull 2005, 145–48.

43. For a critique of organizational culture arguments dealing with the targeting of civilians, see Downes 2012.

44. A related strand focuses more on an organization's structure in explaining the behavior of armed actors (J. Snyder 1984; Weinstein 2007). While structural arguments have not been widely applied to the study of prisoners of war, they suffer from the same limits in accounting for differences in the abuse of captives by the same belligerent.

45. Clausewitz 1984, 232.

46. Downes 2008, 10; Kalyvas 1999, 243–45; Pape 1996, 7–11; Valentino 2004, 3.

47. Downes 2007b; Valentino, Huth, and Croco 2006.

48. Vance 2006, 471.

49. A. Roberts 1993–94, 160–61.

50. Examples in this vein include Bourke 1999; Ferguson 2004; Grauer 2014.

51. On the use of battle-related deaths by the Correlates of War project and the UCDP/PRIO Armed Conflict Dataset, see N. Gleditsch et al. 2002; Sarkees and Wayman 2010, 49–52.

52. Based on figures from Bartov 2001, 107; Sarkees and Wayman 2010, 140.

53. Burrows 2008, 200–201.

54. Mann 2004, 3–5.

55. Kinsella 2011; E. Posner 2003; Price 1998; Price and Tannenwald 1996.

56. Morrow 2007, 2014; Prorok and Appel 2014.

57. Goldsmith and Posner 2005, 167–84; Walzer 2000, 20.

58. Hastings 1987, 305.

59. Hastings 1987, 329.

60. Speed 1990, ix.

61. Piper 1994, 159.

62. Streit 1986, 2.

63. Mueller 1996, 30–31. Though for a more skeptical account, see Burk 1999.

64. Powers 2002, 332–33.

65. On different estimates of the number of persons killed in the Rwandan genocide, see Straus 2006, 51.

1. Repertoires of Violence against Prisoners

1. T. Snyder 2010, 176–82. It is estimated that far more Russian soldiers died from German policies of purposeful starvation than from outright execution during the Second World War (Streit 1986, 9–10).

2. Carnegie Endowment 1993, 112. The report uses the alternative spelling Toundja for the river.

3. Bowman 1976, 19–21; Metzger 1962, 281–88. The letter of one prisoner was typical of the experience endured by many: "I am now in the limboes, in the midst of filth and vermin." Quoted in Metzger 1962, 283.

4. Krammer 2008, 7.

5. *Economist* 2005; Carter 2004; Hersh 2004, 46.

6. Burrows 2008, 22; Metzger 1962, 152.

7. See, for instance, the lengthy ICC trial against the militia leader Germain Katanga for a massacre in a Congolese village in 2003, which involved several questions over the quality and accuracy of the evidence presented. The accused ended up being convicted in a split ruling among the presiding justices of lesser charges as an accessory rather than as a principal perpetrator of the massacre and acquitted on other charges involving rape and the use of child soldiers (Simons 2014).

8. Rogers 2007, 103–8.

9. Best 1980, 63–66.

10. Buzan 2002, 91; Dunlap 2000, 10.

11. Valentino, Huth, and Balch-Lindsay 2004, 383–85.

12. Becker and Shane 2012.

13. AP I, Article 43.

14. The decision in AP I to expand the combatant umbrella to include guerrilla fighters remains controversial and was one of the main reasons why the United States and several other countries refused to ratify the agreement (Reagan 1987). Nevertheless, this rule and many other aspects of AP I are widely considered customary international law even by the United States (International Committee of the Red Cross 2010, Rule 3).

15. Valentino 2004, 13–14.

16. Walzer 2000, 145–46.

17. Downes 2008, 14–15.

18. The acronym FFL is based on the French term, Forces Françaises Libres.

19. Schaffer 1985, 39.

20. Indeed, workers in munitions factories, and the armaments industry more broadly, made up an increasingly significant proportion of foreign labor in Nazi Germany's war effort (Homze 1967, 234–40).

21. For instance, Article 50 of AP I defines civilians in a negative fashion as any individual that is *not* a member of the armed forces, militias, or similar military forces.

22. See Article 4 of the 1949 Third Geneva Convention relative to the Treatment of Prisoners of War, and the accompanying commentaries.

23. See AP I, Article 44.

24. See AP I, Article 47.

25. Bourke 1999, 170.

26. T. Cook 2006, 645.

27. Grossman 1995, 179.

28. Hastings 1987, 287.

29. Kerr 1985, 83–84. Although the conduct toward prisoners held by Japan during the war was usually ruthless, there were times when captives could be shown some mercy and decency (Yap 2012).

30. For a similar definition concerning civilian targeting, see Arreguin-Toft 2001, 101–2; Downes 2008, 15.

31. Gutman, Rieff, and Dworkin 2007, 358.

32. Britt, Castro, and Adler 2006, 95–96; Newman 1944.

33. See Article 38 of the 1949 Third Geneva Convention.

34. See Article 8 of the 1998 Rome Statute of the International Criminal Court.

35. As corollaries for the treatment of prisoners, see Articles 2, 5, 9, 31–32, and 45 from the 1929 Geneva Convention, and Articles 4 through 20 from the Annexes to the 1899 and 1907 Hague Conventions of War on Land.

36. A full accounting of the precursors to the grave breaches is provided in supplementary online appendices accompanying this book. See, in particular, Articles 4, 9(b), 10–11, 21–22, and 61–78 from the Oxford Manual; Articles 11, 13(c)(d), and 23–34 from the Brussels Declaration; and Articles 15, 16, 44, 49–52, 60–61, 67–68, and 71–81 from the Lieber Code. The Lieber Code is particularly interesting since, alongside the aforementioned humanitarian principles, the regulations allowed and sometimes even encouraged reprisals and harsh treatment for certain categories of prisoners. However, these more coercive elements became less prominent or disappeared altogether in later international legal documents. For a broader overview of the principles and tensions embodied in the Lieber Code and its successors, see Witt 2013.

37. MacKenzie 1994, 504–12; Ober 1994, 18.

38. S. Miller 1982, 247–48.

39. Hata 1996, 266–67; Roland 1996, 150.

40. Gordon 1924, 102.

41. Gutman, Rieff, and Dworkin 2007, 119.

42. Weindling 2000, 76–77.

43. Rachamimov 2002, 95.

44. Correlates of War Inter-State War Data Set (v4.0). See Sarkees and Wayman 2010. Following conventional COW practices, an interstate war is defined as a military conflict between two states, in other words two recognized members of the international system, that resulted in a minimum of one thousand battle fatalities among the states involved. An individual state is counted as a participant in the war if it had a minimum of one thousand armed personnel engaged in the hostilities or sustained a minimum of one hundred battle fatalities (Small and Singer 1982, 55).

45. For instance, Article 6 of the 1864 Geneva Convention discusses the treatment of wounded soldiers from the adversary, though Article 8 subsequently allows for many of the details concerning the actual implementation of these and other obligations to be negotiated between the warring parties.

46. Others also divide the Vietnam War into a United States/South Vietnam-North Vietnam conflict from 1965 to either 1973 or 1975, and a subsequent South Vietnam-North Vietnam conflict from either 1973 to 1975 or for 1975 only: see Downes 2008, 43; Reiter and Stam 2002, 39. For the purposes of prisoner abuse, this distinction is less relevant and is not adopted. Both North and South Vietnamese forces continued to hold prisoners from the 1965–73 period after the United States withdrew its armed forces. Separating the treatment of these earlier prisoners from those captured later is thus problematic. Moreover, the general policies of both the North and South Vietnamese sides did not change substantially during this time, which suggests that combining the two periods together presents a more appropriate picture of each state's overall treatment of the other side's enemy combatants.

47. Cases of prisoner treatment by two or more belligerents within the same conflict are likely to be related to one another in some fashion, which introduces concerns over dependence among the observations. The statistical analyses presented in subsequent chapters thus address dependence issues by a variety of means, including the clustering of standard errors according to the relevant war.

48. Springer 2010, 167–68.

49. Hastings 1987, 332.

50. Rowe 1993, 200; Springer 2010, 193.

51. MacKenzie 1995, 83. The case of Canada during the war is interesting, since at times Canadian authorities were willing to take more initiative vis-à-vis their British and later U.S. allies. However, looking at the total experience of Canada during the war, one notable military historian concluded "the government in Ottawa [Canada's capital] remained little more than a spectator to the formulation of Allied POW policy" (Vance 1995, 504).

52. Warmbrunn 1993, 45–48.

53. De Gaury 1966, 35; Wenner 1967, 145.

54. Hata 1996, 262–63.

55. On negative versus impossible cases for the purposes for both qualitative and quantitative analysis, see Mahoney and Goertz 2004, 654–57.

56. Walzer 2000, 306–9.

57. Etkind et al. 2012, 2.

58. P. Cohen 1997, 192; C. Martin 1968, 72; Springer 2010, 166–68.

59. Rachamimov 2002, 34.

60. The mixed success of the ICRC in gaining entry to camps across various wars is well documented in several of the organization's own official histories (Boissier 1985; A. Durand 1984).

61. Davies 1983, 238–39.

62. McCarthy 1918, 1.

63. Quoted in Burrows 2008, 185.

64. Page 1992, 6–11.

65. For example, Downes 2006; Valentino, Huth, and Balch-Lindsay 2004; Valentino, Huth, and Croco 2010. Other studies have chosen to use continuous measures alone or in combination with categorical outcomes, particularly for the number of civilians killed (Downes 2008; Eck and Hultman 2007; Eckhardt 1989; Valentino, Huth, and Croco 2006). The various data issues involved when confronting prisoner treatment generally prevent relying on similar measures. One of the only exceptions is a past study on the determinants of surrender (Reiter and Stam 1997). However, there are numerous critiques of the accuracy of continuous conflict measures, along with cautions regarding the likely presence of substantial biases (Lacina, Gleditsch, and Russett 2006; Peterman et al. 2011; Spagat et al. 2009).

66. This differs from the approach of Morrow and Jo (2006), which does not differentiate between specific types of prisoner violations. Their endeavor is also distinguished by its much greater scope, examining prisoner treatment along with compliance across many other areas, including civilians, cultural property, and war declarations. One consequence of this breadth, however, is that there are many more cases (almost 40 percent) where no specific measure for prisoner treatment is provided.

[210]

67. Downes 2008, 48; Morrow 2007, 564.

68. Even many proponents of events-level conflict data acknowledge their limits, in particular concerning issues of quality control and likely sources of biases (Eck 2012).

69. Beaumont 1996, 286.

70. Carnegie Endowment 1993, 215.

71. Gordon and Trainor 1995, 363.

72. Beaumont 1996, 287–88.

73. Hannikainen, Hanski, and Rosas 1992, 70; McCullagh 1912, 140, 172–73.

74. A. Barker 1975, 177. The official commentaries to the Geneva Conventions on Article 130 dealing with grave breaches discuss in greater detail the threat posed to prisoners from forcible conscription.

75. Kerr 1985, 264–65.

76. Cases were also independently coded by research assistants using the same set of sources; intercoder reliability revealed approximately 70 percent agreement in coding decisions, which is in line with similar studies. See, for instance, Morrow and Jo 2006, 101.

77. Alternatives included using the lowest value across the six component violations, the average value, the median value, or a binary measure for high-level abuses. A discussion of results using these alternative measures is available in supplementary online materials.

78. I was unable to code around 5 percent of the cases due to the lack of available information.

79. On selection biases and interpretive issues for coding based on historical texts, see Lustick 1996, 606; Thies 2002, 362; Trachtenberg 2006, 146–62.

80. De Waal 1991, 311; Kargil Review Committee 2000, 153.

81. McGrath 1975, 6–8.

82. There are even claims, though contested, that the prohibition against torture has attained the status of *jus cogens*, or a peremptory norm of international law from which no derogation is ever permitted (Rodley 2009, 64–81).

83. Tavernier 1992, 130–31.

84. For instance, if a captor engages in the summary execution of prisoners, then this counts as a denial of legal rights, in this case of a fair trial before punishment, and is coded accordingly.

85. Admittedly, the lines between forced military conscription and other forms of abuse can sometimes be blurred. The difference between forced and "voluntary" conscription is not always distinct, as occurred with English offers of better food and living conditions to revolutionary American prisoners in return for enlisting (Bowman 1976, 94). Likewise, many prisoners during the First World War were integrated into labor battalions located in the battle zone and under the direct command of the captor state's armed forces (H. Jones 2011, 127–29). I use the narrower definition for this form of abuse to only include instances where prisoners are forced to take up arms on behalf of the adversary.

86. MacKenzie 1994, 509.

87. Quoted in Hull 2014, 310.

88. Reiter and Stam 2002, 68.

89. Observations for a war are counted in the period when a conflict began. This choice was made to avoid counting twice any wars that happened to be fought across two separate time periods.

90. Liddell Hart 1946, 60–61; Pastor 1983, 113–17. For a more moderate view, see Rachamimov 2002, 67–69, 78–82.

91. Goldstein 2011; Pinker 2012.

2. The Captor's Dilemma

1. Historian John Keegan cautions that contemporary chroniclers likely exaggerated that French corpses were piled "higher than a man" but acknowledges that the "mounds thus raised were big and hideous enough to justify some priestly rhetoric" (1976, 106–7).

2. Burne 1956, 85–86.

3. J. Barker 2005, 289–92.

4. From William Shakespeare's *Henry V*, act 4, scene 7. Quoted in Walzer 2000, 18.

5. Curry 2000, 108–10. Though in a 2010 mock trial presided over by U.S. Supreme Court Justices Ruth Bader Ginsburg and Samuel Alito, among others, Henry V was found guilty for ordering the prisoner killings (A. Jones 2010).

6. The term "captor's dilemma" appears to have first come from Ferguson's work on the First World War (Ferguson 1999, 371). Ferguson primarily refers to the decision of individual soldiers in accepting or refusing the surrender of enemy troops, in contrast to the focus of this book on the decision making of higher government authorities.

7. Beaumont 1996, 287–88; Vance 2006, 129–30.

8. On the frequency of the killing of prisoners and hostages in the medieval period, see Prestwich 1999, 239.

9. Rayfield 2005, 409.

10. Arreguin-Toft 2003; Carr 2002, 11–12.

11. Excerpt from Article 1 of the Convention against Torture, available at http://www.hrweb.org/legal/cat.html.

12. Bellamy 2006, 123; Slater 2006, 193.

13. Green 2005, 34.

14. Biderman 1960, 140–41; Bowden 2003, 57. The scarcity of publically available studies on the effectiveness of torture is not entirely surprising, since governments are likely reluctant to publically admit to torturing research subjects. Furthermore, academic studies are equally unlikely, since "federal guidelines governing the treatment of human subjects almost certainly would prevent the gathering of empirical research comparing whether torture was more effective than less brutal means of gathering information" (Bell 2008, 356).

15. Lelyveld 2005, 40.

16. Quoted in Rejali 2007, 461.

17. Garrett 1981, 217–18.

[212]

18. MacKenzie 2012, 48.

19. Arrigo 2004, 564; Rejali 2007, 446, 480.

20. Davis 1977, 623, though Davis is careful to point out that prisoners can become a net burden on captor economies because of the resources required for their proper care. This drawback, among others, is dealt with in further detail below.

21. See, for instance, Articles 49 through 57 of the 1949 Third Geneva Convention.

22. MacKenzie 1994, 509.

23. Kerr 1985, 83–89.

24. Rachamimov 2002, 111–12.

25. Davis 1977, 626; Lewis and Mewha 1955, 199–200.

26. Rachamimov 2002, 111.

27. Bartov 1991, 44–45. The term *Hiwi* is an abbreviation for the German word *Hilf-swilliger*, meaning "voluntary assistant." Other estimates of the total number of Soviet prisoners forcibly enlisted range from a minimum of 250,000 to upwards of one million (Vance 2006, 460).

28. Walzer 2000, 134. Walzer discusses this reasoning in the context of rape during World War II and alludes to similar thinking by the legal scholar Vitoria with respect to plunder. However, the logic is also largely consistent with prisoner abuse.

29. Ferguson 2004, 158.

30. D. Cohen 2013, 463–66.

31. Rejali 2007, 524–25.

32. Phillips 2012, 132–33.

33. Bartov 1991, 82, 86–89; 2001, 115.

34. French 2004, 3.

35. Ignatieff 1997, 116–17.

36. Liivoja 2013, 158.

37. Keegan 1995, 11.

38. Robinson 2006, 6.

39. Hull 2005, 317–18.

40. Carr-Gregg 1978, 25; MacKenzie 1994, 514–15.

41. Ignatieff 1997, 117, though he goes on to note the importance of such codes for helping to delineate appropriate conduct, for "without them war is not war—it is no more than slaughter."

42. Davis 1977, 629.

43. Article 59 of the Lieber Code says, in part, "All prisoners of war are liable to the infliction of retaliatory measures." By the time of the 1949 Geneva Conventions such acts were generally no longer allowed under international law, with Article 13 of the Third Geneva Conventions plainly stating, "Measures of reprisal against prisoners of war are prohibited."

44. On the selected use of retaliation to foster longer-term cooperation, see Axelrod 1984, 20–21. In the international law literature, reciprocity, retaliation, and reprisals sometimes refer to distinct types of actions or intentions (Hull 2014, 277). Yet for the purposes here, these terms are used interchangeably to refer to violations taken in response to the enemy's wartime conduct.

45. Quoted in Ferguson 1999, 378.

46. Quoted in A. Durand 1984, 70.

47. H. Elliott 1995, 243.

48. Downes and McNabb Cochran 2010.

49. Quoted in Bartov 2001, 118.

50. Ferguson 2004, 149–52.

51. Grauer 2014.

52. Lerner 1981, 43; Shils and Janowitz 1948, 312–13.

53. Clausewitz 1984, 231–32.

54. Carr-Gregg 1989, 103.

55. Ashworth 1980, 46; Axelrod 1984, 73–74.

56. Tollefson 1946, 76–77.

57. Beevor 1998, 58–59.

58. MacKenzie 1994, 508–9.

59. T. Snyder 2010, 175.

60. Ferguson 2004, 171–88.

61. Blainey 1988, 57–60.

62. Beardsley 2011; Regan 2002; Walter 2001.

63. Barnett 2013, 7–8.

64. Finnemore 2004, 83–84; Prorok and Appel 2014.

65. Hafner-Burton 2009; Krain 2014a; Lebovic and Voeten 2009.

66. Hafner-Burton 2008; Maller 2010a; Murdie and Davis 2012.

67. For details of the Keitel judgment, see Avalon Project 2008.

68. Bass 2000, 284–310.

69. Finnemore 1996b.

70. Finnemore and Sikkink 1998, 902–4.

71. United Nations General Assembly 2005, Paragraph 139.

72. Bellamy 2009; Evans 2008.

73. Ki-moon 2009; United Nations Security Council 2006; Wills 2009.

74. This does not mean that condemnation of prisoner abuse does not take place, such as toward the United States in the War on Terror by NGOs like Human Rights Watch and Amnesty International, only that attention for prisoners is substantially lower with fewer consequences to the violator for their mistreatment.

75. Fein 1993, 99; Stohl 1987.

76. Herrmann and Shannon 2001.

77. Finnemore 1996a, 169–75.

78. Bellamy 2012, 31–41.

79. Hultman 2013; Lebovic and Voeten 2006.

80. Hultman 2010; Kathman and Wood 2011; Krain 2005; Shirkey 2012; Wood, Kathman, and Gent 2012. Though also see DeMeritt, forthcoming; Hultman, Kathman, and Shannon 2013.

81. On the ineffectiveness of economic sanctions against human rights violations, see Peksen 2009; Wood 2008. On some of the limits of naming and shaming in the context of ongoing episodes of mass killing, see DeMeritt 2012. For a slightly more optimistic view, see Krain 2012.

82. Krain 2014b; Maller 2010b.

83. Chayes and Chayes 1993, 185; Henkin 1979, 47.

84. Clausewitz 1984, 75.

85. Morgenthau 1985, 295; Waltz 1979, 104–5.

86. Mearsheimer 1994–95, 13; Morgenthau 1985, 295.

87. Aron 2003, 108.

88. Hull 2014, 318.

89. Morrow 2007, 569; 2014, 127–28, though the statistical significance for overall compliance toward prisoners varies depending on the exact model specification.

90. Valentino, Huth, and Croco 2006, 368.

91. Cardenas 2007, 12–13.

92. Leeds, Long, and Mitchell 2000, 687.

93. Schabas 2011, 16–22.

94. Fuller 1969, 46–80.

95. This legitimating function of legal rules has been applied to both domestic and international law (Franck 1990, 185; Tyler 1990, 19–27).

96. Finnemore and Sikkink 1998, 902–4.

97. Best 1994, 136.

98. Morrow 2014, 58–59, 87.

99. Morrow 2007, 560–61.

100. Quoted in Hull 2014, 3.

101. Hull 2014, 279–300.

102. Lyall and Wallace 2011.

103. Prorok and Appel 2014.

104. Guzman 2008, 59.

105. Hevia 2007, 106.

106. Bedjaoui 1992, 292.

107. Baudendistel 2006, 221.

108. Ober 1994, 12–14.

109. Farcau 1996, 61–63; Zook 1960, 101.

110. Jarman 1998, 242.

111. Huntington 1996, 47, 126.

112. Mercer 1995, 241–45.

113. Huntington 1993, 25.

114. Fazal and Greene, forthcoming.

115. Boot 2013, 200–201.

116. MacKenzie 1994, 509.

117. Henderson 1998, 475–76, though the results are not completely clear. Studying war onset from 1820 to 1989, he finds that religious similarity dampened conflict, while ethnic or linguistic ties actually heightened its likelihood. Other research similarly finds an opposite relationship, where cultural similarity enables rather than hinders the resort to violence (Gartzke and Gleditsch 2006).

118. Chiozza 2002, 726; Henderson and Tucker 2001, 328; Russett, Oneal, and Cox 2000, 595.

119. Downes 2006, 174; 2007b, 891; Valentino, Huth, and Croco 2006, 369–70.

120. Downes 2008, 26.

121. Beaumont 1996, 280.

122. Best 1980, 217–18.

123. A. Roberts 1994, 136. The broader civil war literature is more mixed on this point. Some scholars find civil wars based around ethnic or religious differences are longer, bloodier, and more difficult to settle than wars centering on socioeconomic or political issues (Kaufmann 1996, 139–43; Roeder 2003, 523). However, others find little support for ethnoreligious factors (Fearon and Laitin 2003).

124. Dower 1986, 9, 35, 48–52.

125. Rees 2001, 28.

126. Hata 1996, 257–62.

127. Coox 1985, 485.

128. Kinsella 2005, 183.

129. Beaumont 1996, 279.

130. A. Roberts 1993–94, 161; U.S. News and World Report 1992, 123, 143, 174.

131. Christensen 1996, 17.

132. Russett 1993, 30–42.

133. Downes 2008, 21; Valentino, Huth, and Croco 2006, 345–46.

134. Merom 2003, 15; Rummel 1995, 4. Rummel also offers an institutional explanation based on the number and scope of checks and balances that restrain democratic governments. However, he qualifies that institutional checks are reinforced by "the development of a democratic culture and norms that emphasizes rational debate, toleration, negotiation of differences, conciliation, and conflict resolution" (Rummel 1995, 4–5).

135. Engelhardt 1992, 53.

136. Valentino, Huth, and Balch-Lindsay 2004, 382.

137. Gabriel 1984, 8–9; Sarkesian 1989, 44. However, others note that some militaries have insulated themselves from their surrounding domestic society, lessening the influence of broader societal norms (Rosen 1995, 6).

138. Davenport and Armstrong 2004; Fein 1993; Harff 2003; Poe, Tate, and Keith 1999.

139. Dixon 1994, 16–18.

140. Weart 1998, 76–77, 90–92.

141. M. Doyle 1983, 344.

142. Locke (1690) 1980, 93.

143. Russett 1993, 33.

144. Huth and Allee 2002, 111, though their study focuses on relations between states over territorial disputes, making it unclear whether this willingness for retaliation on the part of democracies would carry over to abusing defenseless prisoners where liberal norms of individual rights are more clear-cut. Furthermore, even in the context of territorial disputes, Huth and Allee note that democratic norms still likely provide a brake against escalating to the worst levels of violence.

145. M. Doyle 1997, 292; Forsythe 1992, 393–94; Rosato 2003, 588–89.

146. Fein 1993, 83–84; McClintock 1992, 139.

147. Downes 2008, 23; Powers 2002, 508–11.

148. Reiter and Stam 2002, 151–58.

149. Rejali 2007, 46–47.

150. Davenport 2007b, 173–74.

151. Valentino 2004, 26–27, 237; Valentino, Huth, and Croco 2006, 368–69. Others acknowledge that the greater domestic concentrations of power associated with autocracies may have an impact on the propensity of these states to engage in mass murder but argue that these factors matter much less compared to the opportunities provided by broader contextual events, such as war or decolonization (Krain 1997, 346).

152. Bennett and Stam 1998; Bueno de Mesquita and Siverson 1995; Morgan and Campbell 1991. While democratic leaders may be at a higher risk of losing office, others contend that the more salient question concerns the costs of losing office and whether an ousted leader will face death or similar punishments. These costs pose much greater dangers for autocratic leaders and consequently may make them more sensitive to war outcomes (Chiozza and Goemans 2004; Goemans 2000b, 38–49). More recent work takes a middle ground centered on other attributes affecting the prospects for punishment, such as the extent of a leader's perceived culpability, though even here democratic leaders are found to be much more vulnerable overall to poor wartime outcomes (Croco 2011, 473).

153. Gartner and Segura 1998; Mueller 1973, 60–65. Though for one notable critique, see Gelpi, Feaver, and Reifler 2009, 221–22.

154. These two components are commonly referred to as the selection and warfighting effects (Reiter and Stam 2002, 11).

155. Bueno de Mesquita et al. 2004, 374. Though see Reiter and Stam 2002, 135–36.

156. Valentino, Huth, and Croco 2006, 348.

157. Downes 2007b, 889. Downes finds these enabling effects are strongest in wars of attrition where the pressures to win and minimize costs are likely most salient, though these and related effects for regime type depend on the particular measure used for civilian fatalities (2008, 64–77).

158. Downes 2008, 21–22; Valentino, Huth, and Croco 2006, 345–49.

159. Reiter and Stam 2002, 164–65; Siverson 1995, 481.

160. Democracies could perhaps also be more susceptible to some of the costs from third parties resulting from prisoner abuse that were discussed in the earlier cost-benefit analysis. However, these external pressures are likely less consequential compared to those associated with reciprocity or battlefield dynamics. There is generally much greater disagreement over how much democracies value and are influenced by external pressures compared to other regime types. See, for instance, Gartzke and Gleditsch 2004; Hafner-Burton 2008; Simmons 2000.

[217]

161. McCarthy 1918, 3.

162. Moore 2000, 183. See chapter 4 for a more detailed examination of this case.

163. Levi 1997, 33–35, 205–8.

164. Gilbert 1994, 333–34.

165. C. Powell (2002) 2005, 123.

166. M. Elliott 1981, 192.

167. Bailey 1981, 123.

168. Quoted in Walzer 2000, 136.

169. Holmes 1985, 382.

170. Reiter and Stam 1997, 11–13. This points to a potential complementarity between institutional and normative explanations for wartime conduct. The democratic political culture of individual rights and nonviolence appears to go a long way in shaping the beliefs of enemy soldiers—they see democracies treating their own citizens well and expect they will act the same toward prisoners of war. However, the important point to note is that the motives underlying the decision making of democratic captors is driven more by institutional incentives of capitalizing upon the strategic benefits of good conduct rather than out of any inherent normative commitments.

171. Shils and Janowitz 1948, 313.

172. Committee on Military Affairs 1945, 13. This does not necessarily mean that such promises led individual soldiers to internalize these democratic norms themselves. On the mixed results of subsequent reeducation campaigns to inculcate German prisoners with democratic principles and beliefs, see Robin 1995, 162.

173. Grauer 2014. In an in-depth study of the First World War, Grauer also points to several fascinating ebbs and flows in prisoner taking, as well as variation in surrender rates to allied captors like Britain and France. Rather than focusing on unit-level factors like democracy, Grauer develops a self-preservation theory of surrender, which contends that soldiers take cues from battlefield dynamics when deciding whether to lay down their arms and are especially sensitive to expectations of proper treatment by captors and beliefs over their length of time in captivity. While differing in emphasis in certain respects, ultimately Grauer's argument and the one developed here on democracy should be viewed as complementary. In particular, in a further analysis of broad surrender rates across twentieth-century interstate wars, Grauer finds strong support for the role of both expectations of good treatment and length of captivity. Yet both of these factors are likely closely related to regime type, as democracies have stronger reasons to treat their captives humanely and have also been found to win their wars more quickly, reducing the likely length of prisoners' time in captivity (Bennett and Stam 1996, 253).

174. Reiter and Stam 2002, 67.

175. Lerner 1981, 213.

176. Rowe 1993, 197.

177. Beaumont 1996, 288.

178. Downes 2007b, 876–77.

179. Downes 2008, 23; Valentino 2004, 27–28.

180. Valentino, Huth, and Croco 2010.

181. The Kosovo War is often credited as a shining example of how air power can do it alone in winning wars (Stigler 2002, 125). Critics counter that ground forces played a crucial role in bringing about Serbia's surrender in the form of surrogate forces from the Kosovo Liberation Army (KLA), as well as the importance of the U.S.-led NATO's threat to initiate a ground invasion (Thomas 2006, 17).

182. H. Jones 2011, 164–69; A. Kramer 2007, 63–64.

183. Pape 1996, 12–13.

184. Blainey 1988, 159–61; Goemans 2000b, 3–12; Wittman 1979, 744–49.

185. Reiter 2003, 30–31; Slantchev 2003, 127–28.

186. Pape 1996, 13.

187. Human Rights Watch 2003, 61; Weeramantry 2005.

188. Ober 1994, 18.

189. In the language of the coercion literature, targeting the capabilities of the adversary refers to a denial strategy, while the previous discussion on weakening the enemy's resolve concerns a strategy of punishment (Pape 1996, 13).

190. Blainey 1988, 65–66; Reiter 2003, 31.

191. Diehl and Goertz 2000, 64.

192. For instance, Article 118 of the Third Geneva Convention of 1949 states that "Prisoners of war shall be released and repatriated without delay after the cessation of active hostilities."

193. Bugnion 2003, 101–2.

194. Horowitz and Reiter 2001, 160.

195. Pape 1996, 21–26.

196. Downes and McNabb Cochran 2010, 27; Johnson 2009, 112; Lyall 2009, 336–38.

197. Downes 2008, 38–39.

198. Bartov 2001, 4.

199. H. Jones 2011, 52.

200. Holsti 1991, 12–20.

201. Huth 1996, 6; Vasquez 1993, 124.

202. Midlarsky 2011, 70–72.

203. Downes 2008, 35–36; Valentino, Huth, and Croco 2006, 356.

204. Stachura 2004, 132–33.

205. Kalvoda 1983, 231–33.

206. A. Durand 1984, 123–24.

207. Friedman 2002, 18–20.

208. Fulcher of Chartres 1969, 122.

209. Fried 1914, 4.

210. Hall 2000, 136.

211. Quoted in Browning 2007, 220–21.

212. For discussions of some of the main differences in the nature of territorial conflicts, see Fazal 2007; Goddard 2009; Hassner 2009; Huth 1996.

213. Ferguson 2004, 188–91.

[219]

214. Buzan 2002, 90; Walzer 2000, 132.

215. Edelstein 2004, 50–51.

216. O'Donnell and Schmitter 1986, 39–40.

217. Cordesman 2008, 48–50; R. Doyle 2010, 314.

3. PRISONERS BY THE NUMBERS

1. For one of the main critiques of war as an accident, see Blainey 1988, 141.

2. On the dangers of biases resulting from poor case selection, see Geddes 1990. Collier and Mahoney (1996) offer a middle ground acknowledging some of these selection concerns but still stressing the benefits of this type of methodological approach.

3. Using a dichotomous measure, a country is considered a democracy if it scores a 7 or higher on the Polity index (Marshall, Jaggers, and Gurr 2010).

4. Kendall's Tau-b statistic is used to test for the strength of association between each pair of variables because the prisoner abuse measure is ordinal (Agresti 2007, 60).

5. All calculations performed in Stata 12 using the CLARIFY software package (Tomz, Wittenberg, and King 2003).

6. The percent change is calculated by dividing the absolute change in probability by the initial probability for each variable.

7. Downes 2006; Valentino, Huth, and Croco 2006.

8. Downes 2007b; Harff 2003; Valentino, Huth, and Balch-Lindsay 2004; Valentino, Huth, and Croco 2006.

9. A related concern is that democracies may try to keep their hands clean by transferring prisoners to other countries, especially autocratic ones, who can then carry out more brutal tasks such as employing torture. Allegations of such extraordinary renditions have been made against the United States, which sent suspected militants to partner countries known for engaging in egregious human rights abuses (Mayer 2005). However, the coding scheme for prisoner abuse developed here follows international legal principles, whereby the original captor state continues to bear a great deal of responsibility for the proper treatment of prisoners even after transferring them to a third party. See, for instance, Article 12 of the Third Geneva Convention of 1949.

10. There is some debate over the precise obligations of a party to more recent treaties when the opponent has not also committed to the relevant laws of war. In particular, see Article 2 of the Third Geneva Convention of 1949 and accompanying Commentaries.

11. The full statistical results for these and other supplementary analyses are available in an online appendix accompanying the book.

12. In a related study on compliance across a wider range of issues, Morrow (2007, 567; 2014, 174) finds that joint ratification has significant effects, especially when interacted with the opponent's level of abuse. However, when limited to only prisoner treatment these findings no longer hold in Morrow's own data, nor are they apparent with the alternative prisoner-specific measure used here.

13. Evaluating the effects for the prospects of third-party coercion on the wartime conduct of belligerents is based on measures developed by Prorok and Appel 2014.

[220]

They argue that because of the attachment of democracies to the rule of law and respect for human rights, outside democratic states have a greater willingness to impose costs on belligerents committing violations. Democracies, in turn, will have more levers to influence wartime conduct the greater the extent of a belligerent's relations with democratic governments in military or economic affairs, or common ties in intergovernmental organizations (IGOs). Prorok and Appel create three separate measures for the degree of democratic influence on a given country within each relevant sphere—the proportion of total capabilities possessed by democratic members in alliance networks, IGO networks, and the proportion of total trade involving democratic partners in economic networks. These network variables are then interacted with a dichotomous indicator for the status of international law in the conflict (which equals 1 for joint ratification within each warring-directed-dyad for wars starting in 1899 through 1948, or unilateral ratification by captor states for wars starting after 1948, and 0 otherwise), instead of the three ratification variables used in the main models presented earlier. In their study Prorok and Appel find that external democratic influence in each network has a strong constraining effect on the number of civilians killed by belligerents when international law is in force. Yet when looking at the treatment of enemy combatants, none of the network variables has a significant impact on prisoner abuse under any circumstances.

14. Downes (2008, 51–55) finds that civilians are instead less likely to be victimized in wars taking place after 1945 using the Second World War and the attendant horrors visited upon noncombatants as the turning point. However, he also shows that postwar norms do not significantly alter the conduct of belligerents when using alternative outcomes, such as the incidence of mass killing or the actual number of civilians killed during war.

15. Downes 2008, 51; Valentino, Huth, and Croco 2006, 373.

16. Axelrod 1984, 73–87; MacKenzie 1994, 491.

17. Downes 2007b; Valentino, Huth, and Balch-Lindsay 2004; Valentino, Huth, and Croco 2006.

18. One commonly cited implication of accounts focusing on political culture is that newer democracies may conduct themselves in more violent and unrestrained ways than older democracies (Huth and Allee 2002, 112; Russett 1993, 34). While domestic political institutions can change rapidly, younger democracies may have a less engrained political culture committed to nonviolence and individual rights compared to more mature democratic regimes. To test for this possibility, a country is considered a new democracy once it achieves a score of 7 or higher on the Polity index until it either drops below this threshold or stays at or above this level for at least ten years (Goodliffe and Hawkins 2006, 362; Huth and Allee 2002, 120). An alternative indicator for the strength of democratic norms is a count of the number of years in the preceding twenty-year period that the country achieved a Polity score of 7 or higher (Huth and Allee 2002, 117–19). Analysis reveals no statistically significant differences between newer and older democracies in their treatment of prisoners. Furthermore, when limited only to democratic belligerents, the number of prior years a captor was democratic also was not statistically significant. The relative strength of a democracy's political culture thus does not appear to figure prominently in its overall treatment of prisoners.

19. Cross-tabulations are reported here because the estimation of multiple regression models is complicated by the generally smaller sample sizes and the perfect correlation between several of the explanatory variables and certain of the more specific

prisoner treatment outcomes. Nevertheless, results remain substantially the same when estimated using fully specified regression models for each type of conduct.

20. The pattern remains the same when including all capable captors, irrespective of the level of abuse.

21. De Zayas 1989, 151; Y. Durand 1987, 25.

22. Since in these instances the outcome and explanatory variables are both dichotomous, Pearson's chi-square is instead used to assess whether the relationship is statistically significant.

23. Merom 2003, 21; Rummel 1994, 22–23.

24. Russett 1993, 33.

25. Huth and Allee 2002, 107–12.

26. First violators are excluded since, by definition, they cannot simultaneously be in a position to retaliate against an initial abuse.

27. M. Doyle 1983, 323–25.

28. Rosato 2003, 588–89.

29. The potential strategic advantages coming out of prisoner treatment are partly a function of the adversary's conduct as well. This is based on the balance of soldiers from each side who would prefer to surrender rather than continue fighting, as well as the prisoner policies put in place by each side. If a democracy chooses to engage in prisoner abuse, but the adversary commits proportionally higher levels of violence, then the democratic belligerent could still gain some advantages. These benefits would certainly be less than if it committed little or no abuse at all, since it would still have a harder time convincing enemy soldiers to surrender. But the democracy would likely be assured that even fewer of its own soldiers would lay down their arms because of the even higher level of violence committed by the adversary.

30. The conditional relationship between regime type and wars of attrition may in fact largely account for the overall observed finding that democracies are more likely to target civilians (Downes 2006, 176; 2008, 51).

31. Ferguson 2004.

32. Reiter and Stam 2002, 151–52; Rosato 2003, 588–89.

33. On the impact of democracy on territorial conflicts, see Huth and Allee 2002. For an alternative account that reverses the causal arrow to instead investigate the impact of territorial disputes on a country's long-run democratic prospects, see Gibler 2012.

34. Gutman, Rieff, and Dworkin 2007, 40–41; Morris 2008, 405.

35. Borowiec 2000, 75–76; Lindley 1997, 21–22.

36. Gaubatz 1996; L. Martin 2000. Though for more critical or nuanced positions on the relationship between democracy and international law, see Busch 2000; Dai 2006.

37. Slaughter 1995, 532–33.

38. Lipson 2003, 81; McGillivray and Smith 2000.

39. Morrow 2007, 561. The international law results should also be treated with some caution since the factors initially leading states to ratify a treaty (such as democracy) may also influence their subsequent behavior, which can make isolating the causal effects of international legal forces extremely difficult (Simmons 2010, 290; von Stein 2005, 611–12).

40. There are also some parallel, though less consistent, effects in research on the targeting of civilians (Downes 2008, 66–68).

41. H. Smith 2005.

42. Bueno de Mesquita and Siverson 1995.

43. Reiter and Stam 2002, 10–11. Though for a critique, see Downes 2009.

44. Though these findings are equally problematic, if not more so, for variants stressing the importance of democratic political culture, where democratic targets are expected to differ little from autocracies (Huth and Allee 2002, 111).

45. Collier, Brady, and Seawright 2010, 184–88.

4. WORLD WAR II, DEMOCRACIES, AND THE (MIS)TREATMENT OF PRISONERS

Sauerbrei epigraph: Quoted in Bailey 1981, 156.

1. Quoted in Krammer 2008, 40. Other favorable accounts include R. Cook 2006, 15; Koop 1988, 116; A. Thompson 2010, 134.

2. This is in line with what Ronald Bailey (1981, 156) called the "pragmatic lenience" exhibited by U.S. and British prisoner policies during the war.

3. For a discussion of some of the varying estimates on the death toll from the Second World War, see Clodfelter 2008, 560–61.

4. Forster 1986. The percentage of prisoner deaths across autocracies was based on the average death rates for the autocratic captors (Germany, Japan, and the Soviet Union) from table 4.1, which were then weighted by the total number of prisoners taken.

5. Vourkoutiotis 2003, 189–91.

6. An excerpt from the order makes clear the tension between the legal rights of commando prisoners under international treaties and the contempt for them held by the German leadership: "From now on all enemies on so-called Commando missions in Europe or Africa challenged by German troops, even if they are to all appearances soldiers in uniform or demolition troops, whether armed or unarmed, in battle or in flight, are to be slaughtered to the last man. . . . Even if these individuals, when found, should apparently be prepared to give themselves up, no pardon is to be granted to them on principle." Quoted in Solis 2010, 261.

7. Weingartner 1979, 97–99.

8. Article 50 of the 1929 Geneva Convention only permitted disciplinary punishment against escaped prisoners who were subsequently captured before succeeding in rejoining their own armed forces.

9. Ross and Romanus 2004, 530.

10. Calculations based on figures from table 16 in Ross and Romanus 2004, 530. Food resources for prisoners in fact dwarfed those for U.S. allies by a ratio of almost 5:1.

11. Krammer 1979, xv.

12. Dower 1986, 61–73; Weingartner 1992, 55.

13. The frequency and severity of violations does indeed appear to have been greater in the case of U.S. conduct on the Pacific front in comparison to western Europe. This

was most likely in part a function of reciprocity, since much higher levels of abuse were committed by Japanese forces against U.S. prisoners than by the German Wehrmacht. As the war continued U.S. practices in the Pacific generally trended toward relatively better treatment of Japanese prisoners, which cautions against ascribing U.S. policy purely to racial motives. This case is discussed in greater detail further below.

14. A. Powell 1989, 223–25.

15. Bartov 1991, 83.

16. One potential objection to this line of reasoning is that domestic norms may have been so deeply engrained and accepted that democratic leaders would not actually have openly discussed them all that much. According to this alternative view, such norms would have been taken for granted as unspoken common knowledge. While acknowledging this possibility, the weight of the evidence, especially once taking into account patterns in the substantive behavior rather than simply the statements of the democratic belligerents, suggests otherwise. This point will be returned to later in the case study analysis.

17. Committee on Military Affairs 1945, 4.

18. Porter 1945, 4.

19. Porter 1945, 4.

20. Committee on Military Affairs 1945, 15.

21. *Newsweek* 1945b, 58; Wittels 1945, 18.

22. Keefer 1992, 69. It should be noted that prisoner labor is entirely legal under international humanitarian law, so long as the work does not pose serious risks to the prisoner's health and safety, is not directly related to the war effort, and workers are adequately compensated. For specific labor provisions prevailing during the Second World War, see Articles 27 through 34 from the 1929 Geneva Convention.

23. Committee on Military Affairs 1944, 5–30.

24. Vance 1995, 490–93. The estimates of letters for or against retaliation refer to those received by the Canadian prime minister Mackenzie King, though Vance argues that other allies, including U.S. and British leaders, felt similar pressures from their publics over the treatment of Axis prisoners.

25. Moravcsik 1998, 80–83. On the application of hard sources to such historical work, see Lieshout, Segers, and van der Vleuten 2004.

26. Moore 2000, 183.

27. Quoted in Gilbert 1993, 242–43.

28. Note from Churchill to General Ismay, May 2, 1940 (Gilbert 1993, 1185). Using prisoners to protect targets from military attack contravened Article 9 of the 1929 Geneva Convention.

29. Moore 2000, 183.

30. Ferguson 2004, 153 n.14.

31. Personal minute from Churchill to Anthony Eden, British foreign secretary, July 30, 1944. Quoted in Moore 2000, 190.

32. It should be noted that many Axis prisoners were transferred to camps in countries allied to Britain, such as Canada, Australia, and New Zealand. However, these countries were in a similar position to Britain in that they were also democracies

who had their own troops in combat, meaning they were likely to exhibit a similar sensitivity to the risks of retaliation should they have chosen to abuse Axis prisoners. Moreover, all three largely followed the lead of their larger British ally and Commonwealth patron (Vance 1995), and thus were deemed not to possess an independent prisoner policy for the purposes of this study.

33. A. Durand 1984, 540; A. Roberts 1994, 132–33.

34. Moore 2000, 186.

35. Keefer 1992, 17–18.

36. Moore 2000, 187–94.

37. Moore 2000, 189.

38. Bower 1981, 82–83; A. A. Durand 1988, 300–301.

39. *Newsweek* 1945a, 21.

40. Letter from Churchill to Roosevelt, March 22, 1945 (Loewenheim, Langley, and Jonas 1975, 681–82).

41. Excerpt from original text of telegram from Churchill to Roosevelt, dated March 22, 1945. Quoted in Kimball 1984, 582.

42. MacKenzie 1994, 495–96.

43. Reiter and Stam 2002, 165; Valentino, Huth, and Croco 2010, 530.

44. Margulies 1945, 478.

45. Committee on Military Affairs 1945, 19.

46. Committee on Military Affairs 1945, 3.

47. Lerner 1981, 43.

48. Lerner 1981, 44. The surrender response was the second most favored choice among the list of options offered to the question, "How would you describe the mission of Sykewar [i.e., PWD] in Europe during World War II." The most popular option was "To *weaken* enemy will-to-resist" (emphasis in original). However, the choices were clearly not mutually exclusive, since inducing surrender is in many ways a corollary to weakening enemy resistance. In light of the fact that a range of sometimes overlapping response options was offered, the widespread support for the role of surrender suggests it played a prominent role in PWD members' beliefs regarding their division's planning and operations.

49. PWD/SHAEF 1945, 159.

50. Lerner 1981, 184. Of course, surveys of captured German soldiers need to be considered with some caution, since prisoners may simply want to give responses their captors prefer to hear. A further danger is that a sample limited solely to German prisoners may provide a biased picture, since those most likely or amenable to picking up and reading an Allied leaflet may also be more likely to be influenced by the message and subsequently have chosen to surrender.

51. Lerner 1981, 186–87.

52. Lerner 1981, 306–7.

53. Interestingly, the original design was loosely based on Soviet combat leaflets. Given the brutality of Russian treatment of enemy prisoners during the Second World War, the Russian message was consequently much less effective, though Russian propaganda did become more sophisticated over the course of the war (Ferguson 2004, 191 n.193).

[225]

54. Margolin 1946, 50.

55. Committee on Military Affairs 1945, 13.

56. The Western Allies combined held around thirty-five thousand German POWs by the end of the second quarter of 1944, but this would rise to over two hundred thousand by the end of the third quarter of the same year and to almost five million by the second quarter of 1945, the time of the war's termination. Prisoner figures are from Overmans 1992, 145.

57. United States Strategic Bombing Survey 1976.

58. Smith, Lasswell, and Casey 1946, 133.

59. Gilmore 1998, 148.

60. Shils and Janowitz 1948, 302.

61. Committee on Military Affairs 1945, 13.

62. Bartov 1991, 172; Shils and Janowitz 1948, 307–8.

63. Bischof and Ambrose 1992b, 5.

64. Estimates at the close of hostilities in Europe were 7.8 million prisoners held by the Western allies compared to around 2 million for the Soviet Union (Wyman 1989, 17).

65. Committee on Military Affairs 1945, 3.

66. Dower 1986, 11–12.

67. Vance 2006, 464.

68. MacKenzie 1994, 516; Vance 2006, 462.

69. Benedict 1946, 38.

70. Quoted in Carr-Gregg 1978, 25.

71. At the end of 1942 there were around 1,200 Japanese prisoners in Allied captivity, while near the end of the war that number only increased to a little over 12,000 POWs. Figures come from Gilmore 1998, 155.

72. Hata 1996, 269.

73. Gilmore 1995, 200; Hata 1996, 269.

74. Based on personal correspondence from MacArthur to the commanding general of Alamo Force, May 14, 1944 (Gilmore 1995, 198).

75. Gilmore 1995, 198–99.

76. More direct incentives to encourage U.S. soldiers to capture rather than kill Japanese soldiers included the promise of ice cream and three days' extra leave if a soldier brought in a prisoner alive (Bourke 1999, 172–73).

77. Mann 2004, 55–69.

78. Bacque 1990, 2. Bacque saw the crimes as so ghastly that in a later interview he said that Americans "should take down every statue of Eisenhower and every photograph of him and annul his memory from American history as best they can, except to say, 'Here was a man who did very evil things that we're ashamed of.'" Quoted in Bischof and Ambrose 1992b, 20.

79. Bischof and Ambrose 1992a; MacKenzie 1992; Rummel 1998, 203–4.

80. Cowdrey 1992, 92.

81. Ferguson 2004, 186–88.

82. R. Doyle 2010, 230–31.

83. Even detractors of Bacque's most outlandish claims acknowledge that Allied conduct toward German prisoners at the end of war became increasingly abusive (Ambrose 1991).

84. R. Cook 2006, 15–16.

85. MacKenzie 1994, 503.

86. ICRC 1948, 539–40.

87. Bailey 1981, 165.

88. Beaumont 1996, 282.

89. Gansberg 1977, 136.

90. However, neither the United States nor Great Britain were simply bystanders who acquiesced to the demands of a vindictive French ally. For instance, the British War Office created the Combined Services Detailed Interrogation Centre (CSDIC), which administered a secret prison in occupied Germany that involved the interrogation and torture of former members of the Nazi Party and SS (Cobain 2005).

91. ICRC 1948, 334.

92. Moore 1996, 32.

93. MacKenzie 1994, 502.

94. Quoted in Committee on Military Affairs 1945, 3.

95. Lewis and Mewha 1955, 100.

96. Specific numbers of prisoners in the United States proper are based on statistics from Krammer 1979, 271–72.

97. Keefer 1992, 103; Porter 1945, 4.

98. Proudfoot 1957, 169.

99. Bartov 1991, 44–45; Vance 2006, 460.

100. Proudfoot 1957, 152.

101. Ginsburgs 1957, 360.

102. Dallin and Nicolaevsky 1947, 282.

103. Quoted in M. Elliott 1981, 192.

104. Epstein 1973, 21, 30.

105. Epstein 1973, 15.

106. The full title for the arrangement was *Agreement Relating to Prisoners of War and Civilians Liberated by Forces under Soviet Command and Forces Operating under United States of America Command; February 11, 1945.*

107. Solzhenitsyn 1974, 85 n.45.

108. The entire text of the agreement is available at Avalon Project 2008.

109. M. Elliott 1973, 262.

110. Tolstoy 1977, 51–52.

111. Quoted in Sanders, Sauter, and Kirkwood 1992, 34.

112. Epstein 1973, 33–34.

113. Quoted in Epstein 1973, 38.

114. M. Elliott 1973, 269.

115. Proudfoot 1957, 211.

116. Sanders, Sauter, and Kirkwood 1992, 34.

117. Wyman 1989, 64.

118. Quoted in Epstein 1973, 78. NKVD refers to the acronym used for the Soviet secret police, Narodnyy Komissariat Vnutrennikh Del.

119. Epstein 1973, 81.

120. M. Elliott 1981, 193. Of Russian soldiers and civilians repatriated, only around 15–20 percent were allowed to return to their previous homes. The vast majority received punishments including execution, sentences in labor camps, or exile to frontier regions like Siberia. Based on figures from Tolstoy 1977, 408–9.

121. Quoted in Epstein 1973, 1.

122. R. Doyle 2010, 227; Werth 1999, 230.

123. Sword 1995, 325; Wyman 1989, 63.

124. M. Elliott 1973, 264.

125. Sword 1995, 323.

126. Sword 1995, 325.

127. M. Elliott 1973, 266.

128. Personal correspondence from Churchill to Roosevelt, March 16, 1945 (Loewenheim, Langley, and Jonas 1975, 675–76).

129. Personal correspondence from Roosevelt to Churchill, March 3, 1945 (Kimball 1984, 542).

130. Quote from secret telegram from Churchill to Stalin, March 21, 1945 (Gilbert 1986, 1259).

131. Gilbert 1986, 1159, 1204–5; MacKenzie 1994, 512 n.98.

132. Quote from secret telegram from Stettinius to Grew, February 9, 1945 (Epstein 1973, 45).

133. Betthel 1974, 68.

134. Wyman 1989, 64.

135. Deane 1947, 187.

136. Vance 2006, 223.

137. M. Elliott 1973, 265.

138. R. Doyle 2010, 227–28.

139. Pape 1996, 271–72.

140. Searle 2002.

141. Some civilian and military officials did express moral reservations over bombing civilians, but this was a minority view within the democratic leaderships (Downes 2008, 137–39).

142. Roosevelt 1937.

143. Quoted in Dower 1986, 38.

144. In his work on civilian victimization, Downes (2007b, 876–77) makes an institutional argument that democracies are actually more likely to victimize civilians as they become increasingly desperate to shorten the war and reduce costs. However, Morrow (2007, 570) counters that for many of the cases involving democracies reciprocity provides just as good an explanation, given the opponent had often either already targeted civilians itself or was unable to do so.

[228]

145. Downes 2008, 142–43.

146. This is consistent with the notion of "symmetrical performance," where wartime conduct and compliance in one area has often largely been divorced from others and dealt with by belligerents on its own terms (R. Posner 2002, S324). On the presence of such "firewalls" for compliance across different issue areas, see also Morrow 2014, 80–81.

147. Vance 2006, 186.

148. Vourkoutiotis 2003, 29–31, 186.

149. MacKenzie 1994, 494–95.

150. The Japanese eventually made a clear distinction between Allied pilots and regular soldiers; the former were classified as "captured enemy flyers" rather than prisoners of war and their abuses were usually even more unbearable (Roland 1996, 157).

151. Biddle 2002, 107.

152. Douhet 1983, 9–10. U.S. and British air doctrine initially differed, with the United States placing more emphasis on military targets, but eventually converged toward indiscriminate bombing over the course of the war (Downes 2012, 81–82).

153. Dower 1986, 40–41.

154. Downes 2008, 139–40; Searle 2002, 104.

155. Keown-Boyd 1991, 116.

156. C. Martin 1968, 72.

157. P. Cohen 1997, 189.

158. Keown-Boyd 1991, 115–16.

159. C. Martin 1968, 145; Vance 2006, 51.

160. P. Cohen 1997, 192.

161. C. Martin 1968, 72.

162. P. Cohen 1997, 182.

163. Downes 2008, 60.

164. Bourke 1999, 167; Forsythe 2005, 76.

165. Beaumont 1996, 285.

166. Asprey 2002, 910–11.

167. Moyar 1997, 87–107; Vance 2006, 422.

168. Hall 2000, 136–37.

169. Reiter and Stam 2002, 158.

170. Carnegie Endowment 1993, 148.

5. Territorial Conquest and the Katyn Massacre in Perspective

1. M. Kramer 2012, 572.

2. On memory and the Katyn massacre, see Etkind et al. 2012.

3. Quoted in Kulish and Barry 2010.

[229]

4. From the entry of April 9, 1943 (Goebbels 1948, 318).

5. Etkind et al. 2012, 5.

6. TASS Communiqué on Katyn, April 13, 1990, quoted in Cienciala, Lebedeva, and Materski 2007, 345.

7. Courtois 1999, 2–4; Rummel 1994, 15; Valentino 2004, 91.

8. Liberman 1995, 4–5, 13–14.

9. Downes 2008, 178–83.

10. Zeidner 2005, 108.

11. See, for example, Articles 23 and 27 of the 1929 Geneva Convention, or Articles 44, 49, and 60 from the later Third Geneva Convention of 1949.

12. Beaumont 1983, 74–75.

13. Rachamimov 2002, 55, 98.

14. On the frequency of territorial changes, see Goertz and Diehl 1992, 33–54.

15. Fazal 2007, 101–2.

16. Piotrowski 1998, 304–5.

17. These and other towns and locations are often referred to by different names in Russian, Polish, and Ukrainian. To facilitate the following discussion, Russian names are used unless noted otherwise.

18. Davies 1982a, 408–11.

19. Sanford 2005, 7.

20. Quoted in Davies 1982b, 393–94.

21. Treaty of Nonaggression between Germany and the Union of Soviet Socialist Republics, August 23, 1939, Moscow. Available at Avalon Project 2008.

22. Keegan 1990, 43.

23. Secret Additional Protocol to the Treaty of Nonaggression between Germany and the Soviet Union, August 23, 1939, Moscow. Available at Avalon Project 2008. The secret protocol also contained Soviet claims over the Baltic states and Bessarabia, which will be discussed in greater detail when considering Soviet conduct in other cases where it sought to annex neighboring territories.

24. Zaslavsky 2008, 10–11.

25. Sanford 2005, 21.

26. Clodfelter 2008, 465. Other estimates of Polish battle deaths during the war are in the range of between three thousand and seven thousand killed (Sanford 2005, 23).

27. German-Soviet Boundary and Friendship Treaty, September 28, 1939, Moscow. Available at Avalon Project 2008.

28. Piotrowski 1998, 9.

29. Siemaszko 1991, 230.

30. Polish Ministry of Information 1941, 9.

31. Secret Supplementary Protocol to the German-Soviet Treaty on Friendship and the Border between the USSR and Germany [Establishing Cooperation against Polish Resistance], September 28, 1939, Moscow. Excerpt quoted in Cienciala, Lebedeva, and Materski 2007, 61–62.

32. Sanford 2005, 29–31.

33. Gross 1991, 45–46; Szawlowski 1991, 30.

34. Sanford 2005, 23.

35. Piesakowski 1990, 38–39; Zawodny 1962, 131.

36. Piesakowski 1990, 39; Vance 2006, 222.

37. Rossino 2003, 179.

38. Figures from Sanford 2005, 22.

39. Zaslavsky 2008, 13.

40. Cienciala, Lebedeva, and Materski 2007, 62–63.

41. ICRC 1948, 407–8.

42. Gross 1991, 46.

43. Malcher 1993, 7. Decree of the Presidium of the Supreme Council of the USSR concerning the acquisition of citizenship of the USSR by the inhabitants of the Western districts of the Ukraine and Byelorussia (General Sikorski Historical Institute 1961, 92).

44. Malcher 1993, 7–9.

45. Cienciala, Lebedeva, and Materski 2007, 138–39; Gross 2002, 193–94.

46. Conquest 1978, 218–19.

47. This estimate is based on the widely cited upper figure of 1.5 million persons deported to the Soviet Union out of a total prewar population in Soviet-held Poland of around 13.4 million (Cienciala, Lebedeva, and Materski 2007, 138–39; Sanford 2005, 23).

48. Dallin and Nicolaevsky 1947, 264. Available figures specifically for other ranks of Polish forces captured by the Soviet Union during the war suggest a slightly higher, though comparable, death rate of around 29 percent excluding the Katyn victims (Werth 1999, 209).

49. The occupying force was essentially trying to bring about the entire removal of undesirable elements in a matter of months, a process that had taken a decade in Soviet Russia proper (Dallin and Nicolaevsky 1947, 263).

50. FitzGibbon 1971, 179.

51. Cienciala, Lebedeva, and Materski 2007, 141.

52. Overy 1997, 77.

53. Politburo Decision on Placing POW Reception Points under NKVD Protection (Excerpt), September 18, 1939, Moscow (Cienciala, Lebedeva, and Materski 2007, 48–49).

54. Prisoners of war are supposed to be under the control of the captor's government and subject to the regulations of the captor's armed forces. See, for example, Articles 4 and 8 of the 1899 Hague Convention, and Articles 2, 43, and 45 of the 1929 Geneva Convention. The NKVD would go on to play a prominent role in the case of not only Polish prisoners, but also later Axis captives who were often held for years after the war in labor camps inside the Soviet Union and other occupied areas (Naimark 1995, 376–78).

55. Applebaum 2003, 94.

56. See Secret Order of the USSR People's Commissar of Internal Affairs, September 19, 1939, No. 0309, Moscow (Cienciala, Lebedeva, and Materski 2007, 49). The

acronym UPV is commonly used to refer to the department in many scholarly writings and refers to the Russian name, Upravlenie po Delam Voennoplennykh.

57. Gross 1991, 46.

58. Cienciala, Lebedeva, and Materski 2007, 28; Sanford 2005, 44.

59. Malcher 1993, 24. See, in particular, Top Secret Report on Prisoners of War Received, Dispatched, and Remaining in NKVD Camps, November 19, 1939, Moscow (Cienciala, Lebedeva, and Materski 2007, 81).

60. Cienciala, Lebedeva, and Materski 2007, 29–30.

61. Sanford 2005, 54.

62. Vance 2006, 221.

63. Malcher 1993, 24.

64. G. Roberts 2006, 170.

65. Malcher 1993, 25.

66. Stachura 2004, 131.

67. Piesakowski 1990, 142.

68. Cienciala, Lebedeva, and Materski 2007, 141.

69. Sanford 2005, 64.

70. Beria Memorandum to Joseph Stalin No. 794/B, March 5, 1940, Moscow (Cienciala, Lebedeva, and Materski 2007, 118–20). Indicative of how the business of the politburo could move from the exceptional to the mundane, minutes from the meeting indicate the next item on the agenda concerned preparations for a new sarcophagus at the Kremlin mausoleum for Lenin's body (Sanford 2005, 713–81).

71. Sanford 2005, 76.

72. Sanford 2005, 112–14.

73. For a fuller discussion on estimates of the number of prisoner killed, see Cienciala, Lebedeva, and Materski 2007, 122–36.

74. Beria Order No. 00350, March 22, 1940, Moscow (Cienciala, Lebedeva, and Materski 2007, 154–56).

75. According to the March 5, 1940, Beria memorandum, the various prisons held a larger number of inmates, 18,632, but only around 11,000 of them were identified as Polish (Cienciala, Lebedeva, and Materski 2007, 136).

76. Uncertainty over the deaths from the other NKVD prisons has been compounded by the lack of cooperation from contemporary Belarusian governments, where around half of the killings took place, in and around Minsk. By contrast, recent Ukrainian governments have been more forthcoming, but even in that case the full details may not fully come to light (Sanford 2005, 109–11).

77. Piesakowski 1990, 157.

78. Malcher 1993, 23.

79. Vance 2006, 222.

80. Sanford 2005, 52; Zawodny 1962, 22.

81. Quoted in Cienciala, Lebedeva, and Materski 2007, 118.

82. Cienciala, Lebedeva, and Materski 2007, 120.

83. Sanford 2005, 24.

84. Bor-Komorowski 1951, 140. For an overview of the composition of the Home Army, see Walker 2008, 58–59.

85. Stachura 2004, 132–35.

86. Paczkowski 1999, 368.

87. Report by Grigory Korytov to the Head of the Special Department of Kalinin Oblast NKVD, Vasily Pavlov, no later than March 4, 1940, Ostashkov (Cienciala, Lebedeva, and Materski 2007, 117).

88. Hannikainen, Hanski, and Rosas 1992, 85.

89. Hannikainen, Hanski, and Rosas 1992, 79.

90. Gilbert 1989, 42. It should be noted, however, that Britain and France also had ulterior motives in sending an expedition to Finland. The operation could also be used as a pretext to occupy Norway at the same time, thereby withholding valuable ore deposits from Nazi Germany (Calvocoressi, Wint, and Pritchard 1989, 118). Despite Allied efforts, Germany would eventually succeed in occupying all of Norway later that same spring.

91. Cienciala, Lebedeva, and Materski 2007, 147.

92. Cienciala, Lebedeva, and Materski 2007, 147.

93. Zawodny 1962, 105–6.

94. Zawodny 1962, 132.

95. T. Snyder 2010, 140.

96. Protocol no. 13, Decision of the Politburo: Decision on Guarding the State Borders of the UkSSR and BSSR, March 2, 1940, Moscow (Cienciala, Lebedeva, and Materski 2007, 114–15).

97. Cienciala, Lebedeva, and Materski 2007, 121, 137–38.

98. Sanford 2005, 27.

99. Cienciala, Lebedeva, and Materski 2007, 142. The slightly lower death rates for inmates from the various NKVD prisons may have reflected a smaller number of similar elite military officers and security officials compared to the composition of the three special camps. Yet even in these instances, the death rates were far in excess of those in the general prisoner or civilian populations, suggesting these captives were largely viewed by the Soviets as threatening elements that needed to be eliminated.

100. As an example of the last category, even one general, Jerzy Wołkowicki, managed to survive the Katyn massacre. Wołkowicki surmises that the NKVD favored him because of his experience in the Tsarist Russian Navy during the 1904–5 Russo-Japanese War when he was the only officer who opposed surrendering his ship during the Battle of Tsushima. He believes this single event is what made the difference in saving him, while the other Polish generals were executed (Zawodny 1962, 143–45).

101. There is also a supposition that a few prisoners were spared as a result of Germany's attack against Belgium, France, and the Netherlands starting on May 10 in the midst of the Soviet prisoner killings (Cienciala, Lebedeva, and Materski 2007, 122–23). The westward offensive appears to have taken the Soviet Union by surprise, as it was only notified that same day by Germany's ambassador Friedrich Werner Graf von der Schulenburg. While Starobelsk was reportedly fully emptied

by May 10, the last transport leaving Kozelsk on May 12 did not end up going to the Katyn Forest, suggesting these prisoners may have survived because of Soviet hesitation and concerns over the events unfolding in the west. The problem with this argument is that Ostashkov prisoners continued being sent to their deaths in Kalinin (Tver) as late as May 19, and the last May 10 batch of Starobelsk prisoners would likely have been killed several days later in Kharkov once word of the German military maneuvers had already spread. This suggests the initial developments in western Europe were not crucial to Soviet authorities regarding this series of executions. However, as will be discussed in greater detail below, the solidifying Nazi threat would rapidly come to play an important role in shaping subsequent Soviet treatment of Polish prisoners under its control.

102. Zawodny 1962, 148.

103. Sanford 2005, 83.

104. Weinberg 1994, 107.

105. Earlier, in November 1939, the Soviet Union came to an agreement with the Lithuanian government to allow members of the Polish armed forces interned in Lithuania to voluntarily reenter Soviet-controlled territory if they so desired. While regular enlistees would be sent home, Soviet authorities explicitly kept secret that officers and high-ranking security officials would be separated and detained. See SNK Resolution on the Admission to the USSR of Polish Military Personnel Interned in Lithuania, November 9, 1939, Moscow (Cienciala, Lebedeva, and Materski 2007, 79–80). This means that at least some of those who voluntarily returned might have later become victims of the Katyn massacre, though it is unknown precisely how many Polish soldiers left Lithuania during the period leading up to the Soviet takeover of the Baltic states.

106. Mearsheimer 2001, 196–97.

107. On the general perceived costs and benefits of buffer states, see Partem 1983; Schroeder 1994, 670–91.

108. Fazal 2007, 38–42.

109. Weinberg 1994, 53–58.

110. Keegan 1990, 175–80. On the wider historiography of Soviet decision making in the lead-up to the German invasion, see Petrov 1968, 1–30.

111. Quoted in Erickson 1991, 22.

112. Cienciala, Lebedeva, and Materski 2007, 147–48.

113. Quoted from No. 47/13b Top Secret TsK VKP (b), Note from Beria to Stalin on the Possible Organization of Military Units with Polish and Czech Prisoners of War, November 2, 1940, Moscow (Cienciala, Lebedeva, and Materski 2007, 276–78).

114. Diehl and Goertz 2000, 57–65.

115. Jervis 1976, 266–81.

116. Paul 1991, 49.

117. Cienciala, Lebedeva, and Materski 2007, 142.

118. Sanford 2005, 8.

119. Associated Press 2010.

120. State Archives in Poland 2004.

121. Davies 1983, 3; Ferguson 1999, 394.

122. Klein, Goertz, and Diehl 2006. Further details on the construction of this variable, as well as the subsequent measures, are provided in the appendix.

123. W. Thompson 2001. Thompson codes Soviet Russia and Poland as rivals during this period, while Goertz and Diehl view the two countries as only involved in an isolated conflict.

124. Weinberg 1994, 107.

125. Kochanski 2012, 85.

126. Datner 1962, 10, 21–22. In words reminiscent of the feelings expressed by the Soviet leadership, Adolf Hitler ordered German forces to kill and commit atrocities "without pity or mercy [against] all men, women, and children of Polish descent or language. Only in this way can we obtain the living space we need." Quoted in Lukas 1986, 3.

127. Piotrowski 1998, 29; T. Snyder 2010, 221.

128. Homze 1967, 36; Kamenetsky 1961, 135, 160–61.

129. Cienciala, Lebedeva, and Materski 2007, 61–62.

130. Gross 1979, 47; Lukas 1986, 9.

131. See the discussion in Sanford 2005, 29–31.

132. Quoted from conversation between Churchill and Polish General Władysław Anders, August 22, 1942 (General Sikorski Historical Institute 1961, 422).

133. Sterio 2012, 620.

134. Quoted in Lowe 2012.

135. For instance, a select congressional committee held a number of hearings on the massacre between 1951 and 1952. For key excerpts from the transcripts, see Lauck 1988.

136. Bellamy 2012, 223–25; Dallin and Breslauer 1970, 5–6. For a review of the literature on communist regimes and violence, see Valentino 2004, 91–100, though Valentino develops a more fine-grained typology that distinguishes radical communist regimes from those that for a variety of reasons are less likely to engage in mass killing (2004, 142–49).

137. Fein 1993, 92–93; Poe and Tate 1994, 858.

138. Morrow 2001, 978. This suggests, however, that the Soviet Union would treat officers and other ranks similarly rather than targeting the former as occurred in the case of Poland. Furthermore, the Soviet Union was still a party to the 1899 and 1907 Hague Conventions, which required the proper treatment of prisoners irrespective of rank and clearly disallowed the type of actions perpetrated during the Katyn massacre.

139. Beaumont 1996, 286.

140. R. Miller 1975, 65, 287.

141. Since all communist regimes were autocracies, the effect of communism was compared to other nondemocratic regimes, while all other variables were held constant at their means in a similar manner to the original quantitative results. A more complete discussion of the various communist measures is presented in the appendix.

142. Hagenloh 2009, 8; Naimark 2010, 126–30.

143. Cienciala, Lebedeva, and Materski 2007, 345.

144. Zaslavsky 2008, 4–5.

145. Excerpt from T. A. Taracouzio, *The Soviet Union and International Law*, quoted in Zawodny 1962, 129.

146. Zawodny 1962, 145.

147. Cienciala, Lebedeva, and Materski 2007, 142; Davies 1982b, 452.

148. A. Weeks 2002, 53.

149. In the secret protocol of August 23, 1939, Finland is also included in the list of the Baltic states, but as will be discussed in greater detail below, Soviet aims on this country would ultimately be much more modest. In the protocol, Lithuania is initially listed as falling under the German sphere, but the Soviet Union would eventually annex this country as part of the later secret protocol of September 28, 1939. For the texts of both protocols, see Cienciala, Lebedeva, and Materski 2007, 41, 61.

150. G. Roberts 2006, 43–44; Wettig 2008, 20.

151. Pons 2002, 201.

152. G. Roberts 2006, 56.

153. G. Roberts 2006, 45.

154. Montefiore 2004, 334. As with many Stalinist atrocities, the exact number of victims is difficult to know with certainty. For other figures, see Dunsdorfs 1975, 22; Gorodetsky 1999, 301. Despite differences in the estimates, there is little doubt that thousands were executed during the Soviet takeover.

155. Wettig 2008, 21.

156. Conquest 1986, 219.

157. The area possessed greater historical ties to the earlier Austro-Hungarian Empire rather than Tsarist Russia.

158. Dallin and Nicolaevsky 1947, 263–65; A. Weeks 2002, 71.

159. G. Roberts 2006, 56.

160. In addition to being a major population center, Leningrad and its surroundings accounted for between 30 percent and 35 percent of the entire Soviet defense industry (G. Roberts 2006, 52).

161. Calvocoressi, Wint, and Pritchard 1989, 115.

162. Quoted in G. Roberts 2006, 48.

163. Hannikainen, Hanski, and Rosas 1992, 85–87.

164. Overy 1997, 76; Vance 2006, 460.

165. Bartov 2001, 124.

166. Clubb 1971, 263.

167. Patrikeeff 2002, 85–87.

168. Japanese conduct was generally worse at Changkufeng, while actually at a much lower level at Nomonhan with Soviet prisoners treated in a fairly decent manner (Calvocoressi, Wint, and Pritchard 1989, 889; Coox 1985, 485; Kikuoka 1988, 26). When compared to the more systematic and brutal treatment of prisoners in later wars of conquest against China and in southeast Asia, the extent of territorial ambitions also appeared to play an important role in Japanese conduct.

169. Coox 1977, 345–46; 1985, 403. The Soviets' relatively restrained conduct toward prisoners in these wars also does not provide much support for an alternative account based on rivalry, since at the time both countries were heated rivals.

Conclusion

1. Hultman 2007; Valentino, Huth, and Croco 2006.

2. Lacina, Gleditsch, and Russett 2006. Though on how improvements in military medicine have lowered battle deaths and, in turn, question the alleged dramatic decline in warfare, see Fazal 2014.

3. Sarkees, Wayman, and Singer 2003, 65.

4. As a rough test, the relationship between the war of attrition measure and the start year of a conflict is negative, though fairly modest, with a correlation coefficient of only around −0.11.

5. Clodfelter 2008, 596–97; Weeramantry 2005, 468.

6. Downes 2008, 60.

7. Downes 2007a; Valentino, Huth, and Balch-Lindsay 2004.

8. Beaumont 1996, 285.

9. Biersteker 2002, 163–66; Ruggie 1993, 148–49.

10. Brooks 1999, 655–63.

11. Kahler 2006, 2–3.

12. Huth and Allee 2002, 27–28.

13. Similar to the severity of the fighting, the correlation between wars of territorial annexation and the start year of the conflict is also negative but fairly small (r = −0.05).

14. Clinton 1996, 22–23. For a more measured view, see Russett 1993, 135.

15. Reiter and Stam 2002, 65–69.

16. Goemans 2000a; Lai and Slater 2006; Peceny, Beer, and Sanchez-Terry 2002.

17. J. Weeks 2008.

18. In a novel approach, Jessica Weeks (2012) uses these two dimensions to create a fourfold typology of dictatorships. Elite-constrained leaders facing a civilian audience count as "Machines," such as many one-party states like North Vietnam. Leaders accountable to a military audience are instead "Juntas," typified by many Latin American dictatorships during the Cold War. Unconstrained personalist leaders are instead classified according to their own background, with civilian leaders like Joseph Stalin viewed as "Bosses" and former high-ranking military commanders like Spain's Francisco Franco as "Strongmen." Weeks also creates a residual "Other nondemocracy" category for those dictatorships that do not neatly fit within this typology, such as monarchies or theocracies.

19. J. Weeks 2012; 2014.

20. I thank Jessica Weeks for sharing data on regime type for the main autocratic belligerents during interstate wars covering the years 1929 to the present. Full results are available in accompanying online appendices.

21. Simmons and Danner 2010; Wallace 2012.

22. Though an intriguing wrinkle is that the concern, some say bordering on an "obsession," by democracies like the United States over POW issues may lead them to act in other destabilizing ways. While limiting prisoner abuses, these sensitivities can still encourage democracies to attempt risky rescue operations or prolong military conflicts in ways that can put even more of their soldiers in danger (Tierney 2010, 138–44).

[237]

23. Davenport 2007b, 8–9.

24. Pearlstein 2006, 253.

25. Rejali 2007, 4, 553–56.

26. Rodley 2009, 402–7.

27. Downes 2008, 257; Kono 2006.

28. Davenport 2007a, 18.

29. Mueller 1990; Sarkees and Wayman 2010, 563–65.

30. Sarkees and Wayman 2010, 563.

31. Metzger 1962, 283.

32. Bowman 1976, 104.

33. Quoted in Burrows 2008, 36.

34. Metzger 1962, 153–54.

35. Utley and Washburn 2002, 198, 207.

36. Linn 1989, 79.

37. Vance 2006, 255.

38. Reiter and Stam 2002, 151–52.

39. Though as a middle ground, AP I Article 1 broadens the purview beyond conventional interstate conflicts to include "fighting against colonial domination and alien occupation and against racist régimes in the exercise of their right of self-determination."

40. For instance, distinct provisions are made in AP II for medical personnel (Articles 9–12) and the civilian population (Articles 13–14, 17), but no section deals specifically with prisoner issues. This does not mean that none of the provisions are relevant for the treatment of prisoners, but these protections fall under more general proscriptions (e.g., Articles 4–8). By contrast, AP I devotes an entire section of the agreement to prisoners of war (Articles 43–47), and several other articles touch upon prisoner issues.

41. Though there have been several promising attempts by international organizations to work with rebel groups and other nonstate actors to encourage adherence to humanitarian principles in wartime (K. Gleditsch et al. 2011; Jo and Thomson 2014).

42. Beevor 2006, 405–6; Preston 2007, 305–8.

43. Barnard 2012.

44. Killion 1998, 347–48.

45. Haigh 1995, 12–20; Lee 2011, 91–93.

46. Vance 2006, 119, 443.

47. Though few prisoners would be shown mercy during or after the battle (Weir 1995, 283).

48. Human Rights Council 2014, 2; Sengupta 2014.

49. Ignatieff 1997, 34–39.

50. Davenport 2007b, 168–74.

51. Carlton 1994, 174.

52. Lee 2011, 93.

53. Killion 1998, 347–48.

54. Meet the Press 2001.

55. Stout 2002.

56. Amnesty International 2004, 23.

57. Forsythe 2005, 133.

58. Several large compendia of leaked and officially released government records on detainee issues have been compiled: Danner 2004; Greenberg and Dratel 2005.

59. Gonzales 2002, 2.

60. Gonzales 2002, 3.

61. C. Powell (2002) 2005, 123.

62. Shane 2009, A14.

63. Yoo 2006, viii.

64. Shane and Savage 2011.

65. Rodriguez 2012, xiii.

66. Hosenball 2012.

67. Fontenot, Degen, and Tohn 2005, 419.

68. Hafner-Burton and Shapiro 2010, 416–17.

69. Huddy et al. 2005; Merolla and Zechmeister 2009, 86.

70. Gronke et al. 2010; Wallace 2013.

71. Desch 2010.

72. Greenwald 2012.

73. Bumiller 2009, A1. There are particular concerns over the methodology used in the report and resulting skepticism over the actual danger posed by released terror suspects.

74. Rodley 2009, 460–81.

75. Savage 2011; 2013.

76. Shane 2013.

77. Mazzetti 2013, 216–20.

78. Walzer 2000, 129–33.

Appendix

1. Sarkees and Wayman 2010.

2. The only exceptions are for denial of legal rights, which is a dichotomous measure where 1 equals medium levels of abuse, since this violation on its own does not necessarily exert the same violence upon the bodies and minds of prisoners compared to the other components; and forced military conscription, which is also treated as a dichotomous measure but any violations are automatically valued as high-level abuses because prisoners are put directly back into the line of fire.

3. Marshall, Jaggers, and Gurr 2010.

4. Gleditsch and Ward 1997; Munck and Verkuilen 2002; Treier and Jackman 2008.

5. Downes 2008, 58–59; Russett 1993, 76; Valentino, Huth, and Croco 2006, 361.

6. Downes 2008, 59–60.

7. Abdelal et al. 2006.

8. Henderson and Tucker 2001; Huntington 1993.

9. This is one reason the mean for the prisoner abuse by the opponent measure across the entire set of observations used in the main analysis is slightly lower than that for the prisoner abuse dependent variable focusing on capable captors.

10. Bueno de Mesquita 1981, 103–8; Singer, Bremer, and Stuckey 1972.

11. The main source was the ICRC International Humanitarian Law Treaties and Documents database, available at https://www.icrc.org/applic/ihl/ihl.nsf/. Ratification decisions for countries that no longer exist came from Schindler and Toman 2004.

12. A. Roberts 1994, 122.

13. An alternative measure uses the 1977 Additional Protocol I (AP I) as the relevant international agreement for wars beginning during or after 1977, but results remain substantially the same.

14. Brambor, Clark, and Golder 2006, 66.

15. Jones, Bremer, and Singer 1996.

16. Klein, Goertz, and Diehl 2006, 335–40. Earlier work distinguished between proto- and enduring rivalries, but these are collapsed together in the more recent version. For a comparison to earlier measures, see Diehl and Goertz 2000, 29–48.

17. W. Thompson 2001, 562–68.

18. Jervis 1976, 266–71.

19. The twenty-five-year period, which is equal to approximately one generation, is similar to that used in Reiter and Meek 1999.

20. Downes 2009; Reiter and Stam 2002, 38–57.

21. Many noncapable captors did not end up fighting later wars against the same adversary. One exception involves both China and Taiwan during each of their two wars in the 1950s, though neither was included in the main analysis, which is limited to capable captors. The only relevant observation concerns China in the Second Sino-Japanese War of 1931–33, but the results remain substantially the same if this episode is recoded accordingly.

22. Karnai 1992, 6–7. Countries' histories were drawn from the Library of Congress, available at http://memory.loc.gov/frd/cs/.

23. Other possible starting years for Stalin's rule as unquestionable leader of the Soviet Union could include 1924 after the death of Lenin, or perhaps 1927 when he finally succeeded in expelling some of his main opponents, such as Leon Trotsky, from the Central Committee. The precise choice of start date for Stalin's rule does not matter much for the purposes of the analysis, since the Soviet Union was not involved in any interstate wars during the years 1922–27.

24. The only significant change is for deterrence, which switches sign when including noncapable captors. However, this turnaround in many ways makes sense because noncapable captors score 0 on prisoner abuse, but are also coded 0 for the deterrence variable, which leads to prisoner abuse being much less likely to occur in situations where deterrence does not prevail.

25. Bayer and Bernhardt 2010; Downes 2008, 64–66.

26. M. Doyle 1997, 261–64; Vanhanen 2000.

27. Both the number of battle deaths a state suffered and the duration of the war in days were logged to reduce skewness. Data on battle deaths came from several sources: Clodfelter 2008; Downes 2008; Sarkees and Wayman 2010.

28. Liddell Hart 1946, 60–61.

29. For instance, in some of the alternative versions of prisoner abuse, the statistical significance of cultural differences improves though the results are not consistent.

30. Brambor, Clark, and Golder 2006, 73–74.

References

Abdelal, Rawi, Yoshiko M. Herrera, Alastair Iain Johnston, and Rose McDermott. 2006. "Identity as a Variable." *Perspectives on Politics* 4 (4): 695–711.

Agresti, Alan. 2007. *An Introduction to Categorical Data Analysis*. Hoboken, NJ: Wiley InterScience.

Ambrose, Stephen E. 1991. "Ike and the Disappearing Atrocities." *New York Times*, February 24. http://www.nytimes.com/books/98/11/22/specials/ambrose-atrocities.html.

Amnesty International. 2004. "USA: Human Dignity Denied: Torture and Accountability in the 'War on Terror.'" http://www.amnesty.org/en/library/info/AMR51/145/2004.

Applebaum, Anne. 2003. *Gulag: A History*. New York: Doubleday.

Aron, Raymond. 2003. *Peace and War: A Theory of International Relations*. New Brunswick, NJ: Transaction Publishers.

Arreguin-Toft, Ivan. 2001. "How the Weak Win Wars: A Theory of Asymmetric Conflict." *International Security* 26 (1): 93–128.

———. 2003. "The [F]utility of Barbarism: Assessing the Impact of the Systematic Harm of Non-Combatants in War." Annual Meeting of the American Political Science Association, Philadelphia, August 27–31.

Arrigo, Jean Maria. 2004. "A Utilitarian Argument against Torture Interrogation of Terrorists." *Science and Engineering Ethics* 10 (3): 543–72.

Ashworth, Tony. 1980. *Trench Warfare, 1914–1918: The Live and Let Live System*. New York: Holmes and Meier.

Asprey, Robert B. 2002. *War in the Shadows: The Guerrilla in History*. Lincoln, NE: iUniverse.

Associated Press. 2010. "Gesture to Poland on Katyn Massacre: Vladimir Putin Says Stalin Executed POWs Out of Revenge." April 7. http://www.cleveland.com/world/index.ssf/2010/04/katyn_massacre_gesture_to_pola.html.

Avalon Project. 2008. Lillian Goldman Law Library. Yale Law School. http://avalon.law.yale.edu/default.asp.

Axelrod, Robert. 1984. *The Evolution of Cooperation*. New York: Basic Books.

Bacque, James. 1990. *Other Losses: An Investigation into the Mass Deaths of German Prisoners at the Hands of the French and Americans after World War II*. London: Macdonald.

Bailey, Ronald H. 1981. *Prisoners of War*. Alexandria, VA: Time-Life Books.

Balcells, Laia. 2010. "Rivalry and Revenge: Violence against Civilians in Conventional Civil Wars." *International Studies Quarterly* 54 (2): 291–313.

[243]

Barker, A. J. 1975. *Prisoners of War*. New York: Universe Books.

Barker, Juliet. 2005. *Agincourt: Henry V and the Battle that Made England*. New York: Little, Brown.

Barnard, Anne. 2012. "Missteps by Rebels Erode Their Support among Syrians." *New York Times*, November 8. http://www.nytimes.com/2012/11/09/world/middleeast/in-syria-missteps-by-rebels-erode-their-support.html?smid=pl-share.

Barnett, Michael. 2013. *Empire of Humanity: A History of Humanitarianism*. Ithaca, NY: Cornell University Press.

Barton, Carlin A. 1993. *The Sorrows of the Ancient Romans: The Gladiator and the Monster*. Princeton, NJ: Princeton University Press.

Bartov, Omer. 1991. *Hitler's Army: Soldiers, Nazis, and War in the Third Reich*. New York: Oxford University Press.

———. 2001. *The Eastern Front, 1941–1945: German Troops and the Barbarisation of Warfare*. 2nd ed. Oxford: Palgrave.

Bass, Gary Jonathan. 2000. *Stay the Hand of Vengeance: The Politics of War Crimes Tribunals*. Princeton, NJ: Princeton University Press.

Baudendistel, Rainer. 2006. *Between Bombs and Good Intentions: The Red Cross and the Italo-Ethiopian War, 1935–1936*. New York: Berghahn Books.

Bayer, Resat, and Michael Bernhardt. 2010. "The Operationalization of Democracy and the Strength of the Democratic Peace: A Test of the Relative Utility of Scalar and Dichotomous Measures." *Conflict Management and Peace Science* 27 (1): 85–101.

Beardsley, Kyle. 2011. *The Mediation Dilemma*. Ithaca, NY: Cornell University Press.

Beaumont, Joan. 1983. "Rank, Privilege and Prisoners of War." *War and Society* 1 (1): 67–94.

———. 1996. "Protecting Prisoners of War, 1939–1995." In *Prisoners of War and Their Captors in World War II*, edited by Bob Moore and Kent Fedorowich, 277–97. Oxford: Berg.

Becker, Jo, and Scott Shane. 2012. "Secret 'Kill List' Proves a Test of Obama's Principles and Will." *New York Times*, May 29. http://www.nytimes.com/2012/05/29/world/obamas-leadership-in-war-on-al-qaeda.html?smid=pl-share.

Bedjaoui, Mohammed. 1992. "The Gulf War of 1980–1988 and the Islamic Conception of International Law." In *The Gulf War of 1980–1988: The Iran-Iraq War in International Legal Perspective*, edited by Ige F. Dekker and Harry H. G. Post, 277–99. Dordrecht: Martinus Nijhoff.

Beevor, Antony. 1998. *Stalingrad*. New York: Viking Press.

———. 2006. *The Battle for Spain: The Spanish Civil War, 1936–1939*. London: Penguin.

Bell, Jeannine. 2008. " 'Behind This Mortal Bone': The (In)effectiveness of Torture." *Indiana Law Journal* 83 (1): 339–61.

Bellamy, Alex J. 2006. "No Pain, No Gain? Torture and Ethics in the War on Terror." *International Affairs* 82 (1): 121–48.

———. 2009. *Responsibility to Protect: The Global Effort to End Mass Atrocities*. Cambridge: Polity Press.

———. 2012. *Massacres and Morality: Mass Atrocities in an Age of Civilian Immunity*. Oxford: Oxford University Press.

Benedict, Ruth. 1946. *The Chrysanthemum and the Sword: Patterns of Japanese Culture*. Boston: Houghton Mifflin.

Bennett, D. Scott, and Alan C. Stam. 1996. "The Duration of Interstate Wars." *American Political Science Review* 90 (2): 239–57.

References

————. 1998. "The Declining Advantages of Democracy: A Combined Model of War Outcomes and Duration." *Journal of Conflict Resolution* 42 (3): 344–66.

Best, Geoffrey. 1980. *Humanity in Warfare: The Modern History of the International Law of Armed Conflicts*. New York: Columbia University Press.

————. 1994. *War and Law since 1945*. Oxford: Clarendon Press.

Betthel, Nicholas. 1974. *The Last Secret: The Delivery to Stalin of over Two Million Russians by Britain and the United States*. New York: Basic Books.

Biddle, Tami D. 2002. *Rhetoric and Reality in Air Warfare: The Evolution of British and American Ideas about Strategic Bombing, 1914–1945*. Princeton, NJ: Princeton University Press.

Biderman, Albert D. 1960. "Social-Psychological Needs and 'Involuntary' Behavior as Illustrated by Compliance in Interrogation." *Sociometry* 23 (2): 120–47.

Biersteker, Thomas J. 2002. "State, Sovereignty and Territory." In *Handbook of International Relations*, edited by Walter Carlsnaes, Thomas Risse, and Beth A. Simmons, 157–76. London: Sage.

Bischof, Günter, and Stephen E. Ambrose, eds. 1992a. *Eisenhower and the German POWs: Facts against Falsehood*. Baton Rouge: Louisiana State University Press.

————. 1992b. "Introduction." In *Eisenhower and the German POWs: Facts against Falsehood*, edited by Günter Bischof and Stephen E. Ambrose, 1–25. Baton Rouge: Louisiana State University Press.

Blainey, Geoffrey. 1988. *The Causes of War*. New York: Free Press.

Bloom, Mia. 2005. *Dying to Kill: The Allure of Suicide Terror*. New York: Columbia University Press.

Boissier, Pierre. 1985. *History of the International Committee of the Red Cross*. Vol. 1, *From Solferino to Tsushima*. Geneva: Henry Dunant Institute.

Boot, Max. 2013. *Invisible Armies: An Epic History of Guerrilla Warfare from Ancient Times to the Present*. New York: Liveright.

Bor-Komorowski, Tadeusz. 1951. *The Secret Army*. New York: Macmillan.

Borowiec, Andrew. 2000. *Cyprus: A Troubled Island*. London: Praeger.

Bourke, Joanna. 1999. *An Intimate History of Killing: Face-To-Face Killing in Twentieth-Century Warfare*. New York: Basic Books.

Bowden, Mark. 2003. "The Dark Art of Interrogation." *Atlantic Monthly* 292 (3): 51–76.

Bower, Tom. 1981. *Blind Eye to Murder: Britain, America and the Purging of Nazi Germany—A Pledge Betrayed*. London: Andre Deutsch.

Bowman, Larry G. 1976. *Captive Americans: Prisoners during the American Revolution*. Athens: Ohio University Press.

Brambor, Thomas, William R. Clark, and Matt Golder. 2006. "Understanding Interaction Models: Improving Empirical Analyses." *Political Analysis* 14 (1): 63–82.

Bravin, Jess. 2013. *The Terror Courts: Rough Justice at Guantanamo Bay*. New Haven, CT: Yale University Press.

Britt, Thomas W., Carl A. Castro, and Amy B. Adler. 2006. *Military Life: The Psychology of Serving in Peace and Combat*. Vol. 2, *Operational Stress*. Westport, CT: Praeger Security International.

Brooks, Stephen G. 1999. "The Globalization of Production and the Changing Benefits of Conquest." *Journal of Conflict Resolution* 43 (5): 646–70.

Browning, Christopher R. 2007. *The Origins of the Final Solution: The Evolution of Nazi Jewish Policy, September 1939–March 1942*. Lincoln: University of Nebraska Press.

Bueno de Mesquita, Bruce. 1981. *The War Trap*. New Haven, CT: Yale University Press.

Bueno de Mesquita, Bruce, James D. Morrow, Randolph M. Siverson, and Alastair Smith. 2004. "Testing Novel Implications from the Selectorate Theory of War." *World Politics* 56 (3): 363–88.

Bueno de Mesquita, Bruce, and Randolph M. Siverson. 1995. "War and the Survival of Political Leaders: A Comparative Study of Regime Types and Political Accountability." *American Political Science Review* 89 (4): 791–808.

Bugnion, François. 2003. *The International Commitee of the Red Cross and the Protection of War Victims.* Oxford: Macmillan.

Bumiller, Elisabeth. 2009. "Later Terror Link Cited for 1 in 7 Freed Detainees." *New York Times*, May 21. http://www.nytimes.com/2009/05/21/us/politics/21gitmo.html.

Burk, James. 1999. "Public Support for Peacekeeping in Lebanon and Somalia: Assessing the Casualties Hypothesis." *Political Science Quarterly* 114 (1): 53–78.

Burne, Alfred H. 1956. *The Agincourt War: A Military History of the Latter Part of the Hundred Years War from 1369 to 1453.* Fair Lawn, NJ: Essential Books.

Burrows, Edwin G. 2008. *Forgotten Patriots: The Untold Story of American Prisoners during the Revolutionary War.* New York: Basic Books.

Busch, Marc L. 2000. "Democracy, Consultation, and the Paneling of Disputes under GATT." *Journal of Conflict Resolution* 44 (4): 425–46.

Buzan, Barry. 2002. "Who May We Bomb?" In *Worlds in Collision: Terror and the Future of the Global Order*, edited by Ken Booth and Tim Dunne, 85–94. New York: Palgrave Macmillan.

Calvocoressi, Peter, Guy Wint, and John Pritchard. 1989. *Total War: The Causes and Courses of the Second World War.* New York: Pantheon Books.

Cardenas, Sonia. 2007. *Conflict and Compliance: State Responses to International Human Rights Pressure.* Philadelphia: University of Pennsylvania Press.

Carlson, Lewis H. 1998. *We Were Each Other's Prisoners: An Oral History of World War II American and German Prisoners of War.* New York: Basic Books.

Carlton, Charles. 1994. *Going to the Wars: The Experience of the British Civil Wars, 1638–1651.* New York: Routledge.

Carnegie Endowment. 1993. *The Other Balkan Wars: A 1913 Carnegie Endowment Inquiry in Retrospect.* Washington, DC: Carnegie Endowment for International Peace.

Carr, Caleb. 2002. *The Lessons of Terror: A History of Warfare against Civilians; Why It Has Always Failed, and Why It Will Fail Again.* New York: Random House.

Carr-Gregg, Charlotte. 1978. *Japanese Prisoners of War in Revolt: The Outbreaks at Featherston and Cowra during World War II.* New York: St. Martin's Press.

———. 1989. "An Extension of Humanitarian International Law: The Case of Soviet Soldiers Captured by Afghan Liberation Movements, 1982–1986." *War and Society* 7 (2): 95–105.

Carter, Phillip. 2004. "The Road to Abu Ghraib: The Biggest Scandal of the Bush Administration Began at the Top." *Washington Monthly* 36 (11): 20–29.

Carvin, Stephanie. 2010. *Prisoners of America's Wars: From the Early Republic to Guantanamo.* New York: Columbia University Press.

Chayes, Abram, and Antonia H. Chayes. 1993. "On Compliance." *International Organization* 47 (2): 175–205.

Chiozza, Giacomo. 2002. "Is There a Clash of Civilizations? Evidence from Patterns of International Conflict Involvement, 1946–97." *Journal of Peace Research* 39 (6): 711–34.

Chiozza, Giacomo, and Hein E. Goemans. 2004. "International Conflict and the Tenure of Leaders: Is War Still 'Ex Post' Inefficient?" *American Journal of Political Science* 48 (3): 604–19.

References

Christensen, Thomas J. 1996. *Useful Adversaries: Grand Strategy, Domestic Mobilization, and Sino-American Conflict, 1947–58*. Princeton, NJ: Princeton University Press.

Cienciala, Anna M., Natalia S. Lebedeva, and Wojciech Materski, eds. 2007. *Katyn: A Crime without Punishment*. New Haven, CT: Yale University Press.

Clausewitz, Carl von. 1984. *On War*. Translated by Michael Howard and Peter Paret. Princeton, NJ: Princeton University Press.

Clinton, William J. 1996. *A National Security Strategy of Engagement and Enlargement*. Washington, DC: Government Printing Office.

Clodfelter, Michael. 2008. *Warfare and Armed Conflicts: A Statistical Reference to Casualty and Other Figures, 1494–2007*. Jefferson, NC: McFarland.

Clubb, O. Edmund. 1971. *China and Russia: The "Great Game."* New York: Columbia University Press.

Cobain, Ian. 2005. "The Interrogation Camp that Turned Prisoners into Living Skeletons." *The Guardian*, December 17. http://www.theguardian.com/uk/2005/dec/17/secondworldwar.topstories3.

Cohen, Dara K. 2013. "Explaining Rape during Civil War: Cross-National Evidence (1980–2009)." *American Political Science Review* 107 (3): 461–77.

Cohen, Paul A. 1997. *History in Three Keys: The Boxers as Event, Experience, and Myth*. New York: Columbia University Press.

Collier, David, Henry E. Brady, and Jason Seawright. 2010. "Sources of Leverage in Causal Inference: Toward an Alternative View of Methodology." In *Rethinking Social Inquiry: Diverse Tools, Shared Standards*, edited by Henry E. Brady and David Collier, 161–99. Plymouth: Rowman and Littlefield.

Collier, David, and James Mahoney. 1996. "Insight and Pitfalls: Selection Bias in Qualitative Research." *World Politics* 49 (1): 56–91.

Committee on Military Affairs. 1944. Investigations of the National War Effort: Report of the Committee on Military Affairs, House of Representatives, Seventy-Eighth Congress, Second Session, Pursuant to H. Res. 30, a Resolution Authorizing the Committee on Military Affairs and the Committee on Naval Affairs to Study the Progress of the National War Effort. H.R. Rep. No. 1992.

———. 1945. Investigations of the National War Effort: Report of the Committee on Military Affairs, House of Representatives, Seventy-Ninth Congress, First Session, Pursuant to H. Res. 20, a Resolution Authorizing the Committee on Military Affairs to Study the Progress of the National War Effort. H.R. Rep. No. 728.

Conquest, Robert. 1978. *Kolyma: The Arctic Death Camps*. New York: Viking Press.

———. 1986. *The Harvest of Sorrow: Soviet Collectivization and the Terror-Famine*. New York: Oxford University Press.

Cook, Ruth B. 2006. *Guests behind Barbed Wire: German POWs in America; A True Story of Hope and Friendship*. Birmingham, AL: Crane Hill Publishers.

Cook, Tim. 2006. "The Politics of Surrender: Canadian Soldiers and the Killing of Prisoners in the Great War." *Journal of Military History* 70 (3): 637–66.

Coox, Alvin D. 1977. *The Anatomy of a Small War: The Soviet-Japanese Struggle for Changkufeng-Khasan, 1938*. Westport, CT: Greenwood Press.

———. 1985. *Nomonhan: Japan against Russia, 1939*. Vol. 1. Stanford, CA: Stanford University Press.

Cordesman, Anthony H. 2008. *Iraq's Insurgency and the Road to Civil Conflict*. Westport, CT: Praeger Security International.

Courtois, Stéphane. 1999. "Introduction: The Crimes of Communism." In *The Black Book of Communism: Crimes, Terror, Repression*, edited by Stéphane Courtois, Nicolas Werth, Jean-Louis Panné, Andrzej Paczkowski, Karel Bartosek, and Jean-Louis Margolin, 1–31. Cambridge, MA: Harvard University Press.

[247]

Cowdrey, Albert E. 1992. "A Question of Numbers." In *Eisenhower and the German POWs: Facts against Falsehood*, edited by Günter Bischof and Stephen E. Ambrose, 78–92. Baton Rouge: Louisiana State University Press.

Croco, Sarah E. 2011. "The Decider's Dilemma: Leader Culpability, War Outcomes, and Domestic Punishment." *American Political Science Review* 105 (3): 457–77.

Curry, Anne. 2000. *The Battle of Agincourt: Sources and Interpretations*. Woodbridge: Boydell Press.

Dai, Xinyuan. 2006. "The Conditional Nature of Democratic Compliance." *Journal of Conflict Resolution* 50 (5): 690–713.

Dallin, Alexander, and George W. Breslauer. 1970. *Political Terror in Communist Systems*. Stanford, CA: Stanford University Press.

Dallin, David J., and Boris I. Nicolaevsky. 1947. *Forced Labor in Soviet Russia*. New Haven, CT: Yale University Press.

Danner, Mark. 2004. *Torture and Truth: America, Abu Ghraib, and the War on Terror*. New York: New York Review of Books.

Datner, Szymon. 1962. *Crimes Committed by the Wehrmacht during the September Campaign and the Period of Military Government*. Poznan: Institute for Western Affairs.

Davenport, Christian. 2007a. "State Repression and Political Order." *Annual Review of Political Science* 10:1–23.

———. 2007b. *State Repression and the Domestic Democratic Peace*. Cambridge: Cambridge University Press.

Davenport, Christian, and David A. Armstrong. 2004. "Democracy and the Violation of Human Rights: A Statistical Analysis from 1976 to 1996." *American Journal of Political Science* 48 (3): 538–54.

Davies, Norman. 1982a. *God's Playground: A History of Poland*. Vol. 1, *The Origins to 1795*. New York: Columbia University Press.

———. 1982b. *God's Playground: A History of Poland*, Vol. 2, *1795 to the Present*. New York: Columbia University Press.

———. 1983. *White Eagle, Red Star: The Polish-Soviet War, 1919–20*. London: Orbis.

Davis, Gerald H. 1977. "Prisoners of War in Twentieth-Century War Economies." *Journal of Contemporary History* 12 (4): 623–34.

de Gaury, Gerald. 1966. *Faisal: King of Saudi Arabia*. London: Arthur Barker.

de Waal, Alex. 1991. *Evil Days: 30 Years of War and Famine in Ethiopia*. New York: Human Rights Watch.

de Zayas, Alfred M. 1989. *The Wehrmacht War Crimes Bureau, 1939–1945*. Lincoln: University of Nebraska Press.

Deane, John. 1947. *The Strange Alliance: The Story of Our Efforts at Wartime Co-operation with Russia*. New York: Viking Press.

DeMeritt, Jacqueline H. R. 2012. "International Organizations and Government Killing: Does Naming and Shaming Save Lives?" *International Interactions* 38 (5): 597–621.

———. Forthcoming. "Delegating Death: Military Intervention and Government Killing." *Journal of Conflict Resolution*.

Desch, Michael C. 2010. "The More Things Change, the More They Stay the Same: The Liberal Tradition and Obama's Counterterrorism Policy." *PS: Political Science & Politics* 43 (3): 425–29.

Diehl, Paul F., and Gary Goertz. 2000. *War and Peace in International Rivalry*. Ann Arbor: University of Michigan Press.

Dixon, William J. 1994. "Democracy and the Peaceful Settlement of International Conflict." *American Political Science Review* 88 (1): 14–32.

Douhet, Giulio. 1983. *The Command of the Air*. Translated by Dino Ferrari. Washington, DC: Office of Air Force History.

Dower, John W. 1986. *War without Mercy: Race and Power in the Pacific War*. New York: Pantheon Books.

Downes, Alexander B. 2006. "Desperate Times, Desperate Measures: The Causes of Civilian Victimization in War." *International Security* 30 (4): 152–95.

———. 2007a. "Draining the Sea by Filling the Graves: Investigating the Effectiveness of Indiscriminate Violence as a Counterinsurgency Strategy." *Civil Wars* 9 (4): 420–44.

———. 2007b. "Restraint or Propellant? Democracy and Civilian Fatalities in Interstate Wars." *Journal of Conflict Resolution* 51 (6): 872–904.

———. 2008. *Targeting Civilians in War*. Ithaca, NY: Cornell University Press.

———. 2009. "How Smart and Tough Are Democracies? Reassessing Theories of Democratic Victory in War." *International Security* 33 (4): 9–51.

———. 2012. "Military Culture and Civilian Victimization: The Allied Strategic Bombing of Germany in World War II." In *Civilians and the Ideology of War*, edited by Daniel Rothbart, Karina V. Korostelina, and Mohammed Cherkaoui, 72–95. London: Routledge.

Downes, Alexander B., and Kathryn McNabb Cochran. 2010. "Targeting Civilians to Win? Assessing the Military Effectiveness of Civilian Victimization in Interstate War." In *Rethinking Violence: States and Non-State Actors in Conflict*, edited by Erica Chenoweth and Adria Lawrence, 23–56. Cambridge, MA: MIT Press.

Doyle, Michael W. 1983. "Kant, Liberal Legacies, and Foreign Affairs, Part 2." *Philosophy and Public Affairs* 12 (4): 323–53.

———. 1997. *Ways of War and Peace: Realism, Liberalism, and Socialism*. New York: W. W. Norton.

Doyle, Robert C. 1994. *Voices from Captivity: Interpreting the American POW Narrative*. Lawrence: University Press of Kansas.

———. 2010. *The Enemy in Our Hands: America's Treatment of Prisoners of War from the Revolution to the War on Terror*. Lexington: University Press of Kentucky.

Dunlap, Charles J., Jr. 2000. "The End of Innocence: Rethinking Noncombatancy in the Post-Kosovo Era." *Strategic Review* 28 (3): 9–17.

Dunsdorfs, Edgars. 1975. *The Baltic Dilemma*. New York: R. Speller.

Durand, André. 1984. *History of the International Committee of the Red Cross*. Vol. 2, *From Sarajevo to Hiroshima*. Geneva: Henry Dunant Institute.

Durand, Arthur A. 1988. *Stalag Luft III: The Secret Story*. Baton Rouge: Louisiana State University Press.

Durand, Yves. 1987. *La vie quotidienne des prisonniers de guerre dans les stalags, les oflags, et les kommandos: 1939–1945*. Paris: Hachette.

Eck, Kristine. 2012. "In Data We Trust? A Comparison of UCDP GED and ACLED Conflict Events Datasets." *Conflict and Cooperation* 47 (1): 124–41.

Eck, Kristine, and Lisa Hultman. 2007. "One-Sided Violence against Civilians in War: Insights from New Fatality Data." *Journal of Peace Research* 44 (2): 233–46.

Eckhardt, William. 1989. "Civilian Deaths in Wartime." *Bulletin of Peace Proposals* 20 (1): 89–98.

Economist. 2005. "Just a Few Bad Apples?" January 20. http://www.economist.com/node/3577249.

Edelstein, David M. 2004. "Occupational Hazards: Military Occupations Succeed or Fail." *International Security* 29 (1): 49–91.

[249]

Elliott, H. Wayne. 1995. "Hostages or Prisoners of War: War Crimes at Dinner." *Military Law Review* 149 (3): 241–74.

Elliott, Mark. 1973. "The United States and Forced Repatriation of Soviet Citizens, 1944–47." *Political Science Quarterly* 88 (2): 253–75.

———. 1981. *Pawns of Yalta: Soviet Refugees and America's Role in Their Repatriation*. Urbana: University of Illinois Press.

Engelhardt, Michael J. 1992. "Democracies, Dictatorships and Counterinsurgency: Does Regime Type Really Matter?" *Conflict Quarterly* 12 (3): 52–63.

Epstein, Julius. 1973. *Operation Keelhaul: The Story of Forced Repatriation from 1944 to the Present*. Old Greenwich, CT: Devin-Adair.

Erickson, John. 1991. "The Red Army's March into Poland, September 1939." In *The Soviet Takeover of the Polish Eastern Provinces, 1939–1941*, edited by Keith Sword, 1–27. New York: St. Martin's Press.

Etkind, Alexander, Rory Finnin, Uilleam Blacker, Julie Fedor, Simon Lewis, Maria Mälksoo, and Matilda Mroz. 2012. *Remembering Katyn*. Malden, MA: Polity Press.

Evans, Gareth. 2008. *The Responsibility to Protect: Ending Mass Atrocity Crimes Once and for All*. Washington, DC: Brookings Institution.

Farcau, Bruce. 1996. *The Chaco War: Bolivia and Paraguay, 1932–1935*. Westport, CT: Praeger.

Fazal, Tanisha M. 2007. *State Death: The Politics and Geography of Conquest, Occupation, and Annexation*. Princeton, NJ: Princeton University Press.

———. 2014. "Dead Wrong?: Battle Deaths, Military Medicine, and Exaggerated Reports of War's Demise." *International Security* 39 (1): 95–125.

Fazal, Tanisha M., and Brooke C. Greene. Forthcoming. "A Particular Difference: European Identity and Civilian Targeting." *British Journal of Political Science*.

Fearon, James D., and David D. Laitin. 2003. "Ethnicity, Insurgency, and Civil War." *American Political Science Review* 97 (1): 75–90.

Fein, Helen. 1993. "Accounting for Genocide after 1945: Theories and Some Findings." *International Journal on Group Rights* 1 (2): 79–106.

Ferguson, Niall. 1999. *The Pity of War*. New York: Basic Books.

———. 2004. "Prisoner Taking and Prisoner Killing in the Age of Total War: Towards a Political Economy of Military Defeat." *War in History* 11 (2): 148–92.

Finnemore, Martha. 1996a. "Constructing Norms of Humanitarian Intervention." In *The Culture of National Security: Norms and Identity in World Politics*, edited by Peter J. Katzenstein, 153–85. New York: Columbia University Press.

———. 1996b. *National Interests in International Society*. Ithaca, NY: Cornell University Press.

———. 2004. *The Purpose of Intervention: Changing Beliefs about the Use of Force*. Ithaca, NY: Cornell University Press.

Finnemore, Martha, and Kathryn Sikkink. 1998. "International Norm Dynamics and Political Change." *International Organization* 52 (4): 887–917.

FitzGibbon, Louis. 1971. *Katyn*. London: Tom Stacey.

Fontenot, Gregory, E. J. Degen, and David Tohn. 2005. *On Point: The United States Army in Operation Iraqi Freedom*. Annapolis, MD: Naval Institute Press.

Forster, Jürgen. 1986. "The German Army and the Ideological War against the Soviet Union." In *The Policies of Genocide: Jews and Soviet Prisoners of War in Nazi Germany*, edited by Gerhard Hirschfeld, 15–29. London: Allen and Unwin.

Forsythe, David P. 1992. "Democracy, War, and Covert Action." *Journal of Peace Research* 29 (4): 385–95.

———. 2005. *The Humanitarians: The International Committee for the Red Cross*. Cambridge: Cambridge University Press.

References

———. 2011. *The Politics of Prisoner Abuse: The United States and Enemy Prisoners after 9/11*. Cambridge: Cambridge University Press.

Franck, Thomas M. 1990. *The Power of Legitimacy among Nations*. New York: Oxford University Press.

French, Shannon E. 2004. *The Code of the Warrior: Exploring Warrior Values Past and Present*. New York: Rowman and Littlefield.

Fried, Alfred H. 1914. "A Few Lessons Taught by the Balkan Wars." *International Conciliation* 74:3–14.

Friedman, Yvonne. 2002. *Encounter between Enemies: Captivity and Ransom in the Latin Kingdom of Jerusalem*. Boston: Brill.

Fulcher of Chartres. 1969. *A History of the Expedition to Jerusalem, 1095–1127*. Translated by Frances R. Ryan. Knoxville: University of Tennessee Press.

Fuller, Lon L. 1969. *The Morality of Law*. New Haven, CT: Yale University Press.

Gabriel, Richard A. 1984. *Operation Peace for Galilee: The Israeli-PLO War in Lebanon*. New York: Hill and Wang.

Gansberg, Judith. 1977. *Stalag: USA*. Toronto: Fitzhenry & Whiteside.

Garrett, Richard. 1981. *P.O.W.* London: David and Charles.

Gartner, Scott S. 1998. "Opening up the Black Box of War: Politics and the Conduct of War." *Journal of Conflict Resolution* 42 (3): 252–58.

Gartner, Scott S., and Gary M. Segura. 1998. "War, Casualties, and Public Opinion." *Journal of Conflict Resolution* 42 (3): 278–300.

Gartzke, Erik, and Kristian S. Gleditsch. 2006. "Identity and Conflict: Ties that Bind and Differences that Divide." *European Journal of International Relations* 12 (1): 53–87.

———. 2004. "Why Democracies May Actually Be Less Reliable Allies." *American Journal of Political Science* 48 (4): 775–95.

Gaubatz, Kurt T. 1996. "Democratic States and Commitment in International Relations." *International Organization* 50 (1): 109–39.

Geddes, Barbara. 1990. "How the Cases You Choose Affect the Answers You Get: Selection Bias in Comparative Politics." *Political Analysis* 2 (1): 131–50.

Gelpi, Christopher, Peter D. Feaver, and Jason Reifler. 2009. *Paying the Human Costs of War: American Public Opinion and Casualties in Military Conflicts*. Princeton, NJ: Princeton University Press.

General Sikorski Historical Institute, ed. 1961. *Documents on Polish-Soviet Relations, 1939–1945*. Vol. 1, *1939–1943*. London: Heinemann.

Gibler, Douglas M. 2012. *The Territorial Peace: Borders, State Development, and International Conflict*. Cambridge: Cambridge University Press.

Gilbert, Martin. 1986. *Winston S. Churchill, 1941–1945*. Vol. 7, *Road to Victory*. London: Heinemann.

———. 1989. *The Second World War: A Complete History*. New York: Henry Holt.

———, ed. 1993. *The Churchill War Papers*. Vol. 1, *At the Admiralty, September 1939 – May 1940*. New York: W. W. Norton.

———. 1994. *The First World War: A Complete History*. New York: Henry Holt.

Gilmore, Allison B. 1995. " 'We Have Been Reborn': Japanese Prisoners and the Allied Propaganda War in the Southwest Pacific." *Pacific Historical Review* 64 (2): 195–215.

———. 1998. *You Can't Fight Tanks with Bayonets: Psychological Warfare against the Japanese Army in the Southwest Pacific*. Lincoln: University of Nebraska Press.

Ginsburgs, George. 1957. "The Soviet Union and the Problem of Refugees and Displaced Persons 1917–1956." *American Journal of International Law* 51 (2): 325–61.

Gleditsch, Kristian S., Simon Hug, Livia I. Schubiger, and Julian Wucherpfennig. 2011. "International Conventions and Non-State Actors: Selection, Signaling, and

[251]

Reputation Effects." Unpublished Manuscript. http://www.unige.ch/ses/spo/static/simonhug/gc/gc_peio.pdf>

Gleditsch, Kristian S., and Michael D. Ward. 1997. "Double Take: A Reexamination of Democracy and Autocracy in Modern Polities." *Journal of Conflict Resolution* 41 (3): 361–83.

Gleditsch, Nils Petter, Peter Wallenstein, Mikael Eriksson, Margareta Sollenberg, and Havard Strand. 2002. "Armed Conflict 1946–2001: A New Dataset." *Journal of Peace Research* 39 (5): 615–37.

Goddard, Stacie E. 2009. *Indivisible Territory and the Politics of Legitimacy: Jerusalem and Northern Ireland.* Cambridge: Cambridge University Press.

Goebbels, Joseph. 1948. *The Goebbels Diaries, 1942–1943.* Translated by Louis P. Lochner. Garden City, NY: Doubleday.

Goemans, Hein E. 2000a. "Fighting for Survival: The Fate of Leaders and the Duration of War." *Journal of Conflict Resolution* 44 (5): 555–79.

———. 2000b. *War and Punishment: The Causes of War Termination and the First World War.* Princeton, NJ: Princeton University Press.

Goertz, Gary, and Paul F. Diehl. 1992. *Territorial Changes and International Conflict.* New York: Routledge.

Goldsmith, Jack L. 2009. *The Terror Presidency: Law and Judgment Inside the Bush Administration.* New York: W. W. Norton.

Goldsmith, Jack L., and Eric A. Posner. 2005. *The Limits of International Law.* Oxford: Oxford University Press.

Goldstein, Joshua S. 2011. *Winning the War on War: The Decline of Armed Conflict Worldwide.* New York: Penguin.

Gonzales, Alberto R. 2002. "Memorandum for the President. Decision RE Application of the Geneva Convention on Prisoners of War to the Conflict with Al Qaeda and the Taliban." Washington, DC: National Security Archives.

Goodliffe, Jay, and Darren G. Hawkins. 2006. "Explaining Commitment: States and the Convention against Torture." *Journal of Politics* 68 (2): 358–71.

Gordon, Mary L. 1924. "The Nationality of Slaves under the Early Roman Empire." *Journal of Roman Studies* 14:93–111.

Gordon, Michael R., and Bernard E. Trainor. 1995. *The Generals' War: The Inside Story of the Conflict in the Gulf.* Boston: Little, Brown.

Gorodetsky, Gabriel. 1999. *Grand Delusion: Stalin and the German Invasion of Russia.* New Haven, CT: Yale University Press.

Grauer, Ryan. 2014. "Why Do Soldiers Give Up? A Self-Preservation Theory of Surrender." *Security Studies* 23 (3): 622–55.

Green, Adam. 2005. "Normalizing Torture, One Rollicking Hour at a Time." *New York Times*, May 22. http://query.nytimes.com/gst/fullpage.html?res=9806E2D D1639F931A15756C0A9639C8B63&smid=pl-share.

Greenberg, Karen J., and Joshua L. Dratel, eds. 2005. *The Torture Papers: The Road to Abu Ghraib.* New York: Cambridge University Press.

Greenwald, Glenn. 2012. "Obama's Justice Department Grants Final Immunity to Bush's CIA Torturers." *The Guardian*, August 31. http://www.guardian.co.uk/commentisfree/2012/aug/31/obama-justice-department-immunity-bush-cia-torturer.

Gronke, Paul, Darius Rejali, Dustin Drenguisa, James Hicksa, Peter Millera, and Bryan Nakayama. 2010. "U.S. Public Opinion on Torture, 2001–2009." *PS: Political Science & Politics* 43 (3): 437–44.

Gross, Jan T. 1979. *Polish Society under the German Occupation: The Generalgouvernement, 1939–1944.* Princeton, NJ: Princeton University Press.

References

———. 1991. "Polish POW Camps in the Soviet-Occupied Western Ukraine." In *The Soviet Takeover of the Polish Eastern Provinces, 1939–1941*, edited by Keith Sword, 44–56. New York: St. Martin's Press.

———. 2002. *Revolution from Abroad: The Soviet Conquest of Poland's Western Ukraine and Western Belorussia*. Princeton, NJ: Princeton University Press.

Grossman, Dave. 1995. *On Killing: The Psychological Cost of Learning to Kill in War and Society*. Boston: Little, Brown.

Gutman, Roy, David Rieff, and Anthony Dworkin, eds. 2007. *Crimes of War: What the Public Should Know*. New York: W. W. Norton.

Guzman, Andrew T. 2008. *How International Law Works: A Rational Choice Theory*. Oxford: Oxford University Press.

Hafner-Burton, Emilie M. 2008. "Sticks and Stones: Naming and Shaming the Human Rights Enforcement Problem." *International Organization* 62 (4): 689–716.

———. 2009. *Forced to Be Good: Why Trade Agreements Boost Human Rights*. Ithaca, NY: Cornell University Press.

Hafner-Burton, Emilie M., and Jacob N. Shapiro. 2010. "Tortured Relations: Human Rights Abuses and Counterterrorism Cooperation." *PS: Political Science & Politics* 43 (3): 415–19.

Hagenloh, Paul. 2009. *Stalin's Police: Public Order and Mass Repression in the USSR, 1926–1941*. Baltimore: Johns Hopkins University Press.

Haigh, Philip A. 1995. *The Military Campaigns of the Wars of the Roses*. Stroud: Alan Sutton.

Hall, Richard C. 2000. *The Balkan Wars: Prelude to the First World War*. London: Routledge.

Hannikainen, Lauri, Raija Hanski, and Allan Rosas. 1992. *Implementing Humanitarian Law Applicable in Armed Conflicts: The Case of Finland*. Boston: Martinus Nijhoff.

Harff, Barbara. 2003. "No Lessons Learned from the Holocaust? Assessing Risks of Genocide and Mass Murder since 1955." *American Political Science Review* 97 (1): 57–73.

Harris, William V. 1985. *War and Imperialism in Republican Rome, 327–70 B.C.* Oxford: Oxford University Press.

Hassig, Ross. 1988. *Aztec Warfare: Imperial Expansion and Political Control*. Norman: University of Oklahoma Press.

Hassner, Ron E. 2009. *War on Sacred Grounds*. Ithaca, NY: Cornell University Press.

Hastings, Max. 1987. *The Korean War*. New York: Simon and Schuster.

Hata, Ikuhiko. 1996. "From Consideration to Contempt: The Changing Nature of Japanese Military and Popular Perceptions of Prisoners of War through the Ages." In *Prisoners of War and Their Captors in World War II*, edited by Bob Moore and Kent Fedorowich, 253–76. Oxford: Berg.

Henderson, Errol A. 1998. "The Democratic Peace through the Lens of Culture, 1820–1989." *International Studies Quarterly* 42 (3): 461–84.

Henderson, Errol A., and Richard Tucker. 2001. "Clear and Present Dangers: The Clash of Civilizations and International Conflict." *International Studies Quarterly* 45 (2): 317–38.

Henkin, Louis. 1979. *How Nations Behave*. New York: Columbia University Press.

Herrmann, Richard K., and Vaughn P. Shannon. 2001. "Defending International Norms: The Role of Obligation, Material Interest, and Perception in Decision Making." *International Organization* 55 (3): 621–54.

Hersh, Seymour M. 2004. *Chain of Command: The Road from 9/11 to Abu Ghraib*. New York: Harper Collins.

[253]

Hevia, James L. 2007. "Looting and Its Discontents: Moral Discourse and the Plunder of Beijing, 1900–1901." In *The Boxers, China, and the World*, edited by Robert Bickers and R. G. Tiedemann, 93–113. New York: Rowman and Littlefield.

Holmes, Richard. 1985. *Acts of War: The Behavior of Men in Battle*. New York: Free Press.

Holsti, Kalevi J. 1991. *Peace and War: Armed Conflicts and International Order, 1648–1989*. Cambridge: Cambridge University Press.

Homze, Edward L. 1967. *Foreign Labor in Nazi Germany*. Princeton, NJ: Princeton University Press.

Horne, Alastair. 2006. *A Savage War of Peace: Algeria, 1954–1962*. New York: New York Review of Books.

Horowitz, Michael, and Dan Reiter. 2001. "When Does Aerial Bombing Work? Quantitative Empirical Tests, 1917–1999." *Journal of Conflict Resolution* 45 (2): 147–73.

Hosenball, Mark. 2012. "Senate Probe Finds Little Evidence of Effective 'Torture.'" *Reuters*, April 27. http://www.reuters.com/article/2012/04/27/us-usa-congress-torture-idUSBRE83Q07J20120427.

Huddy, Leonie, Stanley Feldman, Charles Taber, and Gallya Lahav. 2005. "Threat, Anxiety, and Support of Antiterrorism Policies." *American Journal of Political Science* 49 (3): 593–608.

Hull, Isabel V. 2005. *Absolute Destruction: Military Culture and the Practices of War in Imperial Germany*. Ithaca, NY: Cornell University Press.

———. 2014. *A Scrap of Paper: Breaking and Making International Law during the Great War*. Ithaca, NY: Cornell University Press.

Hultman, Lisa. 2007. "Battle Losses and Rebel Violence: Raising the Costs for Fighting." *Terrorism and Political Violence* 19 (2): 205–22.

———. 2010. "Keeping Peace or Spurring Violence? Unintended Effects of Peace Operations on Violence against Civilians." *Civil Wars* 12 (1–2): 29–46.

———. 2013. "UN Peace Operations and Protection of Civilians: Cheap Talk or Norm Implementation?" *Journal of Peace Research* 50 (1): 59–73.

Hultman, Lisa, Jacob Kathman, and Megan Shannon. 2013. "United Nations Peacekeeping and Civilian Protection in Civil War." *American Journal of Political Science* 57 (4): 875–91.

Human Rights Council. 2014. Oral Update of the Independent International Commission of Inquiry on the Syrian Arab Republic. http://www.ohchr.org/Docu ments/HRBodies/HRCouncil/CoISyria/OralUpdate18March2014.pdf.

Human Rights Watch. 2003. *The Horn of Africa War: Mass Expulsions and the Nationality Issue (June 1998–April 2002)*. New York: Human Rights Watch.

Huntington, Samuel P. 1993. "The Clash of Civilizations?" *Foreign Affairs* 72 (3): 22–49.

———. 1996. *The Clash of Civilizations and the Remaking of World Order*. New York: Simon and Schuster.

Huth, Paul K. 1996. *Standing Your Ground: Territorial Disputes and International Conflict*. Ann Arbor: University of Michigan Press.

Huth, Paul K., and Todd L. Allee. 2002. *The Democratic Peace and Territorial Conflict in the Twentieth Century*. Cambridge: Cambridge University Press.

Ignatieff, Michael. 1997. *The Warrior's Honor: Ethnic War and the Modern Conscience*. New York: Henry Holt.

International Committee of the Red Cross. 1948. *Report of the International Committee of the Red Cross on Its Activities during the Second World War (1 September, 1939–30 June, 1947)*. Vol. 1, *General Activities*. Geneva: International Red Cross Conference.

———. 2010. Customary International Humanitarian Law Database. http://www. icrc.org/customary-ihl/eng/docs/home?.

———. 2014. Treaties and States Parties to Such Treaties. http://www.icrc.org/ap plic/ihl/ihl.nsf/.

Ishay, Micheline. 2008. *The History of Human Rights: From Ancient Times to the Globalization Era*. Berkeley: University of California Press.

Jarman, Robert L. 1998. *Political Diaries of the Arab World: Saudi Arabia*. Vol. 5, *Annual Reports 1930–1940*. Chippenham: Archive Editions.

Jervis, Robert. 1976. *Perception and Misperception in International Politics*. Princeton, NJ: Princeton University Press.

Jo, Hyeran, and Catarina Thomson. 2014. "Legitimacy and Compliance with International Law: Access to Detainees in Civil Conflicts, 1991–2006." *British Journal of Political Science* 44 (2): 323–55.

Johnson, Patrick. 2009. "The Treatment of Civilians in Effective Counterinsurgency Operations." PhD dissertation, Nortwestern University.

Jones, Andy. 2010. "High Court Justices, Legal Luminaries Debate Shakespeare's 'Henry V.'" *National Law Journal*. March 18. http://www.nationallawjournal. com/id=1202446381186/High-Court-Justices-Legal-Luminaries-Debate-Shake speares-Henry-V.

Jones, Daniel M., Stuart A. Bremer, and J. David Singer. 1996. "Militarized Interstate Disputes, 1816–1992: Rationale, Coding Rules, and Empirical Patterns." *Conflict Management and Peace Science* 15 (2): 163–213.

Jones, Heather. 2011. *Violence against Prisoners of War in the First World War: Britain, France and Germany, 1914–1920*. Cambridge: Cambridge University Press.

Kahler, Miles. 2006. "Territoriality and Conflict in an Era of Globalization." In *Territoriality and Conflict in an Era of Globalization*, edited by Miles Kahler and Barbara F. Walter, 1–24. Cambridge: Cambridge University Press.

Kalvoda, Josef. 1983. "Czech and Slovak Prisoners of War in Russian during the War and Revolution." In *Essays on World War I: Origins and Prisoners of War*, edited by Samuel R. Williamson and Peter Pastor, 215–38. New York: Columbia University Press.

Kalyvas, Stathis N. 1999. "Wanton and Senseless? The Logic of Violence in Civil Wars." *Rationality and Society* 11 (3): 243–85.

———. 2006. *The Logic of Violence in Civil War*. Cambridge: Cambridge University Press.

Kamenetsky, Ihor. 1961. *Secret Nazi Plans for Eastern Europe. A Study of Lebensraum Policies*. New York: Bookman Associates.

Kargil Review Committee. 2000. *From Surprise to Reckoning: The Kargil Review Committee Report*. Thousand Oaks, CA: Sage Publications.

Karnai, Janos. 1992. *The Socialist System: The Political Economy of Communism*. Princeton, NJ: Princeton University Press.

Kathman, Jacob D., and Reed M. Wood. 2011. "Managing Threat, Cost, and Incentive to Kill: The Short- and Long-Term Effects of Intervention in Mass Killings." *Journal of Conflict Resolution* 55 (5): 735–60.

Kaufmann, Chaim. 1996. "Possible and Impossible Solutions to Ethnic Civil Wars." *International Security* 20 (4): 136–75.

Keefer, Louis E. 1992. *Italian Prisoners of War in America, 1942–1946: Captives or Allies?* New York: Praeger.

Keegan, John. 1976. *The Face of Battle*. New York: Viking Press.

———. 1990. *The Second World War*. New York: Viking.

———. 1995. "If You Won't, We Won't: Honour and the Decencies of Battle." *Times Literary Supplement*, November 24, 11.

Keen, David. 2005. *Conflict & Collusion in Sierra Leone*. New York: Palgrave.

Keen, M. H. 1965. *The Laws of War in the Late Middle Ages*. London: Routledge.

Keown-Boyd, Henry. 1991. *The Fists of Righteous Harmony: A History of the Boxer Uprising in China in the Year 1900*. London: Leo Cooper.

Kerr, E. Bartlett. 1985. *Surrender and Survival: The Experience of American POWs in the Pacific 1941–1945*. New York: William Morrow.

Ki-moon, Ban. 2009. Implementing the Responsibility to Protect: Report of the Secretary General. United Nations General Assembly. http://www.unrol.org/files/sg_reporta_63_677_en.pdf.

Kier, Elizabeth. 1997. *Imagining War: French and British Military Doctrine between the Wars*. Princeton, NJ: Princeton University Press.

Kikuoka, Michael T. 1988. *The Changkufeng Incident: A Study in Soviet-Japanese Conflict, 1938*. New York: University Press of America.

Killion, Tim. 1998. *Historical Dictionary of Eritrea*. Lanham, MD: Scarecrow Press.

Kimball, Warren F., ed. 1984. *Churchill and Roosevelt: The Complete Correspondence*. Vol. 3, *Alliance Declining, February 1944 – April 1945*. Princeton, NJ: Princeton University Press.

Kinsella, Helen M. 2005. "Discourses of Difference: Civilians, Combatants, and Compliance with the Laws of War." *Review of International Studies* 31 (Supplement S1): 163–85.

———. 2011. *The Image before the Weapon: A Critical History of the Distinction between Combatant and Civilian*. Ithaca, NY: Cornell University Press.

Klein, James P., Gary Goertz, and Paul F. Diehl. 2006. "The New Rivalry Dataset: Procedures and Patterns." *Journal of Peace Research* 43 (3): 331–48.

Kochanski, Halik. 2012. *The Eagle Unbowed: Poland and the Poles in the Second World War*. Cambridge, MA: Harvard University Press.

Kochavi, Arieh J. 2005. *Confronting Captivity: Britain and the United States and Their POWs in Nazi Germany*. Chapel Hill: University of North Carolina Press.

Kono, Daniel Y. 2006. "Optimal Obfuscation: Democracy and Trade Policy Transparency." *American Political Science Review* 100 (3): 369–84.

Koop, Allen V. 1988. *Stark Decency: German Prisoners of War in a New England Village*. Hanover, NH: University Press of New England.

Krain, Matthew. 1997. "State-Sponsored Mass Murder: The Onset and Severity of Genocides and Politicides." *Journal of Conflict Resolution* 41 (3): 331–60.

———. 2005. "International Intervention and the Severity of Genocides and Politicides." *International Studies Quarterly* 49 (3): 363–87.

———. 2012. "*J'accuse!* Does Naming and Shaming Perpetrators Reduce the Severity of Genocides or Politicides?" *International Studies Quarterly* 56 (3): 574–89.

———. 2014a. "The Effect of Economic Sanctions on the Severity of Genocides or Politicides." Unpublished Manuscript. http://discover.wooster.edu/mkrain/files/2014/01/SanctionsGP1.pdf

———. 2014b. "The Effects of Diplomatic Sanctions and Engagement on the Severity of Ongoing Genocides or Politicides." *Journal of Genocide Research* 16 (1): 25–53.

Kramer, Alan. 2007. *Dynamic of Destruction: Culture and Mass Killing in the First World War*. Oxford: Oxford University Press.

Kramer, Mark. 2012. "What Was Distinctive about Katyn? The Massacres in Comparative Perspective." *Case Western Reserve Journal of International Law* 44 (3): 569–76.

Krammer, Arnold. 1979. *Nazi Prisoners of War in America*. New York: Stein and Day.

———. 2008. *Prisoners of War: A Reference Handbook*. Westport, CT: Praeger Security International.

References

Kulish, Nicholas, Ellen Barry, and Michal Piotrowski. 2010. "Polish President Dies in Jet Crash in Russia." *New York Times*, April 10. http://www.nytimes.com/2010/04/11/world/europe/11poland.html?smid=pl-share.

Lacina, Bethany A., and Nils P. Gleditsch. 2005. "Monitoring Trends in Global Combat: A New Dataset of Battle Deaths." *European Journal of Population* 21 (2–3): 145–65.

Lacina, Bethany A., Nils P. Gleditsch, and Bruce M. Russett. 2006. "The Declining Risk of Death in Battle." *International Studies Quarterly* 50 (3): 673–80.

Lai, Brian, and Dan Slater. 2006. "Institutions of the Offensive: Domestic Sources of Dispute Initiation in Authoritarian Regimes, 1950–1992." *American Journal of Political Science* 50 (1): 113–26.

Lauck, John H. 1988. *Katyn Killings: In the Record*. Clifton, NJ: Kingston Press.

Lebovic, James H., and Erik Voeten. 2006. "The Politics of Shame: The Condemnation of Country Human Rights Practices in the UNCHR." *International Studies Quarterly* 50 (4): 861–88.

———. 2009. "The Cost of Shame: International Organizations and Foreign Aid in the Punishing of Human Rights Violators." *Journal of Peace Research* 46 (1): 79–97.

Lee, Wayne E. 2011. *Barbarians and Brothers: Anglo-American Warfare, 1500–1865*. Oxford: Oxford University Press.

Leeds, Brett Ashley, Andrew G. Long, and Sara McLaughlin Mitchell. 2000. "Reevaluating Alliance Reliability: Specific Threats, Specific Promises." *Journal of Conflict Resolution* 44 (5): 686–99.

Legro, Jeffrey W. 1995. *Cooperation under Fire: Anglo-German Restraint during World War II*. Ithaca, NY: Cornell University Press.

Lelyveld, Joseph. 2005. "Interrogating Ourselves." *New York Times Magazine*, June 12, 36–60.

Lerner, Daniel. 1981. *Psychological Warfare against Nazi Germany: The Sykewar Campaign, D-Day to VE-Day*. Cambridge, MA: MIT Press.

Levi, Margaret. 1997. *Consent, Dissent, and Patriotism*. Cambridge: Cambridge University Press.

Levy, Jack S. 1989. "The Causes of War: A Review of Theories and Evidence." In *Behavior, Society, and Nuclear War*, edited by Philip Tetlock, Jo L. Husbands, Robert Jervis, Paul C. Stern, and Charles Tilly, 209–333. New York: Oxford University Press.

Lewis, George G., and John Mewha. 1955. *History of Prisoner of War Utilization by the United States Army, 1776–1945*. Washington, DC: Department of the Army.

Liberman, Peter. 1995. *Does Conquest Pay? The Exploitation of Occupied Industrial Societies*. Princeton, NJ: Princeton University Press.

Liddell Hart, B. H. 1946. *The Revolution in Warfare*. London: Faber and Faber.

Lieberman, Evan S. 2005. "Nested Analysis as a Mixed-Method Strategy for Comparative Research." *American Political Science Review* 99 (3): 435–52.

Lieshout, Robert S., Mathieu L. L. Segers, and Johanna Maria van der Vleuten. 2004. "De Gaulle, Moravcsik, and the Choice for Europe: Soft Sources, Weak Evidence." *Journal of Cold War Studies* 6 (4): 89–139.

Lightcap, Tracy. 2011. *The Politics of Torture*. New York: Palgrave Macmillan.

Liivoja, Rain. 2013. "Law and Honor: Normative Pluralism in the Regulation of Military Conduct." In *Normative Pluralism and International Law: Exploring Global Governance*, edited by Jan Klabbers and Touko Piiparinen, 143–65. Cambridge: Cambridge University Press.

Lindley, Dan. 1997. "UNFICYP and a Cyprus Solution: A Strategic Assessment." Center for International Studies, Massachusetts Institute of Technology, Cambridge, MA.

Linn, Brian M. 1989. *The U.S. Army and Counterinsurgency in the Philippine War, 1899–1902*. Chapel Hill: University of North Carolina Press.

Lipson, Charles. 2003. *Reliable Partners: How Democracies Have Made a Separate Peace*. Princeton, NJ: Princeton University Press.

Locke, John. (1690) 1980. *Second Treatise of Government*. Indianapolis: Hackett.

Loewenheim, Francis L., Harold D. Langley, and Manfred Jonas, eds. 1975. *Roosevelt and Churchill: Their Secret Wartime Correspondence*. New York: Saturday Review Press.

Lowe, Christian. 2012. "War-Time Allies Hushed Up Katyn Massacre of Poles: Documents." *Reuters*, September 11. http://www.reuters.com/article/2012/09/11/us-usa-poland-katyn-idUSBRE88A0O020120911.

Lukas, Richard C. 1986. *The Forgotten Holocaust: The Poles under German Occupation, 1939–1944*. Lexington: University Press of Kentucky.

Lustick, Ian S. 1996. "History, Historiography, and Political Science: Multiple Historical Records and the Problem of Selection Bias." *American Political Science Review* 90 (3): 605–18.

Lyall, Jason. 2009. "Does Indiscriminate Violence Incite Insurgent Attacks? Evidence from Chechnya." *Journal of Conflict Resolution* 53 (3): 331–62.

Lyall, Jason, and Geoffrey P. R. Wallace. 2011. "Wartime Conduct and the Rise of Postwar Insurgencies." Unpublished manuscript.

MacKenzie, S. P. 1992. "Essay and Reflection: On the 'Other Losses' Debate." *International History Review* 14 (4): 717–31.

———. 1994. "The Treatment of Prisoners of War in World War II." *Journal of Modern History* 66 (3): 487–520.

———. 1995. "The Shackling Crisis: A Case-Study in the Dynamics of Prisoner-of-War Diplomacy in the Second World War." *International History Review* 17 (1): 79–98.

———. 2004. *The Colditz Myth: British and Commonwealth Prisoners of War in Nazi Germany*. Oxford: Oxford University Press.

———. 2012. *British Prisoners of the Korean War*. Oxford: Oxford University Press.

Mahoney, James, and Gary Goertz. 2004. "The Possibility Principle: Choosing Negative Cases in Comparative Research." *American Political Science Review* 98 (4): 653–69.

Malcher, G. C. 1993. *Blank Pages: Soviet Genocide against the Polish People*. Woking: Pyrford Press.

Maller, Tara. 2010a. "Diplomacy Derailed: The Consequences of Diplomatic Sanctions." *Washington Quarterly* 33 (3): 61–79.

———. 2010b. "Diplomatic Sanctions as a U.S. Foreign Policy Tool: Helpful or Harmful?" *PS: Political Science & Politics* 43 (4): 826–27.

Mann, Michael. 2004. *The Dark Side of Democracy: Explaining Ethnic Cleansing*. Cambridge: Cambridge University Press.

Margolin, Leo J. 1946. *Paper Bullets: A Brief Story of Psychological Warfare in World War II*. New York: Froben Press.

Margulies, Newton L. 1945. "Proper Treatment of Prisoners of War: Reason for War Department Management." *Vital Speeches of the Day* 11 (15): 477–80.

Marshall, Monty G., Keith Jaggers, and Ted R. Gurr. 2010. *Polity IV Project: Political Regime Characteristics and Transitions, 1800–2010*. Severn, MD: Center for Systemic Peace.

Martin, Christopher. 1968. *The Boxer Rebellion*. London: Abelard-Schuman.

Martin, Lisa. 2000. *Democratic Commitments: Legislatures and International Cooperation*. Princeton, NJ: Princeton University Press.

References

Mayer, Jane. 2005. "Outsourcing Torture: The Secret History of America's 'Extraordinary Rendition' Program." *New Yorker*, February 14.
———. 2009. *The Dark Side: The Inside Story of How the War on Terror Turned into a War on American Ideals*. New York: Anchor Books.
Mazzetti, Mark. 2013. *The Way of the Knife: The CIA, a Secret Army, and a War at the Ends of the Earth*. New York: Penguin Press.
McCarthy, Daniel J. 1918. *The Prisoner of War in Germany*. New York: Moffat, Yard.
McClintock, Michael. 1992. *Instruments of Statecraft: U.S. Guerilla Warfare, Counterinsurgency, and Counterterrorism, 1940–1990*. New York: Pantheon.
McCoy, Alfred W. 2006. *A Question of Torture: CIA Interrogation, from the Cold War to the War on Terror*. New York: Metropolitan Books.
McCullagh, Francis. 1912. *Italy's War for a Desert: Being Some Experiences of a War-Correspondent with the Italians in Tripoli*. London: Herbert and Daniel.
McGillivray, Fiona, and Alastair Smith. 2000. "Trust and Cooperation through Agent-Specific Punishments." *International Organization* 54 (4): 809–24.
McGrath, John M. 1975. *Prisoner of War: Six Years in Hanoi*. Annapolis, MD: Naval Institute Press.
Mearsheimer, John. 1994–95. "The False Promise of International Institutions." *International Security* 19 (3): 5–49.
———. 2001. *The Tragedy of Great Power Politics*. New York. Norton.
Meet the Press. 2001. "Vice President Dick Cheney Interview with Tim Russert." September 16. http://georgewbush-whitehouse.archives.gov/vicepresident/news-speeches/speeches/vp20010916.html.
Mercer, Jonathan. 1995. "Anarchy and Identity." *International Organization* 49 (2): 229–52.
Merolla, Jennifer L., and Elizabeth J. Zechmeister. 2009. *Democracy at Risk: How Terrorist Threats Affect the Public*. Chicago: Chicago University Press.
Merom, Gil. 2003. *How Democracies Lose Small Wars: State, Society, and the Failures of France in Algeria, Israel in Lebanon, and the United States in Vietnam*. Cambridge: Cambridge University Press.
Metzger, Charles H. 1962. *The Prisoner in the American Revolution*. Chicago: Loyola University Press.
Midlarsky, Manus I. 2005. *The Killing Trap: Genocide in the Twentieth Century*. Cambridge: Cambridge University Press.
———. 2011. *Origins of Political Extremism: Mass Violence in the Twentieth Century and Beyond*. Cambridge: Cambridge University Press.
Miller, Richard I., ed. 1975. *The Law of War*. Lexington, MA: Lexington Books.
Miller, Stuart C. 1982. *Benevolent Assimilation: The American Conquest of the Philippines, 1899–1903*. New Haven, CT: Yale University Press.
Montefiore, Simon S. 2004. *Stalin: The Court of the Red Tsar*. New York: Knopf.
Montesquieu, Charles de Secondat, Baron de. (1748) 1989. *Montesquieu: The Spirit of the Laws*. Cambridge: Cambridge University Press.
Moore, Bob. 1996. "Axis Prisoners in Britain during the Second World War: A Comparative Survey." In *Prisoners of War and Their Captors in World War II*, edited by Bob Moore and Kent Fedorowich, 19–46. Oxford: Berg.
———. 2000. "Unruly Allies: British Problems with the French Treatment of Axis Prisoners of War, 1943–1945." *War in History* 7 (2): 180–98.
Moravcsik, Andrew. 1998. *The Choice for Europe: Social Purpose and State Power from Messina to Maastricht*. Ithaca, NY: Cornell University Press.

Morgan, T. Clifton, and Sally Howard Campbell. 1991. "Domestic Structure, Decisional Constraints, and War: So Why Kant Democracies Fight?" *Journal of Conflict Resolution* 35 (2): 187–211.

Morgenthau, Hans J. 1985. *Politics among Nations: The Struggle for Power and Peace.* New York: McGraw-Hill.

Morina, Christina. 2004. "Instructed Silence, Constructed Memory: The SED and the Return of German Prisoners of War as 'War Criminals' from the Soviet Union to East Germany, 1950–1956." *Contemporary European History* 13 (3): 323–43.

Morris, Benny. 2008. *1948: A History of the First Arab-Israeli War.* New Haven, CT: Yale University Press.

Morrow, James D. 2001. "The Institutional Features of the Prisoners of War Treaties." *International Organization* 55 (4): 971–91.

———. 2007. "When Do States Follow the Laws of War?" *American Political Science Review* 101 (3): 559–72.

———. 2014. *Order within Anarchy: The Laws of War as an International Institution.* New York: Cambridge University Press.

Morrow, James D., and Hyeran Jo. 2006. "Compliance with the Laws of War: Dataset and Coding Rules." *Conflict Management and Peace Science* 23 (1): 91–113.

Moyar, Mark. 1997. *Phoenix and the Birds of Prey: The CIA's Secret Campaign to Destroy the Viet Cong.* Annapolis, MD: Naval Institute Press.

Mueller, John E. 1973. *War, Presidents, and Public Opinion.* New York: Wiley.

———. 1990. "The Obsolescence of Major War." *Bulletin of Peace Proposals* 21 (3): 321–28.

———. 1996. "Policy Principles for Unthreatened Wealth-Seekers." *Foreign Policy* 102:22–33.

Munck, Gerardo L., and Jay Verkuilen. 2002. "Conceptualizing and Measuring Democracy." *Comparative Political Studies* 35 (1): 5–34.

Murdie, Amanda M., and David R. Davis. 2012. "Shaming and Blaming: Using Events Data to Assess the Impact of Human Rights INGOs." *International Studies Quarterly* 56 (1): 1–16.

Naimark, Norman M. 1995. *The Russians in Germany: A History of the Soviet Zone of Occupation, 1945–1949.* Cambridge, MA: Harvard University Press.

———. 2010. *Stalin's Genocides.* Princeton, NJ: Princeton University Press.

Newman, P. H. 1944. "The Prisoner-of-War Mentality: Its Effect after Repatriation." *British Medical Journal* 1 (1): 8–10.

Newsweek. 1945a. "Anger at Nazi Atrocities is Rising but U.S. Treats Prisoners Fairly." May 7, 21.

———. 1945b. "German Atrocities Raise Question: Are Nazi POW's 'Coddled' Here?" May 7, 58–60.

O'Donnell, Guillermo, and Philippe C. Schmitter. 1986. *Transitions from Authoritarian Rule: Prospects for Democracy.* Baltimore: Johns Hopkins University Press.

Ober, Josiah. 1994. "Classical Greek Times." In *The Laws of War: Constraints on Warfare in the Western World,* edited by Michael Howard, George J. Andreopoulos, and Mark R. Shulman, 12–26. New Haven, CT: Yale University Press.

Overmans, Rüdiger. 1992. "German Historiography, the War Losses, and the Prisoners of War." In *Eisenhower and the German POWs: Facts against Falsehood,* edited by Günter Bischof and Stephen E. Ambrose, 127–69. Baton Rouge: Louisiana State University Press.

Overy, Richard J. 1997. *Russia's War: Blood upon the Snow.* New York: Penguin Putnam.

Paczkowski, Andrzej. 1999. "Poland, the 'Enemy Nation.'" In *The Black Book of Communism: Crimes, Terror, Repression,* edited by Stéphane Courtois, Nicolas

References

Werth, Jean-Louis Panné, Andrzej Paczkowski, Karel Bartosek, and Jean-Louis Margolin, 363–93. Cambridge, MA: Harvard University Press.

Page, William F. 1992. *The Health of Former Prisoners of War: Results from the Medical Examination*. Washington, DC: National Academy Press.

Pape, Robert A. 1996. *Bombing to Win: Air Power and Coercion in War*. Ithaca, NY: Cornell University Press.

———. 2003. "The Strategic Logic of Suicide Terrorism." *American Political Science Review* 97 (3): 343–61.

Partem, Michael G. 1983. "The Buffer System in International Relations." *Journal of Conflict Resolution* 27 (1): 3–26.

Pastor, Peter. 1983. "Introduction." In *Essays on World War I: Origins and Prisoners of War*, edited by Samuel R. Williamson and Peter Pastor, 113–17. New York: Columbia University Press.

Patrikeeff, Felix. 2002. *Russian Politics in Exile: The Northeast Asian Balance of Power, 1924–1931*. New York: Palgrave Macmillan.

Paul, Allen. 1991. *Katyń: The Untold Story of Stalin's Polish Massacre*. New York: C. Scribner's Sons.

Pearlstein, Deborah. 2006. "Reconciling Torture with Democracy." In *The Torture Debate in America*, edited by Karen J. Greenberg, 253–55. Cambridge: Cambridge University Press.

Peceny, Mark, Caroline C. Beer, and Shannon Sanchez Terry. 2002. "Dictatorial Peace?" *American Political Science Review* 96 (2): 15–26.

Peksen, Dursun. 2009. "Better or Worse? The Effect of Economic Sanctions on Human Rights." *Journal of Peace Research* 46 (1): 59–77.

Peterman, Amber, Dara K. Cohen, Tia Palermo, and Amelia Hoover Green. 2011. "Rape Reporting during War: Why the Numbers Don't Mean What You Think They Do." *Foreign Affairs*. http://www.foreignaffairs.com/articles/68008/amber-peterman-dara-kay-cohen-tia-palermo-and-amelia-hoover-gree/rape-reporting-during-war.

Petrov, Vladimir. 1968. *June 22, 1941: Soviet Historians and the German Invasion*. Columbia: University of South Carolina Press.

Phillips, Joshua E. S. 2012. *None of Us Were Like This Before: American Soldiers and Torture*. New York: Verso.

Piesakowski, Tomasz. 1990. *The Fate of Poles in the USSR, 1939–1989*. London: Gryf Publications.

Pinker, Steven. 2012. *The Better Angels of Our Nature: Why Violence Has Declined*. New York: Penguin.

Piotrowski, Tadeusz. 1998. *Poland's Holocaust: Ethnic Strife, Collaboration with Occupying Forces and Genocide in the Second Republic, 1918–1947*. Jefferson, NC: McFarland.

Piper, Franciszek. 1994. "Gas Chambers and Crematoria." In *Anatomy of the Auschwitz Death Camp*, edited by Yisrael Gutman and Michael Berenbaum, 157–82. Bloomington: Indiana University Press.

Poe, Steven C., and C. Neal Tate. 1994. "Repression of Human Rights to Personal Integrity in the 1980s: A Global Analysis." *American Political Science Review* 88 (4): 853–72.

Poe, Steven C., C. Neal Tate, and Linda Camp Keith. 1999. "Repression of the Human Right to Personal Integrity Revisited: A Global Cross-National Study Covering the Years 1976–1993." *International Studies Quarterly* 43 (2): 281–313.

Polish Ministry of Information. 1941. *Concise Statistical Year-Book of Poland, September 1939 – June 1941*. Glasgow: Polish Ministry of Information.

Pons, Silvio. 2002. *Stalin and the Inevitable War, 1936–1941*. London: Frank Cass.

Porter, Russell. 1945. "Defends Handling of Nazi Prisoners." *New York Times*, February 14. http://query.nytimes.com/gst/abstract.html?res=9800E2DC1F38EE3B BC4C52DFB466838E659EDE.

Posner, Eric A. 2003. "A Theory of the Laws of War." *University of Chicago Law Review* 70 (1): 297–317.

Posner, Richard A. 2002. "Some Economics of International Law: Comment on Conference Papers." *Journal of Legal Studies* 31 (S1):S321–S329.

Powell, Allan K. 1989. *Splinters of a Nation: German Prisoners of War in Utah*. Salt Lake City: University of Utah Press.

Powell, Colin L. (2002) 2005. "Draft Decision Memorandum for the President on the Applicability of the Geneva Convention to the Conflict in Afghanistan." In *The Torture Papers: The Road to Abu Ghraib*, edited by Karen J. Greenberg and Joshua L. Dratel, 122–25. New York: Cambridge University Press.

Powers, Samantha. 2002. *"A Problem from Hell": America and the Age of Genocide*. New York: Basic Books.

Preston, Paul. 2007. *The Spanish Civil War: Reaction, Revolution, and Revenge*. New York: W. W. Norton.

Prestwich, Michael. 1999. *Armies and Warfare in the Middle Ages: The English Experience*. New Haven, CT: Yale University Press.

Price, Richard. 1998. "Reversing the Gun Sights: Transnational Civil Society Targets Land Mines." *International Organization* 52 (3): 613–44.

Price, Richard, and Nina Tannenwald. 1996. "Norms and Deterrence: The Nuclear and Chemical Weapons Taboos." In *The Culture of National Security: Norms and Identity in World Politics*, edited by Peter J. Katzenstein, 114–52. New York: Columbia University Press.

Prorok, Alyssa K., and Benjamin J. Appel. 2014. "Compliance with International Humanitarian Law: Democratic Third Parties and Civilian Targeting in Interstate War." *Journal of Conflict Resolution* 58 (4): 713–40.

Proudfoot, Malcolm J. 1957. *European Refugees, 1939–52: A Study in Forced Population Movement*. London: Faber and Faber.

PWD/SHAEF. 1945. *The Psychological Warfare Division Supreme Headquarters Allied Expeditionary Force: An Account of Its Operations in the Western European Campaign, 1944–1945*. Bad Homburg: PWD/SHAEF.

Rachamimov, Alon. 2002. *POWs and the Great War: Captivity on the Eastern Front*. Oxford: Berg.

Rayfield, Donald. 2005. *Stalin and His Hangmen: The Tyrant and Those Who Killed for Him*. New York: Random House.

Reagan, Ronald. 1987. "Letter of Transmittal." *American Journal of International Law* 81 (4): 910–12.

Rees, Laurence. 2001. *Horror in the East: Japan and the Atrocities of World War II*. Cambridge, MA: Da Capo Press.

Regan, Patrick M. 2002. "Third-party Interventions and the Duration of Intrastate Conflicts." *Journal of Conflict Resolution* 46 (1): 55–73.

Reiter, Dan. 2003. "Exploring the Bargaining Model of War." *Perspectives on Politics* 1 (1): 27–43.

———. 2009. *How Wars End*. Princeton, NJ: Princeton University Press.

Reiter, Dan, and Curtis Meek. 1999. "Determinants of Military Strategy, 1903–1994: A Quantitative Empirical Test." *International Studies Quarterly* 43 (2): 363–87.

Reiter, Dan, and Allan C. Stam. 1997. "The Soldier's Decision to Surrender: Prisoners of War and World Politics." Annual Meeting of the American Political Science Association, Washington, DC, August 28–30.

———. 2002. *Democracies at War*. Princeton, NJ: Princeton University Press.

Rejali, Darius. 2007. *Torture and Democracy*. Princeton, NJ: Princeton University Press.

Roberts, Adam. 1993–94. "The Laws of War in the 1990–91 Gulf Conflict." *International Security* 18 (3): 134–81.

———. 1994. "Land Warfare: From Hague to Nuremberg." In *The Laws of War: Constraints on Warfare in the Western World*, edited by Michael Howard, George J. Andreopoulos, and Mark R. Shulman, 116–39. New Haven, CT: Yale University Press.

Roberts, Geoffrey. 2006. *Stalin's Wars: From World War to Cold War, 1939–1953*. New Haven, CT: Yale University Press.

Robin, Ron. 1995. *The Barbed Wire College: Reeducating German POWs in the United States during World War II*. Princeton, NJ: Princeton University Press.

Robinson, Paul. 2006. *Military Honour and the Conduct of War: From Ancient Greece to Iraq*. London: Routledge.

Rodley, Nigel S. 2009. *The Treatment of Prisoners under International Law*. Oxford: Oxford University Press.

Rodriguez, Jose A. 2012. *Hard Measures: How Aggressive CIA Actions after 9/11 Saved American Lives*. New York: Threshold Editions.

Roeder, Philip. 2003. "Clash of Civilizations and Escalation of Domestic Ethnopolitical Conflicts." *Comparative Political Studies* 36 (5): 509–40.

Rogers, Anthony. 2007. "Combatant Status." In *Perspectives on the ICRC Study on Customary International Law*, edited by Elizabeth Wilmshurst and Susan Breau, 101–27. Cambridge: Cambridge University Press.

Roland, Charles G. 1996. "Human Vivisection: The Intoxication of Limitless Power in Wartime." In *Prisoners of War and Their Captors in World War II*, edited by Bob Moore and Kent Fedorowich, 149–79. Oxford: Berg.

Roosevelt, Franklin Delano. 1937. Quarantine Speech. http://millercenter.org/president/speeches/speech-3310.

Rosato, Sebastian. 2003. "The Flawed Logic of Democratic Peace Theory." *American Political Science Review* 97 (4): 585–602.

Rosen, Stephen P. 1995. "Military Effectiveness: Why Society Matters." *International Security* 19 (4): 5–31.

Ross, William F., and Charles F. Romanus. 2004. *The Quartermaster Corps: Operations in the War against Germany*. Washington, DC: Center of Military History, U.S. Army.

Rossino, Alexander B. 2003. *Hitler Strikes Poland: Blitzkrieg, Ideology, and Atrocity*. Lawrence: University Press of Kansas.

Rowe, Peter. 1993. "Prisoners of War in the Gulf Area." In *The Gulf War 1990–91 in International and English Law*, edited by Peter Rowe, 188–204. London: Routledge.

Ruggie, John G. 1993. "Territoriality and Beyond: Problematizing Modernity in International Relations." *International Organization* 47 (1): 139–74.

Rummel, R. J. 1994. *Death by Government*. New Brunswick, NJ: Transaction Publishers.

———. 1995. "Democracy, Power, Genocide, and Mass Murder." *Journal of Conflict Resolution* 39 (1): 3–26.

———. 1998. *Statistics of Democide: Genocide and Mass Murder since 1900*. Piscatway, NJ: Transaction Publishers.

Russett, Bruce. 1993. *Grasping the Democratic Peace*. Princeton, NJ: Princeton University Press.

Russett, Bruce M., John R. Oneal, and Michaelene Cox. 2000. "Clash of Civilizations, or Realism and Liberalism Déjà Vu? Some Evidence." *Journal of Peace Research* 37 (5): 583–608.

Sanders, James D., Mark A. Sauter, and R. Cort Kirkwood. 1992. *Soldiers of Misfortune: Washington's Secret Betrayal of America's POWs in the Soviet Union*. Washington, DC: National Press Books.

Sanford, George. 2005. *Katyn and the Soviet Massacre of 1940: Truth, Justice and Memory*. London: Routledge.

Sarkees, Meredith, and Frank W. Wayman. 2010. *Resort to War: 1816–2007*. Washington, DC: CQ Press.

Sarkees, Meredith R., Frank W. Wayman, and J. David Singer. 2003. "Inter-State, Intra-State, and Extra-State Wars: A Comprehensive Look at Their Distribution over Time, 1816–1997." *International Studies Quarterly* 47 (1): 49–70.

Sarkesian, Sam C. 1989. "The American Response to Low-Intensity Conflict: The Formative Period." In *Armies in Low-Intensity Conflict: A Comparative Analysis*, edited by David A. Charters and Maurice Tugwell, 19–48. London: Brassey's Defence Publishers.

Savage, Charlie. 2011. "As Acts of War or Despair, Suicides Rattle a Prison." *New York Times*, April 24. http://www.nytimes.com/2011/04/25/world/guantanamo-files-suicide-as-act-of-war-or-despair.html.

———. 2013. "Despair Drives Guantánamo Detainees to Revolt." *New York Times*, April 24. http://www.nytimes.com/2013/04/25/us/guantanamo-prison-revolt-driven-by-inmates-despair.html?smid=pl-share.

Schabas, William A. 2011. *An Introduction to the International Criminal Court*. Cambridge: Cambridge University Press.

Schaffer, Ronald. 1985. *Wings of Judgment:American Bombing in World War II*. Oxford: Oxford University Press.

Schindler, Dietrich, and Jin Toman, eds. 2004. *The Laws of Armed Conflicts: A Collection of Conventions, Resolutions, and Other Documents*. Boston: Martinus Nijhoff.

Schroeder, Paul W. 1994. *The Transformation of European Politics 1763–1848*. Oxford: Oxford University Press.

Searle, Thomas R. 2002. " 'It Made a Lot of Sense to Kill Skilled Workers': The Firebombing of Tokyo in March 1945." *Journal of Military History* 66 (1): 103–33.

Sengupta, Somini. 2014. "At U.N., a Grim Viewing of Alleged Syrian Torture." *New York Times*, April 15. http://www.nytimes.com/2014/04/16/world/middleeast/at-un-a-grim-viewing-of-alleged-syrian-torture.html?smid=pl-share?.

Shane, Scott. 2009. "Interrogations' Effectiveness May Prove Elusive." *New York Times*, April 23. http://www.nytimes.com/2009/04/23/us/politics/23detain.html.

———. 2013. "Ex-Officer Is First from C.I.A. to Face Prison for a Leak." *New York Times*, January 5. http://www.nytimes.com/2013/01/06/us/former-cia-officer-is-the-first-to-face-prison-for-a-classified-leak.html?smid=pl-share.

Shane, Scott, and Charlie Savage. 2011. "Bin Laden Raid Revives Debate on Value of Torture." *New York Times*, May 3. http://www.nytimes.com/2011/05/04/us/politics/04torture.html.

Shils, Edward A., and Morris Janowitz. 1948. "Cohesion and Disintegration in the Wehrmacht in World War II." *Public Opinion Quarterly* 12 (2): 280–335.

Shirkey, Zachary C. 2012. "When and How Many: The Effects of Third Party Joining on Casualties and Duration in Interstate Wars." *Journal of Peace Research* 49 (2): 321–34.

Siemaszko, Zbigniew. 1991. "The Mass Deportations of the Polish Population to the USSR, 1940–1941." In *The Soviet Takeover of the Polish Eastern Provinces, 1939–1941*, edited by Keith Sword, 217–35. New York: St. Martin's Press.

Simmons, Beth A. 2000. "International Law and State Behavior: Commitment and Compliance in International Monetary Affairs." *American Political Science Review* 94 (4): 819–35.

———. 2010. "Treaty Compliance and Violation." *Annual Review of Political Science* 13:272–96.

Simmons, Beth A., and Allison Danner. 2010. "Credible Commitments and the International Criminal Court." *International Organization* 64 (2): 225–56.

Simons, Marlise. 2014. "Congolese Militia Leader Convicted in Attack on Village." *New York Times*, March 7. http://www.nytimes.com/2014/03/08/world/africa/congolese-militia-leader-convicted-in-attack-on-village.html.

Singer, J. David, Stuart Bremer, and John Stuckey. 1972. "Capability Distribution, Uncertainty, and Major Power War, 1820–1965." In *Peace, War, and Numbers*, edited by Bruce M. Russett, 19–48. Beverly Hills, CA: Sage.

Siverson, Randolph M. 1995. "Democracies and War Participation: In Defense of the Institutional Constraints Argument." *European Journal of International Relations* 1 (4): 481–89.

Slantchev, Branislav L. 2003. "The Power to Hurt: Costly Conflict with Completely Informed States." *American Political Science Review* 97 (1): 123–33.

Slater, Jerome. 2006. "Tragic Choices in the War on Terrorism: Should We Try to Regulate and Control Torture?" *Political Science Quarterly* 121 (2): 191–215.

Slaughter, Anne-Marie. 1995. "International Law in a World of Liberal States." *European Journal of International Law* 6 (1): 505–38.

Small, Melvin, and J. David Singer. 1982. *Resort to Arms: International and Civil Wars, 1816–1980.* Beverley Hills, CA: Sage Publications.

Smith, Bruce Lannes, Harold D. Lasswell, and Ralph D. Casey. 1946. *Propaganda, Communication, and Public Opinion: A Comprehensive Reference Guide.* Princeton, NJ: Princeton University Press.

Smith, David. 2009. "Ghosts of South African Prison Tell What Apartheid Really Meant." *The Guardian*, December 31. http://www.theguardian.com/world/2009/dec/31/south-africa-prison-apartheid.

Smith, Hugh. 2005. "What Costs Will Democracies Bear? A Review of Popular Theories of Casualty Aversion." *Armed Forces & Society* 31 (4): 487–512.

Snyder, Jack L. 1984. *The Ideology of the Offensive: Military Decision Making and the Disasters of 1914.* Ithaca, NY: Cornell University Press.

Snyder, Timothy. 2010. *Bloodlands: Europe between Hitler and Stalin.* New York: Basic Books.

Solis, Gary D. 2010. *The Law of Armed Conflict: International Humanitarian Law in War.* Cambridge: Cambridge University Press.

Solzhenitsyn, Aleksandr I. 1974. *The Gulag Archipelago, 1918–1956: An Experiment in Literary Investigation.* Vol. 1. Translated by Thomas P. Whitney. New York: Harper and Row.

Spagat, Michael, Andrew Mack, Tara Cooper, and Joakim Kreutz. 2009. "Estimating War Deaths: An Arena of Contestation." *Journal of Conflict Resolution* 53 (6): 934–50.

Spaight, James M. 1911. *War Rights on Land.* London: Macmillan.

Speed, Richard B. 1990. *Prisoners, Diplomats and the Great War: A Study in the Diplomacy of Captivity.* New York: Greenwood Press.

Springer, Paul J. 2010. *America's Captives: Treatment of POWs from the Revolutionary War to the War on Terror.* Lawrence: University of Kansas Press.

Stachura, Peter D. 2004. *Poland, 1918–1945: An Interpretive and Documentary History of the Second Republic.* New York: Routledge.

State Archives in Poland. 2004. "Polish-Russian Findings on the Situation of Red Army Soldiers in Polish Captivity (1919–1922)." http://www.archiwa.gov.pl/en/exhibitions/398-polish-russian-findings.html.

Sterio, Milena. 2012. "Katyn Forest Massacre: Of Genocide, State Lies, and Secrecy." *Case Western Reserve Journal of International Law* 44 (3): 615–31.

Stigler, Andrew L. 2002. "A Clear Victory for Air Power: NATO's Empty Threat to Invade Kosovo." *International Security* 27 (3): 124–57.

Stohl, Michael. 1987. "Outside of a Small Circle of Friends: States, Genocide, Mass Killing and the Role of Bystanders." *Journal of Peace Research* 24 (2): 151–66.

Stout, David. 2002. "Geneva Convention to Be Applied to Captured Taliban Fighters." *New York Times*, February 7. http://www.nytimes.com/2002/02/07/international/07CND-DETAIN.html?smid=pl-share.

Straus, Scott. 2006. *The Order of Genocide: Race, Power, and War in Rwanda.* Ithaca, NY: Cornell University Press.

———. 2007. "Second-Generation Comparative Research on Genocide." *World Politics* 59 (3): 476–501.

Streit, Christian. 1986. "The German Army and the Policies of Genocide." In *The Policies of Genocide: Jews and Soviet Prisoners of War in Nazi Germany*, edited by Gerhard Hirschfeld, 1–14. London: Allen and Unwin.

Sword, Keith. 1995. "The Repatriation of Soviet Citizens at the End of the Second World War." In *The Cambridge Survey of World Migration*, edited by Robin Cohen, 323–25. Cambridge: Cambridge University Press.

Szawlowski, Ryszard. 1991. "The Polish-Soviet War of 1939." In *The Soviet Takeover of the Polish Eastern Provinces, 1939–1941*, edited by Keith Sword, 28–43. New York: St. Martin's Press.

Tavernier, Paul. 1992. "Combatants and Non-Combatants." In *The Gulf War of 1980–1988: The Iran-Iraq War in International Legal Perspective*, edited by Ige F. Dekker and Harry H. G. Post, 129–49. Dordrecht: Martinus Nijhoff.

Thies, Cameron G. 2002. "A Pragmatic Guide to Qualitative Historical Analysis in the Study of International Relations." *International Studies Perspectives* 3 (4): 351–72.

Thomas, Ward. 2006. "Victory by Duress: Civilian Infrastructure as a Target in Air Campaigns." *Security Studies* 15 (1): 1–33.

Thompson, Antonio. 2010. *Men in German Uniform: POWs in America during World War II.* Knoxville: University of Tennessee Press.

Thompson, William R. 2001. "Identifying Rivals and Rivalries in World Politics." *International Studies Quarterly* 45 (4): 557–86.

Tierney, Dominic. 2010. "Prisoner Dilemmas: The American Obsession with POWs and Hostages." *Orbis* 54 (1): 130–45.

Tollefson, Martin. 1946. "Enemy Prisoners of War." *Iowa Law Review* 32 (1): 51–77.

Tolstoy, Nikolai. 1977. *Victims of Yalta.* London: Hodder and Stoughton.

Tomz, Michael, Jason Wittenberg, and Gary King. 2003. "CLARIFY: Software for Interpreting and Presenting Statistical Results. Version 2.1." *Journal of Statistical Software* 8 (1): 8–15.

Trachtenberg, Marc. 2006. *The Craft of International History: A Guide to Method.* Princeton, NJ: Princeton University Press.

Treier, Shawn, and Simon Jackman. 2008. "Democracy as a Latent Variable." *American Journal of Political Science* 52 (1): 201–17.

Tyler, Tom R. 1990. *Why People Obey the Law.* New Haven, CT: Yale University Press.

U.S. News and World Report. 1992. *Triumph Without Victory: The Unreported History of the Persian Gulf War.* New York: Random House.

United Nations General Assembly. 2005. Draft Resolution Referred to the High-Level Plenary Meeting of the General Assembly by the General Assembly at its Fifty-Ninth Session: 2005 World Summit Outcome. http://www.who.int/hiv/universalaccess2010/worldsummit.pdf.

United Nations Security Council. 2006. Resolution 1674. http://www.un.org/News/Press/docs/2006/sc8710.doc.htm.

References

United States Strategic Bombing Survey. 1976. *The United States Strategic Bombing Survey*. New York: Garland.

Utley, Robert M., and Wilcomb E. Washburn. 2002. *Indian Wars*. New York: First Mariner Books.

Valentino, Benjamin A. 2004. *Final Solutions: Mass Killing and Genocide in the Twentieth Century*. Ithaca, NY: Cornell University Press.

Valentino, Benjamin A., Paul K. Huth, and Dylan Balch-Lindsay. 2004. " 'Draining the Sea': Mass Killing and Guerrilla Warfare." *International Organization* 58 (2): 375–407.

Valentino, Benjamin A., Paul K. Huth, and Sarah E. Croco. 2006. "Covenants without the Sword: International Law and the Protection of Civilians in Times of War." *World Politics* 58 (3): 339–77.

———. 2010. "Bear Any Burden? How Democracies Minimize the Costs of War." *Journal of Politics* 72 (2): 528–44.

Van Evera, Stephen. 1999. *Causes of War: Power and the Roots of Conflict*. Ithaca, NY: Cornell University Press.

Vance, Jonathan F. 1995. "Men in Manacles: The Shackling of Prisoners of War, 1942–43." *Journal of Military History* 59 (3): 483–504.

———. 2006. *Encyclopedia of Prisoners of War and Internment*. 2nd ed. Millerton, NY: Grey House.

Vanhanen, Tatu. 2000. "A New Dataset for Measuring Democracy, 1810–1998." *Journal of Peace Research* 37 (2): 251–65.

Vasquez, John A. 1993. *The War Puzzle*. Cambridge: Cambridge University Press.

von Stein, Jana. 2005. "Do Treaties Constrain or Screen? Selection Bias and Treaty Compliance." *American Political Science Review* 99 (4): 611–22.

Vourkoutiotis, Vasilis. 2003. *Prisoners of War and the German High Command: The British and American Experience*. New York: Palgrave Macmillan.

Walker, Jonathan. 2008. *Poland Alone: Britain, SOE and the Collapse of Polish Resistance, 1944*. Stroud: History Press.

Wallace, Geoffrey P. R. 2012. "Regulating Conflict: Historical Legacies and State Commitment to the Laws of War." *Foreign Policy Analysis* 8 (2): 151–72.

———. 2012. "Welcome Guests, or Inevitable Victims? The Causes of Prisoner Abuse in War." *Journal of Conflict Resolution* 56 (6): 955–81.

———. 2013. "International Law and Public Attitudes toward Torture: An Experimental Study." *International Organization* 67 (1): 105–40.

Walter, Barbara F. 2001. *Committing to Peace: The Successful Settlement of Civil Wars*. Princeton, NJ: Princeton University Press.

Waltz, Kenneth N. 1979. *Theory of International Politics*. Reading, MA: Addison-Wesley.

Walzer, Michael. 2000. *Just and Unjust Wars*. New York: Basic Books.

Warmbrunn, Werner. 1993. *The German Occupation of Belgium, 1940–1944*. New York: Peter Lang.

Weart, Spencer R. 1998. *Never at War: Why Democracies Will Not Fight One Another*. New Haven, CT: Yale University Press.

Weeks, Albert L. 2002. *Stalin's Other War: Soviet Grand Strategy, 1939–1941*. Lanham, MD: Rowman and Littlefield.

Weeks, Jessica L. 2008. "Autocratic Audience Costs: Regime Type and Signaling Resolve." *International Organization* 62 (1): 35–64.

———2012. "Strongmen and Straw Men: Authoritarian Regimes and the Initiation of International Conflict." *American Political Science Review* 106 (2): 326–47.

———. 2014. *Dictators at War and Peace*. Ithaca, NY: Cornell University Press.

[267]

Weeramantry, J. Romesh. 2005. "Prisoners of War (Eritrea v. Ethiopia), Eritrea's Claim 17/Ethiopia's Claim 4, Partial Awards: Central Front (Eritrea v. Ethiopia), Eritrea's Claims 2, 4, 6, 7, 8 & 22/Ethiopia's Claim 2, Partial Awards." *American Journal of International Law* 99 (2): 465–72.

Weinberg, Gerhard L. 1994. *A World at Arms: A Global History of World War II*. Cambridge: Cambridge University Press.

Weindling, Paul. 2000. *Epidemics and Genocide in Eastern Europe, 1890–1945*. Oxford: Oxford University Press.

Weingartner, James J. 1979. *Crossroads of Death: The Story of the Malmédy Massacre and Trial*. Berkeley: University of California Press.

———. 1992. "Trophies of War: U.S. Troops and the Mutilation of Japanese War Dead, 1941–1945." *Pacific Historical Review* 61 (1): 53–67.

Weinstein, Jeremy M. 2007. *Inside Rebellion: The Politics of Insurgent Violence*. Cambridge: Cambridge University Press.

Weir, Alison. 1995. *The Wars of the Roses*. New York: Ballantine Books.

Wenner, Manfred. 1967. *Modern Yemen, 1918–1966*. Baltimore: Johns Hopkins University Press.

Werth, Nicolas. 1999. "A State against Its People: Violence, Repression, and Terror in the Soviet Union." In *The Black Book of Communism: Crimes, Terror, Repression*, edited by Stéphane Courtois, Nicolas Werth, Jean-Louis Panné, Andrzej Paczkowski, Karel Bartosek, and Jean-Louis Margolin, 33–268. Cambridge, MA: Harvard University Press.

Wettig, Gerhard. 2008. *Stalin and the Cold War in Europe: The Emergence and Development of East-West Conflict, 1939–1953*. Lanham, MD: Rowman and Littlefield.

Wills, Siobhan. 2009. *Protecting Civilians: The Obligations of Peacekeepers*. Oxford: Oxford University Press.

Witt, John F. 2013. *Lincoln's Code: The Laws of War in American History*. New York: Free Press.

Wittels, David G. 1945. "Are We Coddling Italian Prisoners?" *Saturday Evening Post*, March 3, 18–97.

Wittman, Donald. 1979. "How a War Ends: A Rational Model Approach." *Journal of Conflict Resolution* 23 (4): 743–63.

Wood, Reed M. 2008. "'A Hand upon the Throat of the Nation': Economic Sanctions and State Repression, 1976–2001." *International Studies Quarterly* 52 (3): 489–513.

Wood, Reed M., Jacob Kathman, and Stephen E. Gent. 2012. "Armed Intervention and Civilian Victimization in Intrastate Conflicts." *Journal of Peace Research* 49 (5): 647–60.

Wyman, Mark. 1989. *DP: Europe's Diplaced Persons, 1945–1951*. Philadelphia: Balch Institute Press.

Yap, Felicia. 2012. "Prisoners of War and Civilian Internees of the Japanese in British Asia: The Similarities and Contrasts of Experience." *Journal of Contemporary History* 47 (2): 317–46.

Yoo, John. 2006. *War by Other Means: An Insider's Account of the War on Terror*. New York: Atlantic Monthly Press.

Zaslavsky, Victor. 2008. *Class Cleansing: The Katyn Massacre*. Translated by Kizer Walker. New York: Telos Press.

Zawodny, Janusz K. 1962. *Death in the Forest: The Story of the Katyn Forest Massacre*. Notre Dame: University of Notre Dame Press.

Zeidner, Robert F. 2005. *The Tricolor Over the Taurus: The French in Cilicia and Vicinity, 1918–1922*. Ankara: Turkish Historical Society.

Zook, David H. 1960. *The Conduct of the Chaco War*. New York: Bookman Associates.

Index

AB-Aktion, 160
Abkhazia, 176
Abu Ghraib, 4, 16
aerial bombing of cities, 125–28, 228n141, 229n152
Afghanistan, 12, 19, 47, 88, 93, 179
Algerian War, 4, 23
Allee, Todd L., 217n144
al-Qaeda, 5, 19, 23, 185, 186
American Indians. *See* Native Americans
American prisoners. *See* U.S. prisoners
American Red Cross, 104
American Revolutionary War. *See* Revolutionary War
Ancient Greece. *See* Greece, Ancient
annexationist wars. *See* wars of territorial expansion
AP I. *See* Geneva Conventions of 1949: Additional Protocol I (AP I)
AP II. *See* Geneva Conventions of 1949: Additional Protocol II (AP II)
Appel, Benjamin J., 220–21n13
Arab-Israeli War of 1948. *See* Palestine War of 1948
Argentina, 25, 30, 41, 48, 77
Armenia, 2, 38
Armia Krajowa. *See* Home Army (Poland)
armistices, 13, 118–19, 152
assassination of insurgents and suspected terrorists, 17, 188

asylum, 120–21
atrocity and atrocities, 61, 85, 91, 113–15, 129, 130, 235n126. *See also* Katyn massacre
attritional warfare, 9, 66–69, 74–82, 86, 93, 171–74, 182, 190–99; statistics, 77, 82, 92, 190–91, 193, 197–99; Vietnam War, 130; World War II, 93, 155
Australia, 224–25n32
Austria-Hungary, 28, 45, 137
Austro-Hungarian prisoners, 5–6, 22, 136
autocracies (dictatorships), 4, 9, 60–65, 89, 91, 217nn151–52; democracies compared to, 60–63, 76–77, 81, 83, 87–95, 129, 130, 171, 176–77; first violators, 88; rationalization of, 51; rendition to, 220n9; statistics, 190, Weeks typology, 237n18; World War II prisoner mortality, 100
Axis prisoners, 7, 11, 58, 62, 99–109, 231n54; France, 107, 118; Great Britain, 105, 106, 109, 116–19, 224n24, 224–25n32; postwar, 115–20; Soviet Union, 63; transfer of, 224–25n32; United States, 109, 113–19, 224n24; U.S. public opinion and, 104. *See also* German prisoners
Azerbaijan, 2, 38
Aztec Empire, 1

Bacque, James, 116, 117, 226n78
Badme Border War. *See* Ethiopian-Eritrean War (Badme Border War)